A BIBLIOGRAPHY OF AMERICAN EDUCATIONAL HISTORY

CONTRIBUTING EDITORS

A BIBLIOGRAPHY OF AMERICAN EDUCATIONAL HISTORY

An Annotated and Classified Guide

by

Francesco Cordasco
Montclair State College

William W. Brickman
University of Pennsylvania

AMS Press
New York

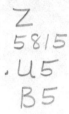

Copyright ©1975 AMS Press, Inc.

All rights reserved. Published in the United States by AMS Press, Inc., 56 East 13th Street, New York, New York 10003

Library of Congress Cataloging in Publication Data

Main entry under title:
A Bibliography of American educational history.

  1. Education—United States—History—Bibliography. I. Cordasco, Francesco, 1920. II. Brickman, William W. III. Binder, Frederick, M.
Z5815.U5B5 [LA212]   016.37'0973   74-29140
ISBN 0-404-12661-8

Manufactured in the United States of America

For

Leonard Covello and Saul Sack
Scholars, Colleagues, Friends

The amount of general educational literature now published is very great. In Germany, during the few years that have elapsed since the repeal of the law controlling the introduction of text-books, their number has greatly increased. A trade catalogue for 1884 enumerates about two thousand books and pamphlets, including new editions, which appeared in the German language during that year. More than three-fourths of these were text-books, and the rest more general pedagogic treatises. One hundred and fifty-seven periodicals, devoted exclusively to education, were published in that language last year. A Berlin firm, in a letter now before me, offers to supply six hundred and eighty-four thousand school reports, of the trade in which it makes a specialty, all for less than sixty thousand dollars, and states that the British Museum has laid in as complete sets of these as could be had since 1863, now some fifty thousand in number. Our own National Bureau of Education has now not far from sixty thousand titles of books and pamphlets and more important magazine articles, mainly pedagogical in character, in its unprinted drawer catalogue, which have accumulated since its establishment, mainly by exchange and gifts, etc., with little effort or funds for systematic purchase.

G. Stanley Hall,
Hints Toward a Select and Descriptive Bibliography of Education
(1886)

TABLE OF CONTENTS

PART I

PART II

Part III

XVIII. THE COLONIAL PERIOD
(1607-1783) *(Robert Sidwell)* .295

XIX. THE GROWTH OF THE AMERICAN
REPUBLIC (1783-1865) *(Frederick M. Binder)* 313

PREFACE

In a trenchant essay-review, Professor Joe Park observes that "there is a tendency among scholars to depreciate the efforts of those who compile bibliographies"; but, as he wryly observes, "nevertheless scholars seek after leads to printed sources as some diligently pursue tips on race horses." [1]

Bibliography, of course, needs little defense: it is the life-blood of scholarship, and beyond the guides and directions it provides for continuing study and investigation, bibliography (as both a discipline and science) has fascinated and attracted the attention of scores of scholars.[2] Ellwood P. Cubberley (certainly, not remembered as a bibliographer) is a case in point. His *Syllabus of Lectures on the History of Education* (which Lawrence A. Cremin characterized as "a rather remarkable work that remains unique in the literature")[3] is a vast bibliographical compendium whose design took the form of a skeletal syllabus in which the framework was held together by hundreds of bibliographical references. Cubberley intended the *Syllabus* to be an instructional tool:

> The Syllabus is based on a combination of the lecture and library methods, with occasional class discussions and reports. Instead of confining students to a few text-books, the aim has been to give them breadth of view by familiarizing them with the literature of the subject, and to provide some training in methods of independent work ... It is a part of a college student's education to become

---

[1] Joe Park, "Some Bibliographies, Old and New," *History of Education Quarterly*, vol. 14 (Summer, 1974), p. 267.

[2] See, in this connection, [Bibliographical Society] *The Bibliographical Society, 1892-1942: Studies in Retrospect* (London: The Society, 1945); and generally, Ray Stokes, *The Function of Bibliography* (London: The Library Association, 1969); and Robert B. Downs and Frances B. Jenkins, eds., *Bibliography: Current State and Future Trends* (Urbana: University of Illinois Press, 1967).

[3] Ellwood P. Cubberley, *Syllabus of Lectures on the History of Education. With Selected Bibliographies and Suggested Readings* (New York: Macmillan, 1902, rev. ed., 1904); Lawrence A Cremin, *The Wonderful World of Ellwood Patterson Cubberley: An Essay on the Historiography of American Education* (New York: Bureau of Publications, Teachers College, Columbia University, 1965), p. 36.

familiar with books, to know the best that has been written on the subject he studies, and to become somewhat familiar with the books themselves. The student in the old college who could browse about in the library had an immense advantage over the university student of today, who seldom gets nearer the stacks than the card catalogue. While the administration of a large library of necessity requires that the stacks be closed to the student body, it is none the less a misfortune to the individual student, and makes it all the more necessary that the instructor should provide the student with the bibliographies which he can no longer prepare, even in part, for himself. The great mass of literature at present available also makes it advisable that students and teachers be provided with a time-saving key.[4]

And in a strict sense all bibliographies are instructional tools.

It was as an instructional tool that the psychologist G. Stanley Hall intended his *Hints Toward a Select and Descriptive Bibliography of Education* (1886), itself the first general and selectively comprehensive bibliography of education in English: "This Bibliography was ... primarily designed as a set of topical reference lists, to be given out in connection with the writer's two-years' course of lectures on education, to post graduate and special students at the Johns Hopkins University, and follows in the main its order of topics, and, indeed, may now be of chief use to such students."[5] Although Will S. Monroe thought of his *Bibliography of Education* (1897) as 'systematic" (*i.e.,* a catalogue of his educational library assembled over some sixteen years), it, too, was intended as an instructional tool, in Monroe's words, "suggestive to others engaged in educational work."[6]

In a strict sense, the bibliographies of Hall and Monroe are the earliest general, selectively comprehensive bibliographies of education in English. There are, of course, hundreds of specialized bibliographies in education;[7] and the

---

[4] Cubberley, *Syllabus,* pp. iii, v.

[5] G. Stanley Hall and John M. Mansfield, *Hints Toward a Select and Descriptive Bibliography of Education* (Boston: D. C. Heath, 1886), p. v. Mansfield was a graduate student at Hopkins whom Hall used for verification of titles. Hall's main sources were two works: Henry Kiddle and Alexander J. Schem, *The Cyclopedia of Education* (New York: Steiger, 1877); and K. A. Schmidt, *Encyclopädia der gesammten Erziehungs-und Unterrichtswesens.* 11 vols. (Gotha: Besser, 1858-71; new edition, 1876-1887, 10 vols.).

[6] Will S. Monroe, *Bibliography of Education* (New York: D. Appleton, 1897), p. xii. Monroe had published an earlier prospectus from which his *Bibliography* derives: *A Pedagogical Library* (Oakland, Calif.: Fisher, 1892), a pamphlet of 16 pages, itself originally published in the *Pacific Educational Journal.*

[7] See, generally, Walter S. Monroe and Louis Shores, *Bibliographies and Summaries in Education to July 1, 1935* (New York: Wilson, 1936), an annotated catalogue of more than 4000 bibliographies published from 1910 to 1935; and *Education Index,* 1929-- (New York: Wilson) which is published monthly (except July and August), with annual cumulations. A vast repository (over 40,000 entries) of research studies in education is [U.S. Office of

massive catalogues of libraries,[8] which classify and describe their holdings, are invaluable bibliographical repositories, but neither the specialized bibliographies nor the catalogue lists qualify as general, comprehensive bibliographies.

It may be that a general, comprehensive bibliography of education, truly universal and retrospective (and even if limited to works published in English), is impracticable. Both Hall's and Monroe's books, if general and comprehensive in their plans, are neither universal nor retrospective. Both are highly selective and limited to some 3000 entries each. (Monroe limited his entries to English language works; Hall drew his entries from the major western European languages [with a preponderance from the German, in keeping with the Germanophilist tendencies of the period].) The enormity of educational literature was apparent even by Monroe's time, and of this Monroe was keenly aware:

> The literature of education is now admittedly large and is growing daily. In the Central Pedagogical Library at Leipzig, founded twenty-five years ago in honor of Comenius, there are 66,604 books and pamphlets on the subject of education. The Musée Pédagogique at Paris, founded in 1879 by the French Government, contains 50,000 pedagogical books. The national pedagogical libraries of Belgium, Switzerland, and Russia each contain over 15,000 volumes. In the city of Berlin there are two such special libraries—the one containing 16,000 and the other 14,500 volumes. In the South Kensington Museum in London there are 10,500 books on the subject of education; and the Teachers' Guild of Great Britain and Ireland has a pedagogical library of more than 6,000 volumes.
>
> In America no less than in Europe there has been marked development in the collection of books on education. The library connected with the Bureau of Education at Washington has over 50,000 books and 150,000 pamphlets on education and subjects more or less directly allied to education.[9]

In the twentieth century, educational bibliography has tended to be specialized, generating a staggering multiplicity of handlists, monographic commentaries, and guides; and when it has attempted general, comprehensive (if selected) conspectuses, it has limited itself, most often, to the educational literature of a

Education] *Bibliography of Research Studies in Education* (Washington: Government Printing Office, 1926-27 - 1940-41) which has been reissued with an introduction by F. Cordasco (5 vols., Detroit: Gale Research Co., 1974). See, also, Arvid J. Burke and Mary A. Burke, *Documentation in Education* (New York: Teachers College Press, 1967), a basic guide to the literature.

8 See, *e.g.*, [Columbia University] Teachers College, *Dictionary Catalog of the Teachers College Library*. 36 vols. (Boston: G. K. Hall, 1970); and [London University] Institute of Education, *Catalogue of the Comparative Education Library*. 5 vols. (Boston: G. K. Hall, 1971).

9 Will S. Monroe, *Bibliography of Education*, p. xi.

particular nation.[10]

A Bibliography of American Educational History is a specialized bibliography whose primary focus is the history of American education. Yet, even with its national and field limitations, its classification schema inevitably comprehends more than that which its delimiting precincts would impose. *Part One* (General Bibliographies and Encyclopedic Works; Collections of Sources; The Historiography of American Education; Comprehensive Histories of American Education), and *Part Three* (The Colonial Period, 1607-1783; The Growth of the American Republic, 1783-1865; The Expansion of American Education, 1865-1900; American Education in the 20th Century) are neatly congruent with the field of American educational history.

Yet, in our judgment, to have limited coverage to the thematic/bibliographical, and chronological schemata of *Parts One* and *Three* would have seriously impaired the value of the work. *Part Two,* as a subject-field schema,[11] adds that dimension and scope to the work which expands its utility and, hopefully, places it in a direct developmental line with the earlier works of Hall and Monroe. Its some 3000 entries (essentially, the same number in Hall and Monroe) are intended as a compact, dimensionally representative, guide to the contemporary literature of American educational history, and its framework allows for adequate notice of some retrospective literature. In this sense, *A Bibliography of American Educational History* is intended both as an instructional and reference tool, and it supplements and extends those other bibliographical works on American education currently available.[12]

Our first indebtedness, in the preparation of this volume, is to the contributing editors who so competently undertook each of their tasks. Each contributing editor had a free hand in the development of an assigned section, *i.e.,* plan and classification, selection of entries; and, beyond the uniformity of style for entires and some minor adaptations, we made very few additions (or deletions) to each of the sections. Of inestimable value was the assistance of Mrs.

---

[10] See, generally, W. Kenneth Richmond, *The Literature of Education: A Critical Bibliography, 1945-1970* (London: Methuen, 1972); also, C. W. J. Higson, *Sources for the History of Education* (London: Library Association, 1967). See, also, [Council of Europe] *Documentation Centre for Education in Europe. Compendium of Basic Bibliographies by Country.* Strasbourg: Council of Europe, 1966; and United Nations Educational, Scientific and Cultural Organization. *International Guide to Educational Documentation, 1960-1965.* 2nd ed. Paris: UNESCO, 1971.

[11] Including, *i.e.,* Elementary Education; Secondary Education; Vocational Education; Histories of Education in the Individual States; Higher Education; Schoolbooks; Teacher Education; Church, State and Education; The Federal Government and Education; The Education of Women; Biographies of American Educators; Contemporary Issues in American Education; Foreign Influences on American Education.

[12] Particularly, Barbara S. Marks, ed., *List of Books in Education* (New York: Citation Press, 1968); Jurgen Herbst, *The History of American Education* (Northbrook, Illinois: AHM Publishing Corp., 1973); and Joe Park, *The Rise of American Education: An Annotated Bibliography* (Evanston, Illinois: Northwestern University Press, 1965).

Molly Morehead, who not only prepared the typescript but also attended to a multitude of editorial details. And a host of individuals, in a number of academic communities, enriched our understanding and aided in defining both the volume's aims and its conceptualization. Special thanks are due to Professor Elliot S. M. Gatner of Long Island University, and Professor Henry J. Perkinson of New York University.

A Bibliography of American Educational History is not a finished work; no bibliography can hope to be, and each is incomplete immediately upon publication. All bibliographers should remember Talleyrand's gratuitous dictum: *Surtout, pas trop de zèle.* Ideally, each user brings to a bibliography his own store of knowledge, preferences, and perspectives. The distinguished economist, John Maynard Keynes, understood this when, in the preface to the bibliography appended to his *Treatise on Probability* (1921), he observed: "At present a bibliographer takes pride in numerous entries, but he would be a more useful fellow, and the labours of research would be lightened, if he could practice deletion and bring into existence an accredited *Index Expurgatorius.* But this can only be accomplished by the slow mills of the collective judgment of the learned, and I have indicated my own favourite authors in copious footnotes to the main body of the text."

Montclair, N.J.

Philadelphia, Pa.

December, 1974

Francesco Cordasco

William W. Brickman

PART I:

BIBLIOGRAPHIES, SOURCE COLLECTIONS,
HISTORIOGRAPHY AND COMPREHENSIVE HISTORIES

I. GENERAL BIBLIOGRAPHIES AND ENCYCLOPEDIC WORKS

A. GENERAL

Bibliography of Publications of the United States Office of Education, 1867-1959. Introductory note by Francesco Cordasco. Totowa, N.J.: Rowman and Littlefield, 1971. A reprint of three important compilations: *List of Publications of the United States Bureau of Education, 1867-1910; List of Publications of the Office of Education, 1910-1936;* and *1937-1959 Publications: Office of Education.* Thoroughly indexed for convenient reference.

Brickman, William W. "Educational History of the United States." *School & Society,* vol. 72 (December 30, 1950), pp. 436-44. A critical bibliographical essay on 31 general works and monographs published during 1947-1950.

Brickman, William W. "An Historical Survery of Foreign Writings on American Educational History." *Paedagogica Historica,* vol. 2, no. 1 (1962), pp. 1-21. A critical commentary, with 60 footnotes, on the historical treatments of education in the United States in French, German, Dutch, and other languages.

Brickman, William W. "Selected Bibliography of the History of Education in the United States." *Paedagogica Historica,* vol. 10, no. 3 (1972), pp. 622-630. An unannotated, classified listing of general and specialized works, collections of source materials, and other works.

Brickman, William W., and Lorraine Mathies. "Education," in Carl M. White, ed., *Sources of Information in the Social Sciences.* Chicago: American Library Association, 1973, pp. 425-607. Comprehensive review of sources in education, keyed to analytical analyses and discussion.

Cordasco, Francesco. "Reference Books in Education: A Bibliographical Commentary." (Stechert-Hafner) *Book News,* vol. 17 (March, 1963), pp. 81-83. Notices of bibliographies, encyclopedias, educational biography, and educational periodicals.

Deighton, Lee C., ed. *The Encyclopedia of Education.* 10 vols. New York: Macmillan, 1971. Deals primarily with American education with some notices of international education, comparative education and foreign systems. Within the body of the work, articles appear in alphabetical order with bibliographies appended. Some 1000 articles, and *Index* (vol. 10). See also, Edward Blishen, ed., *Encyclopedia of Education* (New York: Philosophical Library, 1970).

Gersman, Elinor M. "A Bibliography for Historians of Education." *History of Education Quarterly,* vol. 12 (Spring, 1972), pp. 81-88. An unannotated list, classified by broad topics, of recent articles published in various types of journals on the history of education in the United States and other countries.

Gersman, Elinor M. "A Bibliography for Historians of Education." *History of Education Quarterly,* vol. 12 (Winter, 1972), pp. 531-541. A list of recent journal articles on the educational history of the United States and foreign countries.

Gersman, Elinor M. "A Bibliography of Current Periodical Literature in Educational History." *History of Education Quarterly,* vol. 13 (Spring, 1973), pp. 91-96. A list of recent references on the history of education in the U.S. and abroad and related topics.

Gersman, Elinor M. "A Bibliography for Historians of Education." *History of Education Quarterly,* vol. 13 (Winter, 1973), pp. 447-455. Recent periodical references, mainly on the history of education in the United States.

Gersman, Elinor M. "A Bibliography for Historians of Education." *History of Education Quarterly,* vol. 14 (Summer, 1974), pp. 279-292. An unannotated list of recent periodical writings on the educational history of the United States and other countries.

Gersman, Elinor M. "Textbooks in American Educational History." *History of Education Quarterly,* vol. 13 (Spring, 1973), pp. 41-51. An enlightening, critical commentary on textbooks, source collections, and related works published during 1962-1971.

Hall, G. Stanley, and John M. Mansfield. *Hints toward a Select and Descriptive Bibliography of Education.* Boston: Heath, 1886. Reprinted, Detroit: Gale Research Co., 1973. Brief annotations of a well-classified compilation of works useful for the study of the history of education, including many titles pertinent to the United States. Gale reprint includes new introduction by F. Cordasco.

Herbst, Jurgen, comp. *The History of American Education.* Northbrook, Ill.: AHM Publishing Corp., 1973. A selective, but for most purposes reasonably comprehensive classified, and unannotated compilation of a wide variety of titles. Cross-references and indexed.

Marks, Barbara S., ed. *The New York University List of Books in Education.*

New York: Citation Press, 1968. Lists of titles put together by the departments of the New York University School of Education. Restricted to "books, some pamphlets, yearbooks and a few monographic series." Excellent annotations.

Monroe, Paul, ed. *A Cyclopedia of Education*. 5 vols. New York: Macmillan, 1911-1913. Reprinted, Detroit: Gale Research Co., 1968. This well-known encyclopedic work contains numerous articles with appended bibliographies on all aspects of the history of American education. Especially useful for biographies of educators and histories of institutions. Gale reprint includes introductory essay by W. W. Brickman, F. Cordasco, T. H. Richardson. See F. Cordasco, "The 50th Anniversary of Monroe's Cyclopedia of Education," *School & Society*, vol. 91 (March, 1963), pp. 123-124; and W. W. Brickman and F. Cordasco, "Paul Monroe's *Cyclopedia of Education* with Notices of Educational Encyclopedias Past and Present," *History of Education Quarterly*, vol. 10 (Fall, 1970), pp. 324-337.

Monroe, Walter S., and Louis Shores. *Bibliographies and Summaries in Education to July, 1935*. New York: Wilson, 1936. An annotated listing, arranged by author and subject, of over 4,000 bibliographies and summaries of research reports published during 1910-1935. Bibliographies in the history of education, pp. 195-202.

Monroe, Will S. *Bibliography of Education*. New York: Appleton, 1897. Reprinted, Detroit: Gale Research Co., 1968. An occasionally annotated, well-classified compilation of references, including many which are useful for the history of American education. Especially useful are the summaries of the contents of Horace Mann's annual reports (1838-1849) and William T. Harris's reports of the St. Louis public schools (1867-1879). Gale reprint includes new introduction by F. Cordasco.

Park, Joe, ed. *The Rise of American Education: An Annotated Bibliography*. Evanston: Northwestern University Press, 1965. A good selection of general books and specialized works on the history of elementary, secondary, and higher education in the United States. Includes a substantial chapter on current issues, listings of pertinent dissertations, and miscellaneous references of value to the student of American educational history.

Reisner, Edward H., and R. Freeman Butts. "History of American Education during the Colonial Period." *Review of Educational Research*, vol. 6 (October, 1936), pp. 357-363, 417-422. A bibliographical essay and listing of 137 titles published in the 19th and 20th centuries.

Richey, Herman G. "History of American Education since the Beginning of the National Period." *Review of Educational Research*, vol. 6 (October, 1936), pp. 363-377, 422-429. A commentary on and listing of 161 references of the 19th and 20th centuries.

Richmond, W. Kenneth. *The Literature of Education: A Critical*

Bibliography, 1945-1970. London: Methuen, 1972. British compilation with valuable analysis of trends.

[University of California Department of Pedagogy] *Catalogue of Books in the Pedagogical Section of the University Library.* Rev. ed. Berkeley, Calif.: Regents of the University, 1895. A classified, indexed, unannotated compilation of publications including many on the history of American education and writings throwing light on 19th century education in the United States.

B. ELEMENTARY AND SECONDARY EDUCATION

Brown, Elmer E. "The History of Secondary Education in the United States—Bibliography." *School Review,* vol. 5 (February, 1897), pp. 84-94; (March, 1897), pp. 139-147. A briefly annotated listing of general works, as well as books and articles dealing with the history of secondary education on state and local levels, and histories of individual institutions.

DeBoer, Peter P., and Robert L. McCaul. "Annotated List of *Chicago Tribune* Editorials on Elementary and Secondary Education in the U.S. *History of Education Quarterly,* vol. 3 (Summer, 1973), pp. 201-214. An annotated list of educational editorials published during 1875-1885.

DeBoer, Peter P., and Robert L. McCaul. "Annotated List of *Chicago Tribune* Editorials on Elementary and Secondary Education in the U.S., 1852-1900." *History of Education Quarterly,* vol. 13 (Spring, 1973), pp. 97-107. The first part of a useful guide to public opinion on educational affairs covers the period 1852-1874.

DeBoer, Peter P., and Robert L. McCaul. "Annotated List of *Chicago Tribune* Editorials on Elementary and Secondary Education in the U.S., 1886-1900." *History of Education Quarterly,* vol. 13 (Winter, 1973), pp. 457-485. This list includes editorials which comment favorably on John Dewey's writings and Elementary School (September 10, 1899; December 12, 1899).

Greenwood, James M., and Artemas Martin. "Notes on the History of American Text-Books on Arithmetic," in *Report of the Commissioner of Education for the Year 1897-98.* Vol. I. Washington: Government Printing Office, 1899, pp. 789-868. Description of textbooks used in the 18th and 19th centuries, together with biographical sketches of their authors.

Heartman, Charles F. *American Primers, Indian Primers, Royal Primers.* Highland Park, N.J.: Weiss, 1935. A listing, with facsimile pages, of primers used in American schools prior to 1830.

Packer, Katherine H. *Early American School Books: A Bibliography Based on the Boston Booksellers' Catalogue of 1804.* Ann Arbor: A partially annotated, alphabetized, indexed listing of textbooks used in American schools at the beginning of the nineteenth century. Contains such interesting data as the widespread use of foreign books prior to the Revolution, the change to American works by 1804, and the sale of over 80,000,000 copies of Noah Webster's *American Spelling Book* between 1783 and 1880.

Richey, Herman G. "History of Education in the United States: Preschool Education." *Review of Educational Research,* vol. 9 (October, 1939), pp. 337-339, 412-413. A bibliographical essay on 30 unpublished works on the dame and infant schools, the kindergarten, and the nursery school.

Soper, Wayne W. "History of Education in the United States: Secondary Education." *Review of Educational Research,* vol. 9 (October, 1939), pp. 342-346, 413-414. A commentary on and a listing of 40 titles on general secondary education, the junior high school, and the junior college.

Strayer, George D., Jr. "History of Education in the United States: Elementary Education." *Review of Educational Research,* vol. 9 (October, 1939), pp. 340-341, 413. Comments on seven works dealing with developments and trends.

C. HIGHER EDUCATION

Brickman, William W. "A Bibliographical Introduction to History of U.S. Higher Education," in William W. Brickman and Stanley Lehrer, eds. *A Century of Higher Education: Classical Citadel to Collegiate Colossus.* New York: Society for the Advancement of Education, 1962, pp. 257-285. An unannotated, classified list of works on the general history of U.S. higher education, histories of individual colleges and universities, monographs on various aspects of higher educational history, documentary collections, bibliographies, biographies and autobiographies, and other works.

Carrell, William D. "Biographical List of American College Professors to 1800." *History of Education Quarterly,* vol. 8 (Fall, 1968), pp. 358-374. A listing of references to biographical compilations, articles, and books containing information on the lives of 142 early American college faculty members.

Eells, Walter C., and Ernest V. Hollis. *The College Presidency, 1900-1960: An Annotated Bibliography.* Bulletin 1961, No. 9, U.S. Office of Education. Washington: Government Printing Office, 1961. An annotated, indexed compilation of 695 publications appearing during six decades on the qualifications, duties, and responsibilities of the American college president.

Good, H. G. "History of Education in the United States: Higher Education." *Review of Educational Research,* vol. 9 (October, 1939), pp. 347-351, 415-417. Evaluative analysis and listing of 78 general and specialized works.

Gougher, Ronald L. "Comparison of English and American Views of the German University, 1840-1865: A Bibliography." *History of Education*

Quarterly, vol. 9 (Winter, 1969), pp. 477-491. An annotated list of primary and other works, some of which exerted an impact on the development of American higher education in the 19th century.

Gray, Ruth A. *Doctors' Theses in Education: A List of 797 Theses Deposited with the Office of Education and Available for Loan.* Pamphlet No. 60, U.S. Office of Education. Washington: Government Printing Office, 1935. A compilation of doctoral dissertations sent to the U.S. Office of Education prior to September, 1934.

Ryan, W. Carson, Jr. *The Literature of American School and College Athletics.* Bulletin No. 24. New York: Carnegie Foundation for the Advancement of Teaching, 1929. A well-annotated compilation of 1030 titles, many of which deal with the history of physical education and athletics in American high schools and colleges, with particular reference to the controversy over the overemphasis of collegiate athletics.

Shipton, Clarence K. *Sibley's Harvard Graduates, Volume 16, 1764-1767: Biographical Sketches of Those Who Attended Harvard College in the Classes 1764-1767.* Boston: Massachusetts Historical Society, 1972. The latest installment in a unique, illustrated compilation of long and short biographical accounts, including such personalities as Manasseh Cutler (pp. 138-54) and President Joseph Willard (pp. 253-65). An important reference work.

D. EDUCATORS

Boydston, Jo Ann, ed. *Guide to the Works of John Dewey*. Carbondale: Southern Illinois University Press, 1970. Commentaries in the form of bibliographical essays by philosophers and educators on the various facets of Dewey's thought. Each chapter is followed by a long list of pertinent writings by Dewey.

Boydston, Jo Ann, and Robert L. Andresen, eds. *John Dewey: A Checklist of Translations, 1900-1967.* Carbondale: Southern Illinois University Press, 1969. A comprehensive collection of translations of Dewey's writings in many languages.

Federal Writer's Project, WPA, Massachusetts. *Selective and Critical Bibliography of Horace Mann.* Boston: State Department of Education, 1937. Annotations of the published works by and about the influential educator.

King, Clyde S. *Horace Mann, 1796-1859: A Bibliography.* Dobbs Ferry, N.Y.: Oceana Publications, 1966. A comprehensive, partially annotated compilation of the writings by and about Horace Mann. Especially valuable are the listing of manuscripts and newspaper articles.

Leidecker, Kurt F. "Bibliography: William Torrey Harris in Literature," in Edward F. Schaub, ed., *William Torrey Harris, 1835-1935.* Chicago: Open

Court Publishing Co., 1936, pp. 125-136. A listing of writings on Harris by Europeans and Americans.

Mann, B. Pickman. "Bibliography of Horace Mann," in *Report of the Commissioner of Education for the Year 1896-97*. Vol. I. Washington: Government Printing Office, 1898, pp. 897-927. A comprehensive listing, as of the end of the 19th century, of writings by and about Mann.

Monroe, Will S. *Bibliography of Henry Barnard*. Boston: New England Publishing Co., 1897. A collection of titles by and about Barnard, including several in four European languages.

"Publications from 1898 to 1940 by E. L. Thorndike." *Teachers College Record*, vol. 41 (May, 1940), pp. 699-725. An unannotated listing which supplements the collection by Simpson (see below) of the works by the pioneering educational psychologist.

Simpson, Benjamin R., *et al.* "Annotated Chronological Bibliography of Publications by E. L. Thorndike." *Teachers College Record*, vol. 27 (February, 1926), pp. 466-515. A descriptively annotated compilation of the works, 1898-1925, by the influential educational psychologist.

Thomas, Milton H. *John Dewey: A Centennial Bibliography*. Chicago: University of Chicago Press, 1962. An expanded edition of a comprehensive, chronologically arranged, indexed listing of works by Dewey and English and foreign writings about him. This standard work includes the tables of contents of the volumes and reviews of Dewey's books.

Wilson, Louis N. "Bibliography of the Published Writings of G. Stanley Hall: 1866-1924," in National Academy of Sciences of the United States of America, *Biographical Memoir*, Vol. 12. Washington: National Academy of Sciences, 1929, pp. 155-180. A more complete listing of the works by the psychologist and president of Clark University.

Wilson, Louis N. "Bibliography of the Published Writings of President G. Stanley Hall." *American Journal of Psychology*, vol. 14 (July-October, 1903), pp. 417-430. An unannotated listing of the works by a pioneer in child, adolescent, and educational psychology. Also published in *Publications of the Clark University Library*, vol. 1 (October, 1903), pp. 3-16.

E. SUBJECTS

Bardeen, Charles W. *Catalogue of Rare Books on Pedagogy*. Syracuse, N.Y.: Bardeen, 1894. Helpful references for the history of teacher education in the United States.

Bellack, Arno A. "History of Curriculum Thought and Practice." *Review of Educational Research*, vol. 39 (June, 1969), pp. 283-292. A bibliographical essay covering the writings published during 1964-1968 on the history of and current situation in curriculum theory, problems, issues, and plans.

Davis, Sheldon E. *Educational Periodicals during the Nineteenth Century*. Bulletin 1919, No. 28, U.S. Bureau of Education. Washington: Government Printing Office, 1919. Reprinted, Metuchen, N.J.: Scarecrow Press, 1970. A unique, analytical study of American educational journals followed by an annotated listing of the periodicals in chronological order (pp. 93-112). Scarecrow reprint includes introductory note by F. Cordasco.

Finkelstein, Barbara J. "Schooling and Schoolteachers: Selected Bibliography of Autobiographies in the Nineteenth Century." *History of Education Quarterly*, vol. 14 (Summer, 1974), pp. 293-300. An unannotated listing of autobiographical works containing recollections of schooling and teaching.

Karpinski, Louis C. *Bibliography of Mathematical Works Published in America through 1850*. Ann Arbor: University of Michigan Press, 1940. Covers over 1,000 books in 3,000 editions published in North America until 1850 and in South America until 1800. A valuable compilation for research in the history of the teaching of mathematics in the United States.

Reddick, L. D. "Select Bibliography." *Journal of Educational Sociology*, vol. 19 (April, 1946), pp. 512-516. A partially annotated compilation of 59 publications, most of them dealing with the history of black education in the United States.

Richey, Herman G. "History of Education in the United States: Adult Education." *Review of Educational Research*, vol. 9 (October, 1939), pp. 352-356, 417-419. A commentary on and listing of 45 works.

F. STATE

Green, Paul G. *An Annotated Bibliography of the History of Education in Kansas*. Emporia: Kansas State Teachers College, 1935. A suitably classified compilation of writings, chiefly of a secondary nature.

Jorgenson, Lloyd P. "Materials on the History of Education in State Historical Journals." *History of Education Quarterly*, vol. 7 (Summer, 1967), pp. 234-254. An unannotated listing of articles on the history of education especially of the South, in the historical journals of Alabama, Arkansas, Florida, Kentucky, Mississippi, North Carolina, South Carolina, Texas, and Virginia. Arrangement by year of publication.

Jorgenson, Lloyd P. "Materials on the History of Education in State Historical Journals." *History of Education Quarterly*, vol. 7 (Fall, 1967), pp. 369-389. Articles published in the historical journals of the Midwest—Illinois, Indiana, Iowa, Kansas, and Michigan.

Jorgenson, Lloyd P. "Materials on the History of Education in State Historical Journals." *History of Education Quarterly*, vol. 7 (Winter, 1968), pp. 510-527. A list of articles published in the historical journals of the Midwest—Minnesota, Nebraska, North Dakota, Ohio, and Oklahoma.

Jorgenson, Lloyd P. "Materials on the History of Education in State Historical Journals." *History of Education Quarterly*, vol. 9 (Spring, 1969), pp. 73-87. Articles on educational history published in the historical journals of the East (Delaware, Maryland, New York, Pennsylvania, Vermont, and West Virginia) and of the West (California, Colorado, Montana, Oregon, New Mexico, Washington, and Utah).

Noble, Stuart G. "State Histories of Education." *Review of Educational Research*, vol. 6 (October, 1936), pp. 372-377, 429-431. A critical review and a listing of 54 comprehensive and specialized works on state educational history.

Sheldon, Henry D. *A Critical and Descriptive Bibliography of the History of Education in the State of Oregon*. Eugene: University of Oregon, 1929. A collection of briefly annotated books, dissertations, and articles.

G. INDEXES

Analytical Index to Barnard's American Journal of Education. U.S. Bureau of Education. Washington: Government Printing Office, 1892. A valuable guide to the essays, documents, and other materials on the history of American and European education published in the 31 volumes (1855-1881) under the editorship of Henry Barnard.

Butler, Nicholas M., ed. *Educational Review: Analytical Index to Volumes 26-60; June, 1903, to December, 1915*. Easton, Pa.: Educational Review Publishing Co., 1916. A guide to the contents of periodical reflecting the significant developments in the recent and contemporary education in the United States during the early 20th century.

Nelson, Charles A., ed. *Educational Review: Analytical Index to Volumes 1-25; January, 1891, to May, 1903*. Easton, Pa.: Educational Review Publishing Co., 1904. A guide to articles and book reviews dealing with the history and recent development of education in the United states.

Nelson, Martha F., comp. *Index by Authors, Titles, and Subjects to the Publications of the National Educational Association for Its First Fifty Years, 1857 to 1906*. Winona, Minn.: National Educational Association, 1907. A guide to the addresses, papers, and other writings throwing light on the development of education in the United States during the late 20th century.

Porter, Dorothy B., and Ethel M. Ellis, comps. *The Journal of Negro Education: Index to Volumes 1-31, 1932-1962*. Washington: Howard University Press, 1963. An index of articles by title, subject, and author. Includes articles on the history of the education of Negroes in the United

States.

[Shereshewsky, Murray S., ed.] *History of Education Quarterly Index*. New York: History of Education Society, 1973. A ten year index, vols. 1-10, by title, subject, and author.

[U.S. Bureau of Education] *Index to the Reports of the Commissioner of Education*. Bulletin, 1909, No. 7. Washington: Government Printing Office, 1909. Reprinted, Totowa, N.J.: Rowman and Littlefield, 1970. A comprehensive index of the annual reports of the U.S. Commissioner of Education. Includes authors and subjects, with an analysis of the more important articles for the years 1867-1907 inclusive. Reprint edition includes introduction by F. Cordasco.

II. COLLECTIONS OF SOURCE MATERIALS

A. GENERAL

Best, John H., and Robert T. Sidwell, eds. *The American Legacy of Learning: Readings in the History of Education*. Philadelphia: Lippincott, 1967. A compilation of 131 source materials and theoretical statements from colonial times through the 1950's. Editorial notes, bibliography, and index.

Bremner, Robert H., ed. *Children and Youth in America: A Documentary History*. 3 vols. in 5. Cambridge: Harvard University Press, 1970-1974. An appropriately classified, comprehensive collection of a wide variety of documentary materials on child and adolescent life, labor, and education, in the family, the school, factory, and society, from the colonial period to the present. Editorial introductions, chronologies, bibliographies, and indexes. A unique and valuable work.

Calhoun, Daniel, ed. *The Educating of Americans: A Documentary History*. Boston: Houghton Miffin, 1969. A compilation of 155 source materials covering the development of education in the United States, including European precedents and ideas of the sixteenth and seventeenth centuries. Arranged topically, the documents include laws, programs, addresses, reports, court decisions, and other materials. Brief introductions and an excellent bibliographical essay on source publications.

Cohen, Sol. *Education in the United States: A Documentary History*. 5 vols. New York: Random House, 1974. "Attempts to bring together the most significant documents in the field of American education, extending from the 16th and 17th century English and European background to the earliest colonial beginnings to the present, and to locate them in their historical context." Historical overviews introduce each of the books. Book I: The Planting, 1607-1789; Book II: The Shaping of American Education, 1789-1895; Book III: The Transformation of American Education, 1895-1973.

Crane, Theodore R., ed. *The Dimensions of American Education*. Reading, Mass.: Addison-Wesley, 1974. A compilation of laws, statements, arguments, and book extracts, including secondary writings, throwing light on several aspects of education in the United States from the colonial era to the 1960's. Brief introductions and an appropriately annotated bibliography.

Cremin, Lawrence A., advisory editor. *American Education: Its Men, Ideas, and Institutions.* New York: Arno Press/New York Times, 1970-1971. Two series of volumes (161 vols.) in a massive reprint program of basic materials in the history of American education.

Cubberley, Ellwood P., ed. *Readings in Public Education in the United States.* Boston: Houghton Mifflin, 1934. For some time, a standard collection of sources covering American education from the colonial period to the twentieth century.

Cubberley, Ellwood P., and Edward C. Elliot, eds. *State and County School Administration: Volume II, Source Book.* New York: Macmillan, 1915. A convenient anthology of the texts of the early state constitutional provisions for education, land-grant ordinances for schools, other school grants, court decisions and miscellaneous sources illustrating the development of school administration and finance into the twentieth century.

Gross, Carl H., and Charles C. Chandler, eds. *The History of American Education through Readings.* Boston: Heath, 1964. Theoretical and policy statements, documents, secondary readings and literary writings illustrating the development of education in the United States from the colonial period to 1960. Editorial introductions to each chronological section and an index.

Hillesheim, James W., and George D. Merrill, eds. *Theory and Practice in the History of American Education.* Pacific Palisades, Calif.: Goodyear, 1971. A documentary history of educational thought and practice in the United States, including European philosophical precursors, from the colonial era to the 1960's. The sources include laws, school regulations, constitutional provisions, reports, and court decisions.

Hillway, Tyrus, ed. *American Education: An Introduction through Readings.* Boston: Houghton Mifflin, 1964. A compilation of 41 documents, including eight court decisions, and theoretical statements from the colonial era to 1960. Introductory chapter and chapter introductions by the editor.

Hinsdale, B. A., comp. "Documents Illustrative of American Educational History," in *Report of the Commissioner of Education for the Year 1892-93,* Vol. II. Washington: Government Printing Office, 1895, pp. 1225-1414. A useful collection of sources on the history of American education from the seventeenth century to about 1890.

Katz, Michael B., ed. *School Reform: Past and Present.* Boston: Little, Brown, 1971. An anthology of 56 theoretical and policy statements from 1826 to 1969, on urban public education and social problems, pedagogical principles and practice, black education, and bureaucratic educational administration and organization. Brief introduction by the editor.

Knight, Edgar W., ed. *Readings in Educational Administration*. New York: Holt, 1953. A collection of 191 laws, constitutional provisions, policy statements, court decisions, and other sources on the administrative and organizational development of education, including controversial issues, in the United States from colonial times to the mid-twentieth century. Editorial previews, footnotes, bibliographical notes, and index.

Knight, Edgar W., and Clifton L. Hall, eds. *Readings in American Educational History*. New York: Appleton-Century-Crofts, 1951. An extensive compilation of primary source materials of all types on the development of education in the United States from colonial times to the mid-twentieth century. Some uncommon sources are included.

Monroe, Paul, ed. *Readings in the Founding of the American Public School System*. Ann Arbor, Mich.: University Microfilms, 1940. Considerable source material, reproduced in microfilm form, on the development of education in the United States prior to the Civil War.

Noll, James W., and Sam P. Kelly, eds. *Foundations of Education in America: An Anthology of Major Thoughts and Significant Actions*. New York: Harper & Row, 1970. A compilation of laws, court decisions, and theoretical statements on education in the United States from the colonial period through the 1960's. A substantial portion of the volume is devoted to ancient, medieval, and modern European sources. Interpretative introductions, modern bibliography, and indexes of basic issues.

Rippa, S. Alexander, ed. *Educational Ideas in America: A Documentary History*. New York: McKay, 1969. A collection of philosophical statements in educational and other treatises, letters, reports, laws, and textbooks illustrating the development of educational theory in the United States. Thoughts from ancient and medieval and modern European sources are included.

Smiley, Marjorie B., and John S. Diekhoff, eds. *Prologue to Teaching*. New York: Oxford University Press, 1959. Source materials and recent statements on the teacher, educational aims and policy, curriculum, and sociocultural context from colonial America to the mid-twentieth century. Some sources are from ancient, medieval, and modern European education. Editorial introductions to each section.

Tyack, David B., ed. *Turning Points in American Educational History*. Waltham, Mass.: Blaisdell, 1967. A documentary history of education in the United States, organized by eleven significant topics, from the colonial period to the twentieth century. Interpretative introductions and tables of historical statistics.

Vassar, Rena L., ed. *Social History of American Education.* 2 vols. Chicago: Rand McNally, 1965. An anthology of 73 sources—statements, letters, court decisions, constitutional provisions—emphasizing the development of attitudes and provisions in public education in the United States for diverse social and racial groups. Helpful editorial introductions.

Welter, Rush, ed. *American Writings on Popular Education: The Nineteenth Century.* Indianapolis: Bobbs-Merrill, 1971. A group of 37 documents—reports, letters, addresses, statements, and other sources—illustrating controversies and other aspects of public and private education in the United States from 1810 to 1897. Analytical introduction and bibliography.

B. STATE AND REGIONAL

Chadbourne, Ava H., comp. *Readings in the History of Education in Maine.* Bangor, Me.: Burr, 1932. A collection of source materials from the colonial era through the nineteenth century.

Coon, Charles L., ed. *North Carolina Schools and Academies, 1790-1840.* Raleigh, N.C.: Edwards and Broughton, 1915. Source materials dealing with the development of secondary education in the early decades of the Republic.

Coon, Charles L., ed. *The Beginnings of Public Education in North Carolina*: A Documentary History, 1790-1840. 2 vols. Raleigh, N.C.: Edwards and Broughton, 1908. A comprehensive compilation of complete texts of reports, letters, and other primary source materials.

Cowley, Elizabeth B. *Free Learning.* Boston: Humphries, 1941. Laws, governors' messages, provisions in constitutions, and other sources on education in Massachusetts, Pennsylvania, Michigan, and California from colonial times to the twentieth century.

Eby, Frederick, comp. *Education in Texas: Source Materials.* Austin: University of Texas, 1918. A unique collection of primary sources for the history of education in Texas from the Spanish colonial era to 1890. This 963-page book contains a 72-page bibliography.

Fleming, Walter L. *Documentary History of Reconstruction.* Vol. II. Cleveland: Clark, 1907. Includes letters, newspaper editorials, congressional and other reports, extracts from contemporary discussions, and other sources on educational developments and problems in the postbellum South.

Klain, Zora, ed. *Educational Activities of New England Quakers: A Source Book.* Philadelphia: Westbrook, 1928. A compilation of minutes of meetings, from colonial times to the twentieth century, dealing with educational questions among the Quakers.

Knight, Edgar W., ed. *A Documentary History of Education in the South before 1860.* 5 vols. Chapel Hill: University of North Carolina Press, 1949-1953. A five-volume, comprehensive compilation of source materials of the eighteenth and nineteenth centuries in the various Southern colonies and states. An exemplary work with informative editorial essays and notes. Indispensable for research on Southern educational history, as well as for the history of education in the United States.

Martz, Velorus, and Stanley E. Ballinger. *A Guide to the Source Material Relating to Education in the Laws of the State of Indiana, 1816-1851; Part One: 1816-1838.* Bloomington: Bureau of Research and Field Services, Indiana University, 1953. A compilation, in chronological order, of the legislation on education.

Martz, Velorus, and Henry L. Smith. *Source Material Relating to the Development of Education in Indiana.* Bloomington: Bureau of Cooperative Research and Field Service, 1945. A collection of ordinances, legislative resolutions, acts, letters, petitions, and other source materials, mostly concerned with the eighteenth century.

Pyburn, Nita K., ed. *Documentary History of Education in Florida, 1822-1860.* [Tallahassee:] Florida State University Press, 1951. The documentary materials include laws, newspaper notices, legislative reports, and school vouchers.

Woody, Thomas. *Quaker Education in the Colony and State of New Jersey: A Source Book.* Philadelphia: University of Pennsylvania, 1923. Numerous source materials on the eighteenth and nineteenth centuries.

C. ELEMENTARY AND SECONDARY EDUCATION

Caldwell, Otis W., and Stuart A. Courtis. *Then and Now in Education, 1845-1923.* Yonkers, N.Y.: World Book Co., 1923. A collection of tests, reports, and other sources on school testing in Boston during the nineteenth century.

Clews, Elsie W. *Educational Legislation and Administration of Colonial Governments.* New York: Macmillan, 1899. A valuable collection of laws and other documentary materials on education during the colonial era.

Johnson, Clifton. *Old-Time Schools and School-Books.* New York: Macmillan, 1904. Extracts from eighteenth and nineteenth-century American textbooks together with many facsimile pages.

Littlefield, George E. *Early Schools and School-Books of New England.* Boston: The Club of Odd Volumes, 1904. This volume of essays on education in colonial New England includes facsimiles of title pages and other content of books used for instruction in the seventeenth century.

Livengood, W. W., comp. *Americana as Taught to the Tune of a Hickory Stick*.[n.p.] Women's National Book Association, 1954. Facsimile pages and extracts from nineteenth-century elementary readers, spellers, and arithmetic, geography, and history textbooks. Also included are a few items of the seventeenth and eighteenth centuries. Introduction and notes by the compiler.

Meriwether, Colyer. *Our Colonial Curriculum, 1606-1776.* Washington: Capital Publishing Co., 1907. A study which contains documents and other source materials related to courses of study in colonial schools and colleges.

Raubinger, Frederick M., *et al.*, eds. *The Development of Secondary Education.* [New York:] Macmillan, 1969. Texts of some reports and generous extracts of others on the changes in theory, organization, administration, and curriculum of the American secondary school from the 1890's through 1945. Editorial introductions and epilogue, and a bibliography.

Seybold, Robert F. *The Private Schools of Colonial Boston.* Cambridge: Harvard University Press, 1935. Includes newspaper advertisements of schools, 1706-1776. Useful for the listing of subjects offered in colonial schools.

Seybolt, Robert F. *The Public Schools of Colonial Boston, 1635-1775.* Cambridge: Harvard University Press, 1935. Contains many source materials.

Seybold, Robert F., ed. *Source Studies in American Colonial Education: The Private School.* Urbana: University of Illinois, 1925. Primary source materials showing evidence of the flourishing of private education in early American history.

Sizer, Theodore R., ed. *The Age of the Academies.* New York: Bureau of Publications, Teachers College, Columbia University, 1964. Twelve theoretical statements and other source materials (including John Milton's "Of Education") on development of the academy in the United States, 1749-1885. Introduction, bibliographical commentary, and chapter notes by the editor.

Small, Walter H. *Early New England Schools.* Boston: Ginn, 1914. Includes many extracts from documents related to elementary and secondary education during the seventeenth and eighteenth centuries.

Smith, Henry L., Merrill T. Eaton, and Kathleen Dugdale. *One Hundred Fifty Years of Arithmetic Textbooks.* Bloomington: Bureau of Cooperative Research and Field Service, Indiana University, 1945. Many extracts and facsimile pages from textbooks used in American schools since the Revolution.

Smith, Henry L., *et al. One Hundred Fifty Years of Grammar Textbooks.*

Division of Research and Field Services, Indiana University, 1946. Numerous excerpts and facsimile pages from schoolbooks used in American schools since the Revolution.

D. HIGHER EDUCATION

Brubacher, John S. *The Law and Higher Education: A Casebook.* 2 vols. Rutherford, N.J.: Fairleigh Dickinson University Press, 1971. A convenient compilation of texts of the major Federal and state court decisions of the nineteenth and twentieth centuries regarding student admission and dismissal, professorial appointment and dismissal, academic freedom, administrative issues, academic program, and other problems.

Butterfield, L. H., ed. *John Witherspoon Comes to America.* Princeton, N.J.: Princeton University Library, 1953. A collection of correspondence, 1766-1770, involving the future president of the College of New Jersey, Benjamin Rush, Ezra Stiles, and others. Editorial introduction and useful notes.

Crane, Theodore R., ed. *The Colleges and the Public, 1787-1862.* New York: Bureau of Publications, Teachers College, Columbia University, 1963. Twelve documents, including the writings of George Washington, Thomas Jefferson, and Henry P. Tappan throwing light on the early development and problems of higher education in the United States. Editorial introduction and documentary headnotes.

Dexter, Franklin B., ed. *Documentary History of Yale University.* New Haven: Yale University Press, 1916. Letters, proceedings of trustees' meetings, legislative documents, and other source materials on the early history of Yale, 1701-1745.

Elliott, Edward C., and M. M. Chambers, eds. *Charters and Basic Laws of Selected American Universities and Colleges.* New York: Carnegie Foundation for the Advancement of Teaching, 1934. The texts of the charters and laws concerning the founding of 51 colleges and universities, including Cornell, Harvard, Wisconsin, and Stanford. The appendix reprints the Morrill Acts of 1862 and 1890 and other Federal laws affecting higher education, and adds a list of court decisions on colleges and universities.

Federal Laws and Rulings Relating to Morrill and Supplementary Morrill Funds for Land-Grant Colleges and Universities. Pamphlet No. 91, U.S. Office of Education. Washington: U.S. Government Printing Office, 1940. The texts of laws and rulings thereon from 1862 to 1940.

Hammond, William G. *Remembrance of Amherst.* New York: Columbia University Press, 1946. The diary kept by an undergraduate during 1846-1848. Interesting insight into student life during the mid-nineteenth century.

Hofstadter, Richard, and Wilson Smith, eds. *American Higher Education: A Documentary History*. 2 vols. Chicago: University of Chicago Press, 1961. An anthology of 158 sources—statutes, charters, statements, arguments, plans, reports—on the history of colleges and universities in the United States from 1633 to the mid-twentieth century. Particularly useful for changing ideas of higher education.

Knight, Edgar W. *What College Presidents Say*. Chapel Hill: University of North Carolina Press, 1940. Excerpts from the commencement addresses, speeches, and annual reports of heads of colleges and universities in the nineteenth and twentieth centuries.

Morgan, Joy E. *Horace Mann at Antioch*. Washington: National Education Association, 1938. Includes the addresses and sermons delivered by Mann as president of Antioch College, 1853-1859.

Morison, Samuel E. *Harvard College in the Seventeenth Century*. 2 vols. Cambridge: Harvard University Press, 1936. Includes source materials, particularly the titles of Latin thesis subjects at commencements.

Nissenbaum, Stephen, ed. *The Great Awakening at Yale College*. Belmont, Calif.: Wadsworth Publishing Co., 1972. A group of 50 letters, diaries, memoirs, reports, resolutions, laws, and other sources revealing the impact of George Whitefield's religious revival on Yale faculty and students during 1740-1745. Editorial introductions, chronology, appendix, and a bibliographical essay. A unique, highly specialized source book.

Weaver, David A., ed. *Builders of American Universities: Inaugural Addresses, Privately Controlled Institutions*. Alton, Ill.: Shurtleff College Press, 1950. The texts of the inaugural address of 19 presidents (Charles W. Eliot, Woodrow Wilson, Mark Hopkins, G. Stanley Hall, etc.) of the nineteenth and twentieth centuries.

E. EDUCATIONAL THOUGHT

Archambault, Reginald D., ed. *John Dewey on Education: Selected Writings*. New York: Random House, 1964. Numerous writings by Dewey, from 1897 onward, on the relation of ethics, aesthetics, science, psychology, and society to educational theory and practice.

Arrowood, Charles F., ed. *Thomas Jefferson and Education in a Republic*. New York: McGraw-Hill, 1930. Extracts from Jefferson's letters, reports, and other writings dealing with educational themes. Introduction discusses the life, and educational ideas and contributions by Jefferson.

Babbidge, Homer D., Jr., ed. *Noah Webster: On Being American; Selected Writings, 1783-1828*. New York: Praeger, 1967. Selections from the educational and other writings by the influential lexicographer and author of widely used textbooks. Editorial introductions and commentaries.

Best, John H., ed. *Benjamin Franklin on Education*. New York: Bureau of Publications, Teachers College, Columbia University, 1962. Letters, speeches, essays, and other writings by Franklin on various educational and related themes. Editorial introduction and bibliographical note.

Brubacher, John S., ed. *Henry Barnard on Education*. New York: McGraw-Hill, 1931. A biographical and interpretative introduction precedes several writings by the 19th century educator.

Cremin, Lawrence A., ed. *The Republic and the School: Horace Mann on the Education of Free Men*. New York: Bureau of Publications, Teachers College, Columbia University, 1957. Extracts from the twelve annual reports written by Mann as secretary of the Massachusetts Board of Education, 1837-1848. Editorial introduction and documentary headnotes.

Cross, Barbara M., ed. *The Educated Woman in America: Selected Writings of Catharine Beecher, Margaret Fuller, and M. Carey Thomas*. New York: Teachers College Press, 1965. Thoughts by influential educators on the education of women in the United States during the nineteenth and twentieth centuries. Editorial introduction and documentary headnotes.

Dworkin, Martin S., ed. *Dewey on Education*. New York: Bureau of Publications, Teachers College, Columbia University, 1959. Selected educational writings by John Dewey, 1897-1952. Introductory essay and notes by the editor.

Evans, Henry R., and Edith A. Wright, comps. *Expressions on Education by Builders of American Democracy*. Bulletin 1940, No. 10, U.S. Office of Education. Washington: U.S. Government Printing Office, 1940. Brief statements by political leaders and educators, from the eighteenth to the twentieth century, on the contributions of education to the growth and welfare of the United States.

Filler, Louis, ed. *Horace Mann on the Crisis in Education*. [Yellow Springs, Ohio:] Antioch Press, 1965. Lengthy extracts from the writings of the nineteenth-century educator-statesman on aims and problems of education. General introduction, introductory notes, and chronology by the editor.

Garforth, F. W., ed. John Dewey: *Selected Educational Writings*. London: Heinemann, 1966. Various statements on education by Dewey since 1897. Editorial introduction, bibliography, and notes.

Grattan, C. Hartley, ed. *American Ideas about Adult Education, 1710-1951*. New York: Bureau of Publications, Teachers College, Columbia University, 1959. Sixteen theoretical statements illustrating the development of thought concerning the various aspects of the education of adults in the United States. Brief editorial introduction and documentary headnotes.

Greven, Philip J., Jr., ed. *Child-Rearing Concepts, 1628-1861: Historical*

Sources. Itasca, Ill.: Peacock, 1973. Ten statements by educators, philosophers, and theologians on the nature and education of children. Four of the writers are English, but their influence was felt in America. Introductions by the editor.

Honeywell, Roy J. *The Educational Work of Thomas Jefferson.* Cambridge: Harvard University Press, 1931. A collection of Jefferson's letters and statements dealing with education, preceded by an analysis.

Joncich, Geraldine M., ed. *Psychology and the Science of Education: Selected Writings of Edward L. Thorndike.* New York: Bureau of Publications, Teachers College, Columbia University, 1962. Extracts from Thorndike's writings on curriculum, instruction, intelligence, learning, and measurement, 1901-1939. Editorial introduction and documentary headnotes.

Jones, Howard M., ed. *Emerson on Education.* New York: Teachers College Press, 1966. Seven essays on education and related themes by Ralph Waldo Emerson. Editorial introduction and brief bibliographical notes.

Krug, Edward A., ed. *Charles W. Eliot and Popular Education.* New York: Bureau of Publications, Teachers College, Columbia University, 1961. Nine statements by Eliot, most of them essays, on secondary and other aspects of education in the United States, 1869-1905. Editorial introduction and documentary headnotes.

Lee, Gordon C., ed. *Crusade Against Ignorance: Thomas Jefferson on Education.* New York: Bureau of Publications, Teachers College, Columbia University, 1961. Letters, reports, and statements by Thomas Jefferson on educational and related questions, 1776-1825. General and chapter introductions by the editor.

Mann, Mary P. *Life of Horace Mann.* Washington: National Education Association, 1937. Includes many letters written by the influential educator. Facsimile reprint of the 1865 edition.

Mayer, Frederick, ed. *Introductory Readings in Education.* Belmont, Calif.: Dickenson Publishing Co., 1966. Theoretical statements on American education from the eighteenth through the twentieth century. Editorial introductions and bibliography.

Rudolph, Frederick, ed. *Essays on Education in the Early Republic.* Cambridge: Harvard University Press, 1965. A convenient collection of the texts of eight educational writings by Benjamin Rush, Noah Webster, Samuel Harrison Smith, and other thinkers in eighteenth-century America. Editorial introduction, notes, and index.

Skilbeck, Malcolm, ed. *John Dewey.* London: Collier-Mcmillan, 1970. Many short extracts from Dewey's educational writings, 1900-1952, with an editorial introduction, notes, brief bibliography, and index.

Sloan, Douglas, ed. *The Great Awakening and American Education: A Documentary History*. New York: Teachers College Press, 1973. A group of 28 contemporary statements by individuals and groups on the roles of religion, education, culture in eighteenth-century America. Editorial introduction and bibliographical note.

Smith, Wilson, ed. *Theories of Education in Early America, 1655-1819*. Indianapolis: Bobbs-Merrill, 1973. A collection of 28 fresh and familiar statements by philosophers, theologians, statesmen, and educators on education in the family and school. Editorial introductions, chronology, bibliographies, and index.

Strickland, Charles E., and Charles Burgess, eds. *Health, Growth, and Heredity: G. Stanley Hall on Natural Education*. New York: Teachers College Press, 1965. Twelve statements by Hall, 1885-1923, on psychology, childhood and adolescence, elementary and secondary school, and health and moral education. Editorial introduction and documentary headnotes.

Thomas, Maurice J., comp. *Presidential Statements on Education: Excerpts from Inaugural and State of the Union Messages, 1789-1967*. Pittsburgh: University of Pittsburgh Press, 1967. An anthology of brief extracts illustrating Presidential perceptions of American education at various periods.

Ulich, Robert, ed. *A Sequence of Educational Influences*. Cambridge: Harvard University Press, 1935. Five manuscript letters involving the exchange of educational ideas among European (Johann Heinrich Pestalozzi, Friedrich Froebel, and Adolf Diesterweg) and American (Horace Mann and Henry Barnard) educators. The European letters are in the German original and in translation. A helpful interpretation of the historical significance of the letters.

Winn, Ralph B., ed. *John Dewey: Dictionary of Education*. New York: Philosophical Library, 1959. Quotations on education and related themes from the works of Dewey arranged in alphabetical order by topic. The sources of the quotations are indicated, but minus the page numbers. Cross-references.

Woody, Thomas, ed. *Educational Views of Benjamin Franklin*. New York: McGraw-Hill, 1931. A biographical essay followed by some of Franklin's writings on education.

F. MISCELLANEOUS

Bestor, Arthur E., Jr., ed. *Education and Reform at New Harmony: Correspondence of William MacLure and Marie Duclos Fretageot, 1820-1833*. Indianapolis: Indiana Historical Society, 1948. The letters between the social and educational reformer and his deputy " . . . constitute the only continuous contemporary record of the genesis, culmination, and dissolution of [Robert] Owen's social experiment [Workingmen's Institute at New Harmony] and of the steadier advance of the scientific and educational programs connected with it." Editorial introduction and connecting commentary and an index.

Borrowman, Merle L., ed. *Teacher Education in America: A Documentary History*. New York: Teachers College Press, 1965. A group of sources, mainly theoretical statements, eleven of which deal with the development of teacher education in the United States, 1839-1946. Editorial introduction and documentary headnotes.

Fellman, David, ed. *The Supreme Court and Education*. New York: Teachers College Press, 1969. An updated edition of a compilation of extracts from 22 decisions by the United States Supreme Court, from 1925 to 1968, on church-state-school relations, racial segregation, and academic freedom. Brief editorial introductions.

Fraser, Stewart E., ed. *American Education in Foreign Perspectives: Twentieth Century Essays*. New York: Wiley, 1969. A volume of 39 analyses and evaluations, 1902-1968, presenting "a panorama of some of the facets of twentieth-century education as seen through the eyes of illustrative foreign commentators." The writers, who represent Britain, China, France, Germany, Sweden, the U.S.S.R., and seven other countries, include Sir Michael Sadler, Gunnar Myrdal, and Arnold Toynbee. Editorial introduction, bibliographical essay, and a 57-page bibliography in several languages.

Gartner, Lloyd P., ed. *Jewish Education in the United States: A Documentary History*. New York: Teachers College Press, 1969. A group of 39 documents tracing the growth of American Jewish education from the eighteenth century to 1960. Editorial introduction, bibliographical commentary, and documentary headnotes.

Goodsell, Willystine, ed. *Pioneers of Women's Education in the United States*. New York: McGraw-Hill, 1931. Extracts from the educational writings of nineteenth-century women educators—Emma Hart Willard, Catharine Esther Beecher, and Mary Lyon. There are brief biographical introductions.

Kliebard, Herbert M., ed. *Religion and Education in America: A Documentary History*. Scranton: International Textbook, 1969. Legal and judicial sources, as well as theoretical and policy statements, from the eighteenth century to the late 1960's. Interpretative introductory essay and comments on the documents by the editor. Selected bibliography.

Knight, Edgar W., ed. *Reports on European Education*. New York: McGraw-Hill, 1930. Reports on European schools by John Griscom, Calvin E. Stowe, and Victor Cousin for the enlightenment of American educators and laymen.

Lazerson, Marvin, and W. Norton Grubb, eds. *American Education and Vocationalism: A Documentary History, 1870-1970*. New York: Teachers College Press, 1974. A group of 21 reports, theoretical statements, and other sources on a century of vocational education in the United States. Editorial introduction and bibliographical essay.

Lewis, Elmer A., comp. *Laws Relating to Vocational Education and Agricultural Extension*. Washington: U.S. Government Printing Office, 1941. The texts of laws passed during 1914-1940.

McCluskey, Neil G., S.J., ed. *Catholic Education in America: A Documentary History*. New York: Bureau of Education, Teachers College, Columbia University, 1964. Thirteen documents, all but one of an ecclesiastical source, on the development of Catholic education in the United States from 1792 to 1950. Editorial introduction, bibliographical commentary, and documentary headnotes.

Norton, Arthur O., ed. *The First State Normal School in America: The Journals of Cyrus Peirce and Mary Swift*. Cambridge: Harvard University Press, 1936. The text of the journals of the first principal and a member of the first class, plus other documents on the early history of teacher training in Massachusetts.

Peterson, Houston, ed. *Great Teachers*. New Brunswick: Rutgers University Press, 1946. Statements by former students of distinguished American and other teachers of the nineteenth and twentieth centuries.

Spurlock, Clark. *Education and the Supreme Court*. Urbana: University of Illinois Press, 1955. Extracts from the decisions of the United States Supreme Court in the nineteenth and twentieth centuries on a variety of educational issues, including academic freedom, church-state relations, and racial segregation. Editorial introductions, an index of cases, and a bibliography.

III. THE HISTORIOGRAPHY OF AMERICAN EDUCATION

Bailyn, Bernard. "Education as a Discipline: Some Historical Notes," in John Walton and James L. Kuethe, *The Discipline of Education* (Madison: University of Wisconsin Press, 1963), pp. 125-139. Also, *Comments* by Wilson Smith, *Ibid.*, pp. 139-144.

Bailyn, Bernard. *Education in the Forming of American Society: Needs and Opportunities for Study*. Chapel Hill: University of North Carolina Press, 1960. Education "as the entire process by which a culture transmits itself across the generations." A classic revisionist interpretation.

Barzun, Jacques. "History: The Muse and Her Doctors." *The American Historical Review,* vol. 77 (February, 1972), pp. 36-64.

Beach, Mark. "History of Education." *Review of Educational Research,* vol. 39 (December, 1969), pp. 561-576. An overview and review of the literature keyed to a bibliography.

Berkhofer, Robert F. "Clio and the Culture Concept: Some Impressions of a Changing Relationship in American Historiography." *Social Science Quarterly,* vol. 53 (September, 1972), pp. 297-320.

Brickman, William W. "Conant, Koerner, and the History of Education." *School and Society,* vol. 92 (1964), pp. 135-139.

Brickman, William W. "Educational Literature Review: Educational History of the United States." *School and Society,* vol. 72 (1950), pp. 436-444.

Brickman, William W. *Guide to Research in Educational History*. New York: New York University Bookstore, 1949. Seeks "to analyze the principles and procedures of historical research as applied to the content of the field of education." Includes valuable annotated bibliographies. Reissued with additional material, Norwood, Pa.: Norwood Editions, 1973.

Brickman, William W. "An Historical Survey of Foreign Writings on American Educational History." *Paedagogica Historica,* vol. 2 (1962), pp. 5-21.

Brickman, William W. "Revisionism and the Study of the History of Education."

History of Education Quarterly, vol. 4 (December, 1964), pp. 209-223. Critical of Bailyn and revisionist historiography.

Burgess, Charles, and Merle L. Borrowman. *What Doctrines to Embrace: Studies in the History of American Education.* Glenview, Illinois: Scott, Foreman, 1969. "Taken collectively, the following chapters depict a general chronological progression from 1800 to the present. Taken separately, each chapter should be perceived as an independent essay attempting to stop the movement of history momentarily and examine certain dominant interrelationships of various factors then impinging upon education."

Butts, R. Freeman. "Civilization Building and the Modernization Process: A Framework for the Reinterpretation of the History of Education." *History of Education Quarterly,* vol. 7 (Summer, 1967), pp. 147-174. Revisionism, reinterpretation, reconstruction used synonymously in "tentative efforts to arrive at a schema . . . for the interpretation of the history of education." See "Response to Professor Butts" (George F. Kneller), *Ibid.,* pp. 175-181.

Butts, R. Freeman. "Public Education and Political Community." *History of Education Quarterly,* vol. 14 (Summer, 1974), pp. 165-183. An overview of revisionism in the history of American education. "It is now time to gain some perspective on the revisionist movements as we look ahead to see what shape the historiography of education should take in the next fifteen years."

Butts, R. Freeman. "The Public School: Assaults on a Great Idea." *The Nation,* vol. 216 (April 30, 1973), pp. 553-560. The history of the role of organized public education in building political community in the United States. See also, Butts, "The Public Purpose of the Public School," *Teachers College Record,* vol. 75 (December, 1973), pp. 207-221; and "Public Education and the Public Faith," *Educational Quest,* Memphis State University, 18 (Spring, 1974).

Cartwright, William H., and Richard L. Watson, eds. *The Reinterpretation of American History and Culture.* Washington: National Council for the Social Studies, 1973. Assessments of the revisionist historiography of the 1960's. See also, John Higham, ed., *The Reconstruction of American History* (1962) for the revisionism of the 1950's. On "new left history," see Barton J. Bernstein, ed., *Toward a New Past: Dissenting Essays in American History* (1968); and Irwin Unger, "The 'New Left' and American History," *American Historical Review,* vol. 72 (July, 1967), pp. 1237-1263.

Church, Robert L. "Economists as Experts: The Rise of an Academic Profession in America, 1870-1917," in Lawrence Stone, ed., *The University in Society.* 2 vols. (Princeton: Princeton University Press, 1974), vol. 2, pp. 571-609. The evolution of the social scientists as professional men in late 19th century America, using the demographic/social ("quantifiable evidence") methodologies associated with Lawrence Stone. See also in the same volume, James McLachlan, "The Choice of Hercules: American Student Societies in the Early 19th Century," pp. 449-494; and James M. McPherson, "The New Puritanism: Values and Goals of Freedmen's Education in America," pp. 611-639.

Church, Robert L. "History of Education as a Field of Study," in Lee C. Deighton, ed., *Encyclopedia of Education* (New York: Macmillan, 1971. 10 vols.), vol. 4, pp. 415-24.

Clifford, Geraldine J. " 'Psyching' Psycho-History." *History of Education Quarterly,* vol. 11 (Winter, 1971), pp. 413-425. An essay review and commentary, using Sudhir Kakar, *Frederick Taylor: A Study in Personality and Innovation* (1970) as a point of departure, on history written in Freudian or Eriksonian terms.

Cohen, Sol. "Sir Michael E. Sadler and the Sociopolitical Analysis of Education." *History of Education Quarterly,* vol. 7 (Fall, 1967), pp. 281-294. Sir Michael Sadler (1861-1943), a member of the Bryce Commission, and Professor of Education at the University of Manchester. "Especially for historians of education it may be fruitful to approach education as a branch of public administration, as a political problem, as an instrument of social welfare."

Crane, Theodore R., ed. *The Dimensions of American Education.* Reading, Mass.: Addison-Wesley, 1974. A collection of documents which "seeks to introduce students of education, American history, and American studies to the new historiography and to current controversial literature."

Cremin, Lawrence A. "The Family as Educator: Some Comments on the Recent Historiography." *Teachers College Record,* vol. 76 (December, 1974), pp. 250-265. Historical investigations of the last fifteen years with reference to the problems of education. Includes classified bibliography.

Cremin, Lawrence A. *The Genius of American Education.* Pittsburgh: University of Pittsburgh Press, 1965. The "thesis of this volume is that the genius of American education . . .lies in its commitment to popularization." Cremin's purpose is "to formulate a new, tough-minded progressivism that is at the same time consonant with the best in our tradition and appropriate to contemporary needs." See "A Review Symposium," *History of Education Quarterly,* vol. 7 (Spring, 1967), pp. 102-133. Participants: John L. Childs, Robert Ulich, William W. Brickman, Fred M. Hechinger, Paul Woodring, Brian Holmes, Rush Welter; and reply by Cremin.

Cremin, Lawrence A. "Notes Toward a Theory of Education." *Notes on Education,* Institute of Philosophy and Politics of Education, Teachers College, Columbia University, New York, No. 1 (June, 1973). A generally intellectual and cultural approach to history with stress on education as *paideia* (the total configurations or constellations of educational pursuits of which the "school" is only part), forming the basic themes for his comprehensive history of education which is underway. See also, Cremin, *American Education: Some Notes Toward a New History* (Bloomington: Indiana University, 1972).

Cremin, Lawrence A. "The Recent Development of the History of Education as a Field of Study in the United States." *History of Education Journal,* vol. 7(Spring, 1955), pp. 1-35.

Cremin, Lawrence A. *The Wonderful World of Ellwood Patterson Cubberley: An Essay on the Historiography of American Education.* New York: Bureau of Publications, Teachers College, Columbia University, 1965. Cubberley's *Public Education in the United States* (1919), its influence and importance (and the need for its general reinterpretation), set in a wide-ranging essay on the development of American educational historiography and its prospects. See review, Robert E. Mason, *History of Education Quarterly,* vol. 5 (Fall, 1966), pp. 187-90; and F. Cordasco, *Peabody Journal of Education,* vol. 43 (January, 1966), pp. 249-250.

Cross, Robert D. "Recent Histories of U.S. Catholic Education." *History of Education Quarterly,* vol. 14 (Spring, 1974), pp. 125-130. Observations on selected works published in the last decade.

Cubberley, Ellwood P. *Public Education in the United States: A Study and Interpretation of American Educational History.* Boston: Houghton Mifflin, 1919, 1934. Cremin: "It not only synthesized a wealth of previous scholarship into the now-familiar story of the public school triumphant; it proffered a vision of American education that proved both plausible and persuasive." (*Cubberley,* p. 1). Cubberley's view of the public school's progressive influence remained unchallenged until after World War II. See contemporary reviews by Charles Judd, *Elementary School Journal,* vol. 20 (1919-20), p. 68; Frank H. Palmer, *Education,* vol. 40 (1919-20), p. 194; Ernest C. Moore, *Educational Review,* vol. 60 (1920), pp. 159-162; Kimball Young, *American Journal of Sociology,* vol. 25 (1919-1920), pp. 505-507; I. L. Kandel, *School and Society,* vol. 11 (1920), pp. 205-207; and A. E. Winship, *Journal of Education,* vol.90 (1919), p. 211.

Curti, Merle. *The Social Ideas of American Educators: With a Chapter on the Last Twenty-Five Years.* [1935] Totowa, N.J.: Littlefield, Adams, 1959. An historical analysis of the social thought of American educators. Major attention to Horace Mann, Henry Barnard, Booker T. Washington, William T. Harris, Bishop Spaulding, Francis Wayland Parker, G. Stanley Hall, William James, Edward L. Thorndike, and John Dewey.

Cutler, William W. "Oral History: Its Nature and Uses for Educational History." *History of Education Quarterly,* vol. 11 (Summer, 1971), pp. 184-194. Observations of techniques initiated by Allan Nevins at Columbia University in 1948, and applications to history of education. See, Allan Nevins, "Oral History: How and Why it Was Born," *Wilson Library Bulletin,* vol. 40 (March, 1966), p. 601.

Fisher, Berenice M. "History, Social Science, and Education: Some Kinks in the Academic Procession." *History of Education Quarterly,* vol. 11 (Winter, 1971), pp. 426-434. An essay review on "the problems of historians as an occupational group and their relations to the social science disciplines and/or education." See also, George W. Stocking, "On the Limits of 'Presentism' and 'Historicism' in the Historiography of the Behavioral Sciences," *Journal of the History of the Behavioral Sciences,* vol. 1 (1965), pp. 211-217; and Robert A. Skotheim, *American Intellectual Histories and Historians* (1966).

[Fund for the Advancement of Education]. Committee on the Role of Education in American History. Paul H. Buck, *et al. The Role of Education in American History*. New York: The Fund [1957]. Report/statement of conference held under auspices of Fund for the Advancement of Education "to discuss the need of studying the role of education, not in its institutional forms alone, but in terms of all the influences that have helped shape the mind and character of the rising generation."

[Fund for the Advancement of Education]. Committee on the Role of Education in American History. *Education and American History*. New York: The Fund [1965]. A revision and expansion of the 1957 statement and recommendations.

Gersman, Elinor M. "Textbooks in American Educational History." *History of Education Quarterly*, vol. 13 (Spring, 1973), pp. 41-51.

Good, Harry G. "The Approach to the History of Education." *School and Society*, vol. 20 (1924), pp. 231-237.

Good, Harry G. "Rise of the History of Education." *History of Education Journal*, vol. 8 (Spring, 1957), pp. 81-85.

Greene, Maxine. "The Professional Significance of History of Education." *History of Education Quarterly*, vol. 7 (Summer, 1967), pp. 182-190. Observations on the nature of history *qua* history, "in the possibility it offers . . . to make sense of the inchoate present."

Greer, Colin. *The Great School Legend: A Revisionist Interpretation of American Public Education*. New York: Basic Books, 1972. Purpose is "to urge us to reexamine the historical analysis of American education with an acute awareness of contemporary social crises." See review, A. S. Horlick, "Radical School Legends," *History of Education Quarterly*, vol. 14 (Summer, 1974), pp. 251-258.

Hansen, Allen O. "Integrative Anthropological Method in History of Culture and Education." *Educational Forum*, vol. 1 (1937), pp. 361-378.

Hendrick, Irving G. "History of Education and Teacher Preparation: A Cautious Analysis." *Journal of Teacher Education*, vol. 17 (1966), pp. 71-76.

Herbst, Jurgen. "American College History: Re-Examination Underway." *History of Education Quarterly*, vol. 14 (Summer, 1974), pp. 259-265. An essay review which maintains that historians seem less interested in intellectual/social history and are turning to demographic/social analysis and more sophisticated versions of institutional/administrative history.

Hiner, N. Ray. "Professions in Process: Changing Relations Between Historians and Educators, 1896-1911." *History of Education Quarterly*, vol. 12 (Spring, 1972), pp. 34-56. The informal alliances between the leaders of the education and history professions and subsequent developments. Historicism, early revisionism, the influence of the "German seminars," and reports of American Historical Association committees (1896, 1904, 1907). See also, David D. Van Tassel, *Recording America's Past: An Interpretation of the Development of Historical Studies in America* (Chicago: University of Chicago Press, 1960).

[History of Education]"Doing History of Education." *History of Education Quarterly*, vol. 9 (Fall, 1969). Includes: Edgar B. Wesley, "Lo, the Poor History of Education," pp. 329-324; Laurence R. Vesey, "Toward a New Direction in Educational History: Prospect and Retrospect," pp. 343-359; Henry Hodysh, "Some Neglected Philosophical Problems Regarding History of Education," pp. 360-71; Bruce L. Hood, "The Historian of Education: Some Notes on His Role," pp. 372-375. See also, Paul Nash, ed., *History and Education: The Educational Uses of the Past* (1970).

Horlick, Allan S. "Good History and Historical Questions." *History of Education Quarterly*, vol. 13 (Summer, 1973), pp. 173-183. An essay review with definitions of historical themes. Reviews David H. Fischer, *Historians' Fallacies* (1970); and J. H. Hexter, *The History Primer* (1971). See also, the author's "The Rewriting of American Educational History," *New York University Education Quarterly* (Summer, 1974).

Kaestle, Carl F. "Social Reform and the Urban School." *History of Education Quarterly*, vol. 12 (Summer, 1972), pp. 211-228. An essay review on cultural and radical revisionist themes in American educational historiography. "Most of all, we need a synthesis that adjures the premise that the American school has been an unequivocal failure, for such a premise—like the earlier presumption of success—precludes the explanation of change over time."

Kahn, Albert S. "Relevance: Some Historical Perspectives, Past, Present, and Future." *Journal of Education*, vol. 154 (December, 1971), pp. 49-57.

Kalisch, Philip, and Harry Hutton. "Davidson's Influence on Educational Historiography." *History of Education Quarterly*, vol. 6 (1966), pp. 79-87. Thomas Davidson (1840-1900), with notices of his *History of Education* (1900).

Karier, Clarence, Paul Violas, and Joel Spring. *Roots of Crisis: American Education in the Twentieth Century*. Chicago: Rand McNally, 1973. Twelve essays (some previously published) which assess, from the perspective of revisionist historiography, the role of the school as an agency of social control. See review, Barry Franklin, "Education for Social Control," *History of Education Quarterly*, vol. 14 (Spring, 1974), pp. 131-136.

Katz, Michael B. *The Irony of Early School Reform: Educational Innovation in Mid-Nineteenth Century Massachusetts*. Cambridge: Harvard University Press, 1968. A revisionist history of school reformers. In Katz's view the reformers saw public education as a new instrument of social control that would restore the unities and social connections destroyed by urbanization and industrialism. See review, Neil Harris, *Harvard Educational Review*, vol. 39 (Spring, 1969), pp.

383-389. See also by Katz: *Class, Bureaucracy, and Schools: The Illusion of Educational Change in America* (1971); and *School Reform: Past and Present* (1971). Works on social change, in the framework of the institutional history of public schools, include: Carl F. Kaestle, *The Evolution of an Urban School System: New York City, 1750-1850* (1973); Diane Ravitch, *The Great School Wars: New York City, 1805-1973* (1974); Stanley K. Schultz, *The Culture Factory: Boston Public Schools, 1789-1860* (1973); Patricia A. Graham, *Community and Class in American Education, 1865-1918* (1974); Joseph M. Cronin, *The Control of Urban Schools: Perspectives on the Power of Educational Reformers* (1973); and Marvin Lazerson, *Origins of Urban Education: Public Education in Massachusetts, 1870-1915* (1971).

Katz, Michael B. "From Voluntarism to Bureaucracy in American Education." *Sociology of Education,* vol. 44 (Summer, 1971), pp. 297-332. Refinements of the revisionist interpretations in the author's *The Irony of Early School Reform* (1968), *q.v.*

Katz, Michael B. "The Present Moment in Educational Reform." *Harvard Educational Review,* vol. 41 (August, 1971), pp. 342-59. Suggests that the educational reform movement may be coming to an end because of its inability to resolve conflicts.

Lazerson, Marvin. "Revisionism and American Educational History." *Harvard Educational Review,* vol. 43 (May, 1973), pp. 269-283. An essay review on recently published works, with some refinements of views expressed. See also, Marvin Lazerson, "Urban Reform and the Schools: Kindergarten in Massachusetts, 1870-1915," *History of Education Quarterly,* vol. 11 (Summer, 1971), pp. 115-142.

Lewis, H. Graham. "Bailyn and Cremin on Cubberley and History of Education." *Educational Theory,* vol. 17 (January, 1967), pp. 56-69.

Lilge, Frederic. "The Functionalist Fallacy and the History of Education." *School and Society,* vol. 65 (1947), pp. 241-243.

Lipset, Seymour M., and Richard Hofstadter, eds. *Sociology and History: Methods.* New York: Basic Books, 1968. A collection of sixteen essays which deal with the methodologies of history and sociology. See review, Paul Mattingly, *History of Education Quarterly,* vol. 9 (Summer, 1969), pp. 253-259.

Lord, Daniel C. "The Historian as Villain: The Historian's Role in the Training of Teachers." *The Historian,* vol. 34 (May, 1972), pp. 407-420.

Mattingly, Paul H. "Useful History and Black Identity." *History of Education Quarterly,* vol. 10 (Fall, 1970), pp. 338-350. Maintains "the demand that history be 'useful' impinges especially hard on the profession today in the areas of educational and black history."

Mehl, Bernard. "New Writings and the Status of the History of Education."

History of Education Journal, vol. 8 (Spring, 1957), pp. 108-111.

Patterson, Orlando. "Rethinking Black History." *Harvard Educational Review,* vol. 41 (August, 1971), pp. 297-315. Delineates and analyzes prevailing conceptions of black history and recommends making more use of oral, non-written, and non-literary sources. See, in this connection, Eugene D. Genovese, *Roll Jordan, Roll: The World the Slaves Made* (New York: Pantheon, 1974).

Perkinson, Henry J. *The Imperfect Panacea: American Faith in Education, 1865-1965.* New York: Random House, 1968. Questions that the schools are the panacea for all social problems. Revisionist interpretations of educational history. See also his *The Possibilities of Error* (1971).

Pratte, Richard. *The Public School Movement: A critical Study.* New York: David McKay, 1973. A critical inquiry into the forces which are "competing with and challenging today's Public School Movement."

Rothman, David J. *The Discovery of the Asylum: Social Order and Disorder in the New Republic.* Boston: Little, Brown, 1971. Describes the shift from noninstitutional to institutional solutions. Many parallels of interest to students of educational history.

Roucek, Joseph. "The Foreign Roots of American Educational History." *Educational Forum,* vol. 27 (1962), pp. 47-57.

Ryan, Patrick J. *Historical Foundations of Public Education in America.* Dubuque, Iowa: William C. Brown, 1965. "What is attempted within these pages is the utilization of those social developments which can give cumulative insight to current public educational theory and practice in America."

Scott, Ronald M. "The Social History of Education: Three Alternatives." *History of Education Quarterly,* vol. 10 (Summer, 1970), pp. 242-254. An essay review on the examination of education in the broader context of social experience, social structure, and social change. Works examined are Berenice M. Fisher, *Industrial Education: American Ideals and Institutions* (1967), and Michael B. Katz, *The Irony of Early School Reform* (1968).

Sloan, Douglas. "New Perspectives on the Higher Learning in America." *Notes on Education,* Institute of Philosophy and Politics of Education, Teachers College, Columbia University, New York, No. 1 (June, 1973). Recommends going beyond institutional history of higher education to search among the various "habitats of learning" for all the ways that people pursue higher education.

Smith, Wilson. "The New Historian of American Education: Some Notes for a Portrait." *Harvard Educational Review,* vol. 31 (Spring, 1961), pp. 136-143.

Storr, Richard J. "The History of Education: Some Impressions." *Harvard*

Educational Review, vol. 31 (Spring, 1961), pp. 124-135.

Stoutemeyer, J. H. "The Teaching of the History of Education in Normal Schools." *School and Society,* vol. 7 (1918), pp. 517-580.

Swift, Fletcher H. "The Specific Objectives of a Professional Course in the History of Education." *Teachers College Record,* vol. 23 (1922), pp. 12-18.

Talbott, John E. "The History of Education." *Daedalus* (Winter, 1971), pp. 133-150. The entire issue is devoted to history and methodology, new themes and interdisciplinary investigations, *e.g.,* archaeology and history; political and intellectual history; social history and the history of society; local history; prosopography; quantitative history; psychology in history.

Tyack, David B. "The History of Education and the Preparation of Teachers: A reappraisal." *Journal of Teacher Education,* vol. 19 (1965), pp. 427-431.

Tyack, David B. "New Perspectives on the History of American Education," in Herbert J. Bass, ed., *The State of American History* (Chicago: Quadrangle, 1970), pp. 22-42.

Tyack, David B. *The One Best System: A History of American Urban Education.* Cambridge: Harvard University Press, 1974. The organization revolution in American education and a general interpretative framework for the history of urban education.

Tyack, David B., ed. *Turning Points in American Educational History.* Waltham, Mass.: Blaisdell, 1967. Introductions to a corpus of documents assert "the crucial role of education in shaping American society." See also, Edward A. Krug, *Salient Dates in American Education, 1635-1964* (1966).

"[Urban Education] : Needs and Opportunities for Historial Research." *History of Education Quarterly,* vol. 9 (Fall, 1969). Includes: David K. Cohen, "Education and Race," pp. 281-286; David B. Tyack, "Growing Up Black: Perspectives on the History of Education in Northern Ghettos," pp. 287-297; Sol Cohen, "Urban School Reform," pp. 298-304; Neil Sutherland, "The Urban Child," pp. 305-311; Daniel Calhoun, "The City as Teacher: Historical Problems," pp. 312-325; and comment by Michael Katz.

Welter, Rush. *Popular Education and Democratic Thought in America.* New York: Columbia University Press, 1962. Colonial and republican precedents for the belief in popular education, and their extension and elaboration by representative political thinkers of the Jacksonian era. See also, Gladys A. Wiggin, *Education and Nationalism: An Historical Interpretation of American Education* (1962).

IV. COMPREHENSIVE HISTORIES OF
AMERICAN EDUCATION: A HANDLIST

See generally Willam W. Brinckman, "Selected Bibliography of the History of Education in the United States," *Paedogogica Historia,* vol. 10 (1970), pp. 622-630; Lawrence A. Cremin, *The Wonderful World of Ellwood Patterson Cubberley: An Essay on the Historiography of American Education (1965);* Elinor M. Gersman, "Textbooks in American Educational History," *History of Education Quarterly,* vol. 13 (Spring, 1973), pp. 41-51; and Joe Park, *The Rise of American Education: An Annotated Bibliography* (1965). See, also, "The Historiography of American Education," *supra.*

Baden, Paul. *Beiträge zur Entstehung des amerikanischen Lehrerstandes.* Hamburg: Fusslein, 1932.

Barneaud, Charles. *Origines et Progrès de L'Éducation en Amerique.* Paris: Savaete, 1898.

Bayles, Ernest E., and Bruce L. Hood. *Growth of American Educational Thought and Practice.* New York: Harper & Row, 1966.

Boone, Richard G. *Education in the United States: Its History from the Earliest Settlements.* New York: Appleton, 1889.

Brickman, William W. *Educational Systems in the United States.* New York: Center for Applied Research in Education, 1964.

Butts, R. Freeman, and Lawrence A. Cremin. *A History of Education in American Culture.* New York: Holt, 1953.

Cremin, Lawrence A. *History of American Education.* New York: Harper & Row, 1970–. [Projected as a three-volume comprehensive history] Volume I. *American Education: The Colonial Experience, 1607-1783* (1970).

Cubberley, Ellwood P. *Public Education in the United States: A Study and Interpretation of American Educational History.* Boston: Houghton Mifflin, 1919, 1934.

Dexter, Edwin G. *A History of Education in the United States.* New York:

Macmillan, 1904.

Drake, William E. *The American School in Transition*. New York: Prentice-Hall, 1955.

Edwards, Newton, and Herman G. Richey. *The School in the American Social Order*. 2nd ed. Boston: Houghton Mifflin, 1963.

Finney, Ross G. *The American Public School: A Genetic Study of Principles, Practices, and Present Problems*. New York: Macmillan, 1921.

French, William M. *America's Educational Tradition: An Interpretive History*. Boston: Heath, 1964.

Fuller, Edgar, and J. B. Pearson, eds. *Education in the States: Historical Development and Outlook*. Washington: National Education Association, 1969.

Good, Harry G., and James D. Teller. *A History of American Education*. 3rd ed. New York: Macmillan, 1973.

Gross, Richard E. *Heritage of American Education*. Boston: Allyn and Bacon, 1962.

Gutek, Gerald L. *An Historical Introduction to American Education*. New York: Crowell, 1970.

Henderson, John C. *Our National System of Education*. New York: Dodd, Mead, 1877.

Karier, Clarence J. *Man, Society, and Education: A History of American Educational Ideas*. Chicago: Scott, Foresman, 1967.

Knight, Edgar W. *Education in the United States*. 3rd rev. ed. Boston: Ginn, 1951. Also, Edgar W. Knight. *Fifty Years of American Education*. New York: Ronald, 1952.

Meyer, Adolphe E. *An Educational History of the American People*. 2nd ed. New York: McGraw-Hill, 1967.

Monroe, Paul. *Founding of the American Public School System*. New York: Macmillan, 1940. [Vol. II: a microfilm of documents in typescript, numbering 1775 pp.]

Noble, Stuart G. *History of American Education*. rev. ed. New York: Rinehart, 1954.

Potter, Robert E. *The Stream of American Education*. New York: American Book Co., 1967.

Pulliam, John D. *History of Education in America*. Columbus, Ohio: Merrill, 1968.

Rippa, S. Alexander. *Education in a Free Society: An American History*. 2nd ed. New York: David McKay, 1971.

Slosson, Edwin E. *The American Spirit in Education*. New York: American Book Co., 1900.

Swett, John. *American Public Schools*. New York: American Book Co., 1900.

Thayer, V. T. *Formative Ideas in American Education: From the Colonial Period to the Present*. New York: Dodd, Mead, 1965.

Thwing, Charles F. *A History of Education in the United States Since the Civil War*. Boston: Houghton Mifflin, 1910.

Winship, Albert E. *Great American Educators*. New York: American Book Co., 1900.

PART II:

SUBJECT FIELDS AND MISCELLANEOUS

V. ELEMENTARY EDUCATION AND CURRICULUM

A. THE COMMON SCHOOL AND HISTORICAL BACKGROUNDS

Blow, Susan E. "The History of the Kindergarten in the United States." *Outlook,* vol. 55 (1897), pp. 932-938.

Cremin, Lawrence A. *The American Common School: An Historic Conception.* Teachers College, Columbia University, 1951. A classic study of the emergence of the American common school "as a response to the conditions of American life." Period covered is 1815-1850. Includes a comprehensive bibliography of primary sources.

Endres, Raymond J. "Elementary School Functions in the United States: An Historical Analysis." *Paedagogica Historica,* vol. 7 (1967), pp. 378-416.

Goodlad, John I., *et al. The Changing School Curriculum.* New York: Fund for the Advancement of Education, 1966. Includes an overview of changes since the early 1950's with a valuable annotated bibliography.

Jenkins, Elizabeth. "How the Kindergarten Found Its Way to America." *Wisconsin Magazine of History,* vol. 14 (1930-1931), pp. 48-62.

Mayo, Amory D. "The American Common School in New England from 1790 to 1840." *Report.* [1894-95] Commissioner of Education. [Washington, GPO, 1896], vol. 2, pp. 1551-1615. This (and the articles, *infra*) are the fullest materials assembled on the history of the common school. Amory Dwight Mayo (1823-1907) was a Unitarian clergyman who led the "Christian Amendment Movement" which sought constitutional authority to use the Bible in the public schools.

Mayo, Amory D. "The American Common School in New York, New Jersey, and Pennsylvania During the First Half Century of the Republic." *Report.* [1895-96] Commissioner of Education. [Washington, GPO, 1897], vol. 1, pp. 219-66.

Mayo, Amory D. "The American Common School in the Southern States During the First Half Century of the Republic." *Report.* [1895-96] Commissioner of Education. [Washington, GPO, 1897], vol. 1, pp. 167-338.

Mayo, Amory D. "The Common School in the Southern States Beyond the Mississippi River, from 1830 to 1860." *Report.* [1900-01] Commissioner of Education. [Washington, GPO, 1902], vol. 1. pp. 357-401.

Mayo, Amory D. "The Development of the Common School in the Western States from 1830 to 1865." *Report.* [1898-99] Commissioner of Education. [Washington, GPO, 1900], vol. 1, pp. 357-450.

Mayo, Amory D. "Education in the Northwest During the First Half Century of the Republic, 1790-1840." *Report.* [1894-95] Commissioner of Education. [Washington, GPO, 1896], vol. 2, pp. 1513-50.

Mayo, Amory D. "Henry Barnard." *Report.* [1896-97] Commissioner of Education. [Washington, GPO, 1898], vol. 1, pp. 769-810.

Mayo, Amory D. "Horace Mann and the Great Revival of the American Common School, 1830-1850." *Report.* [1896-97] Commissioner of Education. [Washington, GPO, 1898], vol. 1, pp. 715-67.

Mayo, Amory D. "The Organization and Development of the American Common School in the Atlantic and Central States of the South, 1830 to 1860." *Report.* [1889-1900] Commissioner of Education. [Washington, GPO, 1901], vol. 1, pp. 427-561.

Mayo, Amory D. "The Organization and Reconstruction of State Systems of Common-School Education in the North Atlantic States from 1830 to 1865." *Report.* [1897-98] Commissioner of Education. [Washington, GPO, 1899], vol. 1, pp. 355-486.

Mayo, Amory D. "Public Schools During the Colonial and Revolutionary Period in the United States." *Report.* [1893-94] Commissioner of Education. [Washington, GPO, 1896], vol. 1. pp. 639-738.

Parker, Samuel C. *The History of Modern Elementary Education.* Boston: Ginn 1912. Traces "the development from the first city elementary vernacular schools of the Middle Ages down to the present time." [1912] Reissued, Totowa, N.J.: Littlefield, Adams, 1970 (includes a bibliographical note by F. Cordasco).

Raymond, T. *History of the Education of Young Children.* London: Longmans, Green, 1937.

Reisner, E. H. *Evolution of the Common School.* New York: Macmillan, 1930.

Smith, Frank. *A History of English Elementary Education, 1760-1902.* London: University of London Press, 1931. Reissued, New York: Augustus M. Kelley, 1970. A valuable history for English and European influences on American educational practice.

Weber, Evelyn. *The Kindergarten: Its Encounter with Educational Thought in America.* New York: Macmillan, 1969.

B. GENERAL—CONCEPTUAL AND/OR RESEARCH

Association for Supervision and Curriculum Development. *New Insights and the Curriculum.* Washington: The Association, 1963. An attempt to show the implications of certain views of human potentiality, knowledge, social interaction, cultural values and valuing, citizenship, and creativity for curriculum planning.

Beauchamp, George A. *Curriculum Theory.* Wilmette, Illinois: Kagg Press, 1968. Theoretical approach to developing a theory about curriculum as a field of inquiry.

Berman, Louise M. *New Priorities in the Curriculum.* Columbus, Ohio: Charles E. Merrill, 1968. Describes the dynamic human processes of perceiving, knowing, and organizing and how the curriculum can be planned—using traditional and new ideas—to foster these human processes.

Bloom, Benjamin S., ed. *Taxonomy of Educational Objectives: Cognitive Domain.* New York: Longmans, Green and Co., 1956. This book (with its companion volume, "The Affective Domain"), must be regarded as the standard guide to the clarification and evaluation of objectives at all levels of education.

Burdin, Joel L., and John D. McAulay. *Elementary School Curriculum and Instruction: The Teacher's Role.* New York: The Ronald Press, 1971. Comprehensive view of teaching, knowledge, human development and learning, approaches to curriculum development, as well as present practices and possible trends in classroom procedures.

Chasnoff, Robert E., ed. *Elementary Curriculum: A Book of Readings.* New York: Pitman, 1964. Review of values from which curriculum is derived, followed by practical suggestions for planning to teach—from choreography of the classroom to broad social issues.

Dunkin, Michael J., and Bruce J. Biddle. *The Study of Teaching.* New York: Holt, Rinehart and Winston, 1974. Sophisticated summary of research findings dealing with practical day-to-day issues such as classroom climate, teaching strategies, pupil-teacher interaction, and levels of knowledge as well as theoretical issues such as research methodology and models for describing the teaching process.

Fantini, Mario D., and Gerald Weinstein. *The Disadvantaged: Challenge to Education.* New York: Harper & Row, 1968. Uses a term that was popular in the 1960's. Explains difficulties middle-class teachers have in working with poor children.

Goodlad, John I., and Robert H. Anderson. *The Nongraded Elementary School*. Revised edition. New York: Harcourt, Brace & World, 1963. A proposal for reorganizing the school, in part to accommodate a curriculum organized vertically around fundamental concepts, principles, and modes of inquiry.

Heath, Robert W., ed. *New Curricula*. New York: Harper and Row, 1964. Describes curriculum change in the academic subjects and some of the broader issues involved in the current reform; papers by Paul Woodring, Max Beberman, Jerrold R. Zacharias, Bentley Glass, Lee J. Cranbach, James R. Killian, Jr., Sterling M. McMurrin, and others.

Herrick, Virgil E. *Strategies of Curriculum Development* (edited by James B. MacDonald, Dan W. Anderson, and Frank B. May). Columbus, Ohio: Charles C. Merrill, 1965. A collection of papers from the works of the late Virgil Herrick who devoted a considerable portion of his career to matters of curriculum theory. His discussion of curriculum design, little treated in the literature, is particularly noteworthy and relevant to current curriculum reform.

Hyman, Ronald T. *Ways of Teaching*. New York: J. B. Lippincott, 1970. Develops a concept of teaching and presents examples and analyses of various methods which teachers use. Also deals with the issues of observing and evaluating teaching.

Jackson, Philip W. *Life in Classrooms*. New York: Holt, Rinehart and Winston, 1968. Research report on the thousands of teacher-pupil interpersonal interchanges.

Joyce, Bruce, and Marsha Weil. *Models of Teaching*. Englewood Cliffs, N.J.: Prentice-Hall, 1972. Presents a view of many approaches to creating learning environments. Offers the curriculum-maker alternatives for curriculum design and suggests that teaching styles and curriculum models can be matched to the learning styles of children.

McClure, Robert M. *The Curriculum: Retrospect and Prospect*. The Seventieth Yearbook of the National Society for the Study of Education. Chicago: The Society, 1971. Review of what has been written about the past, the present, and the future of curriculum development by scholars.

Mosston, Muska. *Teaching: From Command to Discovery*. Belmont, Calif.: Wadsworth, 1972. Believing that teachers should have available a repertoire of teaching styles in order that every child's chances of learning be increased, presents a model of styles based upon the decisions which teachers and learners are to make.

Short, Edmund C., and George D. Marcounit, eds. *Contemporary Thought on Public School Curriculum: Readings*. Dubuque, Iowa: Wm. C. Brown, 1968. Selections written by leaders in the field. Focus on basic decisions that must be made to determine the curriculum.

Shumsky, Abraham. *In Search of Teaching Style.* New York: Appleton-Century-Crofts, 1968. For the teacher who wishes to alter, improve or change the style of teaching, explores the climate of the teaching-learning relationship. Deals with the problems of student-teaching, and with the disadvantaged learner.

Shuster, Albert H., and Milton E. Ploghoft. *The Emerging Elementary Curriculum.* Columbus, Ohio: Charles E. Merrill, 1963. Describes the plans teachers must make to permit pupils' experiences to emerge as the focal point of what is happening in school.

Stoddard, George D. *The Dual Progress Plan.* New York: Harper and Row, 1961. A translation of the cultural duality concept into curricular and organizational duality in the elementary school.

Tyler, Ralph W. *Basic Principles of Curriculum and Instruction.* Chicago: University of Chicago Press, 1950. The primer for curriculum planners in any educational enterprise; specifies some basic questions and suggests where some of the answers may be found.

C. SUGGESTIONS TO HELP THE "SPECIAL" CHILD

Connor, James. *Classroom Activities for Helping Hyperactive Children.* New York: The Center for Applied Research in Education, 1974. Many different activities brought together which have proven successful in aiding the hyperactive child to learn.

Golick, Margie. *Deal Me In.* Montreal: Quebec Association for Children with learning Disabilities, 1974. Explores fully the use of the oldest educational toy in the world—a pack of cards.

Levin, Joyce. *Classroom Activities for Encouraging Reluctant Readers.* New York: The Center for Applied Research in Education, 1974. Provides activities that are intended to aid the teacher in setting a new environment for the reluctant reader so that he may gain confidence in reading, acquire new skills in reading, and overcome the reluctance which he formerly had toward reading.

Lucas, Virginia. *Classroom Activities for Helping Slower Learning Children.* New York: The Center for Applied Research in Education, 1974. Practical activities are described which will provide experiences for the slower learning child to be successful.

Murphy, Patricia. *A Special Way for the Special Child in the Regular Classroom.* San Rafael, California: Academic Therapy Publications, 1971. Concrete suggestions are provided for the classroom teacher for helping those children having difficulty. Materials and activities are provided related to skill areas, simple tests the teacher might use and a listing of sources of commercial materials according to skill which should prove invaluable.

Owen, Jacqueline. *Classroom Activities for Motivating Underachieving Children*. New York: The Center for Applied Research in Education, 1974. Numerous activities and techniques which have been found to work to motivate children who are having trouble learning. Suggests other things that can be done by the flexible teacher.

D. PERCEPTION–THE HIDDEN FACTOR IN DEVELOPMENT

Cratty, Bryant J. *Developmental Sequences of Perceptual-Motor Tasks*. Freeport, N.Y.: Educational Activities, Inc., 1967. A guide for suggested movement activities arranged in developmental sequences. The activities are derived from research and experience with handicapped children.

Goodfriend, Ronnie. *Power in Perception for the Young Child*. New York: Teachers College, Columbia University, 1972. Comprehensive program for the development of pre-reading visual perceptual skills. The program though visual, is motor in nature, and at the same time provides experiences in language and concept development without the strain of concentrating on these latter areas.

Magdol, Miriam. *Perceptual Training in the Kindergarten*. San Rafael, California: Academic Therapy Publications, 1971. Clear description of the background of development for the new kindergartens, including research and the author's own interpretation is provided. Included are a wide variety of perceptual experiences for the kindergarten child.

Mourouzis, Ann, *et al*. Dayton, Ohio: MWZ Associates, 1970. Provides information about organizing and implementing a perceptual-motor of body management. Describes a wide variety of activities to develop balance, coordination, perception. Also includes classroom activities, use of appropriate equipment, and suggestions for dealing with children with particular problems.

[Portland Public Schools] *Improving Motor-Perceptual Skills*. Corvallis, Oregon: A Continuing Education Book, 1970. Program of perceptual-motor activities is provided which involves sensory, tactile, auditory and visual perceptions. Survey is included. The format is unusually well put together and serves the teacher well.

Van Witsen, Betty. *Perceptual Training Activities Handbook*. New York: Teachers College, Columbia University, 1967. Behavior problems related to perceptual problems are described. Visual training, auditory perception skills, tactile, olfactory, gustatory and kinesthetic perception activities are included as well as an interesting section on paper folding.

Wright, Genevra E. *Road Game: Part One; Part Two; Part Three*. Johnstown,

Pa.: Mafex Associates, 1971. Three work books of mazes, in sequence, developing eye-hand coordination. These are especially inviting for boys at every age level. Explanations and additional suggestions are found at the end of each book.

Zigmond, Naomi K. *Auditory Learning.* Belmont, California: Fearon Publishers, 1968. Rather complete chapters are included on the development of the auditory processes, disorders of auditory learning, evaluation and implications in teaching the pre-school and school age child. Extensive annotated bibliography.

E. PATTERNS OF CLASSROOM ORGANIZATION

Barth, Roland S. *Open Education and the American School.* New York: Agathon Press, 1972. Includes Barth's assumptions about learning and knowledge, describes the teacher as the curriculum decision maker, and provides an extensive bibliography for further study of the informal movement in education.

Bremer, Anne, and John Bremer. *Open Education: A Beginning.* New York: Holt, Rinehart, and Winston, 1972. An account of the new kinds of teacher attitudes, values, and behaviors and absence of traditional constraints that permit pupils the freedom to learn.

Cutts, Norma, and Nicholas Moseley. *Providing for the Individual Differences in the Elementary School.* Englewood Cliffs, N.J.: Prentice-Hall, Inc., 1960. Each chapter is written by a specialist in the field with extensive first-hand experience in working with children and teachers. Situations are viewed through the teacher's eyes. Various plans of organization and various techniques of instruction are suggested in regard to studying the individual procedures to provide for their differences.

Eisner, Elliot W. *English Primary Schools: Some Observations and Assessments.* Palo Alto: Stanford University, 1973. A scholar's account of schools in which pupils play an important role in the initiation of learning activities. Unlike some other writers, this author views the philosophic roots as derived from John Dewey—the "child as a stimulus-seeking organism who by nature seeks to know . . . ."

Englemann, Siegfried. *Preventing Failure in the Public Schools.* Chicago: Science Research Associates, 1969. Describes techniques for behavior modification using highly structured reinforcement techniques.

Lee, Doris M. *Diagnostic Teaching.* Washington: American Association of Elementary-Kindergarten-Nursery Educators, 1970. Concise explanation of diagnostic teaching, the teacher's role and implications for various curriculum areas.

Madsen, Sheila, *et al. Change for Children.* Pacific Palisades, California:

Goodyear Publishing, 1973. Ideas and activities for individualizing learning are provided. Sample job pages and diagrams of centers are especially helpful.

Moore, George N., and G. Willard Woodruff. *Providing for Children's Differences*. New York: Starting Tomorrow Programs, 1971. A rich fare of techniques we call pupil-team learning. The processes and activities described involve a high degree of mutal aid in learning, children working together and planning together. The processes involve each child moving through a sequence of learning tasks or creative activities at his own individual rate of mastery. The every-pupil-response techniques are especially interesting.

Taylor, Joy. *Organizing the Open Classroom: A Teachers' Guide to the Integrated Day*. New York: Schocken Books, 1972. A practical book that shows how pupils may be afforded many individual choices while the teacher maintains a carefully planned but responsive view of the entire group's activities.

Thomas, George I., and Joseph Crescimbeni. *Individualizing Instruction in the Elementary School*. New York: Random House, 1967. A standard over-all, general curriculum book.

Williams, Lois E. *Independent Learning*. Washington: American Association of Elementary-Kindergarten-Nursery Educators, 1969. Stresses that teachers can and should work with what they have and that they can improve independent learning by experimenting within the self-contained classroom. Suggests setting up free activity periods, learning centers, helping children make choices and checking on their independence.

F. INSTRUCTIONAL METHODS AND MATERIALS

Allegra, James W. *Sequential Mathematics*. New York: Harcourt Brace, Jovanovich, 1973. Two student books and manuals are available, *Addition and Subtraction* and *Multiplication and Division*. The student book may be used standing up on a student desk to be copied or used with a transparent overlay. Each book contains built-in diagnostic testing and a sequential series of exercises. The manual gives suggestions as to programming. This series is especially appropriate for perceptually impaired children or those having difficulty copying from the blackboard.

Bailey, Larry J., and Ronald W. Stadt. *Career Education: New Approaches to Human Development*. Bloomington, Ill.: McKnight, 1973. Presents the need and basis for career education, the development of this curriculum area, and offers models and suggestions for the implementation within the educational organization.

Boning, Richard A. *Picto-cabulary Series: Words to Eat, Words to Meet, Words to Wear*. New York: Barnell Loft, 1972. Designed for grades 3-4, these sets may also be used to advantage on higher level. Unusual foods, clothing of the past and present, and common and uncommon words we meet every day are utilized. Each unit is comprised of a clear picture and paragraph description and a number of multiple-choice questions having to do with the item description.

Botel, Morton. *Communicating*. Lexington, Mass.: D.C. Heath, 1973. Heath's new Language series stresses oral language development. Cartoon illustrations, etc., are motivating and provide a rich experiential background for children. Level I is especially appropriate for children lacking rich experience.

Burke, Barbara P. *The Cambridge Staff Development Program–Reading*. New York: Cambridge Book, 1974. Sequentially designed reading program in the form of *Work-a-texts*. Diagnostic review, unit tests and monitoring programs make it possible for the student to know what objectives or goals in the program are stated as activities. Series is appropriate as a dual or co-reading series.

Byrne, Margaret C. *The Child Speaks*. New York: Harper & Row, 1965. Speech improvement program for Kindergarten and First Grade. Units are provided for each speech sound involving various activities, illustrations and review and reinforcment techniques.

Carlson, Ruth K. *Poetry for Today's Child*. Dansville, New York: The Instructor Publications, 1968. Handbook describing kinds of poetry and appropriate methods of handling them effectively. Topics covered are poetry for enjoyment, the design of poetry, modern children and poetry and children's responses to poetry. An extensive bibliography and an index of poems are provided.

Cherry, Clare. *Creative Movement for the Developing Child*. Belmont, California: Lear Siegler, 1968. A handbook of activities for teachers who are not musicians.

Classroom Math Lab. Aero Educational Products, Chicago, Ill., 1973. A "box" for providing reinforcement in the basic skills. The innovation is that instead of worksheets or workbooks, each child works on a magic slate. The cards fitting over the slates are self-correcting by turning them over.

Cobb, Vicki. *Science Experiments You Can Eat*. New York: J. B. Lippincott Company, 1972. As the title suggests, children may eat their experiments. A novel approach.

Corle, Clyde G. *Skill Games for Mathematics*. Dansville, New York; The Instructor Publications, 1968. Developed to assist teachers with motivational ideas for teaching elementary school mathematics. The items include jingles, games, contests, teaching devices and thought-provoking exercises.

Cratty, Bryant J. *Sounds, Words and Actions*. Freeport, New York: Educational Activities, 1971. Movement games to enhance the language art skills of elementary school children. The games are color coded on 5"x7" cards. Skill clusters provided are letter identification, phonics, linguistic skills, reading and listening.

Dale, Edgar. *Audiovisual Methods in Teaching*. 3rd. ed. New York: Holt, Rinehart and Winston, 1969. Basic text on the variety of methods and materials that range from concrete-direct to abstract experiences.

Darrow, Helen, and R. Van Allen. *Independent Activities for Creative Learning*. New York: Teachers College, Columbia University, 1961. Has all the features that should be included in a how-to-do-it bulletin to help intelligent human beings. A case for a type of independent work which will foster creativity in children.

Donovan, Nancy, *et al*. *Yellow Pages of Learning Resources*. New York: Educational Facilities Laboratories, 1972. Resource directory resembling the Yellow Pages section of the phone book. Community resources are described, illustrated and lists of learning experiences available at each place in the city and field trip follow-up experiences are provided.

Duffy, Joan. *Typing*. Cambridge, Mass.: Educator's Publishing Service, 1974. A linguistically-oriented beginning "touch system" typing manual for students from age six on. Especially useful for students with special learning problems. Progress chart is included.

Dunas,, Enoch. *Arithmetic Games*. Belmont, California: Lear Siegler/Fearon Publishers, 1956. Presents a concise description of the use of games in teaching arithmetic. Games are listed by grade and skill. Games range from the kindergarten to sixth grade level.

Dunn, Lloyd M. *Peabody Language Development Kits*. Circle Pines, Minnesota: American Guidance Service, 1968. Designed to be especially effective with children from economically disadvantaged areas of urban and rural communities. Manuals are comprehensive and a kit accompanies the manual with pictures and records.

Forte, Frank. *Creative Math Experiences for the Young Child*. Nashville, Tenn.: Incentive Publications, 1974. Child-centered presentation of basic number concepts, numerals, sets, sizes, shapes, time, money, measurement, fractions, and math vocabulary are creatively set in attractive, activity-filled pages. For class and individual instruction in loose-leaf binder form.

Forte, Frank. *Kids' Stuff—Reading and Language Experience, Intermediate-Junior High*. Nashville, Tenn.: Incentive Publications, 1974. More than 300 pages of explicit, practical, step-by-step instructions for presenting reading and language arts skills and concepts. It is fully illustrated with special instructions for tailoring ideas to individual instruction. Appendix includes record keeping, room arrangements, time schedules, etc.

Garrison, E. L. *Individualized Reading*. Dansville, New York: The Instructor Publications, 1970. Handbook which discusses individuality and learning and provides a variety of Skill-o-ettes which are activities based on the theory of self-paced individualized instruction.

Geake, Robert R. *Primary Tracking*. Ann Arbor, Michigan: Primary Tracking, 1970. Self-instruction workbook for visual discrimination and perceptual skills in reading. Designed to improve visual skills, left-right direction and skill in following a line of print. May be used as a readiness activity or as a remedial procedure.

Gladstone, Blanche. *Mastering Mathematics*. New York: William H. Sadlier, 1971. Four workbooks [ABCD] are in the series. Non-graded so that a child may begin at his ability level and proceed at his own pace. Designed to give reinforcement along with the basic math program. Correlation chart is presented with each book for the 12 most used series. Each page is self-contained. Models are utilized to introduce concepts and algorithms and are attractively set off by a color block. To avoid complicated verbiage in directions, sample exercises are worked out for the child.

Gould, Annabell, and Warren Schollaert. *Reading Activities*. Dansville, New York: The Instructor Publications, 1967. Variety of activities suitable in the primary grades and covering word recognition, increasing comprehension, using audio-visual equipment, individualizing and interest builders.

Herber, Harold L. *Reading in the Content Areas*. New York: Scholastic Book Services, 1973. Selections in the areas children are expected to function, *e.g.*, literature, social studies, math and science. Following each selection are a variety of questions.

Hightower, Robert, and Lore Rasmussen. *First-Grade Diary*. Forest Hills, N.Y.: Learning Innovations Corp., 1962. A daily log of progress in a first-grade room using a math lab. Extensive plans provide the teacher with a practical, sequential program in primary math.

Johnson, David W., and Frank Johnson. *Joining Together: Group Theory and Group Skills*. Englewood Cliffs, N.J.: Prentice-Hall, 1975. Presents integrated statements of theory and field-tested exercises that can be used.

Kahn, Charles H., and Bradley J. Hanna. *Using Dollars and Sense*. Belmont, California: Fearon Publishers/Lear Siegler, 1973. Practical instruction in the use of money. Money pictures in actual size and color. Restaurant checks, supermarket stubs, etc., as well as other practical experiences are utilized.

Kottmeyer, William. *Reading Booster Code Book*. New York: McGraw-Hill, 1972. A workbook in skill reinforcement. Tapes are available for the child to use in a listening center.

LaCoste, Roberta. *Clues to Consonants. Views on Vowels*. Boston: Allyn and

Bacon, 1971. Patterns, sounds and meanings in these word analysis skills areas. Appropriate for use as reinforcement from grades two and beyond.

[*Lavatelli Program*] A Piaget Program, Parts 1 and 2. Boston: American Science and Engineering, 1973. A math-science program based on Piaget's theory of the development of thinking. Sequential development is stressed. All materials necessary to the program are filed in appropriately labeled drawers.

Luts, Jack. *Expanding Spelling Skills*. Dansville, N. Y.: The Instructor Publications, 1973. Views on time needs, student problems, ways of examining words and various methods teachers have found helpful in expanding spelling skills. The techniques of individualized spelling programs are discussed. Games and activities for all grades.

Mann, Phillip H., and Patricia Suiter. *Handbook in Diagnostic Teaching: A Learning Disabilities Approach*. Boston: Allyn and Bacon, 1974. Comprehensive handbook covering all areas of diagnostic teaching and its application to reading instruction. Theoretical perspectives, spelling inventories, reading inventories, developmental screening, supplementary evaluation, deficit level curriculum, task level curriculum and arithmetic are included.

McLeod, Pierce H. *Readiness for Learning: Clinic*. New York: J. B. Lippincott, 1973. Complete readiness program for kindergarten and first-grade children. A series of activities, games and manipulative materials are provided with a workbook covering eye-hand coordination, upper case letters, lower case letters and recognizing word forms.

Metzner, Seymour. *One-Minute Game Guide*. Belmont, California: Fearon Publishers, 1968. A rather unusual collection of short chalkboard learning games for those in-between moments of the day.

Miel, Alice, ed. *Creativity in Teaching: Invitations and Instances*. Belmont, California: Wadsworth Publishing, 1961. Describes concepts and examples of how teaching can come alive for pupils and teachers alike.

Munson, Howard R. *Science with Simple Things*. Belmont, California: Lear Siegler/Fearon Publishers, 1972. Science with rubber bands, soda straws, paper clips, paper and plastic cups, ping-pong balls and marbles, boxes, needles and the pins, bottles and cans, milk cartons and odds and ends. The perfect answer for the teacher who neglects science because of a lack of materials.

[*Nuffield Mathematics Project*] New York: John Wiley and Sons, 1964. The Nuffield Foundation has developed a series of guides devising a contemporary approach for children from 5 to 13. The stress is on how to learn, not on what to teach. Running through all the work is the central notion that the children must be set free to make their own discoveries and think for themselves and so achieve understanding, instead of mysterious drill. The titles are Mathematics Begins, Beginnings, I Do, and I Understand, Pictorial Representation, and Shape and Size.

Ord, John E. *Elementary School Social Studies for Today's Children*. Washington: American Association of Elementary-Kindergarten-Nursery Educators, 1969. Provides a clear description of the new direction in elementary school physical education. A complete listing of resources for developing movement education programs is provided.

Porter, Lorena. *Movement Education for Children*. Washington: American Association of Elementary-Kindergarten-Nursery Educators, 1969. Provides a clear description of the new direction in elementary school physical education. A complete listing of resources for developing movement education programs is provided.

Rasmussen, Lore, *et al*. *Mathematics Laboratory Materials*. [Primary—edition] Chicago: 1964. Worksheets, workbooks and other materials for the teacher to provide a sequential approach to math. The worksheets provide patterns for cuisinaire rods and other manipulative materials.

Robbins, Edward L. *Tutors Handbook*. *Problem Solving Exercises*. Washington: National Reading Center, 1972. Custom made for the teacher with volunteer or paid para-professional help in the room. Suggestion for tutors and for teachers responsible for tutors are provided. Reading skills checklists; 60 lessons in readiness and beginning reading skills. Problem solving exercises provide two additional reinforcement activities for each lesson.

Saunders, Roger E., *et al*. *Visual, Auditory, Kinesthetic, Tactile Skills*. Cambridge, Mass.: Educators Publishing Service, 1969. Workbook which is highly structured primarily for use with children who display a disability in functioning effectively within some area of the communicative processes. Cursive writing, reading and spelling are combined in the approach.

Science—A Process Approach. New York: Xerox Corporation, 1964. A program sequential in nature to the Lavatelli program. It stresses pupil observation and has material filed in appropriate drawers.

Sharp, F. A. *These Kids Don't Count*. San Rafael, California: Academic Therapy Publications, 1971. A remediation program for children having problems in definite math skill areas. Novel, but practical approaches are used along with suggested worksheets.

Sholinsky, Jane. *Dinosaur Bones*. Scholastic Magazines, 1973. A language stimulating workbook. High interest level and attractive illustrations make language an interesting experience for children.

Smith, Donald E. P. *Symbol Tracking. Word Tracking. Word Attack and Comprehension*. Ann Arbor, Michigan: Ann Arbor Publishers, 1967. Excellent for remediation. Special pens are available for use with the workbooks or transparency overlays might be substituted.

Stanford, Gene and Barbara. *Learning Discussion Skills Through Games*. New York: Citation Press, 1969. A sequence of skill-building games and activities designed to give students the necessary practice in proper discussion techniques; presents a repertoire of remedial devices for use when a group shows signs of a particular weakness in working together.

Tobin, Alexander. *Systemathix*. New York: William H. Sadlier, 1973. A series of five sequential and remedial workbooks in math computation skills. Graphs are utilized as background for the computation.

Ullyette, Jean M. *Guidelines for Creative Writing*. Dansville, N.Y.: The Instructor Publications, 1963. Guides, areas, motivation techniques, word skills, stories, poetry.

Van Allen, Roach, and Claryce Allen. *Language Experiences in Early Childhood*. Chicago: Encyclopedia Britannica Press, 1969. Teacher's resource book of language activities concerning names, environment, movement, reading and resources. A packet of masters made up of letters to parents with suggestions for developing language skills.

Wagner, Guy, *et al*. *Listening Games*. New York: Macmillan Company, 1970. Listening skills are built with "fun" games. Of particular note is the arrangement according to skill and grade level. Many games are provided at the 5th and 6th grade levels.

Witty, Paul A. *Reading for the Gifted and. the Creative Student*. Newark, Delaware: International Reading Association, 1971. Discusses the question of how best to maximize the reading development of gifted and creative students. Problems in identifying the gifted are dealt with in depth as well as the roles of the teacher and the parents involved.

Work-aTexts in Science. New York: Cambridge Company, 1974. Paper bound texts providing for six levels of achievement. Stresses science concepts, processes and the fun of inquiry. Each chapter concludes with a Test Yourself page which may be used as a homework assignment, for self-evaluation, or removed from the book for a formal classroom test.

G. CRITICISM AND THOUGHTS ON IMPROVING

Bruner, Jerome S. *Process of Education*. Cambridge: Harvard University Press, 1960. Presents the concept that structure of subjects can be taught at early age—providing traditionalists with a term, "structure," that was used as a rallying cry during the 1960's.

Featherstone, Joseph. *Schools Where Children Learn*. New York: Liveright, 1971. Describes informal British primary schools.

Goodlad, John I., and Robert H. Anderson. *The Nongraded Elementary School*. New York: Harcourt, Brace & World, 1963. A book that was influential in getting educators to assess the lock-step approaches currently in use.

Gross, Beatrice, and Ronald Gross, eds. *Radical School Reform*. New York: Simon and Schuster, 1969. Accounts of "suppression, irrelevance, inhumanity, manipulation, and systematic stultification of what is most promising in children and youth." Contributors from a wide range of backgrounds.

Herndon, James. *How to Survive in Your Native Land*. New York: Random House, 1971. A personal, highly readable account of a dedicated teacher's experiences with a class.

Holt, John. *How Children Fail*. New York: Pitman Publishing Corporation, 1964. Presents examples of pupils' frustration and a personal account of how a teacher can make school meaningful and alive.

Kohl, Herbert. *36 Children*. New York: New American Library, 1968. Describes how a dedicated teacher helps ghetto children become creative and active learners.

Kozol, Jonathan. *Death at an Early Age*. Boston: Houghton Mifflin, 1967. A teacher's inside account of the school environment and treatment of black students in Boston.

Leonard, George B. *Education and Ecstasy*. New York: Delacorte, 1968. A fantasy of what a school may be like in the future, where people care for one another and where freedom of movement allows for productive learning.

Silberman, Charles. *Crisis in the Classroom*. New York: Random House, 1970. A wide-ranging volume, written in the popular magazine idiom, touching on history, philosophy, and random descriptions of good and bad examples of teaching.

VI. SECONDARY EDUCATION

A. AIMS AND OBJECTIVES

1. General

Brent, Rudyard K., Henry H. Kronenberg, and Charles C. Boardman. *Principles of Secondary Education*. New York: McGraw-Hill, 1970. The most current edition of the 1941 Bent and Kronenberg text, providing a comprehensive overview of secondary education in the United States.

Broudy, Harry S., B. O. Smith, and Joe R. Burnett. *Democracy and Excellence in American Secondary Education*. Chicago: Rand McNally and Company, 1964. Proposal for providing excellence in the educational context of popular or mass democracy—a single-track, nongraded curriculum devoid of electives, stressing the interpretive use of knowledge.

Commission on the Reorganization of Secondary Education. *Reports*. Washington, D.C.: U.S. Government Printing Office, 1914-1921. Includes the reports of the sixteen committees, appointed by a joint commission sponsored by the U.S. Office of Education and the National Education Association, which conducted a comprehensive study of secondary education and effected major changes in American secondary education.

Downey, Laurence W. *The Secondary Phase of Education*. New York: Blaisdell Publishing Company, 1965. An attempt to develop a conceptual system for ordering knowledge in the field of secondary education and for clarifying relationships within the process of education.

Engelhardt, Fred, and Alfred Victor Overn. *Secondary Education, Principles and Practices*. New York: D. Appleton-Century Company, Inc., 1937. An early plea for public education as a unified process extending from nursery school to higher education, providing a valuable overview of the state of secondary school practices during the 1930's.

Griffith, Leroy H., et al. *Secondary Education Today*. New York: David McKay Company, Inc., 1967. Presents a suggested frame of reference as a means by which to understand and interpret secondary education in the mid-sixties.

Hahn, Robert O., and David B. Bidna (eds.). *Secondary Education: Origins and Directions*. 2nd ed. New York: The Macmillan Company, 1970. Collection of readings—presenting conflicting views—emphasizing the origins of secondary education as they relate to contemporary educational problems in the high schools, curriculum trends, instructional procedures, and disadvantaged youth.

Johnson, Mauritz, Jr. *American Secondary Schools*. New York: Harcourt Brace and World, Inc., 1965. A brief overview of American secondary education which makes a plea for a stronger intellectual emphasis—dedicated to the advancement of knowledge and the "preservation of mankind's noblest achievements."

National Association of Secondary School Principals. *Planning for American Youth: An Educational Program for Youth of Secondary-School Age*. Rev. ed. Washington, D.C.: National Education Association, 1951. A summary of *Education for All American Youth*, a 1944 publication of the Educational Policies Commission, NEA, prepared by the Executive Committee and the Committee on Curriculum Planning and Development of the National Association of Secondary School Principals.

National Education Association, Commission on the Reorganization of Secondary Education. *Cardinal Principles of Secondary Education*. Washington, D.C.: U.S. Government Printing Office, 1918. One of the classic statements of objectives for American secondary education, urging the reorganization of secondary education based on the "democratic ideal" and the changes in society, the secondary school population, and educational theory—perhaps the most famous of the Reports of the Commission on the Reorganization of Secondary Education.

National Education Association, Committee of Ten on Secondary School Studies. *Report of the Committee on Secondary School Studies, Appointed at the Meeting of the National Education Association*. New York: Arno Press, 1969. First of a series of national reports on different aspects of American education that had considerable influence on the conduct of the schools—reprint of 1893 edition.

Oliva, Peter F. *The Secondary School Today*. 2nd ed. Scranton: Intext Educational Publishers, 1972. Comprehensive introductory text treating the emergence of the modern secondary school, the curriculum, planning for instruction, the instructional process, guidance, evaluation, etc.

Tanner, Daniel. Secondary Education: *Perspectives and Prospects*. New York: Macmillan Company, 1972. Comprehensive introductory text discussing the development, status, and trends in American secondary education.

Trump, J. Lloyd, and Dorsey Bayham. *Focus on Change: Guide to Better Schools.* Chicago: Rand McNally, 1961. Reflects the work done by the Commission on the Experimental Study of the Utilization of the Staff in the Secondary School, under the directorship of J. Lloyd Trump, suggesting ways of modifying the utilization of staff to achieve educational objectives and thereby improve the secondary schools.

2. Junior High/Middle Schools

Brimm, R. P. *The Junior High School.* New York: Center for Applied Research in Education, 1963. A comprehensive overview of the junior high school, including instructional programs, school services, patterns of reporting student progress, staffing, etc.

Conant, James B. *Recommendations for Education in the Junior High School Years: A Memorandum to School Boards.* New Jersey: Educational Testing Service, 1960. Sequel to *The American High School Today,* containing 14 recommendations to improve the junior high school based on the best practices seen in the 237 schools visited.

Eichhorn, Donald H. *The Middle School.* New York: Center for Applied Research in Education, 1966. Description and analysis of the "middle school," a concept of school organization based on integration of age and growth needs with educational factors.

Gaumnitz, Walter H. (ed.). *Strengths and Weaknesses of the Junior High School.* Washington, D.C.: U.S. Office of Education, 1955. Report of the National Conference on Junior High Schools, Washington, D.C., February 24-26, 1955.

Gaumnitz, Walter H., and J. Dan Hull. *Junior High Schools vs. the Traditional (8-4) High School Organization.* Washington, D.C.: U.S. Office of Education, 1953. A brief circular which analyzes the comparative advantages of the junior high school vs. the traditional (8-4) high school organization.

Grambs, Jean D., et al. *The Junior High School We Need.* Washington, D.C.: Association for Supervision and Curriculum Development, 1961. A report prepared by the ASCD Commission on Secondary Curriculum, recommending directions for junior high school education.

Hansen, John H., and Arthur C. Hearn. *The Middle School Program.* Chicago: Rand McNally, 1971. Introduction to the middle school program: aims and objectives, patterns of organization, instructional procedures, etc.

Howard, Alvin W. *The Junior High and Middle School: Issues and Practices.* Scranton: Intext Educational Publishers, 1970. Discussion and analysis of the major issues of the junior high school and middle school organization, and description of current educational practices.

Popper, Samuel J. *The Middle School.* Boston: Blaisdell Publishing Co., 1967. Presents the case for a clearly defined, autonomous middle school in the total organization of pre-collegiate education.

3. High Schools

American Association of School Administrators. *The High School In a Changing World.* Washington, D.C.: Association of School Administrators, 1958. Thirty-sixth yearbook of the Commission on the High School in a Changing World, under the chairmanship of John H. Fischer.

Conant, James B. *The American High School Today: A First Report to Interested Citizens.* New York: McGraw-Hill, 1959. Critical examination of the organization and functioning of the American high school, and a recommendation of the "comprehensive" high school whose programs correspond to the needs of all the youth of the community.

Conant, James B. *The Comprehensive High School: A Second Report to Interested Citizens.* New York: McGraw-Hill, 1967. A follow-up to *The American High School Today: A First Report to Interested Citizens,* concluding that many of the recommendations of the "first report" had been implemented.

Douglass, Harl R. *Trends and Issues in Secondary Education.* New York: Center for Applied Research in Education, 1962. An evaluation of the major changes taking place in the secondary schools in the 1960's: changing concepts of learning, revised subject matter, use of new technology, flexible grouping and scheduling, and the redesign of school plants to accommodate these new developments.

French, Will, et al. *Behavioral Goals of General Education in High School.* New York: Russell Sage Foundation, 1957. Report representing the combined planning of six national educational agencies working to develop a statement of behavioral objectives or outcomes that can be expected of high school graduates as a result of their high school education.

Gross, Ronald, and Paul Osterman (eds.). *High School.* New York: Simon and Schuster, 1971. A collection of readings by educational reformers dealing with what high schools are like, why they are the way they are, and how they might be—with emphasis on the latter.

Keller, Franklin J. *The Comprehensive High School.* New York: Harper, 1955. Report of a nation-wide study of comprehensive high schools and other forms of educational organization, recommending a comprehensive school which combines the best features of the academic and vocational schools—a sequel to the author's 1953 book, *The Double-Purpose High*

School: Closing the Gap Between the Vocational and Academic Preparation.

Patterson, Franklin K. *High Schools For a Free Society: Education For Citizenship in American Secondary Schools.* Glencoe, Ill.: The Free Press, 1960. Outgrowth of a study conducted by the Tufts University Civic Education Center in 1958-1959, urging the goal of education for citizenship as a major objective of the American high school.

Wiles, Kimball, and Franklin Patterson. *The High School We Need.* Washington, D.C.: Association for Supervision and Curriculum Development, 1959. Report from the ASCD Commission on the Education of Adolescents, prepared by Wiles and Patterson.

4. Future Directions

Alexander, William M. (ed.). *The High School of the Future: A Memorial to Kimball Wiles.* Columbus, Ohio: C. E. Merrill Publishing Co., 1969. A memorial volume to Kimball Wiles presenting predictions and insights of distinguished educators on the shape of secondary education in the year 2000.

Anderson, Wendell G. (ed.). *Direction of the Junior High School in a New Era.* Danville, Ill.: Interstate Printers & Publishers, 1968. A collection of papers presented at the spring and fall, 1968, conference of the Junior High School Association of Illinois.

Eurich, Alvin C. (ed.). *High School 1980: The Shape of the Future in American Secondary Education.* New York: Pitman Publishing Corp., 1970. Twenty-four leading educators present "a provocative guess" at the educational future by evaluating and projecting the impact of environmental, economic, and social change in the secondary school, teachers, and students.

Gorman, Burton W. *Secondary Education: The High School America Needs.* New York: Random House, 1971. Centers on the author's recommendations for the "change that must take place" in high schools to bring them abreast of current challenges.

Nickerson, Neal C. *Junior High Schools Are On the Way Out.* Danville, Ill.: The Interstate Printers & Publishers, 1966. Monograph of the Educational Research and Development Council of the Twin Cities Metropolitan Area, presenting a critical examination of the state of the junior high schools.

B. HISTORY

1. General

Brown, Elmer Ellsworth. *The Making of Our Middle Schools.* New York:

Arno Press, 1969. History of secondary education in America from the seventeenth century Latin grammar schools through the popularization of the high schools at the close of the nineteenth century—reprint of 1905 edition.

Chase, Francis S., and Harold A. Anderson (eds.). *The High School in a New Era*. Chicago: University of Chicago Press, 1958. Collection of papers presented at the Conference on the American High School at the University of Chicago in 1957: reviews the contributions of the high school to American society, analyzes the new demands confronting the high school, and considers how the high school can best adapt to these new conditions.

Counts, George S. *The Selective Character of American Secondary Education*. New York: Arno Press, 1969. A landmark sociological survey of social class bias in American secondary education, and proposals for equalizing educational opportunity—reprint of 1922 edition.

Koss, Leonard V., et al. *Summary: National Survey of Secondary Education*. Washington, D.C.: U.S. Government Printing Office, 1934. Summary of the massive twenty-eight volume survey of secondary education conducted by Leonard V. Koss, documenting the status of American secondary education of the period.

Middlekauff, Robert. *Ancients and Axioms: Secondary Education in Eighteenth-Century New England*. New York: Arno Press, 1963. Traces, through an examination of town records, local newspapers, and school textbooks, the persistence of Puritan traditions in secondary schooling during the eighteenth century.

Miller, George Frederick. *The Academy System of the State of New York*. New York: Arno Press, 1969. Traces the development of the academy system of the State of New York from 1787 to 1900, and their role as preparatory schools and teacher education institutions—reprint of 1922 edition.

Nietz, John A. *The Evolution of American Secondary School Textbooks*. Rutland, Vt.: Tuttle Publishing Company, 1966. Analysis of the books used in Latin and grammar schools from the Colonial period to 1900, documenting some of the changes in curriculum and methodology over time.

Raubinger, Frederick M., et al. *The Development of Secondary Education*. New York: Macmillan, 1969. Valuable collection of studies and reports of various committees and commissions on public secondary education in the United States from 1893 to the mid-twentieth century.

Redcay, Edward Edgeworth (ed.). *Public Secondary Schools for Negroes in the Southern States of the United States*. Washington, D.C.: The Slater

Fund, 1935. Unique occasional paper and historical document providing a complete list of all "public schools for Negroes in the Southern States of the United States that offer any instruction at all on the secondary level, as of October 1, 1933."

Sizer, Theodore R. *The Age of Academies*. New York: Teachers College Press, Columbia University, 1964. A major study of the academy in ante-bellum America, containing selections from primary documents.

Sizer, Theodore R. *Secondary Schools at the Turn of the Century*. New Haven: Yale University Press, 1964. Based on the author's doctoral thesis focusing on the National Education Association's Committee of Ten on Secondary School Studies.

2. Junior High/Middle Schools

Briggs, Thomas H. *The Junior High School*. New York: Houghton Mifflin Company, 1920. Traces the origin and development of the junior high school, describes organizational patterns, curriculum offerings, etc.

Bunker, Frank Forest. *The Junior High School Movement: Its Beginnings*. Washington, D.C.: W. F. Roberts Company, 1935. Description of the origin and development of the junior high school movement from 1909 to 1935.

Van Denberg, Joseph K. *The Junior High School Idea*. New York: H. Holt and Company, 1922. Discussion of the concept of a junior high school and its role in the total pattern of secondary school education.

3. High Schools

Belting, Paul Everett. *The Development of the Free Public High School in Illinois to 1860*. New York: Arno Press, 1969. Presents the emergence of the township high school in the 1850's as both an upward extension of the common school and as an alternative to the private academy—reprint of 1919 edition.

Grizzell, Emit Duncan. *Origin and Development of the High School in New England Before 1865*. New York: Macmillan, 1923. Study of the origin and development of the public high school in New England from 1821 to 1865.

Krug, Edward A. *The Shaping of the American High School*. Madison: University of Wisconsin Press, 1969. Comprehensive two-volume analysis of the major events, individuals and forces responsible for the establishment and development of the American high school: vol. 1, 1880-1920; vol. 2, 1920-1941.

Mulhern, James. *A History of Secondary Education in Pennsylvania*. New

York: Arno Press, 1969. Historical development of secondary education in Pennsylvania from the establishment of the William Penn Charter School, through the academies of the nineteenth century, to the development of the modern public schools—reprint of 1933 edition.

Stout, John Elliot. *The Development of High-School Curricula in the North Central States from 1860 to 1918*. New York: Arno Press, 1969.

Were We Guinea Pigs? New York: Holt, Rinehart and Winston, 1938. Written by the graduating class of the University High School of the Ohio State University, telling of their experiences in a progressive school.

Williams, Sylvia Berry. *Hassling*. Boston: Little, Brown and Company, 1970. Case study of a suburban high school during 1967-1969; students, teachers, parents, and administrators confront one another on the issues of war, race, drugs, politics, and student power.

4. The Eight-Year Study

Aikin, Wilford M. *The Story of the Eight-Year Study*. New York: Harper and Brothers, 1942. Conclusions and recommendations of the Progressive Education Association's classic study of thirty secondary schools (1930-1941) for "the purpose of establishing an improved relationship between school and college."

Hemming, James. *Teach Them To Live*. 2nd ed. London: Longmans, Green, 1957. Presents a summary of the Progressive Education Association's Eight-Year Study of adolescent education.

Progressive Education Association, Commission on the Relation of School and College. *Adventure in American Education*. New York: Harper and Brothers, 1942. The complete five-volume report of the Progressive Education Association's classic Eight-Year Study.

C. ADMINISTRATION

1. General

Anderson, Lester. *Secondary School Administration*. 2nd ed. Boston: Houghton Mifflin, 1972. An introductory text offering a pragmatic approach to secondary school administration.

Corbally, John E., Jr., et al. *Educational Administration: The Secondary School*. Boston: Allyn and Bacon, 1961. Task analysis model of secondary school administration, focusing on the role of the administrator, the problems encountered, and the processes used to respond to these problems.

Douglass, Harl R. *Modern Admministration of Secondary Schools:*

Organization and Administration of Junior and Senior High Schools. 2nd ed. Boston: Ginn, 1963. A revision and extension of *Organization and Administration of Secondary Schools* (1945), offering a comprehensive introduction while stressing both the task-oriented and process-oriented approach to secondary school administration.

Hughes, Meredydd G. *Secondary School Administration: A Management Approach.* New York: Pergamon Press, 1970. Introduction to secondary school administration emphasizing a management approach.

Jones, James J., et al. *Secondary School Administration.* New York: McGraw-Hill, 1969. Introductory text providing a comprehensive overview of secondary school administration.

Kraft, Leonard E. (ed.). *The Secondary School Principal in Action.* Iowa: W. C. Brown, 1971. Compilation of essays dealing with the tasks and problems of secondary school principals and the techniques used to carry out these tasks and respond to these problems.

McLeary, Lloyd E., and Stephen P. Hencley. *Secondary School Administration: Theoretical Bases of Professional Practice.* New York: Dodd, Mead and Co., 1965. Stresses a balance between the theoretical and conceptual approach to secondary school administration.

Ovard, Glen F. *Administration of the Changing Secondary School.* New York: Macmillan, 1966. An introductory text emphasizing the relationship between administrative theory and school practice.

Williams, Stanley W. *Educational Administration in Secondary Schools.* New York: Holt, Rinehart & Winston, Inc., 1964. Examination of the role and function of the secondary school administrator with reference to curriculum, staff, student body, and plant administration.

2. Junior High/Middle Schools

Baughman, M. Dale. *Administration of the Junior High School.* Danville, Ill.: Interstate Printers and Publishers, 1966. A pragmatic "pointers for principals" approach, prepared under the sponsorship of the Illinois Junior High School Principals' Association.

Rock, D. A., and J. K. Hemphill. *Report of the Junior High-School Principalship.* Washington, D.C. National Education Association, 1965. Prepared by the Department of Secondary-School Principals of the NEA, reporting on its study of the junior high school principalship.

3. High Schools

Ackerly, Robert L. *The Reasonable Exercise of Authority.* Washington, D.C.: National Association of Secondary School Principals, 1969.

Analyzes the principal's exercise of authority and the administrator's legal status in relationship to the political activity of high school students.

Barker, Roger G., and Paul V. Gump. *Big School, Small School: High School Size and Student Behavior*. Stanford, California: Stanford University Press, 1964. Recommends that a smaller school provides a more favorable educational climate—based on a study of the effect of school size (enrollment, number of divisions of school organization, etc.) on the educational environment.

Corwin, Ronald G. *Militant Professionalism: A Study of Organizational Conflict in High Schools*. New York: Appleton-Century-Crofts, 1970. A study of staff conflicts and organizational conflict in high schools, based on the author's U.S. Office of Education Cooperative Research Project.

Epstein, Benjamin. *The Principal's Role in Collective Negotiations Between Teachers and School Boards*. Washington, D.C. National Association of Secondary-School Principals, 1965. Analysis of the teacher-administrator-school board relationship, and the task of the principal in collective negotiations.

Fitzwater, Ivan W. *Practical Techniques For High School Administration*. Danville, Ill.: Interstate Printers and Publishers, 1968. A pragmatic approach to high school administration, prepared for the Indiana Public School Study Council.

French, Will, et al. *American High School Administration: Policy and Practice*. 3rd ed. New York: Holt, Rinehart and Winston, 1962. Emphasizes the critical leadership role of the high school administrator and the skills needed to provide effective leadership.

Hemphill, J. K., et al. *Report of the Senior-High School Principalship*. Washington, D.C.: National Education Association, 1965. Study of the senior high school principalship conducted by the Department of Secondary-School Principals of the NEA.

Mitchum, Paul McCoy. *The High School Principal and Staff Plan for Program Improvement*. New York: Teachers College, Columbia University, 1958. Presents the case for a cooperative teacher-administrator relationship approach to school management and program development.

Parody, Ovid Frank. *The High School Principal and Staff Deal with Discipline*. Rev. ed. New York: Teachers College Press, Columbia University, 1965. Proposals for a cooperative administrator-teacher approach to the development of a program of school discipline and control.

D. CURRICULUM

1. General

Brent, Rudyard K., and Adolph Unruh. *Secondary School Curriculum.* Mass.: D. C. Heath, 1969. Basic textbook providing an overview of secondary curricula in the United States.

Bhaerman, Steve, and Joel Denker. *No Particular Place to Go: The Making of a Free High School.* New York: Simon and Schuster, 1972. Narrative account of an alternative free high school, the New Educational Project, founded by the authors with a group of white, middle class Washington, D.C. students (1968-70) and built on the foundation of communal living.

Bremer, John, and Michael von Moschzisker. *The School Without Walls: Philadelphia's Program.* New York: Holt, Rinehart and Winston, 1971. Account of Philadelphia Parkway Program, an innovative attempt to use the community as a laboratory for learning.

Bush, Robert N., and Dwight W. Allen. *A New Design for High School Education: Assuming a Flexible Schedule.* New York: McGraw-Hill, 1964. Introductory discussion of organizational alternatives available in scheduling and staffing a school.

Elizabeth Cleaners Street School Project. *Starting Your Own High School.* New York: Random House, 1972. First-hand account of an innovative attempt to establish an alternative high school.

Everett, Samuel (ed.). *Programs for the Gifted: A Case Book in Secondary Education.* New York: Harper, 1961. Fifteenth yearbook of the John Dewey Society, containing chapters on what is being done to encourage the academically talented.

Tanner, Daniel. *Secondary Curriculum: Theory and Development.* New York: Macmillan, 1971. Comprehensive text on the principles of secondary curriculum development.

Tompkins, Ellsworth. *The Carnegie Unit: Its Origin, Status, and Trends.* Washington, D.C.: U.S. Government Printing Office, 1954. Valuable U.S. Office of Education Bulletin providing the history of the Carnegie unit of school credit, its status in the mid-fifties, and trends of the time.

Trump, J. Lloyd, and Delmas F. Miller. *Secondary Curriculum Improvement: Proposals and Procedures.* Boston: Allyn and Bacon, 1968. Focuses on curriculum practitioners, urging them to examine their own thinking about the curriculum and to develop plans to transfer their ideas into school programs they can accept and manage.

Unruh, Glenys G., and William M. Alexander. *Innovations in Secondary Education*. New York: Holt, Rinehart and Winston, 1970. Comprehensive overview of innovative practices in American secondary education.

2. Junior High/Middle Schools

Alexander, William M., et al. *The Emergent Middle School*. 2nd ed. New York: Holt, Rinehart and Winston, 1969. Detailed description of the middle school, including curriculum plans and criteria for evaluating and developing the curriculum.

American Association of School Administrators. *The Junior High School Curriculum*. Washington, D.C.: National Education Association, 1927. Valuable summary of the status of the school curriculum in the late 1920's, based on the 1926-1927 report of the Commission on the Curriculum, under the chairmanship of Edwin C. Broome.

Heathers, Glenn. *Organizing Schools Through the Dual Progress Plan: Tryouts of a New Plan for Elementary and Middle Schools*. Danville, Ill.: Interstate Printers and Publishers, 1967. Comprehensive description, analysis, and evaluation of a six-year experimental application of the dual progress plan.

Lounsbury, John H., and Jean V. Marani. *The Junior High School We Saw: One Day in the Eighth Grade*. Washington, D.C.: Association for Supervision and Curriculum Development, 1964. Report prepared for the ASCD describing an in-depth study of one school day in the eighth grade.

McCarthy, Robert J. *The Ungraded Middle School*. West Nyack, N.Y.: Parker Publishing Company, 1972. Description of the ungraded middle school, which de-emphasizes age-grade placement and emphasizes individualized instruction and achievement.

3. High Schools

Alexander, William M. (ed.). *The Changing Secondary School Curriculum: Readings*. New York: Holt, Rinehart and Winston, 1969. Book of readings presenting a wide range of opinions on the major issues in curriculum improvement, emphasizing the need for continued and systematic change.

Brown, B. Frank. *The Nongraded High School*. West Nyack, N.Y.: Parker Publishing Company, 1963. Exploration of the need for innovation and change in traditional student grouping; proposals and plans for reorganization based on the author's experience as principal of a nongraded high school in Melbourne, Florida.

Clark, Leonard H., Raymond L. Klein, and John B. Burks. *The American Secondary School Curriculum*. New York: Macmillan, 1965. Describes the theory and substance of the secondary school curricula, including historical background, the status of curriculum practice in the mid-1960's, and suggested courses of action.

Johnston, Edgar G. (ed.). *Vitalizing Student Activities in the Secondary School.* Washington, D.C.: The National Association of Secondary-School Principals, 1941. Bulletin of the National Association of Secondary-School Principals discussing the principles and practices of the student activity program in secondary schools.

Petrequin, G. (ed.). *Individualizing Learning Through Modular-Flexible Programing.* New York: McGraw-Hill Book Company, 1968. Collection of articles by high school faculty members, each article describing a particular aspect of the modular program at John Marshall High School.

Trump, J. Lloyd. *High-School Extracurriculum Activities: Their Management in Public High Schools of the North Central Association.* Chicago: University of Chicago Press, 1944. Critical evaluation of the management of high school extracurricular activities, based on a set of specified criteria, and recommendations for the future direction and management of these activities.

Wiley, W. M., and Lloyd K. Bishop. *The Flexibly Scheduled High School.* West Nyack, N.Y.: Parker Publishing Company, 1968. An introduction to flexible scheduling based on the experiences at Claremont High School of California.

Wright, Grace. *High School Curriculum Organization Patterns, and Graduation Requirements in Fifty Large Cities.* Washington, D.C.: U.S. Office of Education, 1959. Valuable documentation of high school curriculum organization patterns in the 1950's, based on a U.S. Office of Education survey of fifty large cities.

E. TEACHING

1. General

Alcorn, Marvin D., James S. Kinder, and Jim R. Schunert. *Better Teaching in Secondary Schools.* 3rd ed. New York: Holt, Rinehart and Winston, 1970. Introductory text which attempts to correlate principles of the psychology of learning and human development with concrete examples of classroom practice.

Blair, Glenn M. *Diagnostic and Remedial Teaching: A Guide to Practice in Elementary and Secondary Schools.* Rev. ed. New York: Macmillan, 1956. This pragmatic guide to practice is a revision of the 1946 edition, *Diagnostic and Remedial Teaching in Secondary Schools.*

Blount, Nathan S., and Herbert J. Klausmeir. *Teaching in the Secondary*

School. 3rd ed. New York: Harper and Row, 1968. A revision of *Principles and Practices of Secondary School Teaching,* offering a comprehensive analysis of the objectives of secondary education and suggestions for translating the findings of educational research into teaching practice.

Callahan, G. Sterling. *Successful Teaching in Secondary Schools: A Guide for Students and In-Service Teachers.* Rev. ed. Glenview, Ill.: Scott, Foresman and Company, 1971. Revised edition of a popular methods text using illustrative case studies to focus on teaching principles, planning and special teaching problems.

Faunce, Roland C., and Carroll L. Munshaw. *Teaching and Learning in Secondary Schools.* California: Wadsworth Publishing Company, 1964. Emphasizes the connection between goals and methods, and adapting instruction to individual differences.

Grambs, Jean Dresden, John C. Carr, and Robert N. Fitch. *Modern Methods in Secondary Education.* 3rd ed. New York: Holt, Rinehart and Winston, 1970. Most recent edition of a very popular introductory text to instructional practices for secondary school teaching.

Hoover, Kenneth H. *Learning and Teaching in the Secondary School: Improved Instructional Practices.* 3rd ed. Boston: Allyn and Bacon, 1972. A pragmatic volume offering specific suggestions for improving instructional practice, based on the premise that the proper role of the teacher is to work with students in the appropriate selection, organization, and evaluation of educational experiences which facilitate sound thinking.

Keene, Melvin. *Beginning Secondary School Teacher's Guide: Some Problems and Suggested Solutions.* New York: Harper and Row, 1969. Case studies and suggested principles for resolving problems faced by teachers.

Rivlin, Harry N. *Teaching Adolescents in Secondary Schools: The Principles of Effective Teaching in Junior and Senior High Schools.* 2nd ed. New York: Appleton-Century-Crofts, 1961. Introduction to secondary school teaching practices which emphasizes and illustrates the possibilities for developing imaginative teaching strategies.

Taba, Hilda, and Deborah Elkins. *Teaching Strategies for the Culturally Disadvantaged.* Chicago: Rand McNally, 1966. A seminal work focusing on middle school-junior high school age students, and the development of programs to reshape the curriculum, its content, and the way of teaching and learning in order to reach so-called "culturally disadvantaged" students.

Zapf, Rosalind Marie. *Democratic Processes in the Secondary Classroom.*

Englewood Cliffs, N.J.: Prentice-Hall, Inc., 1959. Focuses on the principles and procedures for developing socially interactive learning situations using group work and the committee approach.

2. Junior High/Middle Schools

Baughman, M. Dale (ed.). *Climate for Learning: Focus on the Teacher.* Danville, Ill.: Interstate Printers and Publishers, 1964. Reviews the literature in the field and presents position papers on the role of the junior high school teacher in relationship to the learning climate.

Baughman, M. Dale (ed.). *Junior High School Staff Personnel: Their Preparation and Professional Growth.* Danville, Ill.: Interstate Printers and Publishers, 1966. Collection of papers presented at various conferences of the Junior High School Association of Illinois in 1965.

Howard, Alvin W. *Teaching in Middle Schools.* Scranton: International Textbook Company, 1968. Pragmatic handbook or manual for junior high/middle school teachers.

Van Til, William, et al. *Modern Education for the Junior High School Years.* 2nd ed. Indianapolis: Bobbs, Merrill, 1967. Comprehensive description of general teaching methods and procedures for teaching specific specialized subject areas.

3. High Schools

Alexander, William M., J. Galen Saylor, and Emmett L. Williams. *The High School: Today and Tomorrow.* New York: Holt, Rinehart and Winston, 1971. Description of current principles and practices of high school teaching and curriculum offerings, and prospects for the future.

Hoover, Kenneth H. *A Handbook for High School Teachers.* Boston: Allyn and Bacon, 1970. A pragmatic manual for high school teachers, portions of which were taken from the author's *Learning and Teaching in the Secondary School.*

Inlow, Gail M. *Maturity in High School Teaching.* 2nd ed. Englewood Cliffs, N.J.: Prentice-Hall, Inc., 1970. Designed both as a text and resource book, emphasizing teaching as a subtle process whereby the instructor establishes a learning environment for students.

Parker, Samuel Chester. *Methods of Teaching in High School.* Rev. ed. Boston: Ginn and Company, 1920. A classic text on the status of high school pedagogy in the first quarter of the twentieth century.

Paterson, Carl H. *Effective Team Teaching: The Easton Area High School Program.* West Nyack, N.Y.: Parker Publishing Company, 1966. Detailed account of the introduction of team teaching into the Easton Area High

School in Pennsylvania (1958), and the growth and development of the program.

F. COUNSELING

Holbrook, Harold Lyman, and A. Laura McGregor. *Our Junior High School.* Boston: Allyn and Bacon, 1928. A series of lessons designed for guidance purposes and developed to help junior high school age students develop a clearer understanding of their daily experience.

Indiana Public School Study Council. *Exploring Junior High School Guidance.* Danville, Ill.: Interstate Printers and Publishers, 1965. Consideration of the special needs of guidance and counseling at the junior high school level.

Liggero, John. *A Successful Approach to High School Counseling.* West Nyack, N.Y.: Parker Publishing Company, 1968. Introductory text suggesting principles and practices for counseling at the high school level.

Loughary, John W. *Counseling in Secondary Schools: A Frame of Reference.* New York: Harper and Row, 1961. Presents counseling as the most important function of the school counselor—of greater significance than the non-counseling guidance procedures.

National Education Association. *It's High Time: A Guide for Parents of High School Students.* Washington, D.C.: National Education Association, 1955. A handbook "for every parent of a teenager;" the original manuscript was prepared by Beatrice M. Gudridge for the National Association of Secondary-School Principals, National Public Relations Association, and the National Congress of Parents and Teachers.

Strang, Ruth. *Counseling Technics in College and Secondary School.* 2nd ed. New York: Harper and Row, 1949. Consideration of the personal qualifications of the counselor, the counselor's relationship with the student, and the importance of intelligent application and use of the various counseling techniques.

Williamson, Edmund G. *Counseling Adolescents.* New York: McGraw-Hill, 1950. Emphasizes a personalized and individualized approach to counseling, helping adolescents develop their full personalities, as a means of effectively utilizing human resources.

G. DROPOUTS

Burchill, George W. (ed.). *Work Study Programs for Alienated Youth.* Chicago: Science Research Associates, 1962. A description of nine work-study programs for secondary students combining classroom and job experience to combat student alienation.

Cervantes, Lucius. *The Drop-Out: Causes and Cures*. Ann Arbor: University of Michigan Press, 1965. A study which analyzed the characteristics of 300 youths, half of whom completed high school and half of whom dropped out.

Dentler, Robert A., and Mary E. Warshauer. *Big City Dropouts and Illiterates*. New York: Center for Urban Education, 1965. A study of educational barriers to economic security, comparing high school dropouts and adult illiteracy in over one hundred large cities of the United States.

Greene, Bert I. *Preventing Student Dropouts*. Englewood Cliffs, N.J.: Prentice-Hall, 1966. An analysis of the nature of the dropout problem and the characteristics of the dropout, and the roles which parents and school personnel can and should play.

Lichter, Solomon O., et al. *The Dropouts*. New York: The Free Press, 1962. The report and findings of a three-year treatment study of intellectually able students who dropped out of high school.

Schreiber, Daniel (ed.). *Profile of the School Dropout: A Reader on America's Major Educational Problem*. New York: Random House, 1967. A collection of original essays and articles by twenty leading educators analyzing various aspects of the dropout problem: the issue at stake, early childhood, guidance, statistics, social and historical factors, present and future programs, etc.

Tannenbaum, Abraham J. *Dropout or Diploma: A Socio-Educational Analysis of Early School Withdrawal*. New York: Teachers College Press, Columbia University, 1966. A brief review of the factors affecting early school withdrawal.

Torrance, E. Paul, and Robert D. Strom (eds.). *Mental Health and Achievement: Increasing Potential and Reducing School Dropout*. New York: John Wiley, 1966. Contributions by leading figures in the files of mental health suggesting proposals and procedures for reducing the dropout problem.

H. EVALUATION

Baughman, M. Dale (ed.). *Pupil Evaluation in the Junior High School*. Danville, Ill.: Interstate Printers and Publishers, 1963. A review of the literature, position papers on evaluation, opinions on aspects of evaluation and prevailing practices in selected junior high schools.

Farley, Eugene J., Clyde E. Weinhold, and Arthur P. Crabtree. *High School Certification Through the G. E. D. Tests*. New York: Holt, Rinehart and Winston, 1967. A practical "how to" approach describing the route to high school certification via the General Educational Development tests.

National Study of School Evaluation. *Junior High School/Middle School*

Evaluative Criteria: A Guide for School Improvement. Arlington, Va.: National Study of School Evaluation, 1970. Revised instrument used for identifying, surveying, and evaluating the characteristics of a good secondary school—based on *Evaluative Criteria for Junior High Schools,* issued by the body under its earlier name: National Study of Secondary School Evaluation.

Schwartz, Alfred, and Stuart C. Tiedeman, with the assistance of Donald G. Wallace. *Evaluating Student Progress in the Secondary School.* New York: Longmans, Green, 1957. Introduction to tests and measurements applicable for evaluating student learning at the secondary school level.

Vars, Gordon F. (ed.). *Guidelines for Junior High and Middle School Evaluation.* Washington, D.C.: National Association of Secondary-School Principals, 1966. A summary of position papers of the Department of Secondary-School Principals' Committee on Junior High School Education.

Wright, Grace. *High School Graduation Requirements Established by State Departments of Education, 1963-64.* Washington, D.C.: U.S. Office of Education, 1964. Circular No. 739 of the U.S. Office of Education, updated and revised to summarize the high school graduation requirements established by State Departments of Education.

I. STUDENTS

Ashby, Lloyd W., and John A. Stoops (eds.). *Student Activism in the Secondary Schools: A Practical Outlook.* Danville, Ill.: Interstate Printers and Publishers, 1970. Collection of articles generated by the 1969 Lehigh University Conference on Student Activism.

Birmingham, John (ed.). *Our Time Is Now: Notes from the High School Underground.* New York: Praeger, 1970. Selections from the high school "underground" student newspapers, expressing open revolt against the schools, parents, and a hypocritical society.

Coleman, James S. *The Adolescent Society: The Social Life of the Teenager and Its Impact on Education.* New York: The Free Press, 1961. A study of the adolescent social system in a dozen high schools of varying size and composition, describing social interaction among adolescents and its implications for education.

Divoky, Diane (ed.). *How Old Will You Be In 1984? Expressions of Student Outrage from the High School Free Press.* New York: Avon Books, 1969. Collection of over 250 selections of both writings and graphic art from the "underground" high school student newspapers.

Flanagan, John C., et al. *The American High-School Student: The Identification, Development, and Utilization of Human Talents.* Pittsburgh: University of Pittsburgh, 1964. Final report of a research project conducted by the Project Talent Office of the University of Pittsburgh, following up on earlier studies of educational plans and decisions in relation to aptitude patterns.

Friedenberg, Edgar Z. *Coming of Age In America: Growth and Acquiescence.* New York: Random House, 1965. A study of adolescents in a variety of American high schools, utilizing psychological tests and interviews, which concludes that the school exerts both direct and indirect pressures to oblige students to relinquish their own autonomy, and sacrifice their own desires, on behalf of institutional and social considerations.

Friedenberg, Edgar Z. *The Vanishing Adolescent.* Boston: Beacon Press, 1969. A penetrating sociological study of adolescents and life in the American high school, picturing youth engaged in a gallant, but hopeless struggle with school officials representing the timidity and corruption of the adult world.

Hart, Richard L., and J. Galen Saylor (eds.). *Student Unrest: Threat or Promise?* Washington, D.C.: Association for Supervision and Curriculum Development, 1970. Collection of papers on student unrest, from the proceedings of two ASCD conferences held in 1969.

Libarle, Marc, and Tom Seligson (eds.). *The High School Revolutionaries.* New York: Random House, 1970. Collection of taped interviews and essays by twenty-one students of different ages and backgrounds, presenting their views on the high school protests of the late sixties and conditions they find intolerable.

Mallery, David. *High School Students Speak Out.* New York: Harper and Row, 1962. Report of a study, conducted under the auspices of the Committee on School and College Relations of the Educational Records Bureau of New York, on the impact of high school experiences on youth.

Nordstrom, Carl, Edgar Z. Friedenberg, and Hilary A. Gold. *Society's Children: A Study of Ressentiment in the Secondary School.* New York: Random House, 1967. A sociological and philosophical analysis which attempts to document the malevolent influence of "ressentiment" on school environments—certain types of high schools which inhibit the energy and spirit of students and thereby leave students unfit for productive life.

VII. VOCATIONAL EDUCATION

A. BIBLIOGRAPHIES

Abstracts of Research and Related Materials in Vocational and Technical Education [ARM]. No. 1 ——, 1967 ——. Columbus: ERIC Clearinghouse, Center for Vocational and Technical Education, Ohio State University. Quarterly. Complete bibliographical information and abstracts of each document (200 words or less). Yearly cumulation. See also, *Abstracts of Instructional Materials in Vocational and Technical Education* (1967 ——).

Songe, Alice. *Vocational Education: An Annotated Bibliography of Selected References, 1917-1966.* Washington: U.S. Government Printing Office, 1967. Lists and describes books, monographs, periodical articles, and unpublished doctoral dissertations which trace the history of vocational education in the United States from the early 20th century to the close of 1966.

[United States Bureau of Education] Bulletin, 1913, No. 22. *Bibliography of Industrial, Vocational, and Trade Education.* Washington: Government Printing Office, 1913. Fullest guide to source materials published before World War I.

"Vocational, Technical, and Practical Arts Education." *Review of Educational Research,* vol. 38 (October, 1968), pp. 305-442. A critical review of the literature since 1962, keyed to extensive bibliographies. See also, *Ibid.,* vol. 32 (October, 1962); and *Ibid.,* vol. 26 (October, 1956).

York, Edwin G. *A Compilation of Resource Lists for Vocational Educators: An Annotated Bibliography of Bibliographies in Vocational Education, 1960-1969.* Trenton, N.J.: Bureau of Occupational Research Development, Department of Education, 1969. A register of 579 annotated entries on resources for all phases of vocational education.

B. HISTORIES AND CRITICAL STUDIES

Aldrich, F. R. "Industrial Education in the Early 19th Century." *Elementary School Teacher,* vol. 13 (1913), pp. 478-485. Valuable overview of programs and developments.

Anderson, Lewis F. *History of Manual and Industrial School Education*. New York: Appleton, 1926. Includes notices of developments in Europe and their influence on American schools.

Barlow, Melvin L. *History of Industrial Education in the United States*. Peoria, Illinois: Chas. A. Bennett Co., 1967. The heritage of industrial education from its beginnings to the present.

Bennett, Charles A. *A History of Manual and Industrial Education Up to 1870*. Peoria, Illinois: Manual Arts Press, 1926. Also, Charles A. Bennett. *A History of Manual and Industrial Education, 1870-1917*. Peoria, Illinois: Manual Arts Press, 1937. A universal history from ancient times extending to the passage of the Smith-Hughes Act in 1917. Covers most phases of the manual training movement, and remains the most inclusive source.

Brewer, John M. *A History of Vocational Guidance: Origins and Early Development*. New York: Harper, 1942. The most comprehensive history for the period it covers; see also the author's *The Vocational Guidance Movement* (New York: Macmillan, 1918).

Coates, Charles P. *History of the Manual Training School of Washington University* [St. Louis Manual Training School]. U.S. Bureau of Education. Bulletin #3 (1923). The first major manual training high school in the United States.

Cohen, David K., and Marvin Lazerson. "Education and the Corporate Order." *Socialist Revolution,* vol. 2 (March/April, 1972), pp. 47-72. Vocational education in the framework of American educational change.

Cohen, Sol. "The Industrial Education Movement, 1906-17." *American Quarterly,* vol. 20 (Spring, 1968), pp. 95-110. Explores the connections between the industrial education movement, child labor, and the compulsory education movement.

Cremin, Lawrence A. *The Transformation of the School: Progressivism in American Education, 1876-1957*. New York: Knopf, 1961. Particularly Chapter 2 ("Education and Industry") on the history of the manual training and vocational education movement.

Douglas, Paul H. *American Apprenticeship and Industrial Education* [Columbia University Studies in Economics, History, and Law, XCV, No. 2]. New York: Longmans, Green, 1921. An important history with an excellent summary of the many surveys of the adequacy of traditional schooling, and a major critique of the vocational education movement. See also, George S. Counts, *The Selective Character of American Secondary Education* (1922) for the impact of vocationalism; and Counts, *School and Society in Chicago* (1928) for the controversy which surrounded vocational education; also, for the impact of vocational education on schooling, see Robert and Helen Lynd, *Middletown* (1929).

Fisher, Berenice. *Industrial Education: American Ideals and Institutions.* Madison: University of Wisconsin Press, 1967. An overview of the controversy surrounding vocational training in the first decades of the 20th century, and related developments.

Hawkins, Layton S., Charles Prosser, and John C. Wright. *Development of Vocational Education.* Chicago: American Technical Society, 1951. A massive resource on historical backgrounds, programs, federal legislation, and trends.

Krug, Edward A. *The Shaping of the American High School, 1880-1920.* New York: Harper, 1964; and *The Shaping of the American High School, 1920-1941.* Madison: University of Wisconsin Press, 1972. Invaluable historical contexts for the study of vocational, industrial arts, and practical arts education.

Lazerson, Marvin. *Origins of the Urban School: Public Education in Massachusetts, 1870-1915.* Cambridge: Harvard University Press, 1971. Includes chapters on "Manual Training: The Search for Ideology"; "Manual Training and the Restoration of Social Values"; "From the Principles of Work to the Teaching of Trades"; "The Politics of Vocationalism"; and "Vocationalism and the Equality of Educational Opportunity."

Lazerson, Marvin, and W. Norton Grubb, eds. *American Education and Vocationalism: A Documentary History, 1870-1970.* New York: Teachers College Press, Columbia University, 1974. Representative documents, with essay introduction and valuable bibliographical essay.

Leavitt, Frank M., and Edith Brown. *Prevocational Education in the Public Schools.* Boston: Houghton Mifflin, 1915. The only substantial historical source on prevocational training.

McBride, Paul W. "The Co-Op Industrial Education Experiment, 1900-1917." *History of Education Quarterly,* vol. 14 (Summer, 1974), pp. 209-221. Study of public schools which cooperated closely with local industry in the formulation, control, and staffing of industrial education programs.

Mays, Arthur B. *The Concept of Vocational Education in the Thinking of the General Educator, 1845 to 1945.* Urbana, Illinois: University of Illinois Press, 1946. A theoretical and critical assessment with detailed historical backgrounds. See also the author's *Principles and Practices of Vocational Education* (New York: McGraw-Hill, 1948).

Oberman, Carl E. *A History of Vocational Rehabilitation in America.* Minneapolis: University of Minnesota Press, 1965. Comprehensive history with valuable information on vocational education movement.

Sears, William P., Jr. *The Roots of Vocational Education: A Survey of the*

Origin of Trade and Industrial Education Found in Industry, Education, Legislation and Social Progress. New York: John Wiley, 1931. A comprehensive historical overview, valuable for its considerable detail.

Smith, Ross H. *Development of Manual Training in the United States.* Lancaster, Pa.: Intelligencer Printing Co., 1914. An early history with considerable detail on programs.

Spring, Joel. *Education and the Rise of the Corporate State.* Boston: Beacon Press, 1972. Develops the thesis that the basic failing of the schools resulted from their uncompromising adaptation to the structure and needs of modern, industrial society. Includes a foreword by Ivan Illich.

Stephens, W. Richard. *Social Reforms and the Origins of Vocational Guidance.* Washington: Brookings Institution, 1970. Vocational education and its relationships to social reform, educational change, and the guidance of youth.

Stombaugh, Roy M. *A Survey of the Movements Culminating in Industrial Arts Education in Secondary Schools.* New York: Teachers College, Columbia University, 1936. Historical survey with source materials.

Tesconi, Charles A., and Van Cleve Morris. *The Anti-Man Culture: Bureautechnocracy and the Schools.* Urbana: University of Illinois Press, 1972. Asserts that the schools are the "perpetuator" of bureautechnocracy even as they are its creature. Bureautechnocracy advocates assimilation; the adjustment of individuals to modern, industrial society; and the adoption of scientific methodologies.

True, Alfred C. *A History of Agricultural Education in the United States, 1785-1925.* Washington: Government Printing Office, 1929. Comprehensive history of vocational agriculture in the public schools.

Wendt, Erhard F. "Brief History of Industrial Arts and Vocational Education." *Industrial Arts and Vocational Education,* vol. 35 (April, 1946), pp. 151-154. Useful outlines of history of vocational education with notices of leading figures. Also, *Ibid.,* vol. 35 (May, 1946), pp. 202-203.

Wenrich, R. C., *et al.* "Vocational, Technical, and Practical Arts Education: History of Vocational Education." *Review of Educational Research,* vol. 32 (October, 1962), p. 370 ff. Developments since World War I, with some notices of major figures and federal roles.

Williamson, E. G. "Historical Perspectives of the Vocational Guidance Movement." *Personal and Guidance Journal,* vol. 42 (May, 1964), pp. 854-859. Useful historical outlines and educational backgrounds.

Wirth, Arthur G. *Education in the Technological Society: The Vocational Studies Controversy in the Early Twentieth Century.* Scranton: Intext

Educational Publishers, 1972. The origins of vocational training in the 19th century, and a study of educational policy in the first two decades of the 20th century.

C. FEDERAL LEGISLATION, OFFICIAL REPORTS, AND RELATED DOCUMENTS

Barlow, Melvin L., ed. *Vocational Education*. [National Society for the Study of Education, 64th Yearbook, Part I]. Chicago: University of Chicago Press, 1965. Largely, a commentary on vocational education and the Vocational Education Act of 1963, with examination of different phases of vocational education.

Briggs, L. D. "Support from the Top: Major Areas of Responsibility for Professional Development in Vocational Education." *American Vocational Journal,* vol. 46 (November, 1971), pp. 42-44. Review of federal legislation for vocational education.

Clarke, Isaac E. *Art and Education*. [46th Congress, 2nd Session, U.S. Senate, Executive Documents, 1897], VII, No. 209, pts. 1-4. A comprehensive discussion of "practical" education containing considerable primary source material on manual arts education.

[Commission on Industrial Education] *Report of the Commission on Industrial Education Made to the Legislature of Pennsylvania.* Harrisburg: Edwin K. Meyers, State Printer, 1889. Influential state report.

[Commissioner of Labor] *Industrial Education in the United States*. Twenty-Fifth Annual Report of the Commissioner of Labor. Washington: Government Printing Office, 1911. A massive repository of information on industrial America and its impact on the schools.

[Commissioner of Labor] *Trade and Technical Education*. Seventeenth Annual Report of the Commissioner of Labor. Washington: Government Printing Office, 1902. Valuable source on 19th century programs.

Essex, Martin, *et al. Notes and Working Papers Concerning the Administration of Programs Authorized under the Vocational Education Act of 1963, Public Law 88-210, As Amended.* Washington: U.S. Government Printing Office, 1968. A report by the National Advisory Council on Vocational Education reviewing the administration and status of vocational education programs.

Evans, Rupert N., *et al. Education for Employment: The Background and Potential of the 1968 Vocational Education Amendments.* Ann Arbor, Michigan: University of Michigan, Institute of Labor and Industrial Relations, 1969. A critical analysis of the 1968 report of the Advisory Council on Vocational Education, with outlines of historical trends.

Henry, Nelson B., ed. *Vocational Education.* [National Society for the Study of Education, 42nd Yearbook, Part I]. Chicago: University of Chicago Press, 1943. A comprehensive review of legislation, programs, and problems affecting vocational education. The *Yearbooks* for 1905, 1912, 1916, and 1924 also were addressed to vocational education.

Kliever, Douglas E. *The Vocational Education Act of 1963: A Case Study in Legislation.* Washington: Brookings Institution,1965. A review of federal legislation for vocational education, with exhaustive examination of 1963 Act.

[Massachusetts]. Commission on Industrial and Technical Education. *Report* .... [1906]. Boston: Wright & Potter, 1906. [The Douglas Commission] Chaired by Carroll D. Wright, the Commission's *Report* was the most influential of the state reports.

[National Education Association] *Report of the Committee on the Place of Industries in Public Education.* Washington: The Association, 1910. Professional educators' expressions of approval of certain aspects of vocationalism.

[Office of Science and Technology: Executive Office of the President] *Youth Transition to Adulthood: Report of the Panel on Youth of the President's Science Advisory Committee.* Washington: U.S. Government Printing Office, 1973. Chaired by James Coleman, "the Panel has identified issues and proposed recommendations." Includes materials on the demography of youth, economic problems of youth, the scope of formal schooling, etc.

Proceedings of the National Society for the Promotion of Industrial Education. *Bulletins* (New York: 1907––) Founded in Boston in 1907, the NSPIE was the lobby and chief organ of the alliance between educators and industrialists. At the federal level, the NSPIE influentially promoted national aid to vocational education. Renamed the National Society for Vocational Education in 1920.

Runkle, John D. "The Manual Element in Education," in [Massachusetts State Board of Education] *Forty-First Annual Report of the Board Together with the Annual Report of the Secretary of the Board* [Boston, 1878]. Influential plea for manual training which attracted national attention.

Swanson, J. Chester, ed. *Development of Federal Legislation for Vocational Education.* 2nd ed. Chicago: American Technical Society, 1966. Historical overview with extensive information on the Vocational Education Act of 1963.

[United States Bureau of Education]. Bulletin, 1908, No. 6. Carroll D. Wright. *The Apprenticeship System in Its Relation to Industrial Education.* Washington: Government Printing Office, 1908. Historical backgrounds of the apprentice system and critical appraisal by the Commissioner of Labor.

[U.S. Congress, House of Representatives, 63rd Congress, 3rd Session, 1914, House Document 1004]. *Report of the Commission on National Aid to Vocational Education.* The Commission's recommendations were written into law with the passage of the Smith-Hughes Act of 1917.

[U.S. Department of Health, Education, and Welfare]. *Education for a Changing World of Work.* Washington: Government Printing Office, 1964. The historical development of vocational education and a review of existing programs. Report of John F. Kennedy's Panel of Consultants on Vocational Education.

[U.S. Department of Health, Education, and Welfare]. *Vocational Education: The Bridge Between Man and His Work.* Prepared by the Advisory Council on Vocational Education. Washington: Government Printing Office, 1968. Influential report and the basis for the Vocational Education Amendments of 1968. See also, Garth Mangum, *Reorienting Vocational Education* (1968).

[United States Office of Education]. Bulletin, 1933, No. 15. Lloyd E. Blauch. *Federal Cooperation in Agricultural Extension Work, Vocational Education, and Vocational Rehabilitation.* Washington: Government Printing Office, 1933. The movement to secure federal aid for vocational education between 1910 and 1920.

Venn, Grant. *Education and Work: Post Secondary Vocational and Technical Education.* Washington: American Council on Education, 1964. Derives from a conference called by the American Vocational Association (Washington, September, 1962) whose consensus was that "some assessment of the place of occupational education within education as a whole and within a new technological economy would have to be made." Excellent review of federal role in vocational education.

Whipple, Guy M., ed. *Vocational Guidance and Vocational Education for the Industries.* [National Society for the Study of Education, 23rd Yearbook, Part II]. Bloomington, Indiana: Public School Publications, 1924. Valuable historical resource on schools and industrial contexts in first quarter of 20th century.

D. MISCELLANEOUS

[American Academy of Political and Social Science]. *Industrial Education.* Philadelphia: The Academy, 1909. Vocational education in the early century, with descriptive notices of programs.

Arnold, Walter K., and Russell K. Britton. "Fifty Years of Progress in Trade and Industrial Education." *American Vocational Journal,* vol. 31 (December, 1956), pp. 83-90, 104. A review of programs with some historical source materials.

Astin, A. W., and R. J. Panos. *The Educational and Vocational Development of College Students*. Washington: American Council on Education, 1969. Focus on educational attainment and the determinants of career plans and aspirations.

Banes, Charles E. *Manual Training and Apprenticeship Schools in 1890*. Philadelphia: George H. Buchanan and Co., 1890. An overview of late 19th century practice, with some notices of historical backgrounds.

Barlow, Melvin L. *Principles of Trade and Industrial Education*. Austin: University of Texas Press, 1963. Philosophical and historical basis of industrial education.

Bawden, William T. *Leaders in Industrial Education*. Milwaukee: Bruce, 1950. A review of the work of influential figures, *e.g.,* Woodward, Russell, Bonser, Runkle, Griffith, Harvey, Stout, Struck, Roberts.

Bloomfield, Meyer. *The Vocational Guidance of Youth*. Boston: Houghton Mifflin, 1911. Bloomfield was the most important writer on vocational guidance in the period before World War I. See also the author's *Youth, School, and Vocation* (Boston: Houghton Mifflin, 1915); and *Readings in Vocational Guidance* (Boston: Ginn, 1915).

Brickman, William W., and Stanley Lehrer, eds. *Automation, Education, and Human Values*. New York: School and Society, 1966. Conference papers by specialists in the fields of industry, labor, education, sociology, religion, and psychology.

Burt, Samuel M. *Industry and Vocational-Technical Education: A Study of Education-Advisory Committees*. New York: McGraw-Hill, 1967. Sponsored by the Fund for the Advancement of Education, and intended as a study of the involvement of employers in occupational education.

Carlton, Frank T. *Economic Influences upon Educational Progress in the United States, 1820-1850*. Madison: University of Wisconsin, 1908. Important materials for vocational and practical arts education. See also, Carlton's *Education and Industrial Evolution* (1908).

Clark, Harold F., and Harold S. Sloan. *Classrooms in the Factories: An Account of the Educational Activities Conducted by American Industry*. Rutherford, N.J.: Institute of Research, Fairleigh Dickinson University, 1958. Descriptions of some 300 programs offered by American industry, largely technical and business.

Clark, Harold F., and Harold S. Sloan. *Classrooms on Main Street: An Account of Specialty Schools in the United States that Train for Work and Leisure*. New York: Teachers College, Columbia University, 1966.

Non-traditional programs preparing students for business and industrial employment.

DeCarlo, Charles R. *Education in Business and Industry.* New York: Center for Applied Research in Education, 1966. A discussion of the role of industry and business in education, with historical backgrounds.

Educationally Deficient Adults: Their Education and Training Needs. Washington: Government Printing Office, 1965. The needs of unskilled and deskilled adults with discussion of vocational education programs to meet the needs.

Fee, Edward M. *The Origin and Growth of Vocational Industrial Education in Philadelphia to 1917.* Philadelphia: Westbrook Publishing Co., 1938. A University of Pennsylvania doctoral dissertation which chronicles development of vocational education programs in late 19th and early 20th century urban America.

Feldman, Marvin J. *Making Education Relevant.* New York: Ford Foundation, 1966. A redefinition of vocational education "at least in part as that aspect of an educational experience which helps a person discover, define, and refine his talents and to use them in working toward a career."

Graney, Maurice R. *The Technical Institute.* New York: Center for Applied Research in Education, 1964. The role of the technical institute in providing trained manpower.

Henniger, G. Ross. *The Technical Institute in America.* New York: McGraw-Hill, 1959. A study of developments since 1929 sponsored by the American Society for Engineering Education with a presentation of the Society's views.

Hitchcock, James. "The New Vocationalism," in *On Learning and Change* (New Rochelle, New York: Change Magazine, 1973), pp. 91-103. The new vocationalism and its implications for higher education.

Kaufman, Jacob V. "The Role of Vocational Education in the Transition from School to Work," in Arnold Weber, *et al.*, eds. *Public-Private Manpower Policies.* Madison: University of Wisconsin, 1969. A general conceptual assessment with summaries and critical review of the literature.

Leavitt, Frank M. *Examples of Industrial Education.* Boston: Ginn, 1912. Summarizes the ideology of the industrial education movement, with examples. See also, Arthur D. Dean, *The Worker and the State* (New York: Century Company, 1910).

Leighbody, Gerald B. *Vocational Education in America's Schools: Major Issues of the 1970's.* Chicago: American Technical Society, 1972. Evaluation of programs, and recommendations, with notices of 1968 Amendments of

Vocational Education Act.

Little, J. Kenneth. *Review and Synthesis on the Placement and Follow-up of Vocational Education Students*. Columbus: Ohio State University, 1970. Critical review of literature and reports.

Mays, Arthur B. "Fifty Years of Progress in Vocational and Practical Arts Education." *American Vocational Journal*, vol. 31 (December, 1956), pp. 29-38, 105. A review of programs with some historical source materials.

Prosser, Charles A., and Thomas H. Quigley. *Vocational Education in a Democracy*. Chicago: American Technical Society, 1949. Philosophy, programs, trends, and backgrounds by leading theoreticians in the movement.

Roberts, Roy W. *Vocational and Practical Arts Education: History, Development, and Principles*. 2nd ed. New York: Harper & Row, 1965. Comprehensive review of programs, needs, and federal legislation.

Schaefer, Carl J., and Jacob J. Kaufman. *New Directions for Vocational Education*. Lexington, Mass.: D. C. Heath, 1971. Valuable review of programs, trends, and needs, with critical assessments of reports and literature. Originated as a report prepared for the Massachusetts Advisory Council on Education.

Smith, Leo F., and Lawrence Lypsett. *The Technical Institute*. New York: McGraw-Hill, 1956. Review of various types of institutes and their programs.

Somers, Gerald G., and J. Kenneth Little eds. *Vocational Education: Today and Tomorrow*. Madison: University of Wisconsin Press, 1971. Critical essays on aspects of vocational education with some program assessment.

Struck, F. Theodore. *Foundations of Industrial Education*. New York: John Wiley, 1930. Includes materials on historical backgrounds. Influential statement by leader in field.

Wirth, A. G. "Charles A. Prosser and the Smith-Hughes Act." *Educational Forum*, vol. 36 (March, 1972), pp. 365-371. Backgrounds of the Act, and the role of the profession in its enactment.

Woodward, Calvin M. *The Manual Training School*. Boston: D. C. Heath, 1887. Major source on manual training by a leader in the field. See also Woodward's *Manual Training in Education* (1890).

VIII. EDUCATION IN THE INDIVIDUAL STATES

A. THE UNITED STATES: GENERAL

Bond, Horace Mann. *The Education of the Negro in the American Social Order.* New York: Prentice-Hall, 1934. A documented survey of Negro education since the Civil War.

Chase, Francis S., and Edgar L. Morphet. *The Forty-Eight State School Systems.* Chicago: The Council of State Governments, 1949. Survey of state school systems as organized by 1948.

Cremin, Lawrence A. *The American Common School: An Historic Conception.* New York: Teachers College, Bureau of Publications, Columbia University, 1951. The development of the American public school system during the first half of the nineteenth century. Good bibliography of primary and secondary sources.

B. TERRITORIES AND OUTLYING POSSESSIONS

Calog, Doris S. "Historical survey of Philippine education under American occupation, 1898-1934." Unpublished Master's thesis, Dominican College, San Rafael, California, 1967-68.

Cuesta Mendoza, Antonio. *Historia de la Educación en el Puerto Rico Colonial.* Mexico: 1946-48.

Diaz, Rev. Manuel Rosado. "The Historical Development and Legal Status of the Public Schools in Puerto Rico." Unpublished Doctoral dissertation, University of Denver, 1967.

Osuna, Juan José. *Education in Puerto Rico.* New York: Teachers College, Bureau of Publications, Columbia University, 1933; 2nd ed., 1949.

Reid, Charles Frederick. *Education in the Territories and Outlying Possessions of the United States.* New York: Teachers College, Bureau of Publications, Columbia University, 1941. Brief survey of education in possessions of the United States.

Wilton, Francis W. "An historical investigation of the development of public education on Guam from 1898 to 1950." Master's thesis, Seattle University, 1959-60.

C. SECTIONAL HISTORIES

Baca, Fidel Garcia. "Bilingual Education in Certain Southwest School Districts." Unpublished Doctoral dissertation, University of Utah, Salt Lake City, 1958. Survey of bilingual education in Arizona, California, Colorado, New Mexico, Texas.

Barth, Pius Joseph. *Franciscan Education and the Social Order in Spanish North America (1502-1821).* Chicago: University of Chicago Press, 1945. Efforts of the Franciscans to propagate Christian faith and Spanish culture by formal education of American Indians, producing significant changes in their social order. Presents this education as a model in social reconstruction. Bibliography.

Bullock, Henry Allen. *A History of Negro Education in the South from 1619 to the Present.* Cambridge: Harvard University Press, 1967. Study of Negro education under slavery and freedom.

Hackensmith, Charles W. *Ohio Valley Higher Education in the Nineteenth Century.* Lexington: College of Education, University of Kentucky, 1973. Monograph on beginnings of Indiana, Ohio, and other universities in the Ohio Valley. Special reference to administration and religious controversy.

Hansen, Allen Oscar. *Early Educational Leadership in the Ohio Valley: a Study of Educational Reconstruction through the Western Literary Institute and College of Professional Teachers, 1829-1841.* Bloomington, Ill.: Public School Publishing Company, 1923. Historical significance of the convention of those interested in education, meeting annually from 1829 to 1840, to consider objectives of education in relation to Western needs, public schools to unify the diverse peoples, state support and control of teaching to improve public schools, development of the teaching profession, curricula on various levels, methods of instruction.

Lottich, Kenneth V. *New England Transplanted, a Study of the Development of Educational and other Cultural Agencies in the Connecticut Western Reserve in their National and Philosophical Setting.* Dallas, Texas: Royal Publishing Company, 1904. Study of the influence of Puritan-Congregational culture in the present state of Ohio.

D. INDIVIDUAL STATES

1. Alabama

   Clark, Willis G. *History of Education in Alabama, 1702-1889.* [H. B. Adams, ed., *Contributions to American Educational History*]

Washington: United States Bureau of Education, 1889. Old, somewhat dated, but only history of Alabaman education which is even partially comprehensive.

2. Alaska

Marsh, William R. *North to the Future: Department of Education and Education in Alaska, 1785-1967*. Juneau: State of Alaska, Department of Education, 1967. An Alaskan Centennial publication by a State Department.

3. Arizona

Gladen, Frank Henry, Jr. "An Historical Survey of Public Land and Public Education in the State of Arizona from 1863 to 1960." Unpublished Doctoral dissertation, University of Arizona, 1962.

4. Arkansas

Weeks, Stephen B. *History of Public School Education in Arkansas*. Washington: Government Printing Office, 1912. Ante-bellum private schools, public school system 1827-1861, Murphy administration, reconstruction, restoration of home rule, early twentieth century, city schools, and permanent school fund.

5. California

Falk, C. J. *The Development and Organization of Education in California*. New York: Harcourt, Brace & World, Inc., 1968. Comprehensive regarding public education.

Swett, John. *History of the Public School System in California*. San Francisco: A. L. Bancroft & Company. 1876. Reprinted 1969 by Arno Press as *Public Education in California*. Collection of source materials, disconnected and filled with statistics, but an important source of information.

6. Colorado

Le Rossignol, Edward. *History of Higher Education in Colorado*. [H. B. Adams, ed., Contributions to American Educational History] Washington: United States Bureau of Education, 1903.

Slechtiky, Sr. Mary A. "Sisters of Loretto—Pioneer Educators of Colorado." Unpublished Master's thesis, De Paul University, 1953-54.

7. Connecticut

Griffin, Orwin B. *The Evolution of the Connecticut State School System,*

1

with Special Reference to the Emergence of the United States. New York: Teachers College, Bureau of Publications, Columbia University, 1913. [Contributions to Education No. 293] Reprinted 1973 by AMS Press as *The Evolution of the Connecticut State School System.* Good source for early data.

8. Delaware

Wilson, Etta J. *The Story of Delaware's Effort to Awaken All of her People.* Newark: College of Education, University of Delaware, 1968.

9. Florida

Pyburn, Nita Katharine. *The History of Development of a Single System of Education in Florida, 1822-1903.* Tallahassee: Florida State University, 1954. Fairly recent study. Good bibliography.

10. Georgia

Orr, Dorothy. *A History of Education in Georgia.* Chapel Hill: University of North Carolina Press, 1950.

11. Hawaii

Wist, Benjamin O. "A Century of Public Education in Hawaii, October 15, 1840 to October 15, 1940." *Hawaii Educational Review,* Honolulu, Hawaii, 1940.

12. Idaho

No publications available, i.e., none found.

13. Illinois

The Sesquicentennial: One Hundred and Fifty Years of Illinois Education. Springfield: Office of the Superintendent of Public Instruction, 1967. A public treatise.

14. Indiana

Boone, Richard G. *A History of Education in Indiana.* New York: D. Appleton & Co., 1892. Dated, prejudiced.

Cotton, Fassett A. *Education in Indiana, 1793 to 1934.* Bluffton, Ind.: The Progress Publishing Co., 1934. Fairly good, emphasis on tax-supported education.

15. Iowa

Aurner, C. R. *History of Education in Iowa*. Iowa City: 1920.

16. Kansas

Green, Paul G. *An Annotated Bibliography of the History of Education in Kansas*. Emporia: Kansas State Teachers College, 1935. A classified list mainly of secondary sources.

Throckmorton, Adel F. *Kansas Educational Progress, 1858-1967*. Topeka: State Department of Public Instruction, 1967. Brief review of education in Kansas and the role of the State Department of Public Instruction in the period.

17. Kentucky

Hackensmith, Charles W. *Out of Time and Tide: the Evolution of Education in Kentucky*. Lexington: College of Education, University of Kentucky, 1970. Study of the beginnings of education in Kentucky through the 1930's.

McVey, Joseph Anderson. *The Gates Open Slowly: a History of Education in Kentucky*. Lexington: University of Kentucky Press, 1949.

18. Louisiana

Fay, Edwin Whitfield. *The History of Education in Louisiana*. [H. B. Adams, ed., *Contributions to American Educational History*] Washington: United States Bureau of Education, 1898. Dated but still valuable.

Robertson, Minns Sledge. *Public Education in Louisiana after 1898*. Baton Rouge: Bureau of Educational Materials and Research, College of Education, Louisiana State University and Agricultural and Mechanical College, 1952.

19. Maine

Chadbourne, Ava H. *A History of Education in Maine*. Lancaster, Pa.: The Science Press, 1936. Materials dealing with the colonial period and the nineteenth century, collected by the author, published as *Readings in the History of Education in Maine* by Burr Publishing of Bangor, reprinted 1972 by AMS Press.

Nickerson, Kermit S. *One Hundred and Fifty Years of Education in Maine*. Augusta, Maine: 1970. Sesquicentennial history of Maine's educational system and the growth and development of the Maine State Department of Education.

20. Maryland

Stapleton, Edward G. *Educational Progress in Maryland Public Schools since 1916.* Baltimore: Maryland State Department of Education, 1959.

Steiner, Bernard C. *History of Education in Maryland.* [H. B. Adams, ed., *Contributions to American Educational History*] Washington: United States Bureau of Education, 1894.

21. Massachusetts

Mann, Horace. *The Massachusetts System of Common Schools.* Boston: Dutton and Wentworth, 1849. Enlarged revised edition of Mann's *Tenth Annual Report.* Brief history of popular education in Massachusetts and a complete reproduction of all laws regarding education in force at the time.

Martin, George H. *Evolution of the Massachusetts Public School System.* New York: D. Appleton and Company, 1894. Aims to show how the public schools of Massachusetts evolved and how they related to the social environment.

Smith, Sherman M. *The Relation of the State to Religious Education in Massachusetts.* Syracuse, N.Y.: Syracuse University Book Store, 1920. Detailed and documented.

22. Michigan

Dain, Floyd Russell. *Education in the Wilderness.* Lansing: Michigan Historical Committee, 1968.

Wichers, Wynand, ed. *A History of Education in Michigan.* Detroit: Wayne State University Press, 1963.

23. Minnesota

Greer, John N. *The History of Education in Minnesota.* [H. B. Adams, ed., *Contributions to American Educational History*] Washington: United States Bureau of Education, 1902.

24. Mississippi

Mayes, Edward. *History of Education in Mississippi.* [H. B. Adams, ed., *Contributions to American Educational History*] Washington: United States Bureau of Education, 1899.

Noble, Stuart Grayson. *Forty Years of the Public Schools in Mississippi.* New York: Teachers College, Bureau of Publications, Columbia University, 1918. Special reference to the education of the Negro.

Weathersby, William H. *A History of Educational Legislation in Mississippi from 1798 to 1860.* Chicago: University of Chicago Press, 1921. Good Background for students of Mississippi education.

25. Missouri

Snow, M. S. *Higher Education in Missouri.* [H. B. Adams, ed., *Contributions to American Educational History*] Washington: United States Bureau of Education, 1898.

Stellhorn, August C. *Schools of the Lutheran Church–Missouri Synod.* St. Louis: Concordia Publishing House, 1963. Comprehensive, completely documented history of more than one and a half centuries of educational activity.

26. Montana

Tash, Dale Raymond, Jr. "The Development of the Montana Common School System: 1864-1884." Unpublished Doctoral dissertation, Montana State University, 1968.

27. Nebraska

Caldwell, Howard W. *Education in Nebraska.* [H. B. Adams, ed., *Contributions to American Educational History*] Washington: United States Bureau of Education, 1902.

28. Nevada

Gillies, Inez. "History of elementary education in Nevada, 1934-1950." Unpublished Master's thesis, University of Nevada, 1957-58.

Wall, C. Leon. "History of Indian education in Nevada from 1861 to 1951." Unpublished Master's thesis, University of Nevada, 1951-52.

29. New Hampshire

Bishop, Eugene Alfred. *The Development of a State School System: New Hampshire.* New York: Teachers College, Bureau of Publications, Columbia University, 1930. The New Hampshire school system from colonial beginnings to the twentieth century; effects on educational attainment of various administrative policies; development from local to centralized organization.

30. New Jersey

Apgar, Ellis A. *History of our School System, Report of the Board of Education, New Jersey, 1878-1879.* A report of historical interest.

Burr, Nelson R. *Education in New Jersey, 1630-1871*. Princeton: Princeton University Press, 1942. Seemingly collected reports on schools run by various secular and religious bodies, suffering in some cases from institutionally approved language.

Leach, Carl Graydon. "The Constitutional and Legal Basis of Education in New Jersey." Doctoral dissertation, University of Pennsylvania, 1932. Good summary and analysis (to 1932) of laws and provisions for public education in New Jersey. Briefly discusses teacher training and education under Catholic auspices. Bibliography.

31. New Mexico

Moyers, Robert Arthur. "A History of Education in New Mexico." Unpublished Doctoral dissertation, George Peabody College for Teachers, 1941.

Ritch, W. G. *Education in New Mexico: Third Annual Report to the Commissioner of Education, 1876.*

32. New York

Boese, Thomas. *Public Education in the City of New York: Its History, Condition, and Statistics*. 1869. Education in New York City 1614-1868: Dutch and English schools, the Free School Society, religious questions, juvenile delinquency, school houses, laws on public education.

Finegan, Thomas E. *Free Schools: a Documentary History of the Free School Movement in New York State*. Albany: University of the State of New York, 1921.

Horner, Harlan Hoyt, compiler and editor. *Education in New York State, 1784-1954*. Albany: University of the State of New York Press, 1954.

33. North Carolina

Coon, Charles L., ed. *The Beginnings of Public Education in North Carolina: a Documentary History, 1790-1840*. 2 vols. Raleigh: Edwards and Broughton, 1908. Early documents concerning schools, grouped by counties, with guide to topics in documents. Influence of the State University; school buildings and equipment; teacher qualifications and salaries; methods of teaching, courses of study; Lancaster, military, and law schools; financial support; beginnings of colleges.

————, ed. *North Carolina Schools and Academies, 1790-1840*. Raleigh: Edwards and Broughton, 1915. Similar to the above.

Gilliom, Morris Eugene. "The Development of Public Education in North Carolina during Reconstruction, 1865-1876." Unpublished Doctoral dissertation, Ohio State University, 1962.

Knight, Edgar W. *Public School Education in North Carolina*. Westport, Conn.: Negro Universities Press, 1969. Comprehensive treatment of North Carolina educational history.

Noble, Marcus C. S. *A History of the Public Schools of North Carolina*. Chapel Hill: University of North Carolina Press, 1930. How the State merged the education of indigent orphans with the encouragement of private schools, eventually leading to public schools for all. Touches on separate schools for whites and Negroes. Discusses work of Calvin H. Wiley.

34. North Dakota

No data available.

35. Ohio

Bossing, Nelson L. "The History of Educational Legislation in Ohio from 1851 to 1925." *The Ohio Archaeological and Historical Publications*. Vol. 39, 1930.

Knight, George W., and John R. Commons. *The History of Higher Education in Ohio*. [H. B. Adams, ed., *Contributions to American Educational History*] Washington: United States Bureau of Education, 1891.

36. Oklahoma

No data available.

37. Oregon

A Report on Oregon Schools, 1832-1960. Salem, Oregon: 1960. Sheldon, Henry D. *A Critical and Descriptive Bibliography of the History of Education in the State of Oregon*. Eugene: University of Oregon, 1929. Compilation of briefly annotated books, dissertations, and articles.

38. Pennsylvania

McCadden, Joseph J. *Education in Pennsylvania, 1801-1835 and its Debt to Robert Vaux*. Philadelphia: University of Pennsylvania Press, 1937. The educational development in the city and county of Philadelphia and the Commonwealth of Pennsylvania during the period, emphasizing the part played by the founder and president of the Pennsylvania Society for the Public Schools.

Walsh, Louise Gilchriese, and John Matthew Walsh. *History and*

Organization of Education in Pennsylvania. Indiana Pa.: published by the authors, 1928. Influence of various national, religious, social, and political elements (Quaker, German, Scotch-Irish) on education in Pennsylvania. The fight for free schools, higher education, teacher education, administration of education. Appendix contains important documents.

Wickersham, James P. *A History of Education in Pennsylvania.* Lancaster, Pa.: The Inquirer Publishing Company, 1885. Reprinted 1969 by Arno Press, New York. Topical history of William Penn's educational policies regarding Indian and Negro schools; the University of Pennsylvania; charity schools; Anglicizing the Germans; public schools; technical and special education; secondary schools; soldiers' orphan schools; education of teachers. Author was superintendent of public instruction in the state, and president of the NEA. Out of date, but considered one of the best state histories.

39. Rhode Island

Flaherty, Thomas Francis. "The History of the Public School Movement in the State of Rhode Island and Providence Plantations from 1827 to 1857." Unpublished Doctoral dissertation, Boston College, 1969.

Tolman, W. H. *History of Higher Education in Rhode Island.* [H. B. Adams, ed., *Contributions to American Educational History*] Washington: United States Bureau of Education, 1894.

40. South Carolina

Ramage, B. J. *Local Governments and Free Schools in South Carolina.* New York: Johnson Reprint Corporation, 1973. (Reprint of 1883 edition.)

41. South Dakota

Bruner, Charles W. "A Study of the History of the Elementary Schools of the Lutheran Church—Missouri Synod in the State of South Dakota, 1906-1967." Unpublished Master's thesis, Northern State College, South Dakota, 1968-69.

Solon, James J. "A History of the Public School System, Lemmon, South Dakota." Unpublished Master's thesis, University of South Dakota, 1957-58.

42. Tennessee

Holt, Andrew Davis. *The Struggle for a State System of Public Schools in Tennessee, 1903-1936.* New York; Teachers College, Bureau of Publications, Columbia University, 1938.

43. Texas

Eby Frederick. *The Development of Education in Texas*. New York: The Macmillan Company, 1925. A thorough treatment by a recognized scholar.

————————, compiler. *Education in Texas: Source Materials*. Austin: University of Texas Press, 1918. From the Spanish colonial period in the late eighteenth century to 1890. Extensive bibliography.

44. Utah

Bennion, Milton L. *Mormonism and Education*. Salt Lake City: Department of Education, Church of Jesus of Latter-Day Saints, 1939. A denominational publication.

Coates, Lawrence George. "A History of Indian Education by the Mormons, 1830-1900." Unpublished Doctoral dissertation, Ball State University, 1969.

Moffitt, John Clifton. *The History of Public Education in Utah*. Provo City, Utah: Published by the author, 1946. Establishment of schools by the Mormons en route to and in Utah. Discussion of attempt to introduce the Deseret alphabet into the schools, perhaps to keep believers from the outside world. More modern aspects of Utah in greater detail. Good documentation.

45. Vermont

Stone, Mason S. *History of Education: State of Vermont, 1727-1927*. Montpelier: Capital City Press. (n.d.). Written by the head of the State Public School System for nineteen years. Index, no bibliography. Collection of miscellaneous, poorly organized information and statistics about many details of Vermont education.

46. Virginia

Bell, Sadye. *The Church, the State, and Education in Virginia*. New York: Arno Press, 1969. (reprint) Exhaustive dissertation on the history of religious education in Virginia, seventeenth to twentieth centuries. Excellent documentation.

Buck, James Lawrence Blair. *The Development of Public Schools in Virginia, 1607-1952*. Commonwealth of Virginia State Board of Education, 1952.

Heatwole, Cornelius J. *A History of Education in Virginia*. New York: The Macmillan Company, 1916. Elementary history of Virginia education prepared for teachers and students.

47. Washington

Bolton, Frederick E., and Thomas W. Bibb. *History of Education in Washington*. Office of Education, Bulletin 1934, No. 9. Washington: U.S. Government Printing Office, 1935. A good history of public and private education.

48. West Virginia

Ambler, Charles Henry. *A History of Education in West Virginia, from early Colonial Times to 1949*. Huntington, W. Va.: Standard Printing and Publishing Company, 1951.

49. Wisconsin

Doudna, Edgar George. *The Making of Our Wisconsin Schools, 1848-1948*. Madison, Wis.: State Centennial Committee, 1948.

Jorgenson, Lloyd P. *The Founding of Public Education in Wisconsin*. Madison, Wis.: State Historical Association of Wisconsin, 1956. Bibliographical essay, original records.

50. Wyoming

Bartholow, John. "The Development of Public Elementary and Secondary Education in Wyoming from 1917 to 1945." Unpublished Doctoral dissertation, University of Wyoming, 1967.

Fromong, Terrence D. "The Development of Public Elementary and Secondary Education in Wyoming, 1869-1917." Unpublished Doctoral dissertation, University of Wyoming, 1962.

IX. HIGHER EDUCATION

A. BIBLIOGRAPHY AND GENERAL WORKS

1. Bibliography

Altbach, Philip G. *A Select Bibliography on Students, Politics, and Higher Education.* (rev. ed.) St. Louis, Mo.: United Ministries in Higher Education and Center for International Affairs, Harvard University, 1970. Emphasizes the role of the student in society and in higher education and is "intended to facilitate comparative and cross cultural research" in student politics and in the broader issues of higher education. Brings together approximately 1800 items predominantly in English, French, Spanish, and German. There is some topical arrangement, but the bulk of the entries are listed by geographical region and by country. This is a companion volume to Altbach's *Higher Education in Developing Countries: A Select Bibliography.*

Cordasco, Francesco. "Academic Freedom in the Last Decade: A Preliminary Annotated Bibliography." *Peabody Journal of Education,* vol. 36 (November, 1958), pp. 166-169. A review of the literature with brief annotations.

Dressel, Paul L., and Sally B. Pratt. *The World of Higher Education: An Annotated Guide to the Major Literature.* San Francisco, Calif.: Jassy-Bass, 1971. Emphasizes studies related to institutional research on higher education.

Ebbers, Larry H., et al., comps. *Residence Halls in U.S. Higher Education: A Bibliography.* Ames, Iowa: Iowa State University Library, 1973. This compilation includes materials which date back to the beginning of the twentieth century.

Harmon, Linda A., comp. *Status of Women in Higher Education: A Selective Bibliography.* Ames, Iowa: Library, Iowa State University, 1972. A survey of pertinent literature published in the preceding ten years.

Mayhew, Lewis B. *The Literature of Higher Education.* San Francisco,

Calif.: Jossey-Bass, 1972. This is the fourth in a series of bibliographies compiled by Dr. Mayhew. The preceding volume, *The Literature of Higher Education, 1971* (1971) was also published by Jossey-Bass; the two earlier ones, published by the American Association for Higher Education, are: *The Literature of Higher Education, 1968,* and *The Literature of Higher Education During 1969.*

Meeth, L. Richard. *Selected Issues in Higher Education. An Annotated Bibliography.* New York: Teachers College Press, 1965. Readings on "various subjects related to the establishment of policy in, and the operations of, colleges and universities." Contains approximately 1000 entries arranged in 39 categories.

National Board on Graduate Education. *An Annotated Bibliography on Graduate Education: 1971-1972.* Washington, D.C.: National Board on Graduate Education, 1972. Includes material on students, faculty, administration, curricula, costs, instruction, research, and suggestions for change.

Rarig, Emory W., Jr., ed. *The Community Junior College: An Annotated Bibliography.* New York: Teachers College Bureau of Publications, Columbia University, 1966. Lists books, articles and reports. Subject categories include: purposes, organization, administration, programs, students, personnel, facilities, research, and history.

2. General

Brubacher, John S. *The Courts and Higher Education.* San Francisco, Calif.: Jossey-Bass, 1971. A selection of recent court decisions illustrating the growing impact of judicial bodies on the campus and on the historic concept of university autonomy. The implications of the precedents established by these cases require serious consideration by educators.

Harris, Seymour E. *A Statistical Portrait of Higher Education.* New York: McGraw-Hill, 1972. This volume has assembled an encyclopedic variety of data. There are 700 tables accompanied by clear explanations. The main concerns are students, enrollment, faculty, income, expenditures, and productivity.

Mayhew, Lewis B. *The Carnegie Commission on Higher Education. A Critical Analysis of the Reports and Recommendations.* San Francisco, Calif.: Jossey-Bass, 1973. Summarizes more than fifty sponsored studies, policy reports, technical reports, and recommendations. Mayhew analyzes their implications for colleges and universities.

Newman, Frank, et al. *Report on Higher Education, March, 1971.* Washington, D.C.: U.S. Government Printing Office, 1971. It is time for a change in the system. Federal funding should adopt a marketing approach where the student takes an institutional grant plus his individual grant to the college that offers the best program for him. Also advocates the reduction of discrimination against women, minorities, and older students.

B. CURRICULA AND PROGRAMS

1. Contemporary

Ackerman, James, *et al. The Arts on the Campus: The Necessity for Change*. Greenwich, Conn.: New York Graphic Arts Society, 1970. Teaching and learning are arts that can be practiced and perfected and coordinated with the traditional arts. One chapter presents a hopeful view of the future of higher education.

Akenson, Donald H., and Lawrence F. Stevens. *The Changing Uses of the Liberal Arts College: An Essay in Recent Educational History*. New York: Pageant Press, 1969. Presents an analysis of approximately 10,000 Harvard undergraduates in the ten classes from 1957 to 1966. The authors believe that Harvard can be used as a model because it develops the "pattern that will eventually be repeated in most of the better colleges . . . ." This study deals with the early aspirations, plans, and academic behavior as well as the hopes and plans of undergraduates just prior to the completion of their baccalaureate work. It was found that succeeding classes had increasing percentages of those who planned to go on to graduate and professional schools.

Astin, Alexander W., and Calvin B. T. Lee. *The Invisible College: A Profile of Small, Private Colleges with Limited Resources*. New York: McGraw-Hill, 1972. A study of 494 institutions identified as "invisible," i.e., non-prestigious. It raises a great many questions and suggests a few possible answers. Among the questions are: how can state funds be used to help these small colleges to survive without jeopardizing their integrity as private institutions? If public funds are made available what kinds of controls will be employed? Should state coordinating agencies accept responsibility for private institutions? The conclusion is that these "invisible" institutions are worth saving and that they need a clarification of their role and mission.

Axelrod, Joseph, *et al. Search for Relevance: The Campus in Crisis*. San Francisco, Calif.: Jossey-Bass, 1969. Viewing the contemporary college as "a nineteenth-century convention," poorly equipped to deal with the dynamics and complexity of today's world, the authors propose "sweeping changes in the organization of colleges and universities, in learning and teaching arrangements," and in the relationships between students and faculty. Much of what is advocated is rooted in a theory of personality development based on challenge and response.

Baskin, Samuel, ed. *Higher Education: Some Newer Developments*. New York: McGraw-Hill, 1965. A useful review of recent developments, with emphasis on the effect on quality in education. Lewis B. Mayhew deals with the new colleges and McGrath and Meeth discuss curriculum changes. It is not a comprehensive survey, but it does deal with the more interesting and significant innovations in higher education. The various authors see the problems as increased enrollments, the rapid growth of knowledge, decreasing availability of faculty, rising costs, multiplying career opportunities, and increasing specialization. They find merit in independent study, honors courses, general education, reduction in the number of course offerings, year-round study, off-campus experiences, the residence hall as a center of learning, inter-institutional cooperation, and the use of new media and technology.

Ben-David, Joseph. *American Higher Education: Directions Old and New*. New York: McGraw-Hill, 1972. An analysis of American higher education as a social system through the eyes of a foreign observer. The author comments on our egalitarianism, the increasing politicalization of our universities, the withering of liberal education, the emphasis on graduate education and research. He says that racial discrimination is currently "in favor of black students."

The Carnegie Commission on Higher Education. *Reform on Campus: Changing Students, Changing Academic Programs*. New York: McGraw-Hill, 1972. A report of the findings of a nationwide survey in 1969-70 of 70,000 undergraduates, 30,000 graduate students, and 60,000 faculty members. Despite the public attention given to student protests and calls for greater relevance, most students reported that they were satisfied with the education they were getting. Among the findings of the study are: teaching effectiveness, rather than research, should be the main criterion for faculty promotion, and graduate education should not be expanded without careful consideration.

Chickering, Arthur W. *Education and Identity*. San Francisco, Calif.: Jossey-Bass, 1969. A thought-provoking statement of the form and purpose of contemporary higher education. Winner of the 1969 Education Book Award of the American Council on Education.

Commager, Henry Steele. *The Commonwealth of Learning*. New York: Harper and Row, 1968. Examines the development of American higher education and the position of the scholar in American society. Deals with such problems as: big-time sports programs, the organization of subject-matter disciplines, teaching methods, tuition for publicly supported universities, and the college versus the university. Dr. Commager also discusses the probable effects of changes in American life on the university and university's influence on America.

Cordasco, Francesco. "Higher Education in the Metropolis: Old Challenges and New Postures." *Congressional Record*, 90th Congress, February 28, 1967. Notes on the history of the American college, the liberal arts tradition, the advent of professional eduction, and graduate education.

Cordasco, Francesco, and Louis Romano. "The Promethean Ethic: Higher Education and Social Imperatives." *Peabody Journal of Education,* vol. 44 (March, 1967) pp. 195-199. Discusses the question: to whose needs should higher education address itself, and what should be taught?

Dobbins, Charles G., and Calvin B. T. Lee, eds. *Whose Goals for American Higher Education?* Washington, D.C.: American Council on Education, 1968. Dobbins and Lee ask some provocative questions: What are the means and ends of higher education? How may they best be achieved? A variety of answers are provided by students, faculty, administrators, and trustees.

Dressel, Paul L., et al. *The Confidence Crisis.* San Francisco, Calif.: Jossey-Bass, 1970. Data from fifteen universities lead to the conclusion that the academic department is the locus of most of today's problems in higher education. A few departments in large universities have resources which exceed those of a small liberal arts college. Most are relatively autonomous and "out of control," bureaucratic, and resistant to curriculum changes.

Eisendrath, Craig R., and Thomas J. Cottle. *Out of Discontent: Visions of the Contemporary University.* Morristown, N.J.: General Learning Press, 1972. Recommends that each institution should tailor its programs to its own academic body. It finds no universal situations and no universal solutions.

Fensch, Thomas. *Films on the Campus.* New York: A. S. Barnes, 1970. A comprehensive analysis of film programs, film-making, and related studies and activities on college and university campuses in the United States.

Gallagher, Buell G. *Campus in Crisis.* New York: Harper and Row, 1974. Dr. Gallagher believes that the crisis in higher education is the result of the failure of our value system. His prescription for its cure is to develop our controlling purposes and our moral choices to the "level of sophisticated excellence we have demonstrated in our technology."

Graubard, Stephen R., and Geno A. Balliotti. *The Embattled University.* New York: Braziller, 1970. A collection of essays which reflect on the altered nature of American colleges and universities as a result of a decade of upheaval. There is some speculation upon the future course of these institutions. One writer says that "the curriculum of the university ought to be interesting" and "the government of the university ought to be fair"; he also notes that fairness is more important than participation.

Harcleroad, Fred F., ed. *Issues of the Seventies: The Future of Higher Education.* San Francisco, Calif.: Jossey-Bass, 1970. Collected papers of the 1969 conference of the American College Testing Program. These essays relate to student needs, society's concerns, and institutional responses.

Hardison, O. B., Jr. *Toward Freedom and Dignity: The Humanities and the Idea of Humanity*. Baltimore, Md.: Johns Hopkins University Press, 1973. Humanities offer the "only practical option we have" if the world is going to be worth living in. The jumble of courses and competing educational philosophies make humanistic education an impossibility in most colleges and universities. A distorted relationship between teacher and taught has contributed to demoralization and alienation. Education should liberate rather than intimidate. Employ technology for human ends. Free students from limiting, social determined goals and liberate their imaginations.

Higher Education for Everybody? Issues and Implications, edited by W. Todd Furniss. Washington, D.C.: American Council on Education, 1971. Collected papers of the 1970 Annual Meeting of the American Council on Education. The consensus opinion is that universal higher education, properly defined, is both desirable and feasible. These essays also call for a reexamination and a redefinition of "the college student," an increase in nontraditional programs, a deemphasis of current emergencies, and an increase in long-term planning for reform. Lifelong higher education requires a broad spectrum of alternative programs.

Horn, Francis H. *Challenge and Perspective in Higher Education*. Carbondale, Ill.: Southern Illinois University Press, 1971. Dr. Horn has collected sixteen of his addresses in one handy volume. They deal with the crucial academic issues of our time: objectives, problems, students, and administration. He believes that methods, not content, make a liberal education. Education is viewed as the "key hope for civilization." Accelerated programs and student participation in governance are recommended.

Houle, Cyril O. *The Design of Education*. San Francisco, Calif.: Jossey-Bass, 1972. A handbook for planning, establishing, supporting, and evaluating adult education programs. Dr. Houle offers a flexible system that can be adapted to any kind of adult and continuing education.

Jencks, Christopher, and David Riesman. *The Academic Revolution*. Garden City, N.Y.: Doubleday, 1968. An attempt to provide a sociological and historical analysis of American higher education. Combines first-hand data from a sampling of 150 institutions with secondary material from a variety of sources. Considers such problems as "the generation gap," social stratification, mass higher education, and the reform of graduate schools. Some chapters are devoted to special groups of colleges, such as those intended primarily for Catholics, Negroes, Protestants, and Women. This book, as its authors say, "is primarily descriptive and is not a polemic on behalf of any given program or policy."

Joyce, Bruce, and Marsha Weil. *Perspectives for Reform in Teacher Education.* Englewood Cliffs, N.J.: Prentice-Hall, 1972. Describes the model for teacher education developed at Teachers College, Columbia University, with a 1968 Office of Education grant. This program which, it is hoped, will influence the preparation of teachers throughout the country, emphasizes "inquiry group" teams, democracy, community, wide-ranging contacts with children and schools, and "differential training" models adapted to individual requirements.

Kaysen, Carl, ed. *Current and Context: Essays on College Education.* Hightstown, N.J.: McGraw-Hill, 1973. Presents ten essays, sponsored by the Carnegie Commission on Higher Education, whose focus is on the "characteristics, development and current problems" of the major divisions in institutions of higher education. Also devotes some attention to the interaction between colleges and universities and society in general.

Lawlor, John, ed. *Higher Education: Patterns of Change in the 1970's.* Boston, Mass.: Routledge and Kegan Paul, 1972. Considers the problems of British universities, particularly those related to planning and to efforts to coordinate institutions with disparate goals.

Levine, Arthur E., and John R. Weingart. *Reform of Undergraduate Education.* San Francisco, Calif.: Jossey-Bass, 1973. Data from research concerning 26 representative institutions. Presents analyses of experimentation and innovation concerning student services, examinations and grading, general education, and student-centered curricula.

Martin, Warren B. *Conformity: Standards and Change in Higher Education.* San Francisco, Calif.: Jossey-Bass, 1969. In the past, conformity has been the goal and has become the characteristic of American higher education. What is needed for the future is increased diversity—especially in values.

Morison, Jack. *The Rise of the Arts on the American Campus.* New York: McGraw-Hill, 1973. An examination of the role of the arts at seventeen selected institutions. Considers enrollments, budgets, faculty, admissions policies and programs.

Riesman, David, and Verne A Stadtman, eds. *Academic Transformation: Seventeen Institutions Under Pressure.* New York: McGraw-Hill, 1973. This volume brings together seventeen perceptive essays sponsored by the Carnegie Commission on Higher Education. All of them deal with the campus unrest of the 1960's and institutional responses to student demands. With the exception of the issue of student rights and participation in governance, most protests were not directly related to the campus or to the academic functions of the universities.

Sanford, Nevitt. *Where Colleges Fail.* San Francisco, Calif.: Jossey-Bass,

1967. Those being educated and those doing the educating must assess the college's effect on the total growth and development of the student. Effective education is not a prescribed total of course credits or some accounting measure of accumulated facts, but it is development and integration.

Snelling, W. Rodman, and Robert F. Boruch. *Science in Liberal Arts Colleges: a Longitudinal Study of 49 Selective Colleges.* New York: Columbia University Press, 1972. Results of a Research Corporation study of 30,000 science and mathematics majors who graduated in a ten-year period. An attempt to probe for "factors which seemed to have some significance on productivity in the sciences." The sample was made up primarily of individuals who were "Caucasian and Protestant" and whose family origins were English or West European.

Wilson, Logan, ed. *Emerging Patterns in American Higher Education.* Washington, D.C.: American Council on Education, 1965. An examination of the changing environment in higher education. Focuses on new developments in the structure, function, and administration of institutions. There is some discussion of the conflict between autonomy and centralization and of the increasing trend toward consortia and regional agreements.

Wolfle, Dael. *The Home of Science: The Role of the University.* New York: McGraw-Hill, 1972. Traces the development of science in American universities. Concludes that scientific research in the United States is now primarily a function of these institutions.

2. Innovative

Altman, Robert A. *The Upper Division College.* San Francisco, Calif.: Jossey-Bass, 1970. A history of attempts to modify the conventional four-year baccalaureate degree system in American education. The proliferation of community and junior colleges is providing impetus to the increasing development of colleges that admit students to the junior and senior years and to the first year of postgraduate study.

The Carnegie Commission on Higher Education. *Less Time, More Options.* Hightstown, N.J.: McGraw-Hill, 1971. A brief report on enrollments and degrees. Recommends the encouragement of life-long educational opportunities, the reduction of B.A. programs by one year, and the preparation of M.D.'s and Ph.D.'s by one to two years.

Commission on Non-Traditional Study. *Diversity by Design.* San Francisco, Calif.: Jossey-Bass, 1973. This is the Commission's final report. It advocates the expansion and strengthening of postsecondary educational opportunities and the encouragement of all who are capable of benefiting to take the fullest advantage of them. The report recommends more options in programs of study, more flexible arrangements, a lifelong process of learning, and the use of new instructional technologies. It does not advocate the termination of existing programs or the elimination of traditional institutions.

Coyne, John, and Tom Hebert. *This Way Out: A Guide to Alternatives to Traditional College Education in the United States, Europe, and the Third World*. New York: Dutton, 1972. Beginning with the premise that traditional college curricula do not prepare students for the present, and certainly not for the future, this volume offers a catalog of alternative schools and programs. Evaluations are based on whether or not a program is: intellectually rigorous, personalized, and provides some means for applying theory to the world outside the classroom.

Dressel, Paul, and Mary M. Thompson. *Independent Study. A New Interpretation of Concepts, Practices and Problems*. San Francisco, Calif.: Jossey-Bass, 1973. A comprehensive, nationwide review of current practices with specific recommendations for changing present approaches. Ability to "engage in self-directed learning" throughout one's lifetime is a major goal of all liberal education. However, faculty members are antagonistic to the introduction of innovative programs of independent study that go beyond "honors" courses. The authors present a new conception of the role of independent study in higher education. They take a broad view and relate independent study to the movement toward lifelong learning systems.

Evans, Richard I. *Resistance to Innovation in Higher Education*. San Francisco, Calif.: Jossey-Bass, 1968. A social psychological exploration of the role of university faculty in promoting innovation. Resistance to change has increased in proportion to the interest in innovation.

Goff, Jerry G., et al. *The Cluster College*. San Francisco, Calif.: Jossey-Bass, 1970. A description of collegiate organization that combines physical proximity, cooperative services, and administrative autonomy. This type of federation has gained recent popularity because it provides for greater diversity, flexibility, efficiency, and economy.

Gould, Samuel B., and Patricia Cross, eds. *Explorations in Non-traditional Study*. San Francisco, Calif.: Jossey-Bass, 1972. This volume sets forth the values of extending learning opportunities in dynamic democracies and shows available alternatives to traditional education within "a community of scholars." Warns against some of the dangers inherent in such an extension of the concept of higher education. The necessity of further study on a number of issues in higher education is suggested.

Heiss, Ann M. *An Inventory of Academic Innovation and Reform*. (Carnegie Commission on Higher Education Technical Report). Berkeley, Calif.: The Carnegie Commission on Higher Education, 1973. Provides a guide to attempts by colleges and universities to give relevant responses to present needs and circumstances.

Henderson, Algo D. *The Innovative Spirit: Change in Higher Education*. San Francisco, Calif.: Jossey-Bass, 1970. Analyzes the current shortcomings of higher education, and describes some programs considered to be sound. Recommends problem-oriented curricular, work-study programs, and the inclusion of all elements of the university in the decision-making process.

Hesburgh, Theodore M., et al. *Patterns for Lifelong Learning*. San Francisco, Calif.: Jossey-Bass, 1973. This volume recommends: self-education, institutional consortia, independent study, advanced placement, life experience credits, and governmental financial support for students in every age group.

Houle, Cyril O. *The External Degree*. San Francisco, Calif.: Jossey-Bass, 1973. This study, sponsored by the Commission on Non-Traditional Study, is a thorough assessment of the external degree. It examines some of the best programs in the United States and abroad and discusses major ideas and themes. Houle warns against the uncritical acceptance of programs based solely on their novelty. A related volume is the Commission's *Diversity by Design,* also published in 1973.

Kallen, Denis, and Karl Bengtsson. *Recurrent Education: A Strategy for Lifelong Learning*. Paris: Organization for Economic Co-operation and Development, 1973. "Recurrent Education," defined here as a concept of lifelong "alternation between education [i.e., *schooling*] and other activities," is offered as an alternative strategy for achieving equality of educational opportunity in technologically advanced societies. The basic assumption underlying this presentation is that "Recurrent Education" has the potential to facilitate a shift in goal areas "to provide better opportunities for individual development, greater educational and social equality, and better interplay between the educational and other social sectors, including a better contribution to the potential for necessary growth." Its aim is to clarify the educational and socioeconomic policy making. Much the same ground is traversed in greater brevity in K. Patricia Cross's *The Integration of Learning and Earning: Cooperative Education and Non-traditional Study* (1973).

Lahti, Robert E. *Innovative College Management*. San Francisco, Calif.: Jossey-Bass, 1973. Recommends that business management principles and techniques be applied to colleges. Management-by-objectives systems can be adapted to increase productivity, personnel satisfaction, and organizational efficiency.

Lichtman, Jane. *Bring Your Own Bag: A Report on Free Universities*. Washington, D.C.: American Association for Higher Education, 1973. Surveys the new "universities" in the United States designed to counter the stagnation, complexity, uniformity, and bureaucracy of conventional institutions of higher education. Finds that these alternate colleges develop concepts and programs which, if successful, are incorporated in traditional institutions. They also serve as escape valves for taking the pressure off the older colleges in times of crisis.

Milton, Ohmer. *Alternatives to the Traditional*. San Francisco, Calif.: Jossey-Bass, 1972. Based on documentary evidence and twenty years of classroom teaching and experimentation, this volume harpoons many of the myths and misconceptions about learning. The important questions raised include: Are small classes more effective than large ones? Does the scramble for grades hinder learning? Are some students harmed by being kept in school too long? Is there a positive or negative relationship between formal education and on-the-job performance?

Milton, Ohmer, and Edward Joseph Shoben, Jr. *Learning and the Professors*. Athens, Ohio: Ohio University Press, 1968. Suggests the following to improve higher education: eliminate the freshman year and substitute advanced placement tests; reduce the emphasis on research and publication; increase independent study, seminars, and discussions; make better use of graduate students as teachers; institutional research; study of learning theories; adapt the instructional strategies to the local population and situation.

Moore, William, Jr. *Against the Odds*. San Francisco, Calif.: Jossey-Bass, 1970. An advocacy of "open-door" policies. Questions the use of entrance examinations and seeks the cause of a continuing increase in the dropout rate.

Watts, Anthony Gordon. *Diversity and Choice in Higher Education*. Boston, Mass.: Routledge and Kegan Paul, 1972. Considers the question of freedom of choice among diverse institutions to be one of the most important policy questions currently facing higher education. Emphasis is on British experience.

3. Facing the Future

Brewster, Kingman, et al. *Educating for the Twenty-First Century*. Urbana, Ill.: University of Illinois Press, 1969. An assessment of the role of higher education in shaping America's future. Discusses the university's role in making foreign policy, in city planning, and in the science of politics. It also deals with the goals and consequences of the technological revolution in higher education.

Caffrey, John, ed. *The Future Academic Community*. Washington, D.C.: American Council on Education, 1969. Consideration of the possible ways of resolving the tensions created by the need for change in our institutions.

The Carnegie Commission on Higher Education. *The Purposes and Performance of Higher Education in the United States: Approaching the Year 2000*. Hightstown, N.J.: McGraw-Hill, 1973. This volume presents a redefinition of the purposes and a reevaluation of the functions and performance of higher education. It offers as the main purpose of higher education now and for the prospective future: "The provision of opportunities for the intellectual, aesthetic, ethical, and skill development of individual students" and the construction of campus environments conducive to their more general development. A total of 23 recommendations are made "——for the sake of society's self-renewal."

Eurich, Alvin C., ed. *Campus 1980.* New York: Delacorte Press, 1968. Imaginative, but not improbable, conjectures about the future of higher education. However, its contributors provide no practical approach for the deployment of men, money, and talent to facilitate desirable outcomes and to prevent the development of undesirable ones.

Hostrop, Richard, ed. *Foundations of Futurology in Education.* Homewood, Ill.: ETC Publications, 1973. Opposes Alvin Toffler's view that education is a backward-looking system. The three sections of the book are: "Introducing the Future," "Forecasting and Specifying Educational Futures," and "Conceptual Views of the Future."

McGrath, Earl J., ed. *Prospect for Renewal. The Future of the Liberal Arts College.* San Francisco, Calif.: Jossey-Bass, 1972. Nine distinguished educators, firm in their belief that unique and valuable contributions emanate from the liberal arts colleges, argue for their rescue through renewal. They advocate emphasizing the distinctive qualities of these colleges and the utilization of the new learning concepts and the new instructional technology. Attempt to provide practical solutions for diminishing attractiveness, dissipation of academic resources, fiscal problems, and for the tendency to imitate the universities. These writers suggest the necessity for an analysis and improvement of operations and the application of marketing research and marketing techniques.

Mood, Alexander McFarlane. *The Future of Higher Education; Some Speculations and Suggestions.* (Sponsored by the Carnegie Commission on Higher Education.) New York: McGraw-Hill, 1973. Tries to identify "ways in which colleges and universities can make the most effective use of the resources available to them." Attacks higher education as a status-conferring monopoly. The author advocates apprenticeship training, lifelong learning, use of video cassettes, and the removal of degree and certification requirements for college faculty.

C. MINORITY EDUCATION

Bayer, Alan E. *The Black College Freshman: Characteristics and Recent Trends.* Washington, D.C.: American Council on Education, 1972. Blacks attending predominantly white colleges tend to have better academic records than those at black-oriented institutions. Characteristics of students at black colleges indicate, generally, that: they were older, less religious, more liberal in politics, more likely to think they needed remedial work in English and reading, but less in science and mathematics, and less ambitious in their academic plans. Three-fifths had parents whose incomes were less than $8,000 and most were concerned with the problem of financing their education.

Bowles, Frank, and Frank A. De Costa. *Between Two Worlds: A Profile of Negro Higher Education.* New York: McGraw-Hill, 1971. Attempts to present the past, the present, and the future of higher education in predominantly black colleges. It is best in delineating current conditions. Offers some explanation of the slow rate of innovation in these institutions.

The Carnegie Commission on Higher Education. *From Isolation to Mainstream: Problems of the Colleges Founded for Negroes.* New York: McGraw-Hill, 1971. Urges the redefining of the objectives of black colleges to meet the problems of the current era and the future. These institutions are deemed to be especially well equipped to understand the problems of black Americans, to formulate solutions, and to supply needed leadership.

The Carnegie Commission on Higher Education. *Opportunities for Women in Higher Education: Their Current Participation, Prospects for the Future and Recommendations for Action.* New York: McGraw-Hill, 1973. Contains 24 major proposals for reforming higher education in respect to women. Advocates the ending of all sex bias in admissions policies for all programs, the strengthening of occupational counseling, the end of discrimination in the hiring of women, and the revision of regulations that militate against part-time study.

Clark, Kenneth Bancroft, and the staff of the MARC Corporation. *A Possible Reality: A Design for the Attainment of High Academic Achievement for Inner-City Students.* New York: Emerson Hall, 1972. Presents a comprehensive design for raising disadvantaged students to middle class academic standards and to develop the full powers of human beings as free men. It advocates recognition and rewards for good teaching.

Cordasco, Francesco. "College Admissions: Viable Criteria for the Societally Deprived." *Congressional Record,* 89th Congress, June 14, 1965. Projects a new college population from minority constituencies, admissions policy, and viable plans.

Corson, William R. *Promise or Peril: The Black College Student in America.* New York: Norton, 1970. Based on interviews conducted at Howard University, this study concludes that black students have a potential for radicalization which could detonate a social explosion in America.

Hall, Laurence and Associates. *New Colleges for New Students.* San Francisco, Calif.: Jossey-Bass, 1974. Case studies of innovative programs designed for minority group students, women, older people, and the urban and rural poor.

Knoell, Dorothy M. *Black Student Potential*. Washington, D.C.: American Association of Junior Colleges, 1970. Black high school graduates of the class of 1968 were the subject of this study. Among the conclusions: junior colleges are a prime factor in providing higher education for minorities, and especially for black women; traditional tests are grossly inadequate and unfair instruments for evaluating minorities.

Le Melle, Tilden J., and Wilbert J. Le Melle. *The Black College: A Strategy for Relevancy*. New York: Praeger, 1969. Proposes new goals of service and leadership directly connecting black colleges with the whole black community of the United States. Black colleges can play an important role in solving major problems for all Americans, not just for black Americans alone. The current shortcomings of these colleges is minor in comparison with their over-all effectiveness. Advocates emphasis on the "socialization" and "tool functions" of education.

McGrath, Earl J. *The Predominantly Negro Colleges and Universities in Transition*. New York: Published for the Institute of Higher Education by the Bureau of Publications, Teachers College, Columbia University, 1965. Reports the results of a study sponsored by the Carnegie Corporation of New York. Statistics relate to about 79 institutions. Finds that this group of institutions "will need several hundred million dollars in the next five or ten years merely to keep pace with the growing needs of their potential student bodies and the unprecedented advancements in higher education."

Milner, Murray, Jr. *Illusion of Equality: The Effect of Education on Opportunity, Inequality, and Social Conflict*. San Francisco, Calif.: Jossey-Bass, 1972. Educational disparity between blacks and whites can be reduced through the increase of financial aid. The primary obstacles to occupational equality are discriminatory hiring and promotion policies and are not an indication that higher education does not affect status.

Napper, George. *Blacker Than Thou: The Struggle for Campus Unity*. Grand Rapids, Mich.: William B. Erdmans, 1973. This volume derives its basic data from interviews with forty black college students associated with the 1969 Berkeley strike. The game of "blacker than thou" is one-upmanship in black politics and impedes campus unity. At Berkeley, the black community rejected its previous assimilationist position and projected blacks into a conflict of roles as both students and as participants in the black power movement.

Nichols, David C., and Olive Mills, eds. *The Campus and the Racial Crisis*. Washington, D.C.: American Council on Education, 1970. This is a collection of papers and addresses from the 1969 annual meeting of the American Council on Education. Calls for the restructuring of political, social, and economic forces to reverse the historic trend to inhumanity. These forces "must be manipulated to bar such evils as racism and political domination." Universities must change; black students' demands must be met and compensatory measures must be written into college curricula.

Rempson, Joe L. *Minority Access to Higher Education in New York*. New York: City Almanac, 1972. Lists and discusses the educational programs for minority students. It includes precollegiate and open admissions programs. Some recommendations are made on the basis of an analysis of the results of the survey.

Sowell, Thomas. *Black Education: Myths and Tragedies*. New York: David McKay Co., 1973. The future of black students in white colleges is more promising than in black colleges. Highly talented blacks should seek entry to the most prestigious white institutions.

Women in Higher Education. Edited by W. Todd Furniss [and] Patricia Albjerg Graham. Washington, D.C.: American Council on Education, 1974. Contains 38 selected papers from the Fifty-fifth Annual Meeting (1972) of the American Council on Education. There is unanimous agreement that discrimination against women should be ended. Other topics considered include: Women's colleges, women's movement, coeducation, nepotism, graduate education for women, maternity leave, affirmative action, and the woman professional in higher education. Most essays call for a single standard in deciding all matters relating to women and men in higher education.

D. FACULTY

Bornheimer, Deane G., *et al. The Faculty in Higher Education*. Danville, Ill.: Interstate, 1973. A succinct statement of the rights, responsibilities, roles, and restrictions of the faculty. The decline in the importance and quality of teaching is attributed to: faculty control of the curriculum, primary loyalty vested in an academic specialty rather than in the institution, autonomous departments, and the lack of strong administrative leadership.

Brown, David G. *The Mobile Professors*. Washington, D.C.: American Council on Education, 1967. Describes the marketplace for academic personnel. Shows how institutions and individuals use the marketplace which, the author concludes, is not a free market. Supplements *The Academic Marketplace* by Caplow and McGee (1965).

Caplow, Theodore, and Reece J. McGee. *The Academic Marketplace*. New York: Doubleday, 1965. Describes the process by which individuals obtain positions, move from one institution to another, and establish their professional reputations. This study is amplified by David G. Brown's *The Mobile Professors* (1967).

Carr, Robert K., and Daniel K. Van Eyck. *Collective Bargaining Comes to the Campus*. Washington, D.C.: American Council on Education, 1973. A comprehensive study of collective bargaining in higher education. Discusses faculty dissatisfactions, morale, grievance-arbitration systems, negotiation and administration of contracts, the role of the faculty and the administration, and educational policy. The volume also contains some discussion of other alternatives for meeting the problems of institutional governance.

Chambers, M. M. *The Colleges and the Courts: Faculty and Staff Before the Bench*. Danville, Ill.: Interstate Printers and Publishers, 1973. This volume is the latest in a series begun in 1936; among the other titles are: *The Colleges and the Courts, 1946-50; The Colleges and the Courts, 1962-1966;* and, *The Colleges and the Courts: the Developing Law of the Student and the College* (1972). Dr. Chambers provides an analysis of recent court decisions affecting personnel policies and practices in institutions of higher education. Specific cases are cited to show that the judicial process is beset by many uncertainties—with conflicting decisions in courts with different jurisdictions. In particular, it demonstrates that the U.S. Supreme Court does not view the guarantees of the "Bill of Rights" and the Fourteenth Amendment as absolute.

Daniels, Arlene Kaplan, et al. *Academics on the Line: The Faculty Strike at San Francisco State*. San Francisco, Calif.: Jossey-Bass, 1970. Deals with the sociological and psychological aspects of the 1968-1969 strike that opposed faculty and students to the administrators and trustees. It is an attempt to explain the motives of the participants, the educational issues, and the results.

Duryea, E. D., et al. *Faculty Unions and Collective Bargaining*. San Francisco, Calif.: Jossey-Bass, 1973. Presents a variety of realistic views of academic unionism today. Lawyers, scholars, and administrators are represented.

Elam, Stanley, ed. *Employment Relations in Higher Education*. Bloomington, Ind.: Phi Delta Kappa, 1969. Presents five papers from a symposium sponsored by Phi Delta Kappa. Describes the variety of faculty associations and assesses their ability to engineer collective negotiations for the solution of academic and economic problems. Faculty senates are viewed as inefficient and ineffective. Collective bargaining and unionization are gaining in popular support.

McGee, Reece. *Academic Janus: The Private College and its Faculty*. San Francisco, Calif.: Jossey-Bass, 1971. Primarily concerned with small, non-prestigious institutions. Examines them as both social and educational systems. Job mobility is an important problem: who gets offers of better positions, and why; who changes positions; why are offers of better jobs accepted or rejected?

Miller, Richard I. *Development Programs for Faculty Evaluation*. San Francisco, Calif.: Jossey-Bass, 1974. An attempt to identify the principal factors that implement an efficient and effective faculty evaluation program. This volume supplements and complements Miller's *Evaluating Faculty Performance* (1972).

Miller, Richard I. *Evaluating Faculty Performance*. San Francisco, Calif.:

Jossey-Bass, 1972. Presents basic assumptions and operational procedures. Deals with the professor as teacher as well as in his non-teaching activities; overall performance rating. Contains research summaries of rating instruments and sample evaluation forms.

Smith, Bardwell L. and Associates. *The Tenure Debate*. San Francisco, Calif.: Jossey-Bass, 1973. An examination of tenure, pro and con, from a variety of perspectives. Among the questions propounded are: What is the right of the academic profession to lifetime contracts? Does tenure actually protect academic freedom? Does tenure lock deadwood into an institution and prevent change? Will the abolition of tenure encourage faculty unionization in the search for job security?

E. INSTRUCTION

The Carnegie Commission on Higher Education. *The Fourth Revolution: Instructional Technology in Higher Education*. New York: McGraw-Hill, 1972. Suggests that electronic and optical media can reduce instructional costs, provide more flexibility and a richer variety of content for the student.

Flournoy, Don M., et al. *The New Teachers*. San Francisco, Calif.: Jossey-Bass, 1972. Descriptions of innovative experiments in college classrooms. Discusses methodologies and presents failures as well as successes.

Hyman, Ronald T. *Ways of Teaching*. Philadelphia, Pa.: Lippincott, 1970. Hyman provides a brief statement for the understanding of what teaching is, followed by a thorough analysis of the variety of available teaching methodologies. 2nd ed., 1974.

Levien, Roger E., ed. *The Emerging Technology: Instructional Uses of the Computer in Higher Education*. New York: McGraw-Hill, 1972. Describes the increasing applications of computers on campus for research, administration, library science, and instruction. It also provides a basis for analyzing the potential for instructional computing and recommends strategies for development in individual institutions as well as nationally.

Morris, William H., ed. *Effective College Teaching: The Quest for Relevance*. Washington, D.C.: American Council on Education, 1970. Directed toward the beginning college teacher. Finds the road to improved instruction lies through increased knowledge of the principles of teaching, more knowledge of disciplines other than one's own, and a better understanding of the complexity of the contemporary university.

Tickton, Sidney G., ed. *To Improve Learning: An Evaluation of Instructional Technology*. New York: Bowker, 1970-71. 2 vols. These volumes bring together more than 100 papers dealing with almost every aspect of instructional technology. Major categories are: theory, general applications, practical considerations, and economic implications.

F. STUDENTS AND ACTIVISM

Adams, Frank C., and Clarence W. Stephens. *College and University Student Work Programs: Implications and Implementations*. Carbondale, Ill.: Southern Illinois University Press, 1970. This volume provides a philosophy of student work; it also gives an historical summary and relates work programs to vocational planning, self-help, and financial aid. Some attention is given to the evaluation of student work experience. Suggests the need for the development of more sophisticated work programs in the future. One conclusion is that success depends on the quality of the supervisor.

Anderson, C. Arnold, et al. *Where Colleges Are and Who Attends: Effects of Accessibility on College Attendance*. New York: McGraw-Hill, 1972. This study, sponsored by the Carnegie Commission on Higher Education, concludes that the major determinants of college attendance are "ability and family status." Students with poor prior academic performance records and those with low socio-economic backgrounds will be encouraged to attend college by proximity only when coupled with low cost, moderate admissions requirements, and remedial programs. Mere "spatial accessibility" is not an important consideration.

Aptheker, Bettina. *The Academic Rebellion in the United States*. Citadel, 1972. A radical view of the causes of campus rebellion. Attacks the behaviorists and corporate control of the universities and research; condemns higher education's subservience to government policy. Merits comparison with Lipset's *Rebellion in the University* (1972) and Jencks and Riesman's *The Academic Revolution* (1968).

Buckman, Peter. *The Limits of Protest*. Indianapolis, Ind.: Bobbs-Merrill, 1970. Examines the recent struggle to establish universities as ideological communications command posts. The author finds the roots of campus protest in man's essential discontent.

The Carnegie Commission on Higher Education. *College Graduates and Jobs: Adjusting to a New Labor Market Situation*. New York: McGraw-Hill, 1973. Offers specific recommendations for higher education as a supplier of highly trained personnel. Rejects the idea that university programs should be adjusted to the market for their graduates.

The Carnegie Commission on Higher Education. *New Students and New Places: Policies for the Future Growth and Development of America's Higher Education*. New York: McGraw-Hill, 1971. Expresses a need for increased numbers of community colleges and comprehensive colleges in metropolitan areas with populations of 500,000 or more. More students will come from the lower half of the socio-economic scale and 230 to 280 new community colleges should be created by 1980. It also recommends the strengthening of private colleges and universities.

Clarke, Helen I., and Martha Ozawa. *The Foreign Student in the United*

States. Madison, Wis.: School of Social Work, University of Wisconsin, 1970. Part diary and part handbook, it lists the common problems of foreign students on American campuses.

Cohen, Joseph W., ed. *The Superior Student in American Higher Education: An Analysis of Honors Programs*. New York: McGraw-Hill, 1966. Essays providing a comprehensive survey of the various aspects of current honors work. This volume constitutes the final statement of the Inter-University Committee on the Superior Student (1957-1965). Recommends experiments and innovations.

Cross, K. Patricia. *Beyond the Open Door: New Students to Higher Education*. San Francisco, Calif.: Jossey-Bass, 1971. Employing data derived from such national surveys as: "Project Talent," "ETS Growth Study," "SCOPE," and the "Comparative Guidance and Placement Program," this study of the interests, abilities, and aspirations of the "New Students" observes that most institutions are not geared to meeting their needs. Characteristically, these new students are older, more pragmatic, and have lower verbal skills than traditional students. By way of dealing with these challenges, this study calls for the provision of new educational experiences and for the implementation of programs respecting the diversity of these students.

De Conde, Alexander, ed. *Student Activism: Town and Gown in Historical Perspective*. New York: Scribner, 1972. This volume brings together contemporary views of important student uprisings from the 12th century down to the present. These selections bring today's American campus activism into geographical and historical perspective, and lead to the conclusion that the university does change, but it does survive.

Dennis, Lawrence, and Joseph Kauffman, eds. *College and the Student*. Washington, D.C.: American Council on Education, 1966. An examination of the intellectual climate of "big" education. It provides new definitions of rights and responsibilities in the college-student relationship.

Eichel, Lawrence E., et al. *The Harvard Strike*. Boston, Mass.: Houghton, Mifflin, 1970. The historical record of the 1968 strike based on personal on-the-scene observations, interviews, tape recordings, leaflets, and news releases. Undue "police brutality" caused large-scale participation by the "moderate" students.

Feldman, Kenneth A., and Theodore M. Newcomb. *The Impact of College on Students*. San Francisco, Calif.: Jossey-Bass, 1969. 2 vols. Summarizes and critically evaluates approximately 1500 studies of the effects of the campus experience on college students.

Frankel, Charles. *Education and the Barricades*. New York: W. W. Norton, 1968. A judicious and dispassionate statement of the issues involved in the student protest movement. Frankel declares that colleges have been short-changing students for years: faculty members and trustees are the principal obstacles to change. Much of the campus disruptions, however, do not arise out of the educational deficiencies of the colleges; they are a "reaction to the world beyond the cloister."

Harrington, Thomas F. *Student Personnel Work in Urban Colleges*. New York: Intext, 1974. Attempts to identify the characteristics of urban institutions and the needs of commuting students. Outlines the problems of various kinds of student decision-making. Suggests methods for improving student personnel services.

Heath, G. Louis. *The Hot Campus: The Politics that Impede Change in the Technoversity*. Metuchen, N.J.: Scarecrow Press, 1973. Finds the source of conflict in the technologically oriented university. Analyzes activism at Berkeley and Stanford and considers the effects of women's liberation, the Black Panthers, and open admissions.

Karagueuzian, Dikran. *Blow it Up! The Black Student Revolt at San Francisco State College and Emergence of Dr. Hayakawa*. Boston, Mass.: Gambit, 1971. An account of the 1968 uprising at San Francisco State College, said to be the first serious effort by a group of black students to remold an American college. Members of the Black Student Union went on strike to protest the suspension of George Murray, a militant black instructor, and to retaliate for the suspected attempt to sabotage the new Black Studies Department. It was this upheaval that brought Dr. S. I. Hayakawa to national prominence.

Leemon, Thomas A. *The Rites of Passage in a Student Culture: A Study of the Dynamics of Transition*. New York: Teachers College Press, 1973. A day-by-day account of an eight-week fraternity initiation of a "Middle-Atlantic" college in 1963. The author's interpretations derive from theories expounded by Arnold van Gennep in *Les Rites de Passage*.

Litwak, Leo, and Herbert Wilner. *College Days in Earthquake Country*. New York: Random House, 1972. Two personal points of view about their own involvement and the understandings they gained from the campus upheavals at San Francisco State College in 1968-1969.

Minneman, Charles E., ed. *Students, Religion and the Contemporary University*. Ypsilanti, Mich.: Eastern Michigan University Press, 1970. Contemporary students are dissatisfied with the world that technology has created. They are seeking to develop a world of faith, morals, religious values, and more real humanity. The university, no longer the substitute parent, must create another model which gives importance to faith, love, and other humane values.

Wight, E., and Mary S. Bakke. *Campus Challenge: Student Activism in Perspective*. Hamden, Conn.: Archon Books, 1971. Contains data on student activism in Colombia, India, Japan, and Mexico from 1962 through 1970. It analyzes more than 1500 interviews conducted at 65 universities. Attempts to find basic characteristics and a common denominator that relate to student activism in the United States.

Yankelovich, Daniel. *The Changing Values on Campus: Political and Personal Attitudes of Today's College Students.* New York: Pocket Books, 1972. A report of the results of a 1971 survey of more than 1200 students in 53 colleges and universities. Finds commitment to: the "new naturalism," "community vs. the individual," the non-rational, and the "search for the sacred in nature." Presents student views on authority, competition, marriage, morality, violence and other concerns. Concludes that major institutions need fundamental change and that the system, although imperfect, is reformable.

G. ADMINISTRATION, ORGANIZATION, AND GOVERNANCE

1. Administration and Organization

Budig, Gene A., ed. *Perceptions in Public Higher Education.* Lincoln, Neb.: University of Nebraska Press, 1970. A compilation of ten essays by administrative officers and faculty members at the University of Nebraska. They discuss the roles of administrators in various campus tasks. Most are concerned with their overlapping relationships to each other.

Caffrey, John, and Charles J. Mosmann. *Computers on Campus.* Washington, D.C.: American Council on Education, 1967. Considers the computer as both a tool for solving analytical problems as well as the core of a new system for dealing with research, instruction, management, and finances. It also deals with the computer as a subject for research and instruction.

Feinstein, Otto. *Higher Education in the United States: Economics, Personalism, Quality.* Lexington, Mass.: D. C. Heath, 1971. Tries to determine the underlying assumptions about educational quality and personalism used in planning reports and in estimating needs, demands, and costs. There is also some consideration of planning systems.

Hefferlin, J. B. Lon, and L. Phillips Ellis, Jr. *Information Services for Academic Administration.* San Francisco, Calif.: Jossey-Bass, 1971. This volume is a handy reference book designed to facilitate decision-making. It also provides suggestions for improving information systems and "make them more open, responsive, and effective."

Hungate, Thad L. *Management in Higher Education.* New York: Teachers College Bureau of Publications, Columbia University, 1964. Analyzes methods for implementing efficient management. A philosophy is derived from four functions of management and a consensus of policy formation. The four functions of management are: the organizing and delegating function, the directive function, the operative function, and the evaluative function. For further implications of financial management in higher education, see Dr. Hungate's earlier volumes: *Financing the Future of Higher Education* (1946), *Finance in Educational Management of Colleges and Universities* (1954), and *A New Basis of Support for Higher Education* (1957).

Jellema, William W., ed. *Efficient College Management*. San Francisco, Calif.: Jossey-Bass, 1972. This volume emphasizes the financial aspects of college management and suggests some new ways of reducing institutional costs. The four major sections deal with: program budgeting and institutional research; internal governance and external cooperation; student costs; and financial problems of private institutions.

Knowles, Asa A., ed. *Handbook of College and University Administration*. New York: McGraw-Hill, 1970. 2 vols. A monumental collection of practical information contributed by 85 experts. Covers the spectrum of topics from Alumni Relations to Space Requirements.

Lessinger, Leon, and Associates. *Accountability: Systems Planning in Education*. Homewood, Ill.: ETC Publications, 1973. A broad, in-depth presentation of accountability, cost effectiveness, and systems. Offers clear descriptions, numerous examples, illustrations, and implementing forms. Shows how these principles can be used in classroom and office to ensure that learning is enhanced while remaining humane.

Mosmann, Charles. *Academic Computers in Service. Effective Uses for Higher Education*. San Francisco, Calif.: Jossey-Bass, 1973. A practical, non-technical source book for information about the value and use of computers. Summarizes effective uses in research, explains how to acquire or update a system, discusses problems of management and policy-making, and suggests methods of financing computer services.

Rogers, Rutherford D., and David C. Weber. *University Library Administration*. New York: H. W. Wilson, 1971. A basic handbook of administration for librarians. Views all activities from the standpoint of policy decisions in the Director's office. Considers such topics as acquisitions, automation, book collections, budgets, measurement and evaluation, planning of library buildings, reader's services, personnel, and technical services.

2. Governance

Altbach, Philip G., et al. *Academic Supermarkets: A Critical Case Study of a Multiversity*. San Francisco, Calif.: Jossey-Bass, 1971. Analyzes the problems of academic governance in a large, complex, multi-purpose state university. Its 19 essays deal only with the University of Wisconsin, but are applicable to all similar institutions. The authors find that the base of power has shifted from the faculty to the administration. Little hope is offered that drastic reforms can be undertaken by an essentially conservative faculty whose power is vested in overlapping committees that must contend against autonomous departments. Some of the lessons derived from the crisis situations that rocked Wisconsin in the 1960's could help to avert future upheavals.

Ashby, Eric. *Adapting Universities to a Technological Society*. San Francisco, Calif.: Jossey-Bass, 1974. Presents ten lectures on various aspects of the university with the central thesis that it is not adapting rapidly enough to social change, and that the traditional idea of a university, with its concepts of academic freedom and institutional autonomy, is being threatened by the demands of a technological society. Universities, on the one hand, are the producers of the skilled manpower on which technological adaptation and economic growth depend; but, on the other hand, they are the only shelters in which reflections about the future and innovations with respect to values can take place, disengaged from the politics of expediency. Although the emphasis is on the characteristics of British universities, there is considerable reference to the problems of European and American institutions so that it becomes a discussion of fundamental and universal questions.

Baldridge, J. Victor, ed. *Academic Governance: Research on Institutional Politics and Decision Making*. Berkeley, Calif.: McCutchan, 1971. A collection of research reports dealing with the organization and problems of state universities. Many of the contributors are political scientists and sociologists. Each of these groups tends to view the university as either a bureaucracy or an association of equals, depending on their academic specialization.

Barzun, Jacques. *The American University: How it Runs and Where it is Going*. New York: Harper and Row, 1968. Self-motivated reform offers the only salvation for the "new" American university which has developed since the end of World War II. Barzun views the contemporary university as a "residual" institution, taking on all the social tasks that other agencies could not or would not take on themselves. No assessment of whether these tasks are germane to the idea of a university has been made. The university, as a result, is doing many things poorly because it is inadequately equipped to carry them out. It has also drained money, energy, and talent from its primary function, the transmission of culture.

Bennis, Warren. *The Leaning Ivory Tower*. San Francisco, Calif.: Jossey-Bass, 1972. Presents an inside view of the presidential search process. Contains recommendations for leadership succession, resignation, effecting educational reform, and for dealing with the problem of dissent.

Blau, Peter Michael. *The Organization of Academic Work*. New York: Wiley-Interscience, 1973. A study of the effects of academic bureaucracy on scholarship based on data gathered from more than 100 American universities. Blau concludes that increasing bureaucratization tends to decrease productivity and to weaken faculty morale.

Booz, Allen, and Hamilton, Inc. *Problems in University Library Management*. Washington, D.C.: Association of Research Libraries, 1970. Reports the results of a study conducted for the Association of Research Libraries and the American Council on Education in 1969. Field visits were made to six universities, and 150 administrators, faculty, librarians, and students were interviewed. It concludes that: "Access to library resources will have to be improved in light of scholarly demands for more rapid and reliable access to the growing body of recorded knowledge. These demands will strain the capacity of a single library to meet the teaching and research requirements of its constituency and will necessitate more aggressive pursuit of interinstitutional linkages among libraries and the application of new technology in storing, retrieving, and transmitting knowledge."

Burns, Gerald P. *Trustees in Higher Education*. New York: Independent College Funds of America, 1966. Dr. Burns presents a brief history of the development of trusteeship in America, followed by an encyclopedic handbook of the variety of problems faced by administrators and trustees. He also reviews the responsibilities of governing boards.

Connery, Robert H., ed. *The Corporation and the Campus*. New York: Praeger, 1970. A collection of conference papers. Emphasizes the increasing financial needs of American higher education and the interdependence of campus and corporation. Contains data on costs, spending, and institutional growth.

Dressel, Paul L., and William H. Faricy. *Return to Responsibility*. San Francisco, Calif.: Jossey-Bass, 1972. Excessive institutional autonomy underlies many of the ills of higher education today. Government intervention and an enforced "return to responsibility" are necessary if higher education is to survive. Discussions include the relationship between autonomy and academic freedom, the need for faculty review, and the effects of collective bargaining. Public service and teaching functions should be upgraded and suitably rewarded. Proposes the establishment of statewide coordinating boards for long-range planning and budgeting and for management information systems to increase operational efficiency.

Gould, John Wesley. *The Academic Deanship*. New York: Teachers College Bureau of Publications, Columbia University, 1964. An analysis of the role and responsibilities of the dean of a liberal arts college. It is based on data provided by approximately 250 college officials.

Hodgkinson, Harold L., and L. Richard Meeth, eds. *Power and Authority: Transformation of Campus Governances*. San Francisco, Calif.: Jossey-Bass, 1971. This is a collection of thirteen essays emanating from the Carnegie Foundation for the Advancement of Teaching and a conference sponsored by Higher Education Executive Associates. The authors emphasize the need for more student participation and take note of the fact that universities are becoming increasingly instruments of public policy; both of these will dilute controls now exercised by faculty and trustees. Not all, however, agree that representation is the fulcrum for university improvement.

Mayhew, Lewis B. *Arrogance on Campus*. San Francisco, Calif.: Jossey-Bass, 1970. All elements have been guilty of arrogance—including trustees and minorities. Mayhew recommends a greater spirit of tolerance for others and greater economy—"economy in the use of means to ends." Through these, arrogance on campus will diminish and public backlash will fade.

McGrath, Earl J. *Should Students Share the Power? A Study of their Role in College and University Governance*. Philadelphia, Pa.: Temple University Press, 1970. Urges a reversal of the historic trend by transferring a larger share of power back to the students. Suggests that the structure of governance should reflect a spirit of community. Universities strongly resist power shifts that will erode the present power structure.

Ridgeway, James. *The Closed Corporation*. New York: Random House, 1968. A critical assessment of contemporary American higher education. Trustee control assures collusion between the university and business; this is reenforced by the growing numbers of faculty and administrators who sit on corporate boards or serve as consultants. According to Ridgeway, the "community of scholars" is a myth. Universities are primarily interested in making money and in expanding their real estate holdings.

H. ECONOMICS AND GOVERNMENT SUPPORT

1. Economics

Advisory Committee on Endowment Management. *Managing Educational Endowments. Report to the Ford Foundation, 1972*. An updated version of a report issued in 1970. Stresses "the importance of establishing maximum long-term total return as the primary objective of endowment management, rather than stressing either income or appreciation at the expense of the other."

Arthur, William J. *A Financial Planning Model for Private Colleges. A Research Project*. Charlottesville, Va.: The University Press of Virginia, 1973. Outlines a systematic approach to the coordination of the diverse educational and financial objectives of the private colleges. Suggests methods of effective long-range planning.

Budig, Gene A., ed. *Dollars and Sense: Budgeting for Today's Campus*. Chicago, Ill.: College and University Business Press, McGraw-Hill, 1972. A collection of articles dealing with administrative budget-building, factors used by governors and state legislators in reviewing higher education budgets, and the packaging and selling of budgets to the public.

The Carnegie Commission on Higher Education. *Higher Education: Who Pays? Who Benefits? Who Should Pay?* Hightstown, N.J.: McGraw-Hill, 1973. Provides thirteen specific recommendations for the solution of some of the problems involved in financing higher education. The principal suggestions include: Increased governmental subsidies to reduce tuition costs at junior colleges, proportion tuition rates to actual costs at different academic levels, and to raise tuition for graduate courses. Special assistance should be given to private colleges to help them remain competitive.

Cheit, Earl F. *The New Depression in Higher Education: A Study of Financial Conditions at 41 Colleges and Universities.* New York: McGraw-Hill, 1971. This report, sponsored by the Carnegie Commission on Higher Education, indicates that colleges will be forced to become more efficient as a result of the current financial crisis. Continued increases in student fees are seen as self-defeating for the small colleges although they may work for the large prestigious private institutions. A second volume, *The New Depression in Higher Education: Two Years Later* (Berkeley, Calif.: The Carnegie Commission on Higher Education, 1973) is based on a resurvey of the same 41 institutions studied in 1971. It shows that there have been dramatic cuts in expenditures resulting in "a fiscal plateau."

Danière, André. *Higher Education in the American Economy.* New York: Random House, 1964. Applies the analytical tools of welfare economics to higher education. Dr. Danière considers such factors as costs, pricing, market imperfections, diversification, loans, and social value. He advocates an increase in the availability of student loans because they give the beneficiaries "a substantial share in the task of balancing costs and returns and in the responsibility to engage resources in education." Larger enrollments are more efficient because they reduce unit costs. Public planning and private control should be combined so as to ensure the decentralization of economic decisions and to make the "product" of the educational process a reflection of individual preferences.

Eckhaus, Richard. *Estimating the Returns to Education: A Disaggregated Approach.* (Carnegie Commission on Higher Education Technical Report.) Berkeley, Calif.: The Carnegie Commission on Higher Education, 1973. The calculation of returns on investments in education, using the disaggregated method, shows that expenditure for education does not return as much as previously assumed.

Hansen, W. Lee, and Burton A. Weisbrod. *Benefits, Costs, and Finance of Public Higher Education.* Chicago, Ill.: Markham Publishing Company, 1970. In California, public support of higher education tends mostly to benefit students from relatively high income families. More attention should be given to public support of alternate forms of higher education.

Harris, Seymour E. *Higher Education: Resources and Finance*. New York: McGraw-Hill, 1962. A discussion of methods for providing the additional resources for higher education required as a result of increasing enrollments and the pressure for improved standards and quality. Contains suggestions for raising the necessary funds and the manner in which the money can be most effectively used. Other volumes by Dr. Harris on the economics of higher education include: *The Economics of Harvard* (1970), *Education and Public Policy* (1965), and *Higher Education in the United States: The Economic Problems* (1960).

Higher Education and the Labor Market, edited by Margaret S. Gordon. (Essays sponsored by the Carnegie Commission on Higher Education.) New York: McGraw-Hill, 1974. Studies the impact of education on income. Provides a comprehensive analysis of labor market adjustments required by the increasing numbers of college graduates in the work force. There is some discussion of decision-making affecting the supply of graduates entering the professions.

Jellema, William W. *From Red to Black?* San Francisco, Calif.: Jossey-Boss, 1973. Based on data from a survey conducted by the Association of American Colleges, it describes the current financial conditions of the nation's private institutions. It does not, however, provide any major new solution to financial problems, as suggested by its title. Tells where the money comes from and where it goes.

2. Government Support

The Carnegie Commission on Higher Education. *The Capitol and the Campus: State Responsibility for Postsecondary Education*. New York: McGraw-Hill, 1971. Argues for the continuation of states as the major supporters of higher education in America rather than for the development of a single national system. States are urged to broaden their support for all forms of postsecondary education and to provide some support for private institutions. Advocates institutional autonomy balanced by a fair measure of public accountability.

Chambers, M. M. *Higher Education in the Fifty States*. Danville, Ill.: Interstate Printers and Publishers, 1970. A state-by-state statistical compendium which includes: a tabulation of state tax funds for higher education, tax and expenditure rates per capita, the extent of legislative control, and the organization of the state-wide top echelon administration of colleges and universities. It covers the period from 1959 to 1969.

Horn, Robert E., ed. *The Guide to Federal Assistance for Education*. New York: Appleton-Century-Crofts, 1972. A looseleaf reporting service providing information about: the kinds of funds available for education; deadlines for applications; eligibility requirements; and persons to contact. This material is updated monthly.

Olson, Keith W. *The G.I. Bill, the Veterans, and the Colleges*. Lexington, Ky.: University Press of Kentucky, 1973. The Servicemen's Readjustment Act of 1944 was conceived as "an antidepression measure," but was subsequently liberalized. The result was an unprecedented boom in college attendance and phenomenal academic achievements by the veterans. It showed that mass higher education was a realistic goal. Government support was encouraged and it was recognized that funds spent for higher education was "an investment which paid rich dividends to society."

Rainsford, George N. *Congress and Higher Education in the Nineteenth Century*. Knoxville, Tenn.: University of Tennessee Press, 1972. An examination of the formative era in federal aid to higher education. There is an attempt to provide reasons for the composition and direction of current programs. The book also offers some clues to the probable future course of assistance. It provides a concise and well-organized history of federal aid from the Northwest Ordinance of 1787 to the Smith-Hughes Act of 1917. Rainsford views grants to education as a means of achieving non-educational goals.

I. COMMUNITY AND JUNIOR COLLEGES

Brick, Michael. *Forum and Focus for the Junior College Movement. The American Association of Junior Colleges*. New York: Teachers College Bureau of Publications, Columbia University, 1964. Presents an account of the growth of the Junior College movement in America. Emphasizes the role of the American Association of Junior Colleges in promoting the dynamic development of two-year institutions.

Bushnell, David S. *Organizing for Change: New Priorities for Community Colleges*. New York: McGraw-Hill, 1973. Presents a statement of the findings of a nationwide study of community colleges sponsored by the Kellogg Foundation. Deals with the backgrounds, expectations, and attitudes of students, faculty, administrators, and trustees. There is some discussion of the problems and priorities of the two-year colleges.

Cohen, Arthur M., and Associates. *A Constant Variable. New Perspectives on the Community College*. San Francisco, Calif.: Jossey-Bass, 1971. An unconventional view of the community colleges which shows that they are not living up to their promise. Presents the best current research on each aspect of the two-year college. It also offers recommendations for change and improvement.

Gleazer, Edmund J., Jr. *Project Focus: A Forecast Study of Community Colleges*. New York: McGraw-Hill, 1973. Considers the nature, extent, and direction of change in the two-year colleges. Focuses on trends in organization, governance, programs, financial support, students, and community responsiveness.

Johnson, B. Lamar. *Islands of Innovation Expanding: Changes in the Community Colleges.* Beverly Hills, Calif.: Glencoe Press, 1969. A guide to promising innovative practices based on an assessment of the work being done in about 250 two-year institutions. Discusses some of the factors which discourage innovation. New things which deserve approval are: programmed instruction, games and simulation, cooperative work-study programs, and the systems approaches. Advises colleges to borrow new ideas from each other.

Koos, Leonard V. *The Community College Student.* Gainesville, Fla.: University of Florida Press, 1971. A comprehensive review of nearly 300 research studies relating to "later adolescents" and junior college students. Indicates the need for changes in curricula and improvement in student services.

Mesker, Leland L., and Dale Tillery. *Breaking the Access Barriers: A Profile of Two-Year Colleges.* New York: McGraw-Hill, 1971. Two-year institutions show an infinite variety in their goals, programs, faculty, and students; they do, however, have a number of common characteristics. The authors report a great many facts relating to these institutions which currently comprise the fastest growing category in American higher education.

Monroe, Charles R. *Profile of the Community College.* San Francisco, Calif.: Jossey-Bass, 1972. The primary functions of the two-year colleges are: general education, vocational education, and transfer programs. Dr. Monroe gives consideration to objectives, curriculum development, the pros and cons of the "open-door" concept, work-study programs, and the roles of students and faculty in decision-making and in governance.

Moore, William, Jr. *Blind Man on a Freeway: The Community College Administrator.* San Francisco, Calif.: Jossey-Bass, 1971. Suggests ways in which the preparation of administrators could be improved. Considers the source of most administrative problems to be "student activists, women's liberation, minority groups, and militant faculty."

Palinchak, Robert S. *The Evolution of the Community College.* Metuchen, N.J.: Scarecrow Press, 1973. Conceives of the comprehensive community college as a unique form of two-year institution. Palinchak concludes that its full potential is still untapped.

J. URBAN HIGHER EDUCATION

The Carnegie Commission on Higher Education. *The Campus and the City: Maximizing Assets and Reducing Liabilities.* New York: McGraw-Hill, 1972. Recommends that urban campuses deepen their involvement in big city problems and increase the access of urban dwellers to higher education. Institutions must respond to the problems of cities through renewed emphasis on public service as well as through formal education and research activities.

Advocates open admissions. Suggests a standard of more than 2.5 student spaces per 100 of population and the creation of satellite campuses.

Hoppe, William A., ed. *Policies and Practices in Evening Colleges, 1971*. Metuchen, N.J.: Scarecrow Press, 1972. An analysis of data from 146 evening colleges that responded to a survey by the Research Committee of the Association of University Evening Colleges in 1970-71. Considers admissions policies, faculty, fees, organization and scheduling. Supplements a 1969 volume with the same title under the same editorship.

Klotsche, J. Martin. *The University of Wisconsin—Milwaukee: An Urban University*. Milwaukee, Wis.: University of Wisconsin—Milwaukee, 1972. Klotsche, Chancellor of Wisconsin—Milwaukee, has headed the institution since its founding in 1955. In this volume he provides specific illustrations for the general thesis in his earlier study. Here he describes the search for an "urban mission," the fight for independence from its parent institution. He observes, with regret, that American colleges and universities tend to become increasingly alike.

Klotsche, J. Martin. *The Urban University: And the Future of Our Cities*. New York: Harper and Row, 1966. A study of the effects of the urbanization of the American population on the growth and nature of the urban university. Klotsche's thesis is that the urban university has a special mission in relation to its environment. Emphasizes the necessity for creating an intellectual community and working partnerships with other cultural institutions and research-oriented industry. Advocates programs which take cognizance of the commuter-student's need to work while attending college, off-campus study, and the unlimited opportunities for involvement in community action.

Nash, George. *The University and the City: Eight Cases of Involvement*. New York: McGraw-Hill, 1973. Shows that interaction between urban communities and educational institutions was mutually beneficial. Four major categories of activity are distinguished: as educator, as a provider of services, as a good neighbor and good citizen, and as a model for desirable organization and change for society.

K. GRADUATE AND PROFESSIONAL EDUCATION

Blauch, Lloyd E., et al. *The Podiatry Curriculum*. Washington, D.C.: American Association of Colleges of Podiatric Medicine, 1970. Primarily designed for those interested in the development of the profession of podiatry, it deals with student selection, curricula, and student learning. However, the material is presented in a way that makes it applicable to all fields of higher education.

Calvert, Jack G., et al. *Graduate School in the Sciences: Entrance, Survival, and Careers*. New York: Wiley-Interscience, 1972. An analysis of the problems facing students planning to enter academic, governmental, or industrial fields at high levels of competence and responsibility.

Cordasco, Francesco. *The Shaping of American Graduate Education: Daniel Coit Gilman and the Protean Ph.D.* Totowa, N.J.: Rowman and Littlefield, 1972. This biographical study emphasizing Gilman's contributions to the development of graduate education in America and his presidency at the Johns Hopkins University is a reissue of a work originally published in 1960. Dr. Cordasco's thesis is that Gilman created a uniquely American curriculum rather than transplanting the German Ph.D. program. For additional material, see also: Daniel Coit Gilman, *The Launching of a University* (1906); Abraham Flexner, *Daniel Coit Gilman, Creator of the American Type of University* (1946); and Hugh Hawkins, *Pioneer: A History of the Johns Hopkins University, 1874-1889* (1960).

Fein, Rashi, and Gerald I. Weber. *Financing Medical Education: An Analysis of Alternative Policies and Mechanisms.* New York: McGraw-Hill, 1971. Examines the characteristics of medical students, their financial problems, and the effect of student finances on failure rates. This volume also contains an analysis of the sources and uses of medical school funds in performing the triple mission of teaching, research, and service.

Heiss, Ann M. *Challenges to Graduate Students.* San Francisco, Calif.: Jossey-Bass, 1970. A study of Ph.D. programs in ten prestigious universities. Analyzes the deficiencies in graduate education and offers some suggestions for improvement.

Mayhew, Lewis B. *Graduate and Professional Education.* (Report sponsored by the Carnegie Commission on Higher Education.) New York: McGraw-Hill, 1970. Surveys institutional plans for the expansion of graduate and professional education through 1980. Although some planning is motivated by concern for status, prestige, and growth, much is a sincere response to perceived manpower needs. Mayhew finds that no abatement of the headlong expansion should be anticipated in this decade. He raises some questions about governmental and institutional policies.

National Board on Graduate Education. *Doctorate Manpower Forecasts and Policy.* Washington, D.C.: National Board on Graduate Education, 1973. Places increasing onus on the federal government for better long-range planning, better Ph.D. market data reporting, and for joint action with the universities to insure the success of affirmative action programs and the completion of degree programs by members of minority groups. The continuing flow of young faculty members into academic departments should be assured.

National Board on Graduate Education. *Graduate Education: Purposes, Problems, and Potential.* Washington, D.C.: National Board on Graduate Education, 1973. Presents the Board's views on the various facets of graduate education. Offers assistance in resolving some of the major problems.

Panel on Alternate Approaches to Graduate Education. *Scholarship for Society*. Princeton, N.J.: Educational Testing Service, 1973. America's graduate schools have been prevented from making significant changes to accommodate the needs of new types of students by outdated notions, by unfounded and overstated opinions, and by the erroneous belief that our system of advanced education is already over-developed.

Welch, Claude. *Graduate Education in Religion—A Critical Appraisal*. Chambersburg, Pa.: Council on the Study of Religion, 1971. This study, sponsored by the American Council of Learned Societies, concludes that about one-third of the graduate departments of religion in the United States should go out of business.

L. BIOGRAPHY AND PERSONAL POINTS OF VIEW

Birenbaum, William M. *Overlive*. New York: Delacorte Press, 1969. Describes an American society with surplus living power: overproduction and overconsumption, in which minorities have not shared proportionally. Universities must adapt to their new role in this society of abundance. Birenbaum views the universities as the Cerberuses of social mobility. Faculty members are the chief culprits; they are inordinately concerned with tenure, "scholarly detachment," research and publication, and isolate themselves from the demands of the student and the community. The author concludes that some form of urban-grant university is essential to the renewal of higher education.

Birenbaum, William M. *Something for Everybody is Not Enough. An Educator's Search for his Education*. New York: Random House, 1971. A witty and provocative account of the author's development from Iowa schoolboy to leading spokesman for urban higher education. There are many perceptive views of the problems and tasks that face the educational administrator.

Conant, James B. *My Several Lives: Memoirs of a Social Inventor*. New York: Harper and Row, 1970. One section of Conant's autobiography recounts developments at Harvard during the Depression years, another deals with post-war Harvard. Other chapters are devoted to the vicissitudes and rescues of the Graduate School of Education, the invention of the Master of Arts in Teaching degree, and academic freedom. Additional discussions relevant to higher education are scattered throughout the volume.

Kriegel, Leonard. *Working Through: A Teacher's Journey in the Urban University*. New York: Saturday Review Press, 1972. This is a distillation of personal experience as an undergraduate at Hunter (City University of New York), graduate student at Columbia and New York University, and a teacher at Long Island University's Brooklyn campus and at City College. Views the urban university as the mirror of urban America. It offers some comments on various aspects of urban higher education including: facilities, the characteristics of the students, and institutional "mentality."

Minogue, Kenneth R. *The Concept of a University*. Berkeley, Calif.: University of California Press, 1973. Opposes the "new vocationalism" and the notion that the university exists "for the good of society." Advocates individuality and intellectuality.

Ness, Frederic W. *Uncertain Glory*. San Francisco, Calif.: Jossey-Bass, 1971. This is a distillation of Dr. Ness's long experience as a faculty member and college administrator. It offers candid reflections on the role of deans and presidents.

M. HISTORY

Brubacher, John S., and Willis Rudy. *Higher Education in Transition: A History of American Colleges and Universities, 1636-1968*. Rev. and enl. New York: Harper & Row, 1968. A revised, enlarged, and updated version of the authors' earlier (1958) volume dealing with the period from 1636 to 1958. Emphasizes the broadening and democratization of Western European antecedents in the American setting. Discusses patterns of organization and instruction in the colonial colleges. This volume also gives good coverage to the development of state universities in the latter half of the nineteenth century and to the growth of professional education in this century.

Clark, Burton R. *The Distinctive College: Antioch, Reed and Swarthmore*. Chicago, Ill.: Aldine Pub. Co., 1970. This is a comparative historical study of the special mission of each of these fairly unique institutions. In each case, one creative and charismatic president gave the impetus to the development of its curriculum and goals. William Foster gave Reed its high academic standards and its determination not to be dominated by its local community; Arthur Morgan gave Antioch its pioneering work-study program and its faculty-student participation in the decision-making process; and Frank Aydelotte inaugurated independent study, honors courses, and high academic standards at Swarthmore.

Curti, Merle, and Roderick Nash. *Philanthropy in the Shaping of American Higher Education*. New Brunswick, N.J.: Rutgers University Press, 1965. Curti and Nash present an interesting historical account of one of the significant factors in the shaping of America's unique species of colleges and universities. Each era in our development had its educational philanthropoists who influenced the creation of a characteristic kind of program or institution.

Handlin, Oscar, and Mary F. Handlin. *The American College and American Culture: Socialization as a Function of Higher Eduation*. (Report sponsored by the Carnegie Commission on Higher Education.) New York: McGraw-Hill, 1970. Presents the goals of colleges and universities from colonial times to the present. The one persistent aim has been to prepare young people for the problems and responsibilities of adult life.

Hawkins, Hugh. *Between Harvard and America: The Educational Leadership of Charles W. Eliot.* New York: Oxford University Press, 1972. Explores "the action and reaction between the university and the society at large." Eliot had changing views regarding higher education, but he always tried to combine the old and the new in a changing society. Religion was a stumbling block in the attempt to adapt the university to science and to the urban industrial society.

Kelley, Brooks Mather. *Yale: A History.* New Haven, Conn.: Yale University Press, 1974. Covers Yale's growth from 1701 through 1963. Kelley's thesis is that Yale has never really been a "private" institution; throughout more than two and a half centuries it has always received a considerable portion of its funds from the colonial, state, and national governments. The colonial period is dealt with in more detail in Richard Warch's, *School of the Prophets: Yale College, 1701-1740* (1974), and the period from 1871 through 1937 in George W. Pierson's two-volume *Yale: College and University, 1871-1937* (1952-1955).

Knepper, George W. *New Lamps for Old: One Hundred Years of Urban Higher Education at the University of Akron.* Akron, Ohio: University of Akron, 1970. A broad and balanced narrative of student, faculty, and administration activities. Recounts Akron's history from its founding as Universalist Buchtel College in 1871 through periods of crisis through its conversion into a publicly supported institution. President Park Kolbe transformed it into a municipal university system in 1913. In 1967, Akron became part of the state university system.

Lee, Calvin B. T. *The Campus Scene, 1900-1970. Changing Styles in Undergraduate Life.* New York: David McKay, 1970. Each college generation has a character of its own, generally related to the *Zeitgeist* of the nation. Lee distinguishes seven major eras in this century; the first two decades are the "Good Old Days;" the Twenties are the "Jazz Age;" the Depression created the somber Thirties; the veterans dominated the Forties; students in the Fifties were the "Silent Generation;" and the Sixties gave us our campus activism. There is also a chapter devoted to "The Black Student."

Nisbet, Robert. *The Degradation of the Academic Dogma: The University in America, 1945-1971.* New York: Basic Books, 1971. Universities have become degraded and endangered as a result of a massive infusion of foundation and governmental funds. Professors have become "academic entrepreneurs" and have created semi-autonomous "centers," "projects,' and "institutes." Advocates a return to a commitment to scholarship and free inquiry.

Smith, G. Kerry, ed. *Twenty-Five Years: 1945-1970.* Washington, D.C.: American Association for Higher Education, 1970. Thirty leading educators assess the problems and events of the quarter century since the close of World War II and their impact on higher education. The essays in this volume were selected from the best in the *Current Issues in Higher Education* yearbooks.

Vesey, Laurence R. *The Emergence of the American University*. Chicago, Ill.: University of Chicago Press, 1965. A morphological history of American higher education with special emphasis on the development of the contemporary university. It examines the origins of the controversy between the advocates of pure scholarship and the partisans of pragmatism and professional specialization. Colleges and universities are viewed as products of their social environment.

Whitehead, John S. *The Separation of College and State: Columbia, Dartmouth, Harvard, and Yale, 1776-1876*. New Haven, Conn.: Yale University Press, 1973. This multi-institutional historical study illustrates the quasi-public character of private colleges during the first century of the republic. All were dependent to some extent on state funds for support. Conversely, public universities founded before 1890 were never clearly the financial responsibility of the states. Post revolutionary charters of private colleges provided for governmental supervision.

X. SCHOOLBOOKS, CHILDREN'S LITERATURE, AND ETHNIC BIAS IN INSTRUCTIONAL MATERIALS

A. BIBLIOGRAPHIES AND GENERAL RESOURCES

[American Library Association]. Children's Services Division. *Notable Children's Books, 1940-1970*. Chicago: American Library Association, 1973. Annual Supplements.

Arnold, Arnold. *Pictures and Stories from Forgotten Children's Books*. New York: Dover, 1969. (Reprint) Facsimiles of title pages with selected excerpts from rare texts. See also, Baldwin, Littlefield, Johnson, Rosenbach, Thwaite, Tuer, *infra*.

Baldwin, Ruth, M. *100 Nineteenth-Century Rhyming Alphabets in English*. Carbondale: Southern Illinois University Press, 1972.

Barnard, Henry. "American Textbooks." *American Journal of Education*, vol. 13 (1863), pp. 202-222, 401-408, 626-640; vol 14 (1864), pp. 751-757; vol. 15 (1865), pp. 639-675. Essentially, bibliographical checklists. See F. Cordasco, "Henry Barnard's *American Journal of Education*," *History of Education Quarterly*, vol. 11 (Fall, 1971), pp. 328-332.

Dunfee, Maxine, ed. *Eliminating Ethnic Bias in Instructional Material: Comment and Bibliography*. Washington: Association for Supervision and Curriculum Development, 1974. Discussion and analysis followed by appended bibliographies. Includes materials on pluralism, ethnic bias, efforts to change, resources for educators, with schema for evaluating textbooks for racism, sexism.

Ellis, Alec. *How to Find Out About Children's Literature*. 3rd. ed. New York: Pergamon, 1973. Analytical guide with discussion of history, development, and examples of children's literature.

Haviland, Virginia. *Children's Literature: A Guide to Reference Sources*. Washington: Library of Congress, 1966. First Supplement, 1972. Encompasses eight categories including history and criticism, authorship, illustration, and international studies. Valuable for bibliographic citations.

Jackson, Clara O., and Harriet B. Quimby. "Building a Children's Literature Collection: A Suggested Basic Reference Collection for Academic Libraries." *Choice* [Association of College and Research Libraries], vol. 11 (November, 1974), pp. 1261-1274. A valuable bibliographical overview and analysis of texts, history, authors, illustrators, anthologies, selection aids, reviewing journals, etc., with appended references.

Johnson, Clifton. *Old Time Schools and Schoolbooks.* New York: Macmillan, 1904. Reissued, New York: Dover Publications, 1963 with a new introduction by Carl Withers. Includes copious extracts and illustrations from early primers, spellers, readers, geographies, histories and other textbooks down to *c.* 1850. See also, Clifton Johnson, *The Country School* (New York: Appleton, 1893).

Littlefield, George E. *Early Schools and Schoolbooks of New England.* Boston: Club of Odd Volumes, 1904. Includes illustrations and plate facsmiles. See also, G. E. Littlefield, *Early Boston Booksellers, 1642-1711* (Boston: Club of Odd Volumes, 1900).

Rosenbach, A. S. W. *Early American Children's Books.* Portland, Maine: Southworth Press, 1933. Reissued, New York: Dover Publications, 1970. Bibliographical descriptions of rare schoolbooks from Dr. Rosenbach's collection.

Smith, Elva S. *The History of Children's Literature.* Chicago: American Library Association, 1937. Includes a detailed outline and descriptive bibliography.

Thwaite, Mary F. *From Primer to Pleasure in Reading.* Boston: Horn Book, 1973.

Tuer, Andrew W. *Pages and Pictures from Forgotten Children's Books.* Detroit: Gale Research Company, 1969. (Reprint) See also, A. W. Tuer, *History of the Hornbook* (London: Leadenhall Press, 1897).

Welch, d'Alté. *A Bibliography of Children's Books Printed Prior to 1821.* Charlottesville: University of Virginia Press, 1974. A project undertaken with the American Antiquarian Society. Lists 1478 individual titles, along with all known editions of each.

B. HISTORICAL AND OTHER STUDIES

Adams, Bess. *About Books and Children: A Historical Survey of Children's Literature.* New York: Holt, Rinehart and Winston, 1953.

Arbuthnot, May H., and Zena Sutherland. *Children and Books.* 4th ed. Glenview, Illinois: Scott, Foresman, 1972. Most up-to-date comprehensive text with detailed bibliographies. See also, Adams, *supra.*

Black, Marian W. "The Battle over Uniformity of Textbooks in Florida, 1868-1963." *History of Education Quarterly,* vol. 4 (1964), pp. 106-118.

Brown, Ralph. "The American Geographies of Jedidiah Morse." *Annals* [Association of American Geographies], vol. 31 (1941), pp. 145-217.

Carpenter, Charles. *History of American Schoolbooks.* Philadelphia: University of Pennsylvania Press, 1963. "A general portrayal of American textbooks, and along with this, as a requisite accompaniment, a picture of the pioneer-day school system—this latter only insofar as it had to do with schoolbook production and early usage." Includes excellent annotated bibliography.

Commager, Henry Steele. "Noah Webster, 1758-1958." *Saturday Review,* vol. 41 (October 18, 1958), pp. 12 ff.

Donnally, Williams. "The Haymarket Riot in Secondary School Textbooks." *Harvard Educational Review,* vol. 8 (1938), pp. 105-216.

Earle, Alice Morse. *Child Life in Colonial Days.* Norwood, Pa.: Norwood Editions, 1974. Originally published 1899. Includes chapters on "Hornbook and Primer," "Schoolbooks," "Diaries and Commonplace Books," and "Story and Picture Books."

Elson, Ruth M. "American Schoolbooks and 'Culture' in the Nineteenth Century." *Mississippi Valley Historical Review,* vol. 46 (1959-1960), pp. 411-435.

Elson, Ruth M. *Guardians of Tradition: American Schoolbooks of the Nineteenth Century.* Lincoln: University of Nebraska Press, 1964. Largely, an interpretative index of reactions of 19th century textbooks as compendia of approved ideas of the time. Includes a "Bibliography of Textbooks Used [1776-1900]."

England, J. Merton. "The Democratic Faith in American Schoolbooks of the Republic, 1783-1861." *American Quarterly,* vol. 15 (1963), pp. 191-199.

Fell, Marie L. *The Foundations of Nativism in American Textbooks, 1783-1860.* Washington: Catholic University of America Press, 1941. A Ph.D. dissertation where object "is to determine to what extent the textbooks used . . . laid the foundations of the anti-Catholic and anti-foreign attitudes, which had their political conclusions in the nativist movements of the 1830's and 1840's and in the Know Nothing party of the 1850's."

Ford, Paul L., ed. *The New England Primer: A History of Its Origin and Development. With a Reprint of the Unique Copy of the Earliest Known Edition and Many Fac-simile Illustrations and Reproductions.* New York: Dodd, Mead, 1897. Reprinted, Teachers College, Columbia University, 1962, with a preface by Lawrence A. Cremin: "Ford's essay remains the best brief introduction to the *Primer* [the first edition of which may have been published before 1687/1688], its antecedents in England, and its successive versions in the New World; and the 1727 edition of the *Primer,* which Ford reprinted, is still the earliest extant copy."

Garfinkle, Norton. "Conservatism in American Textbooks, 1800-1860." *New York History,* vol. 35 (1954), pp. 49-63.

Hamilton, Sinclair. *Early American Book Illustrators and Wood Engravers.* Princeton: Princeton University Library, 1958. A *catalogue raisonné* with considerable material on early schoolbooks and on the work of Alexander Anderson, the school text illustrator.

Kiefer, Monica. *American Children Through their Books, 1700-1835.* Philadelphia: University of Pennsylvania Press, 1970. A detailed sociological analysis, with valuable bibliographical documentation.

Martin, Helen. *Nationalism in Children's Literature.* Chicago: American Library Association, 1936.

Meigs, Cornelia, *et al. A Critical History of Children's Literature.* Rev. ed. New York: Macmillan, 1969. Literature from the earliest times to 1967; comprehensive in its scope.

Minnich, Harvey C., ed. *Old Favorites from the McGuffey Readers.* New York: Macmillan, 1936. Reissued, Detroit: Singing Tree Press [Gale Research Co.], 1969. A centennial collection of 150 selections from McGuffey *Readers* commemorating the hundredth anniversary of the first McGuffey *Reader* (1836).

Minnich, Harvey C. *William Holmes McGuffey and His Readers.* New York: American Book Co., 1936. A biographical and critical study of the textbook author, William Holmes McGuffey (1800-1873). Includes a complete list of the various issues of the *Readers* and an extended bibliography on McGuffey.

Mosier, Richard D. *Making the American Mind: Social and Moral Ideas in the McGuffey Readers.* Rev. ed. New York: Kings Crown Press, 1965. Largely on the influence of the *Readers.* See also, Alice McGuffey Ruggles, *The Story of the McGuffeys* (New York, 1930); and Henry Ford, *The McGuffey Readers* (1936), a bibliographical and illustrative compendium put together at the Ford Museum. Henry Ford assembled a large collection of McGuffey *Readers.*

Muir, Percival H. *English Children's Books, 1600-1900.* New York: Praeger, 1969. English sources of influence in America; includes bibliographies.

Nietz, John A. *The Evolution of American Secondary School Textbooks* . . . Rutland, Vt.: Tuttle, 1966. A detailed survey of books used in Latin and grammar schools from the Colonial period to 1900.

Nietz, John A. *Old Textbooks: Spelling, Grammar, Reading, Arithmetic, Geography, American History, Civil Government, Physiology, Penmanship. Art, Music—As Taught in the Common Schools from Colonial Days to 1900.* Pittsburgh: University of Pittsburgh Press, 1961.

Nietz, John A. "Why the Longevity of the McGuffey Readers." *History of Education Quarterly,* vol. 4 (1964), pp. 119-125.

Shankland, Rebecca H. "The McGuffey Readers and Moral Education." *Harvard Educational Review,* vol. 31 (1961), pp. 60-72.

Shoemaker, Ervin C. *Noah Webster: Pioneer of Learning.* New York: Columbia University Press, 1936. See also, Emily Ellsworth, *et al., A Bibliography of the Writings of Noah Webster* (New York, 1958); Horace E. Scudder, *Noah Webster* (Boston, 1881); and Emily Ellsworth Fowler Ford, *Notes on the Life of Noah Webster,* 2 vols. (New York, 1912).

Spieseke, Alice W. *The First Textbooks in American History and their Compiler, John McCulloch.* New York: Teachers College, Columbia University, 1938. John McCulloch (1754?-1824). Includes "Books Printed by John McCulloch, Alone or with Others," pp. 107-116; and "Almanacs Printed by John McCulloch, Alone or with Others," pp. 117-121.

Vail, Henry H. *A History of the McGuffey Readers.* Rev. ed. Cleveland: [Privately Printed], 1911. A brief history with bibliographical data. Includes three portraits.

Warfel, Harry R. *Noah Webster, Schoolmaster to America.* New York: Macmillan, 1936. The fullest biography of Noah Webster (1758-1843), with elaborate "sources and bibliography," pp. 439-449.

[Noah Webster] *Noah Webster's American Spelling Book.* New York: Bureau of Publications, Teachers College, Columbia University, 1962. Includes an introductory essay by Henry Steele Commager. Reprints the 1831 revised impression of Webster's "blue-backed speller" which appeared originally in 1783, and which by 1837 had sales over 15 million. It continued to sell over a million copies a year for the rest of the 19th century (D. Appleton editions).

Weiss, Harry B. *Printers and Publishers of Children's Books in New York City, 1698-1830.* New York: New York Public Library, 1948. Largely a bibliographical checklist with historical notes.

Younker, Donna L. "The Moral Philosophy of William Holmes McGuffey." *Educational Forum,* vol. 28 (1963), pp. 71-77.

C. ETHNIC BIAS IN INSTRUCTIONAL MATERIALS

This section has been adapted from La Mar P. Miller, "Evidence of Ethnic

Bias in Instructional Materials," in Maxine Dunfee, ed., *Eliminating Ethnic Bias in Instructional Materials* (Washington: ASCD, 1974), pp. 14-19.

Abel, Midge B. "American Indian Life as Portrayed in Children's Literature." *Elementary English,* vol. 50 (February, 1973), pp. 202-208.

Abramowitz, Jack. "Textbooks and Negro History." *Social Education,* vol. 33 (March, 1969), pp. 306-309.

Alilunas, Leo J. "What Our Schools Teach About Booker T. Washington and W. E. B. DuBois." *Journal of Negro Education,* vol. 40 (Spring, 1973), pp. 176-86.

Allen, Van S. "An Analysis of Textbooks Relative to the Treatment of Black Americans." *Journal of Negro Education,* vol. 40 (Spring, 1971), pp. 140-45.

Banks, James A. "A Content Analysis of the Black American in Textbooks." *Social Education,* vol. 33 (December, 1969), pp. 954-57.

Barr, Alwyn. "The Negro in American History Texts." *Indiana Social Studies Quarterly,* vol. 22 (Autumn, 1969), pp. 28-34.

Bennett, Lerone, Jr. "The Negro in Textbooks: Reading, 'Riting, and Racism." *Ebony,* vol. 22 (March, 1967), pp. 130-32.

Bernstein, J. E. "Minority Group Representation in Contemporary Fiction for American Children Between the Ages of 3 and 7." *Urban Review,* vol. 5 (May, 1972), pp. 42-44.

Bingham, Jane. "The Pictorial Treatment of Afro-Americans in Books for Young Children 1930-1968." *Elementary English,* vol. 48 (November, 1971), pp. 880-85.

Black, Hillel. *The American Schoolbook.* New York: William Morrow and Company, Inc., 1967.

Blatt, Gloria T. "The Mexican American in Children's Literature." *Elementary English,* vol. 45 (April, 1968), pp. 446-51.

Bosmajian, Haig A. "The Language of White Racism." *College English,* vol. 31 (December, 1969), pp. 163-72.

Caliguri, Joseph P. "Teacher Bias in the Selection of Social Studies Textbooks." *Journal of Negro Education,* vol. 40 (Fall, 1971), pp. 322-29.

Collier, Marilyn. "An Evaluation of Multi-Ethnic Basal Readers." *Elementary English,* vol. 44 (February, 1967), pp. 152-57.

Davis, Lucian. "Current Controversy: Minorities in American History

Textbooks." *Journal of Secondary Education,* vol. 41 (November, 1966), pp. 291-94.

Davison, William E. "Michigan Committee Reports: Textbooks Unfair to Minorities." *Michigan Education Journal,* vol. 46 (September, 1968), pp. 41-42.

Deane, Paul C. "The Persistence of Uncle Tom: An Examination of the Image of the Negro in Children's Fiction Series." *Journal of Negro Education,* vol. 37 (Spring, 1968), pp. 140-45.

[Detroit Public School Staff] "What About Us? Our Textbooks Do Not Meet Our Needs." *Education Product Report,* vol. 3 (November, 1969), pp. 12-38. An analysis of textbooks included.

Dieterich, Daniel J. "Books That Lie and Lullabye." ERIC/RCS Report. *Elementary English,* vol. 49 (November, 1972), pp. 1000-1009.

Donaldson, O. Fred. "Geography and the Black American: The White Papers and the Invisible Man." *Journal of Geography,* vol. 70 (March, 1971), pp. 138-49.

Drachler, Norman. "Shortcomings of American Textbooks." *The Bulletin of the National Association of Secondary School Principals,* vol. 54 (April, 1970), pp. 15-25.

Edelson, Malorie. "What About Us? Evaluation and Confrontation: Keys to Textbook Change." *Educational Product Report,* vol. 3 (November, 1969), pp. 6-11.

Elkin, Sol M. "Minorities in Textbooks: The Latest Chapter." *Teachers College Record,* vol. 66 (March, 1965), pp. 502-508.

Gast, David K. "Dawning of the Age of Aquarius for Multi-Ethnic Children's Literature." *Elementary English,* vol. 47 (May, 1970), pp. 661-65.

Gast, David K. "Minority Groups in Children's Literature." *Elementary English,* vol. 44 (January, 1967), pp. 12-23.

Gibson, Emily Fuller. "The Three D's: Distortion, Deletion, Denial." *Social Education,* vol. 33 (April, 1969), pp. 405-409.

Glancy, Barbara J. "Black Barbeque: An Essay Review." *Teachers College Record,* vol. 70 (April, 1969), pp. 661-84.

Goldman, Martin S. "The Academic Subversion of Black Studies." *Social Studies,* vol. 65 (January, 1974), pp. 26-34.

Gurule, Kay. "Truthful Textbooks and Mexican Americans." *Integrated*

Education: A Report on Race and Schools, vol. 11 (March-April, 1973), pp. 35-42.

Harris, Judah. *The Treatment of Religion in Elementary School Social Studies Textbooks.* New York: Anti-Defamation League of B'nai B'rith, n.d.

Harris, Nelson H. "The Treatment of Negroes in Books and Media Designed for the Elementary School." *Social Education,* vol. 33 (April, 1969), pp. 434-37.

Henry, Jeanette, ed. *Textbooks and the American Indians.* San Francisco: The Indian Historian Press, n.d.

"How Michigan Rates Textbook Treatment of Negro History." *Nation's Schools,* vol. 82 (September, 1968), pp. 62-63.

Jones, James P. "Negro Stereotypes in Children's Literature: The Case of Nancy Drew." *Journal of Negro Education,* vol. 40 (Spring, 1971), pp. 121-25.

Josephy, Alvin M., Jr. "Indians in History." *The Atlantic,* vol. 225 (June, 1970), pp. 121-25.

Kane, Michael B. *Minorities in Textbooks.* Chicago: Quandrangle Books, 1970. [Anti-Defamation League of B'nai B'rith.]

Koblitz, Minnie W. *The Negro in Schoolroom Literature: Resource Materials for the Teacher of Kindergarten Through the Sixth Grade.* New York: Center for Urban Education, 1966.

Krug, Mark M. "Freedom and Racial Equality: A Study of 'Revised' High School History Texts." *School Review,* vol. 28 (May, 1970), pp. 297-354.

Lange, Richard A., and William T. Kelley. "The Problem of Bias in Writing of Elementary History Textbooks." *Journal of General Education,* vol. 22 (January, 1971), pp. 257-67.

Larrick, Nancy. "The All-White World of Children's Books." *Saturday Review,* vol. 48 (September 11, 1965), pp. 84-85.

Lester, Richard I. "The Treatment of Minorities in Our Textbooks." *California Teachers Association Journal,* vol. 66 (January, 1970), pp. 46, 48.

Marcus, Lloyd A. *The Treatment of Minorities in Secondary School Textbooks.* New York: Anti-Defamation League of B'nai B'rith, 1961.

Margolis, Richard J. "The Trouble With Textbooks." *Redbook Magazine,* vol. 124 (March, 1965), pp. 64-65, 123-29.

McDiarmid, Garnet, and David Pratt. *Teaching Prejudice*. Toronto: Ontario Institue for Studies in Education, 1971. An analysis of social studies texts for prejudical content.

Mock, Roberta Sue. "Racial and Religious Prejudice in American Literature Textbooks." *Indiana Social Studies Quarterly,* vol. 22 (Autumn, 1969), pp. 15-18.

NCTE Task Force on Racism and Bias in the Teaching of English. "Criteria for Teaching Materials." *College English,* vol. 32 (March, 1971), pp. 713-15.

[National Education Association, Commission on Professional Rights and Responsibilities.] "The Treatment of Minorities in Textbooks." *School & Society,* vol. 95 (Summer, 1967), pp. 323-24.

Newby, I. A. "Historians and Negroes." *Journal of Negro History,* vol. 54 (January, 1969), pp. 32-47.

Parker, Lenore D., and E. K. Campbell. "A Look at Illustrations in Multi-Racial First Grade Readers." *Elementary English,* vol. 48 (January, 1971), pp. 67-74.

Polos, Nicholas C. "Textbooks and the Invisible Man." *The Educational Forum,* vol. 31 (May, 1967), pp. 477-80.

Price, Robert D., and Thelma L. Spencer. "Elementary Social Studies Textbooks and Their Relevance to the Negro Child." *Social Studies,* vol. 61 (April, 1970), pp. 168-73.

Robinson, Donald W. "European Textbooks and America's Racial Problem." *Social Education,* vol. 33 (March, 1969), pp. 310-13.

Roderick, Juanita. "Minority Groups in Textbooks." *Improving College and University Teaching,* vol. 18 (Spring, 1970), pp. 129-32.

Sloan, Irving. *The Negro in Modern American History Textbooks*. Fourth edition. Washington: American Federation of Teachers, 1972.

Sloan, Irving. *The Treatment of Black Americans in Current Encyclopedias*. Washington: American Federation of Teachers, 1970.

Slotkin, A. N. "The Treatment of Minorities in Textbooks: The Issues and the Outlook." *Education Digest,* vol. 30 (October, 1964), pp. 21-23.

Soderbergh, Peter A. "Bibliographical Essay: The Negro in Juvenile Series Books 1899-1930." *The Journal of Negro History,* vol. 58 (April, 1973), pp. 179-86.

Stampp, Kenneth M., *et al*. "The Negro in American History Textbooks."

Integrated Education, vol. 2 (October-November, 1964), pp. 9-26.

Stewart, Maxwell S. *Prejudice in Textbooks.* New York: Public Affairs Committee, Inc., 1950.

"Textbook Bias Toward Alaskan Natives." Report made part of the record of the hearings of the Subcommittee in Indian Education, Senate Committee on Labor and Public Welfare, Alaska University, Department of Education. *Integrated Education,* vol. 9 (March-April, 1971), pp. 44-49.

Textbook Report. Detroit: Intergroup Relations Department, School-Community Relations Division, Detroit Public Schools, 1968.

Textbooks and the American Indian. San Francisco: The Indian Historian Press, 1970.

[Department of Public Instruction, Lansing, Michigan] *The Treatment of Minority Groups in Textbooks.* Lansing, Michigan: Department of Public Instruction, 1963.

Trezise, Robert L. "The Black American in American History Textbooks." *Social Studies,* vol. 60 (April, 1969), pp. 164-67.

Turner, Richard C., and John A. Dewar. "Black History in Selected American History Textbooks." *Educational Leadership Research Supplement,* vol. 6 (February, 1973), pp. 441-44.

Ylvisaker, Miriam. "Our Guilt." *English Journal,* vol. 58 (February, 1969), pp. 193-95. [List of books by and about Afro-Americans.]

Zuercher, Roger. "The Treatment of Asian Minorities in American History Textbooks." *Indiana Social Studies Quarterly,* vol. 22 (Autumn, 1969), pp. 19-27.

XI. THE TEACHING PROFESSION

A. THE TEACHER

1. Teacher Roles in the Profession

Adelson, J. "The Teacher as a Model," in N. Sanford, ed. *The American College*. New York: John Wiley, 1962, pp. 396-417. Discusses barriers to understanding the topic of the teacher as a model. Proceeds to examine the concept of identification, the idea of accepting or resisting of models by students, the many sides to a good teacher, and finally—the anti-model and disappointing model.

Barzun, Jacques. *Teacher in America*. Boston: Little, Brown, 1945. Offers insight into the professional, scholarly, recreational, and human side of the teacher's life and work. Puts forth his views on general and specific issues related to the teacher's role.

Brooks, Rugg. *The Teacher in School and Society*. Yonkers-on-Hudson, New York: World, 1950. A broad outline and analysis of the teacher's role in the American culture and his profession and how to operate as a professional in the culture. Part I: The School in the American Culture offers material dealing with the teacher's relationships to American society. Part II: The Art of Teaching deals with the teacher's professional activities.

Burrup, Percey E. *The Teacher and the Public School System* New York: Harper and Row, 1967. Discusses the role of the teacher as a community voice on educational matters. The need for teachers to act professionally outside the classroom—especially in the community known to those supporting the school—is emphasized. Criteria offered for ethical relationships between the various people in the school system and the community.

Castle, E. B. *The Teacher*. New York: Oxford, 1970. Historical survey of teachers in relation to critical social and cultural realities of their time. Well-known individuals from each historical period are selected, and their teaching roles are illustrated in terms of political, social, and cultural results.

Chandler, B. J., Daniel Powell, and William Hazard. *Education and the New Teacher*. New York: Dodd, Mead, 1971. The first half deals with background material focusing on problems related to nature and organization of American public schools. The second part deals with professional issues such as who should teach, teacher preparation, the work of the teacher, and professional opportunities.

Goff, J. G., and R. C. Wilson. "The Teaching Environment." *AAUP Bulletin,* vol. 57 (1971), pp. 475-493. A survey of 1,085 faculty members at six institutions—a large state university, a large state college, a public junior college, a medium-sized private university, a small liberal arts college, and a small Protestant college. Results indicated that a large number of faculty considered their advisory role important. It also showed that faculty members considered teaching ability primary consideration for teaching rewards, and felt that quality of teaching was not presently given enough stress.

Greene, Maxine. *Teacher as Stranger*. Belmont, Calif.: Wadsworth, 1973. Indicates that first and foremost a "teacher" is one who modifies changes, or reinforces values and ideas of those in his or her charge. For this reason, regardless of the teacher's subject matter discipline, the professional educator must grapple with the issues of ideological systems, platforms, social theories, and current programs with his students. In other words, the teacher, in order to teach well, must "do philosophy."

Heald, James E., and Samuel A. Moore. *The Teacher and Administrative Relationships in School Systems*. New York: Macmillan, 1968. Presented in the book are a number of facets of a school system and how each relates to the other in terms of social, legal, economic, and political forces. Interactions between the various parts of school systems as they relate to the teacher's role are a valuable component of the book.

Heath, Louis G. *The New Teacher*. New York: Harper and Row, 1973. Considers the need to broaden the professional field to include members of the community in the sharing of educational responsibilities. Included are general predictions regarding the future problems of teachers.

Hilsum, Sidney. *The Teacher at Work*. New York: Fernhill, 1972. Summary of findings of a report in full in *The Teacher's Day, 1971,* in which 129 teachers were surveyed. How teachers spend their time, and how much time (working hours) is given to their professional duties, are major thrusts of the study.

Phelps, William F. *The Teacher's Hand-Book*. New York: A.S. Barnes, 1874. A nineteenth century view of the challenges facing the educator relative to the development of better citizens and statesmen with separate chapters offering advice to the instructor in specific areas and situations. Broader professional topics are included in the last two parts of the book.

Rafferty, Max. *Max Rafferty on Education*. New York: Devin-Adair, 1968. A well-known conservative educator discusses his views on a variety of educational topics in a traditional and common-sense manner. In the first section called "Educator's twelve Labors" he deals with general and current professional issues. In all there are thirteen groups of articles reflecting separate topics ranging from curriculum to extensive notices of the training of teachers.

Rosenthal, Alan. *Pedagogues and Power: Teacher Groups in School Politics*. Syracuse: Syracuse University Press, 1969. Study of orientations and activities of teacher groups, their role in influencing educational issues, and their impact on school politics. The author discusses relationships between certain levels of teacher affiliations as well as the characteristics and forces which help to shape and influence such groups.

Sterling, Philip, ed. *The Real Teachers*. New York: Random House, 1972. Collection of conversations with 30 inner-city public school classroom teachers. The conversations with a heterogeneous selection of teachers cover such topics as who they are, how they teach, and why they teach in a big city.

Strayer, George Drayton. *The Classroom Teacher at Work in American Schools*. New York: American Book, 1920. The book presents the responsible teacher, first as a figure affecting democratic society, and then as a professional with specific roles. Analyses of teaching types lead to information on the training and classification of pupils.

2. Teacher Personality and Behavior

Aspy, David N. *Toward a Technology for Humanizing Education*. Champaign, Ill.: Research Press, 1972. Discussion of various teacher behaviors as they relate to improved instruction. Attempts to provide teachers with tools for making class and classroom instruction more humane. Author defends the policy of involvement for teachers.

Ernst, Morris L. *The Teacher*. Englewood Cliffs, N.J.: Prentice-Hall, 1967. A collection of reminiscences of teachers and school experiences of twenty-six well-known figures. The stories recall human and professional traits as they were influential to the narrators or meaningful to the students of their time.

Hahn, Robert O. *Creative Teachers: Who Wants Them?* New York: Wiley, 1973. Describes the qualities of a creative teacher and then proceeds to narrate a series of experiences which reflect the difficulties and rewards of such a teacher. The book includes conflicts between a creative teacher and various individuals and forces traditionally identified as villains fighting against creative attitudes and methods in education.

Knoblock, Peter, and Arnold P. Goldstein. *The Lonely Teacher*.

Rockleigh, N.J.: Allyn and Bacon, 1971. Through the use of tapes, 17 conversational sessions with six teachers are related to teachers' feelings of loneliness, inadequacy, frustration, etc. Although the problem of loneliness, due to limited and impersonal peer relations as well as traditions affecting personal relationships, flows through the text, many other teacher-related issues are discussed.

Marsh, J. Frank. *The Teacher Outside the School.* Yonkers-on-Hudson, New York: World, 1928. A teacher's guide to success in matters affecting his happiness and satisfaction outside the school. The author directs the teacher to those means which can aid him in forming out-of-school contacts, activities, and habits beneficial to his over-all growth.

Natalicio, L. F. S., and C. F. Hereford, eds. *The Teacher as a Person.* Dubuque, Ia.: William C. Brown, 1971. Including authors as diverse as Skinner and Rogers, the editors have presented ten selections which deal with human personality as it relates to the teacher's role. The material could be used to motivate teachers and teacher-trainees to consider their own personality in terms of their professional role.

Ryans, David G. *Characteristics of Teachers.* Washington, D.C.: American Council on Education, 1960. A research study by the author and his colleagues of teacher traits and their relationship to teacher success in various situations.

Wilson, Charles H. *A Teacher is a Person.* New York: Henry Holt, 1956. In autobiographical form, travels through a variety of educational experiences making professional value judgments on educational issues and activities abstracted from his life. Though very subjective, the material represents an interesting view of a particular teacher as a person going through American life.

Zeigler, Harmon. *The Political Life of American Teachers.* Englewood Cliffs, N.J.: Prentice-Hall, 1967. Describes the behavior of teachers as teachers, and generalizes about the political inferences of teacher behavior. Distinguishes between male and female perceptions, and then investigates such topics as verbal mobility, teachers' associations, classroom politics, and finally—sanctions and the roots of fear.

3. Teacher Organization and Power

Bain, H. "Self-governance Must Come First, Then Accountability." *Phi Delta Kappan,* vol. 51 (1970), p. 413. Argues that before teachers are held accountable for teaching quality or learning standards, they must be given the legal power to make policy decisions relative to the standards of teaching.

Bourne, Richard, and Brian MacArthur. *A Struggle for Education, 1870-1970: A Pictorial History of Popular Education and the National*

Union of Teachers. New York: Philosophical Library, 1970. The record of NUT struggles for professional benefits and educational goals over a 100-year span. Along with photographs, press material, and graphs, the book includes introductory and summary essays for each section.

Braun, Robert J. *Teacher and Power.* New York: Simon and Schuster, 1972. A defense of professional control of education through organizations. The author, through an analysis of AFT's growing power in education, traces the effects of organized teacher power upon the status and quality of education.

Bruker, Robert M. "Color Me Humble." *The Clearing House,* vol. 42 (September, 1967), pp. 33-35. Points to the inadequacies of major professional organizations in education, and offers reasons for their weeknesses. The image of the profession and its lack of professional standards lead the author to recommend drastic actions for a more unified teaching profession.

Cole, Stephen. *The Unionization of Teachers.* New York: Praeger, 1969. An analysis of the growth of the teacher union movement in New York City along with a developmental study. The work touches upon problematic relationships between the educational profession, society, and other professions.

Edinger, Lois V. "Challenge of Professionalization." *The High School Journal,* vol. 51 (January, 1968), pp. 151-157. Discusses the threat to professionalism by non-professionals who control educational standards through state boards. The assertion is made that tradition, custom, and varied interests often influence the course and standards of education more than professional values. Calls for greater control of the decision-making process by teachers, and states that professional organizations can help bring about such a development.

Rand, M. John, and English Fenwick. "Towards a Differentiated Teaching Staff." *Phi Delta Kappan,* vol. 49 (January, 1968), pp. 164-168. Proposes a new system for renumerating teachers and criticizes the single salary schedule. Compensation would be considered in terms of responsibilities rather than just in terms of years of service. Predicts that a change away from the single salary schedule will come before long.

Schmid, William W. *Retirement Systems of the American Teacher.* New York: Fleet Academic Editions, 1971. Study of retirement systems in each of the 50 states. Crucial personnel issues such as financial operations and benefits for retired teachers, death and survivor benefits, are discussed.

4. Teachers' Rights and Academic Freedom

Dennison, Charles P. *Faculty Rights and Obligations.* New York: Bureau of Publications, Teachers College, Columbia, 1955. Outgrowth of a study made in eight colleges in order to determine how faculty rights might be realized through greater formal expression. The first chapter presents an academic bill of rights with related obligations; chapters two and three offer a comparison of the eight colleges studied and other selected colleges, and chapter four discusses the implications of the findings for college governance.

Fischer, Louis, and David Schimmel. *The Civil Rights of Teachers*. New York: Harper and Row, 1963. Deals with the protection of the teacher in his civil rights emphasizing the need to gain protection through better laws and institutions. Efforts to rid the profession of external restraints are discussed.

MacIver, Robert M. *Academic Freedom in Our Time*. New York: Columbia University Press, 1955. Written as a result of the American Academic Freedom Project. Discusses the climate of opinion in the 50's, the relationship between academic government and academic freedom, forces influencing academic freedom, and the problems of academic freedom as related to students. Recommendations are given at the end.

Metzger, Walter P. *Academic Freedom in the Age of the University*. New York: Columbia University Press, 1955. A view of the cultural, political, business, and philosophical forces which have threatened and do threaten academic freedom. Student freedom when affecting the course of professional freedom, is also discussed. The influences upon academic freedom are first presented in an historical manner.

Rubin, David. *The Rights of Teachers: The Basic ACLU Guide to a Teacher's Constitutional Rights*. New York: Baron, 1973. ACLU handbooks are a series on constitutional rights of special interest groups. The first of the series, and deals with three general areas: academic freedom, non-interference with freedoms of teachers in their private lives, and due process as it relates to the professional teacher.

United States Commission on Civil Rights (Bernard, B. I., ed.). *Civil Rights U.S.A., Public Schools: Cities in the North and West*. New York: Greenwood Press, 1962. Series of studies on civil rights cases involving school systems in the North and West. Reports to the commission include studies involving the civil rights of educators in Highland Park, Mich.; New Rochelle, N.Y.; Philadelphia, Pa.; Chicago, Ill.; and St. Louis, Mo.

Urofsky, Melvin I., ed. *Why Teachers Strike: Teachers' Rights and Community Control*. Garden City, New York: Doubleday, 1970. Written transcripts from tapes on various authorities involved in recent strike activities. Included in the work are transcripts by Mario Fantini, Albert Shanker, and others involved in the New York City strike. From the questions to and answers from these people, the reader learns about some of the causes and results of strike movements and related confrontations.

B. TEACHING

1. General Principles and Practices of Teaching

Allen, Charles R. *The Instructor, The Man and the Job*. Philadelphia: J. B. Lippincott, 1919. General outline of principles and practices for teaching in industrial situations. Tries to relate professional instructional methods to areas of trade learning in order to aid in effective industrial training.

Allen, Dwight W., and Eli Seifman, eds. *The Teacher's Handbook*. Glenview, Ill.: Scott, Foresman, 1971. Eighty-five authors have contributed essays especially for the handbook. The works cover a broad spectrum of topics valuable to both the new and experienced teacher. Much of the analytical data and descriptive material is a result of long research and gives specific information about methods, tools, programs and activities identified with the profession.

Bruner, Jerome S. *Toward a Theory of Instruction*. Cambridge: Harvard University Press, 1966. A collection of essays on various themes presented in a sequence designed to reflect certain theoretical bases of the learning process.

Foster, John, and Hugh Lytton. *Creativity and Education*. New York: Schocken, 1972. Tries to indicate just what the educational implications are from the research on creativity. The pervasive message in the text for educators is that teachers should "develop and extend a wide range, a veritable explosion of abilities."

Freeland, George E. *The Improvement of Teaching*. New York: Macmillan, 1924. After studying the activities and results of teachers judged to be successful by set criteria, sets forth procedures that can lead to more successful instruction. Specific descriptions of what good teachers do, and how they do it are offered in very concrete form.

Ginott, Haim. *Teacher and Child, A Book for Parents and Teachers*. New York: Macmillan, 1972. Offers tools and skills for dealing with daily situations and psychological problems faced by all teachers. Presents a great deal of information on the best and worst ways to communicate with, or relate to children in regard to specific desired results.

Grant, Barbara M., and Dorothy Grand Hennings. *The Teacher Moves*. New York: Teachers College Press, Teachers College, Columbia University, 1971. A study of factors, other than verbal, which influence teaching and learning in the classroom. The first part deals with description and analysis of teacher motions as they relate to the teacher's role, the teaching process, and the teaching style. The second part deals with ideas and recommendations related to the improvement of teacher motion for better instruction.

Green, Thomas F. *The Activities of Teaching*. New York: McGraw-Hill, 1971. Independent inquiries into the various philosophic or conceptual problems involved in the activities of teaching and learning. The emphasis is on analysis with special concern for linguistic analysis in relation to instruction. On teaching which stresses the correlation between analysis and the epistemological problems of instruction, this work is geared toward those who are looking for direct relationships between educational theory and instructional process. Green has written an important book which is directed to a synthesis of philosophic and conceptual problems. It is one of the best introductions to the relationship between instructional theory and process. See Hyman, *infra*.

Gruber, Frederick C., ed. *Teaching in America*. Forty-Third Annual Schoolmen's Week Proceedings. Philadelphia: University of Pennsylvania Press, 1956. A sampling of papers from the Schoolmen's Week proceedings including topics related to teaching in American schools. Specific instructional and role-playing problems are discussed under the headings of elementary and secondary education.

Haring, Norris G., and Alice H. Hayden, eds. *Improvement of Instruction*. Seattle, Washington: Special Child Publications, 1972. Compilation of papers concerned with the improvement of teaching through behavior modification. Using a theoretical framework of behavioristic values, the authors offer selections on teaching, decisions preceding teaching, and decisions based on the child's response to the environment.

Hosford, Philip L. *An Instructional Theory: A Beginning*. Englewood Cliffs, N.J.: Prentice-Hall, 1973. Presentation of an instructional theory followed by explanations of the theory as an operational concept and its implications. Included along with the author's theory are general criteria for the development of theory on instruction.

Hyman, Ronald T. *Ways of Teaching*. J. B. Lippincott, 2nd edition, 1974. A textual outgrowth of teaching experiences of the author, other teachers, and students. Covers the challenge of instruction first through a general overview and then through analysis of four methodological approaches. The overview stresses behavioral objectives and the three general areas of instructional processes are: discussion, recitation and lecture, role-playing, and questioning-observing-evaluating.

Joyce, Bruce R., and Berj Harootunian. *The Structure of Teaching*. Chicago: Science Research Associates, 1967. An introduction to teaching, presenting a complex of ideas to be used in analyzing and viewing the objectives and methods of teaching. Offers professional advice to the novice on the assumption that, as a successful teacher, he must be capable in five particular areas of teaching process, all defined in the first chapter.

Melvin, A. Gordon. *Teaching*. New York: John Day, 1944. A general teaching manual for those interested in variables influencing good instruction whether in kindergarten or the university.

Mosston, Muska. *Teaching: From Command to Discovery*. Belmont, Calif.: Wadsworth, 1972. Presents a variety of approaches and styles for teaching, giving sympathetic treatment to all. The different styles or approaches include "Command," "Individual Program," Guided Discovery," and others.

Putnam, Daniel. *Manual of Pedagogics*. New York: Silver, Burdett, 1895. An analysis of the general application of psychology to the science and art of teaching. General background on education and children leads to discussions about factors affecting the teacher's role in his professional relationship to the student.

Raub, Albert N. *Methods of Teaching: Including the Nature, Objectives, and Laws of Education, Methods of Instruction, and Methods of Culture*. Lock Haven, Pa.: E. L. Raub, 1884. Designed as a handbook as well as a text for use in Normal Schools, the book presents in praising terms practices of teaching which, according to the author, have proved successful while condemning those which seem impractical.

Russell, Charles. *Teaching for Tomorrow*. New York: Prentice-Hall, 1937. Presents theoretical, practical, evaluative material concerning the factors influencing learning process. Discusses how, why, when and what children learn; growth in skills, knowledge and ideals, and deals with both analytical material and recommendations.

Salmon, David. *The Art of Teaching*. New York: Longmans, Green, 1898. Deals with general principles related to instruction and teacher responsibility; general problems of order; attention and discipline; and specific instructional demands in academic and skill areas.

Siegel, Laurence, ed. *Instruction: Some Contemporary Viewpoints*. San Francisco: Chandler Publishing, 1967. Various authorities in educational psychology present theoretical positions in regard to instructional matters. Each contributor reflects the biases of the particular educator.

Strebel, Ralph F., and Grover C. Morehart. *The Nature and Meaning of Teaching*. New York: McGraw-Hill, 1929. Broad collection of professional devices, practices, and attitudes offered to the teaching novice in the simplest terms. Theory to subject matter, from general process to the smallest mechanism. The variables affecting good instruction.

Thorndike, Edward L. *The Principles of Teaching*. New York: A. G. Seiler, 1916. Scientific and pragmatic approach to the study of teaching. Offers a comprehensive view of the cultural, psychological, and scientific factors influencing the teaching process.

Wellington, C. Burleigh, and Jean Wellington. *Teaching for Critical*

Thinking. New York: McGraw-Hill, 1960. Not insisting on one approach, or one method other than a concern for democracy, indicates that good teaching is more a matter of talent through study and effort. A true professional discovers and develops which aim of teaching should be emphasized; then—through experience and careful analysis—he learns which methods and approaches are essential to fulfill that aim. Offers general ideas regarding critical thinking for talent development, and offers specific techniques that should be helpful to the "thinking teacher."

Wiles, Kimball. *Teaching for Better Schools.* Englewood Cliffs, N.J.: Prentice—Hall, 1959. Discusses different phases of good teaching in an attempt to assist the teacher in the task of relating worthwhile personal-life qualities to certain teaching qualities. Recognizing that teachers rarely excel in all teaching attributes, discusses various types of "quality teaching" so that each teacher can work on a type which complements his own practices and goals.

Yamamoto, Kaorie. *Teaching.* New York: Houghton Mifflin, 1969. Group of essays and readings on subjects related to good teaching. On the "why," "who," "whom," "when and where," "what," "how," and "how well" of teaching.

2. Criticism and Reform in Teaching Practices and Goals

Cantor, Nathaniel. *Dynamics of Learning.* New York: Agathon, 1972. Emphasizes the negative or weak points in American public education, especially at the level of higher education. After indicating the problems relative to such weaknesses, goes on to offer plans for the improvement of the instructional process. Attacks the emphasis in schools upon knowledge gathering for its own sake.

Cremin, Lawrence A. *The Genius of American Education.* Pittsburgh: University of Pittsburgh Press, 1965. A landmark book. Discusses the purpose behind American educational structures and methods. Makes a defense for universal education in the Jeffersonian tradition, and takes an optimistic view as to the results in terms of learning for a better society and for a better graduate.

Drews, Elizabeth Monroe. *Learning Together: How to Foster Creativity, Self-Fulfillment, and Social Awareness in Today's Students and Teachers.* Englewood Cliffs: Prentice-Hall, 1972. Presents the irrelevancies of present compartmentalized, educational processes. Recommending an interdependent exchange of ideas, proposes an alternative to those who feel frustrated by the lack of creativity in education. Offers suggestions for the development of creativity in teachers as well as new possibilities for a more liberated instruction of pupils.

Eble, Kenneth E. *Professors as Teachers.* San Francisco: Jossey-Bass, 1972. A reflection on the author's participation in the Project to Improve

College Teaching (1969-1971). Studied the recognition and evaluation of teaching, the career development of effective college teachers, and the development of good working conditions for effective teaching. Many disturbing findings included as well as conclusions neither good nor bad concerning the status and performance of professors.

Freire, Paulo. *Pedagogy of the Oppressed*. New York: Herder and Herder, 1970. Radical educational approach to cultural revolution. Directs the reader to certain pedagogical methods for freeing the oppressed from the intellectual and material chains which those in power have imposed upon them. Teaching methods are seen as fruitful only when acting as a liberating force.

Hart, Leslie. *The Classroom Disaster*. New York: Teachers College Press, Teachers College, Columbia University, 1969. Intended for professionals, pre-professionals, and citizens interested in education. Re-examines the teacher-and-class arrangement in America. Tries to convince the professionals and interested laymen that an alternative to the "covered-wagon" approaches to learning must be developed. Has an appendix containing sampling of American schools which have instituted innovations.

Holt, John Caldwell. *Freedom and Beyond*. New York: E. P. Dutton, 1972. Searches for reasons why the educational structures and methods are not freedom-oriented even when, in theory, the educators believe in an educational process of liberation. After analyzing the problems related to freedom and choice, delves into the schooling process as potential for freedom. Looks beyond the schools to society and leaders to find forces which can aid in the cause of education for freedom.

Holt, John Caldwell. *How Children Fail*. New York: Pitman, 1964. Assertion that most children fail in school in varying degrees and in different ways. Feels failure is due to fear, boredom, and confusion. Talks of a strategy to deal with these factors. Separate chapters on "Fear and Failure," "Real Learning," and "How the Schools Fail."

Lembo, John M. *Why Teachers Fail*. Columbus, Ohio: Charles E. Merrill, 1971. Along with various educational practices that supposedly limit the instructional process, attacks basic causes related to faulty practice. Purports that the root of trouble lies in misconception that students have to be coerced in regard to subject matter and school or learning activities. Thinks it would be better if educators were to concentrate more on the uniqueness of the learner, rather than on the need to direct the learner toward successful competition, greater efficiency, and irrelevant standards.

Leonard, George Barr. *Education and Ecstasy*. New York: Delacorte Press, 1968. After a brief overview of education illustrated by thorough glimpses of the teacher, the classroom, the principal, and the institution, reaches for the great potential of education as a force for making life and learning more complementary and more joyous. Offers practical suggestions based upon happenings in innovative schools, brain-research laboratories, and experimental communities.

Rafferty, Max. *Suffer Little Children.* New York: Devin-Adair Co., 1962. Alarmed about various negative forces affecting teaching, proposes new departures and techniques, including leadership schools for the gifted, and for those who are uneducable.

Reeder, Edwin Hewett. *Simplifying Teaching.* New York: Laidlaw, 1929. Calls for the simplification of the educational system aiding the learning process. Attention is given to adverse effects of language complexity upon instruction. Multiplication of technical expressions and lack of understanding behind language used are two of the problems discussed.

Richmond, W. Kenneth. *The Teaching Revolution.* London: Methuen, 1967. After outlining the various factors which precipitated the modern educational revolution, analyzes various fresh approaches which have developed from this revolution. New concepts of educational goals, team teaching practices, new approaches to subject matter, and new teaching aids are among the modern outcomes discussed.

Ruediger, William Carl. *Vitalized Teaching.* Cambridge: Riverside Press, 1923. Attacks the attempt to make schools a complete reproduction of the outer world, yet warns against the tendency of schools to become artificial. Advises the teacher to revitalize education on a balance of realistic and naturalistic procedures. Divided into three parts: the problem of verbalism; exhibiting subject matter; and enlisting the activities of pupils.

Ryan, Kevin, and James M. Cooper. *Those Who Can, Teach.* Boston: Houghton Mifflin, 1972. After an investigation of schools, school life, instruction and curriculum, focuses on the teacher and his instructional challenges. Contemporary issues in teaching such as accountability, performance, contracting, and open classrooms are discussed.

Sanderlin, Orvenita. *Creative Teaching.* New York: A. S. Barnes, 1971. A criticism of certain facets of American schools and American instruction. Tries to acquaint the reader with alleviative settings and methods which could result in a more creative system of education.

Schroder, Harold M., Marvin Karlins, and Jacqueline O. Phares. *Education for Freedom.* New York: Wiley, 1973. Claims that the task of teachers is to cultivate in students the ability to seek and form new information, to make the most of new relationships, and to be "flexible and adaptive." Using case studies to illustrate theories, indicates how methods, curriculum, and teacher pupil relations can be positively related to these goals.

Silberman, C. E. *Crisis in the Classroom.* New York: Random House, 1970. Using the results of a study commissioned by the Carnegie Corp. of New York, explains how and why many American schools are failing to offer teaching in a manner that leads to change, value formation, or meaningful relationships and goals. Too much time is devoted to teaching efficiently and not enough time to teaching for a better humanity.

Thatcher, David A. *Teaching, Loving, and Self-Directed Learning.* Pacific Palisades, California: Goodyear, 1973. Text for those who wish to become more capable as classroom guides for independent, self-directed learning. Stresses the relationship between interpersonal relations and individual achievement, and presents material through an anecdotal style.

Tumin, Melvin. "Teaching in America." *Childhood Education,* vol. 44 (February, 1968), pp. 347-353. Criticizes the general competitive nature of schooling in America and states the need for greater emphasis on certain qualities in teacher education which would move schooling toward a less competitive and negative pattern. Teachers must develop a commitment to the equal rights of pupils, a desire to be professionally competent, a grasp of professional knowledge relating to curricular goals, and a commitment to continue educational and professional growth.

3. Innovational Approaches to Teaching

Barth, Roland S. *Open Education and the American School.* New York: Agathon, 1972. A general synthesis of theories and practices related to the open school. Devotes a chapter to the role of the teacher in the open classroom. Teaching techniques of the open school are also discussed especially in the light of certain assumptions about learning and knowledge held by open school advocates.

Borg, W. R., *et al. The Minicourse: A Micro-teaching Approach to Teacher Education.* Beverly Hills, California: Macmillan Educational Services, 1970. Descriptive material on completely developed form of micro-teaching instruction. Includes a series of mini-courses, described in detail with reports on empirical results.

Dunlop, Richard S. "Toward Improved Professional Practice Under Flexible-Modular Scheduling." *The Journal of Teacher Education,* vol. 19 (Summer, 1968), pp. 159-164. Recommends modular scheduling and greater flexibility in general in regard to teachers' schedules. Proposes that greater independence in use of time will improve communication between all school personnel, in spite of the fact that certain resistance will come from older conservative teachers.

Gingell, Lesley P. *The ABC's of the Open Classroom.* Homewood, Ill.: ETC Publications, 1973. Analysis of teaching methods used in the open schools, including samples of instructional situations involving young students, mostly 9-11. Comparisons made between open school teaching in America and England.

Goldhammer, R. *Clinical Supervision*. New York: Holt, Rinehart, and Winston, 1969. Discusses the contract plan in which teachers can participate in analysis of instruction. Teacher competency judged by the results of teaching rather than by "preferred methods."

Hanna, Lavone A., *et al. Unit Teaching in the Elementary Schools*. New York: Holt, Rinehart, and Winston, 1963. Application of modern educational theory to actual classroom situations. General merits of unit teaching are explained in the light of recent findings and developments.

Holtzman, Wayne H., ed. *Computer-Assisted Instruction, Testing and Guidance*. New York: Harper and Row, 1970. Based on papers prepared for a conference at the University of Texas, 1968. Discusses the implications of computer teaching, testing, and counseling. Some of the contributors defend programs for computer application while others question the value of such a commitment to technology in education.

Hough, J. B., and B. Revsin. "Programmed Instruction at the College Level: A Study of Several Factors Influencing Learning." *Phi Beta Kappa*, vol.44 (1963), pp. 286-291. Compares effects of various types of programmed instruction for prospective teachers. No significant differences were found in overall achievement between those using different materials. Though some preference for teaching machines rather than books became evident, the preference was not strong enough to justify the greater expense of such machines.

Johnson, J. A. "What's New in Teaching." *Illinois Education*, vol. 56 (April, 1968), pp. 328-330. An outline of various innovative approaches to teacher education found in a number of Illinois teacher education institutions. Included are such areas as micro-teaching, simulation, outdoor education, and video-taping of student teachers.

Kapfer, Philip G., and Miriam B. Kapfer, eds. *Learning Packages in American Education*. Englewood Cliffs, N.J.: Educational Technology, 1972. Collection of 21 essays on programs for teaching and learning. Though varied in organizational make-up, the packages do reflect a positive outlook toward individualization of instruction, pre- and post-testing, concern for cognitive behavior, and competency-based objectives.

Lange, Phil C., ed. Programmed Instruction. *The Sixty-sixth Yearbook of the National Society for the Study of Education*. Part II. Chicago: University of Chicago Press, 1967. Materials from which to fashion a balanced, constructive, and comprehensive understanding of the theory and practice of programmed instruction. Section I deals with the Foundations of Instructional Programming; Section II with Program

Development, and Section III with Issues and Problems Related to Programmed Instruction.

Levien, Roger E., ed. *The Emerging Technology: Instructional Uses of the Computer in Higher Education*. New York: McGraw-Hill, 1972. On the use of computers in higher education. Describes the growth of campus computing in research, instruction, administration, and library science. Focuses on instruction about and by means of computers, and provides a basis for forecasting the prospects for instructional computing.

Lillard, Paula Polk. *Montessori: A Modern Approach*. New York: Schocken Books, 1972. Critical analysis of the basic theories and practices of Montessori. Relationship between Montessori theory and Montessori practice, and relationship between the Montessori approach and contemporary issues are important emphases.

Martin, Jane R. *Explaining Understanding, and Teaching*. New York: McGraw-Hill, 1970. Analytical and philosophical approach to presentation of materials and concepts for the attainment of understanding. Part I: covers William Dray's historical views with preferences for more pragmatic interpretations. Part II: gap-filling, question-answering, reason-giving, and linguistic view of teaching are explained and defined. Part III: considers two views of understanding. Part IV: explaining and understanding are related to education.

Menaske, Louis, and Ronald Radosh. *Teach-ins, U.S.A.* New York: Praeger, 1967. Reports on American teach-ins with documents and opinions.

4. Teaching Experiences and Problems

Ashton-Warner, Sylvia. *Spearpoint: Teacher in America*. New York: Knopf, 1972. Description of direction of instruction at a new Colorado school. The author's methods which proceed from the theory that staff, parents and children are all equal, are presented in an honest manner admitting to the unsuccessful experiences without losing the reader's interest in the possible validity of approach.

Dreeben, Robert. *The Nature of Teaching*. Glenview, Ill: Scott, Foresman, 1970. Instead of invitational euphemisms on teaching or theoretical approaches to teaching, presents teaching as it is and as it may become. Is designed to increase understanding of the teacher's work-a-day world with its various occupational influences.

Faunce, Roland C., and Morrel J. Clute. *Teaching and Learning in the Junior High School*. Belmont, Calif.: Wadsworth, 1961. Learning process explained in terms of particular junior high school problems. Development and organization of the senior high presented as a basis of understanding. Describes the particular qualities of junior high age groups as they affect the learning process. A number of professional topics such as student activities, school-parent relationships and guidance, are discussed against the background of adolescent needs and aspirations. Emphasis is placed upon teaching activities within the scope of these topics.

Hershey, Myrless. *Teacher Was a White Witch*. Philadelphia: Westminster, 1973. Recalls the struggles, failures, and successes of a white teacher in a black ghetto school. Gives many examples of approaches and techniques which may help.

Kaufman, Bea. *Up the Down Staircase*. Englewood Cliffs, N.J.: Prentice-Hall, 1964. Best-selling novel about a teacher in daily conflicts with personal and institutional factors which tend to block good instruction. Teaching experiences, told through a variety of forms, many of which represent means of communications in school, ring true primarily because they reflect real-life experiences.

O'Shea, M. V. *Everyday Problems in Teaching*. Indianapolis: Bobbs-Merrill, 1912. Offers concrete examples of teaching practices with discussion of the principles involved. Problems of attaining discipline, motivating pupils to "think and to execute" are illustrated through observations of actual instructional situations.

Otty, Nicolas. *Learner Teacher*. Baltimore: Penguin, 1972. Written in diary form, recalls experiences over two years as a teacher intern. Accounts of teaching assignments center on personal accountability for students' success and failures. Tells about assignments as a learner in this British teacher-training program which stresses development of technical abilities and understanding of problems related to the instructional process.

5. Teaching and Evaluation

Ingils, C. R. "Let's Do Away with Teacher Evaluation." *The Clearing House,* vol. 44 (1970), pp. 451-456. Analysis of teacher evaluation program in 70 districts in 38 states. Findings indicate common purposes and common weaknesses among the teacher evaluation programs.

Miller, Richard I. *Evaluating Faculty Performance*. San Francisco: Jossey-Bass, 1972. Examination of the problems related to evaluation of faculty performance. Deals with trends and forces affecting the cause of faculty evaluation such as unionization and concern for accountability; deals specifically with the teacher and the means of evaluation. The evaluating process for educational roles other than classroom teaching as well as over-all evaluation.

Sciara, Frank J., and Richard K. Janta, eds. *Accountability in American Education*. Boston: Allyn and Bacon, 1972. Selection of writings on the theoretical justifications and attacks on accountability. Information on measurements related to accountability. Traces the ideological and practical development of teacher accountability without avoiding such issues as "threat to teacher autonomy" or "safeguarding the taxpayer's pockets."

Spaights, E. "Students Appraise Teachers' Methods and Attitudes." *Improving College and University Teaching,* vol. 15 (1967), pp. 15-17. Correlation study of student ratings of teachers' characteristics and student achievement. High achievers did not feel teachers were aloof; whereas low achievers felt they were.

Stone, Richard. *The Good Teacher: How Teachers Judge Teachers.* New York: Philosophical Library, 1970. What makes a good teacher in the opinion of those who are supposed to know best—professional teachers. How teachers in a specific school system judged teacher quality as an indication of what some teachers admire in their colleagues.

Strom, Robert D., and Charles Gallaway. "Becoming a Better Teacher." *The Journal of Teacher Education,* vol. 18 (Fall, 1967), pp. 285-292. The present criteria used to define good teaching are attacked as invalid for the identification of good teachers. Suggests that the attempts to identify good teachers have been too objective, too academic, or too impersonal. A more personal, human, and partially subjective assessment might present a more honest appraisal of the teacher as successful professional.

Tuckman, B. W., K. M. McCall, and R. T. Hyman. "The Modification of Teacher Behavior: Effects of Dissonance and Coded Feedback." *American Educational Research Journal,* vol. 6 (1969), pp. 607-619. Asserts that verbal feedback from an outside source must be communicated to the teacher in order to bring about change in a teacher's classroom behavior. Self-observation, if it is to contribute to change, must be combined with verbal feedback from another person, preferably at the professional level of the teacher in question.

C. TEACHER EDUCATION

1. General Scope and Status of Teacher Education

Anderson, Dan W. *Competency Based Teacher Education.* Berkeley, California: McCutchan, 1973. Collection of thought of the original model project directors of the U.S. Office of Education's Elementary Teacher Education Models Program. Provides opinions of the status and promises of the Competency Based Teacher Education Movement.

Bereday, George Z., and Joseph A. Lauwerys. *The Education and Training of Teachers.* The Yearbook of Education, 1963. New York: Harcourt, Brace and World, 1963. Extensive analysis of teacher education encompassing background scope and organization of the field, as well as the social and economic problems involved. Deals with experimentation in teacher education.

Borrowman, Merle L. *The Liberal and Technical in Teacher Education.* New York: Teachers College, 1956. Problem-oriented study of teacher education focusing on the search for balance between two educational functions. Historical presentation starting with issues prior to 1865 and ending with "New Guides to Teacher Education, 1930-1952."

Fen, Sing-Nan. "Professional and Liberal Education of Teachers." *Peabody Journal of Education,* vol. 45 (November, 1967), pp. 158-161. Discusses the relationship between liberal education and the successful application of methods to academic material. Worth of teacher is related to ability to use methods for relevant and useful ends.

Fund for the Advancement of Education. *Teachers for Tomorrow.* New York: Fund for the Advancement of Education, Bulletin No. 2, Nov., 1955. Analytical data on the population and institutions as they relate to the education of teachers. Statistical information in chart form included to illustrate status of certain variables related to teacher education. Isolates particular problems in the field of teacher education and clarifies the prognosis of such problems through data gathered from a variety of reports.

Glenman, T. Keith, and Irwin T. Sanders. "Education and World Affairs," in *The Professional School and World Affairs.* New York: The Committee, 1967. In a report on the role of teacher education in strengthening education as a force related to world affairs, data were compiled on policies of teacher education institutions, characteristics of teacher education programs, and viewpoints of selected authorities toward certain related professional issues.

Haberman, Martin, and T. M. Stinnett. *Teacher Education and the New Profession of Teaching.* Berkeley, Calif.: McCutchan, 1973. Analysis of criteria for deciding which proposals for teacher education make sense. Looks at the selection process in teacher education as well as the various facets of teacher education programs as they confront those who are being admitted as future teachers. Also considered are the areas of teacher education research, teacher education evaluation, and teacher education accreditation.

Johnson, J. S. "Change in Student Teacher Dogmatism." *The Journal of Education Research,* vol. 62 (1969), pp. 224-226. Using Rokeach's scale, an attempt was made to determine whether or not a degree of dogmatism of supervising teachers affects the change in dogmatism of student teachers. Within a population of 80 student teachers and 80 supervisors, a significant influence upon student change was noted.

Lane, R. U. "Toward the Improvement of Teacher Education." *Illinois*

School Journal, vol. 48 (Spring, 1968), pp. 9-15. Analysis of general educational problems as they relate to the improvement of teacher education. Considerations of the social, personal, and professional status of teachers are included. Recommends the establishment of an educational development group in teacher education institutions.

Monroe, Walter S. *Teaching-Learning Theory and Teacher Education 1890 to 1950.* New York: Greenwood Press, 1952. Appraisal of the present status of teaching through a view of the teacher education development in America. Tries to explain how approaches, methods, and attitudes have changed and will change in relationship to values, theories, and practices found in teacher education.

Nineteenth Annual Indiana Teacher Education Workshop. "Pressure Groups and Political Forces in Teacher Education." *Teachers College Journal,* vol. 39 (October, 1967), pp. 5-18. Variety of articles which deal with teacher education as it is influenced by certain social and political forces. Federal, state, and local levels of influence are covered.

Peik, W. E. *The Professional Education of High School Teachers.* Minneapolis: University of Minnesota Press, 1930. Critical analysis of teacher education programs and courses from data gathered from judgments of professionals as well as from instruments designed to elicit objective information. Teacher concerns included in the analysis of training as they relate to instructional problems.

Richey, Robert W. *Planning for Teaching.* New York: McGraw-Hill, 1952. An aid to teacher education-institutions in their attempt to prepare future teachers; introduces pre-professionals to the field of education. Focuses upon three concepts: planning a career in education, the competencies required for teaching, and the function of education in democracy.

Rosner, Benjamin (chairman). *The Power of Competency-Based Teacher Education: A Report.* Boston: Allyn and Bacon, 1972. Presents insights and ideas for the improvement of teacher education programs. Members from the Committee on National Program Priorities in Teacher Education offer recommendations in a number of areas in which teacher education can be improved through competency-based principles.

Sebaly, A. L., ed. *Teacher Education and Religion.* Oneonta, New York: The American Association of Colleges for Teacher Education, 1959. The place of religion in a teacher education program as well as the relationship between teacher education and religious values. Specific information is offered on separate areas of teaching such as humanities, social science and natural science.

Smith, E. Brooks, *et al.,* eds. *Partnership in Teacher Education.* Washington: The American Association of Colleges for Teacher Education and The Association for Student Teaching, 1966. Report of the 1966

Workshop-Symposium on "School-College Partnerships in Teacher Education." Presents additional relevant thinking considered vital to the continued refinement of concepts of partnership programs in teacher education.

Starbird, Richard O., and Frederick Ellis. "Excellence in Education Courses." *Improving College and University Teaching*, vol. 16 (Spring, 1968), pp. 128-130. Explains how many teacher education courses are being improved after many years of criticism from other disciplines and from members of the profession. Certain significant facets of professional education are examined with suggestions for bridging theory and practice in graduate and independent courses.

Steeves, Frank L. *Issues in Student Teaching: A Casebook with Related Problems in Teacher Education*. New York: Odyssey, 1963. Description of the case study as a method for teaching and learning; also analyzes organizational and supervisory problems in teacher education. Makes suggestions for group procedures in the student teaching process and in the evaluative process.

Stiles, Lindley J., *et al. Teacher Education in the United States*. New York: Ronald, 1960. Designed to aid in the achievement of excellence in teacher education programs. Describes the status of American teacher education in concise but comprehensive terms. Virtually every issue and every area of teacher education from student teaching to post-graduate teacher education is explored, and presented in factual and descriptive terms.

Taylor, Harold. *The World and the American Teacher*. Washington: The American Association of Colleges for Teacher Education, 1968. Examination of teacher education in area of world affairs. After analyzing the various problems related to teaching about world society, concludes with both general and specific recommendations for professional educators in attempts to be influential in developing citizens with greater consciousness of world-wide interactions. The benefit of an international perspective for teachers, and the need to change teacher education in a manner that more practically includes broad cultural views also reflected in recommendations.

Weldon, Lynn L. "Is Teacher Education an Illusion?" *The Journal of Teacher Education*, vol. 19 (Summer, 1968), pp. 193-196. Development of graduate occupational programs to take place of present teacher training programs is offered as an alternative which could eliminate the arguments between liberal arts and teacher education as to which offers better road to effective teaching.

2. Criticism, Controversy, and Reform in Teacher Education

American Association of Colleges for Teacher Education. *Teacher*

Education: Issues and Innovations. Washington: The Association, 1968. Presentation of the papers from the annual meeting of the AACTE. Material includes the possible influences of the federal government on educational practices and policies with indications of positive developments in teacher education through institutional evolution.

Armstrong, W. E. "Further Education of Teachers in Service." *The Journal of Teacher Education,* vol. 19 (Spring, 1968), pp. 33-38. Asserting that too much pressure is placed upon educational institutions to provide graduate and in-service opportunities for teachers, recommends certain practical changes in policy to make the in-service challenge easier to bear.

Burkhart, Robert C., and Hugh M. Neil. *Identity and Teacher Learning.* Scranton, Pennsylvania: International, 1968. Asserts that teachers would experience better professional growth with more self-evaluation, self-reflection and less coercion from educational authorities. In order to bring the excitement of learning to the class, teacher must first be excited about learning.

Cardozier, V. R. "Preparing College Teachers." *Improving College and University Teaching,* vol. 16 (Spring, 1968), pp. 131-133. Contends that while future college teachers are prepared in subject matter and in methods of research, they are lacking in preparation so far as teaching methodology is concerned.

Combs, Arthur. "Teacher Education: A Problem in Becoming." *Partnership in Teacher Education.* Washington: American Association of Colleges for Teacher Education and Association for Student Teaching, 1968. Emphasizes the value of self-growth as an effective means of improving one's professional stature and ability. Indicates that the focus has been too much on how to teach rather than how to become teachers or educators.

Cordasco, Francesco. "Reforming Teacher Education in the 1970's." *Intellect,* vol. 101 (March, 1973), pp. 381-384. Presents a five-point reformative schema dealing with a national teacher education foundation, direct support for pre-service education, direct support for in-service education, course content improvement, and project-oriented research.

Etten, John F. "Expanding the School Plant for Teacher Education Facilities." *Education,* vol. 88 (February-March, 1968), pp. 238-240. To attain maximum use of new teaching materials and resources, school plants should be expanded. States a need for greater cooperation between architects who plan schools, and educators who know what schools will need in terms of plant space and material.

Fox, Willard. "Let's Not Train Teachers." *Improving College and University Teaching,* vol. 16 (Spring, 1968), p. 113. A shift of emphasis in teacher education from "training" to "preparation." Feels that the word "preparation" and what it implies more suitably represents what teacher education should be.

Hodenfield, G. K., and T. M. Stinnett. *The Education of Teachers*. Englewood Cliffs, N.J.: Prentice-Hall, 1961. Presentation of conflicts arising midst the development of teacher education institutions. The issues surrounding higher education and the preparation of teachers are revealed through an analysis of three national conferences between 1958 and 1960.

Horn, Francis. "Teachers in Step with the New World." *The Record,* vol. 69 (March, 1968), pp. 569-580. Makes certain educational recommendations designed to alleviate problems of an advanced industrial society. For those enrolled in teacher education programs, advocates first-hand experience in unfamiliar cultural settings and travel outside the United States.

Hostrop, Richard W. "International Experience in Teacher Education." *Phi Delta Kappan,* vol. 49 (December, 1967), pp. 227-230. Report on reactions of Japanese student teachers to the American schools to which they were assigned in the Tokyo area. Lack of moral instruction and the grouping of children seemed to bother the Japanese student teachers.

Joyce, Bruce, and Marshall Weil, eds. *Perspectives for Reform in Teacher Education*. Englewood Cliffs, N.J.: Prentice-Hall, 1972. Analysis of the foundations upon which the Columbia Teachers College model for teacher education was built. Besides identifying the major problems involved in the education and training of teachers, indicates certain directions reform in teacher education should take.

King, Edmond J. *The Education of Teachers: A Comparative Analysis*. New York: Holt, Rinehart, and Winston, 1971. Calls for the universal consideration of challenges and issues of teacher preparation and how teacher training is related to the education of man and man's future. Offers scholarly information on the relationship between teaching principles and cultural and professional outcomes in various countries.

Klopf, Gordan J., and Garda W. Bowman. *Teacher Education in a Social Context*. New York: Mental Health Materials Center, 1966. Study on the preparation of school personnel for working with disadvantaged pupils. Offers provocative profiles on programs which have implications for teacher education.

Openshaw, M. Karl. "Research in Teaching." *Partnership in Teacher Education*. Washington: American Association of Colleges for Teacher Education, 1968. Relates general knowledge growth to behavior changes in teachers. Claims that teachers, in order to promote learning in students, must first develop behavior patterns which hold potential intellectual growth when put in contact with others. Teacher education can be valid only when the knowledge gained in such programs has specific use for teachers in the classroom. Does not feel that education, as a discipline, can be as broad as a general liberal arts program.

Pearl, A., *et al.* "Opinions Differ on Teacher Education." *National Education Association Journal,* vol. 57 (May, 1968), pp. 14-18. Two positions on the status of teacher education are offered. Indicates that we are failing in the preparation of teachers because of attempts to broaden professional responsibilities beyond the point of relevance or efficiency. A great deal of important development is neglected. Defends the changes which have taken place in American schools as positive forces affecting teacher education.

Sarason, Seymour B., *et al. The Preparation of Teachers: An Unstudied Problem in Education.* New York: Wiley, 1962. Charges that teacher education procedures are and have been irrelevant to the actual teaching task. This irrelevancy in teacher preparation has been the source of certain educational problems which have caused controversies. Discusses the irrelevancies, problems, and controversies, and examines the educational implications.

Smith, E. Brooks. "Teacher Education: Joint Responsibility." *National Education Association Journal,* vol. 57 (May, 1968), pp. 19-20. Asserts that greater cooperation is needed between schools and colleges in order to provide a realistic and relevant preparation for teachers. Some autonomous authority not completely tied to either institution is offered as a solution to either institution giving less than total commitment to the program.

Stone, J. C. "Reform or Rebirth?" *National Education Association Journal,* vol. 57 (May, 1968), pp. 23-25. A criticism of past and present ties between public schools and teacher education institutions. Failure in achieving real change for excellence in teacher education is related to the inhibiting forces of the culture which have traditionally influenced the public schools and teacher training institutions. A new institutional structure is recommended.

3. Teacher Education Conferences and Reports

Armstrong, W. Earl, *et al. The College and Teacher Education.* Washington: American Council on Education, 1944. Report of a cooperative study of special efforts to improve teacher education at a representative sample of American colleges. Describes the Commission's work, the activities in affiliated centers, and sets forth interpretations and conclusions.

Bigelow, Donald N., ed. *The Liberal Arts and Teacher Education: A Confrontation.* Lincoln: University of Nebraska Press, 1971. Conference held at the time of Kent State events. Records confrontations between liberal arts promoters and the defenders of teacher education. Addresses and reports are included.

Brown, Bob Burton, and Tom R. Vickery. "Belief Gap in Teacher Education." *Journal of Teacher Education,* vol. 18 (Winter, 1967), pp. 417-422. Four-year study of the differences between teacher performance and teacher preparation. Gap between goals and values of some practitioners and the goals and values of education professors is particularly noted.

Conant, James B. *The Education of American Teachers.* New York: McGraw-Hill, 1963. Two-year study of certification policies and teacher-training programs in America with certain proposals for radical alteration in teacher education.

Cottrell, Donald P., ed. *Teacher Education for a Free People.* Oneonta, New York: The American Association of Colleges for Teacher Education, 1956. An outgrowth of the institutional self-study program of the American Association of Colleges for Teacher Education, 1952-1954. Assuming that teacher education in America must be related to democratic goals and customs, suggests principles, policies, and concrete programs considered worthy for the improvement of teacher education.

Elam, Stanley, ed. *Improving Teacher Education in the United States.* Bloomington, Ind.: Phi Delta Kappa, Inc., 1967. A report of the symposium of Phi Delta Kappa to examine certain problems of teacher education in the United States. Teacher education is considered in developmental, environmental and problematic terms.

Ellis, Harlan Reed, II. "Education Professions Development Act." *American Education,* vol. 9 (October, 1967), pp. 20-21. Report on 1967 legislation to coordinate federal programs in teacher education with workable flexible plans. Deals with provisions for professional in-service and graduate training programs.

Emmer, E. T., *et al. The Effect of Feedback Expectancy on Teacher Trainees' Preferences for Teaching Styles.* R and D Report Series No. 29, Austin, Texas: The University of Texas, The Research and Development Center for Teacher Education, 1970. Experimental study of 44 teacher education students taken through a three-stage process simulated teaching experience, and instructional contacts with black and Mexican volunteer students were included. Five facets of teacher performance were measured through the process.

Sharp, Alexander. "Intensive Teacher Training Program." *The Urban Review,* vol. 2 (December, 1967), p. 2. Description of New York City teacher training experiment which was to prepare teachers in seven weeks. Difficulties are discussed and the facets of the program are assessed.

Meeting of competency objectives were not necessarily more correlative to the special training methods than to the experience of teaching in general.

Smith, B. Othanel, ed. *Research in Teacher Education.* Englewood Cliffs, N.J.: Prentice-Hall, 1971. Summary report on American Educational Research Association symposium. Issues and problems discussed focus on the preparation of teachers, especially in terms of teacher behavior, and student growth in relationship to teacher performance criteria.

Stiles, Lindley J., and Fred D. Carver. "Who Makes Policy for Teacher Education? *The Record,* vol. 69 (December, 1967), pp. 209-211. Survey on data concerning who participates in and affects teacher education policies and practices. Indicates a shared responsibility between liberal arts professors and education professors. Recommendations in higher education favor shared responsibility through interdisciplinary approaches.

Woodring, Paul. *New Directions in Teacher Education.* New York: Fund for the Advancement of Education, 1957. Report on projects in teacher education supported by the Fund for the Advancement of Education. Presents the Fund's general outlook, as well as the stance of general traditional thought on American teacher education. Current projects and difficulties of evaluating projects and programs are discussed culminating with final look at the future.

4. Teacher Education and Student Teaching

Carpenter, E. B., and W. Guess. "Student Teachers Are People Too!" *Business Education World,* vol. 48 (January, 1968), pp. 29-30. Indicates that the possibility of effective student teaching is significantly weakened by the fact that student teachers are not accepted as regular faculty members. Various areas of professional "discrimination" are discussed in light of greater advantages for regular faculty.

Jordan, Archie C. "Improving Student Teacher Evaluation." *Peabody Journal of Education,* vol. 45 (November, 1967), pp. 139-142. Seven-part plan is projected for improved student teaching. First step suggested is to write the basic goals and objectives of the program. Other logical steps follow concluding with the recommendation that a final evaluation be made with two functions: attainment of a course grade for academic purposes and attainment of a measurement for screening entrance into the profession.

Lantz, D. L. "Changes in Student Teachers' Concepts of Self and Others." *Journal of Teacher Education,* vol. 15 (1964), pp. 200-203. Study of 36 female student teachers which indicated that the student teaching experience improved the self-evaluation of the interns.

Perrodin, A. F. "In Support of Supervising Teacher Education Programs." *Journal of Teacher Education,* vol. 12 (1961), pp. 36-38. Study of student teachers and professional attitudes as measured by the MTAI. Indicates that student teacher attitudes improved significantly when the interns are placed with cooperating teachers specially prepared in the supervision of student teachers.

Rancour, L. E. "Student Teacher." *Minnesota Journal of Education,* vol. 48 (December, 1967), p. 24. Presents teaching and student teaching as professional activities in which attributes of the teacher or student teacher relate to the quality of the experience as well as to the professional satisfaction of the teacher.

Schact, Elmer J. "The Building Approach to Student Teaching." *Partnership in Teacher Education.* Washington: American Association of Colleges for Teacher Education, 1968. Recommends that student teaching be approached from the view of team supervision. Every team, along with broad use of material resources, should include a school principal, a college advisor, a school advisor, and a school faculty member.

Wittrock, M. C. "Set Applied to Student Teaching." *Journal of Educational Psychology,* vol. 53 (1962), pp. 175-180. Experiment with student teachers conducted to determine the relationship between student teacher rewards and pupil performance. When rewards for student teachers were given on the basis of pupil performance, pupils achieved at a higher level.

XII. CHURCH, STATE, AND EDUCATION

A. BACKGROUND

1. Books

Ahlstrom, Sydney E. *A Religious History of the American People*. New Haven and London: Yale University Press, 1972. A monumental work going from our European prologue to the present, covering all major religions in the United States.

Beck, Walter Herman. *Lutheran Elementary Schools in the United States*. 2nd ed. St. Louis, Mo.: Concordia Publishing House, 1965. The subtitle describes the work: *A History of the Development of Parochial Schools and Synodical Educational Policies and Programs*.

Buetow, Harold A. *Of Singular Benefit: The Story of U.S. Catholic Education*. New York: The Macmillan Co., 1970. Describes Church and other issues in Catholic education in six chronological periods: to 1783, Colonial period of transplantation; 1784-1828, formative foundations; 1829-1957, maturing process; and 1958-present, contemporary soul-searching and ferment.

Clebsch, William A. *From Sacred to Profane America: The Role of Religion in American History*. New York: Harper and Row, 1968. The chief features of the American dream were formed by people's religious concerns, and they came into realization outside the sanctuary.

Cogley, John. *Religion in America: Original Essays on Religion in a Free Society*. New York: Meridian Books, 1958. Essays originally sponsored by the Fund for the Republic by competent authors on various sides of issues.

Ebersole, Luke. *Church Lobbying in the Nation's Capital*. New York: Macmillan, 1951. An investigation of the Church lobbies that seek to influence Congress.

Fell, Marie Leonore. *The Foundations of Nativism in American Textbooks, 1783-1860*. Washington, D.C.: The Catholic University of

America Press, 1941. Gives evidence of the polarity between public schools and outside influences like Catholicism.

Greeley, Andrew M., and Peter H. Rossi. *The Education of Catholic Americans*. Chicago: Aldine Publishing Co., 1966. A sociological study of such areas of Catholic education as attendance, religious consequences, divisiveness, and achievement.

Marty, Martin E. *The Fire We Can Light: The Role of Religion in a Suddenly Different World*. Garden City, N.Y.: Doubleday, 1973. Reports on the purported conservative direction in religion at the time of writing, and calls for a combination of Christian humanism with the biblical prophetic note.

Marty, Martin E. *Righteous Empire: The Protestant Experience in America*. New York: Dial Press, 1970. U.S. Protestantism from the invention of new forms for a new people in a new land to the date of writing.

Neuwien, Reginald A., ed. *Catholic Schools in Action*. Notre Dame, Ind.: University of Notre Dame Press, 1966. A sociological study of such aspects of Catholic schools as enrollment staff, teacher preparation, understanding, student attitudes and opinions, and parental views.

Phenix, Philip Henry. *Religious Concerns in Contemporary Education*. New York: Teachers College, Columbia University, 1959. Outlines religious concerns in several aspects of contemporary education: school, teacher, curriculum, and administrative process.

Rian, Edwin Harold. *Christianity and American Education*. San Antonio, Texas: The Naylor Company, 1949. The tragic plight of U.S. Protestant education in the light of the current secularism of the public schools and the philosophy of the Catholic educational pattern.

Schiff, Alvin Irwin. *The Jewish Day School in America*. New York: Jewish Education Committee Press, 1966. The most comprehensive work on the subject.

Shaw, Russell, and Richard J. Hurley, eds. *Trends and Issues in Catholic Education*. New York: Citation Press, 1969. Articles in such areas as the why of Catholic education, teachers, organization and policy-making, financing, the disadvantaged, trends in curriculum and instruction, and the future.

Sherrill, Lewis Joseph. *Presbyterian Parochial Schools, 1846-1870*. New Haven, Conn.: Yale University Press, 1932. The only general study delineating Presbyterian parochial schools in their heyday.

Shuster, George N. *Catholic Education in a Changing World*. New York:

Holt, Rinehart & Winston, 1967. Sources of the Catholic education commitment, present Catholic achievements and problems, and new directions especially on the higher education level.

2. Articles

"Churches and Zoning," *Harvard Law Review*, vol. 70 (June, 1957), pp. 1428-1438. Legal considerations in zoning ordinances against the building of religious structures in residential areas.

Cordasco, Francesco. "Historical Perspectives and Contemporary Realities of Catholic Education." *School and Society*, vol. 99 (March, 1971), pp. 149-152. The major problem of Catholic education is not money, but commitment to goals.

Duesenberg, Richard W. "Jurisdiction of Civil Courts over Religious Issues." *Ohio State Law Journal*, vol. 20 (Summer, 1959), pp. 508-548. This is a complicated field, and the government must protect maximum effective free action by individuals.

Evans, John Whitney. "Catholics and the Blair Education Bill." *Catholic Historical Review*, vol. 46 (October, 1960), pp. 273-298. The Blair bill for federal support of education, first introduced in Congress in 1881, was a significant landmark whose debates shed light on a number of political, sectional, and social issues.

Klinkhamer, Maria Carolyn. "The Blaine Amendment of 1875: Private Motives for Political Action." *Catholic Historical Review*, vol. 42 (April, 1956), pp. 15-49. Background of Maine's James G. Blaine and his proposal of an amendment prohibiting federal aid to any sectarian institution.

Pratt, John W. "Religious Conflict in the Development of the New York City Public School System." *History of Education Quarterly*, vol. 5 (June, 1965), pp. 110-120. Presents the typical church-state issues in the development of urban school systems.

McCadden, Joseph J. "Bishop Hughes versus the Public School Society of New York." *Catholic Historical Review*, vol. 50 (July, 1964), pp. 188-207. The vigorous but unsuccessful activities of New York's first archbishop toward state aid for parochial schools that triggered the establishment of New York City's secular public-school system.

McSweeney, Patrick F. "Christian Public Schools." *The Catholic World*, vol. 44 (March, 1887), pp. 788-797. Points to a Princeton professor's view that there is no such thing as religiously neutral education, that the public schools must remain Protestant Christian, and that Roman Catholic schools have remained true to the educational theories of America's founding fathers.

Rossi, Peter Henry, and Alice Schaerr Rossi. "Background and Consequences of Parochial School Education." *Harvard Educational Review,* vol. 27 (Summer, 1957), pp. 168-199. Historical survey and sociological study concluding that the parochial school system was likely to survive only under conditions in which both a religious and an ethnic motivation prevailed, and there isn't much difference between parochial-school and other Catholics.

Schall, James V. "Caesar as God." *Commonweal,* vol. 91 (February 6, 1970), pp. 505-510. Reply by P. Steinfels, vol. 91 (February 13, 1970), p. 526. The state alone cannot govern mankind, is not the solution to modern ills, and must remain finite.

Van Alstyne, Arvo. "Tax Exemption of Church Property." *Ohio State Law Journal,* vol. 20 (Summer, 1959), pp. 461-507. The policy of exempting church property from taxation is firmly rooted in the best traditions of American Law.

Widen, Irwin. "Public Support for Parochial Schools: Why the Issue Has Re-emerged." *History of Education Journal,* vol. 4 (Winter, 1953), pp. 58-72. The issue re-emerged because of Catholics' expanded influence, parochial school need, the Federal aid movement, and the reaction against the secular character of public education; it will continue for some time to come.

B. BIBLIOGRAPHIES AND SOURCE MATERIAL

American Association of School Administrators. Commission on Religion in the Public Schools. *Religion in the Public Schools, A Report.* New York: Harper and Row, 1965.

American Council on Education. Committee on Religion and Education. *The Function of the Public Schools in Dealing with Religion; A Report on the Exploratory Study made by the Committee on Religion and Education.* Washington, D.C.: The Council, 1953. Illustrations of avoidance of religion in public schools, opinions of educational and religious leaders, need for education of teachers for teaching religion, and recommendations.

American Council on Education. Committee on Religion and Education. *The Relation of Religion to Public Education; the Basic Principles.* (American Council on Education. Studies. Series I, Reports of Committees and Conferences, N. 26, Vol. XI, April, 1947.) Washington, D.C.: the Council, 1947.

American Council on Education. Conference on Religion and Public Education. *The Study of Religion in the Public Schools; An Appraisal.* Washington, D.C.: The Council, 1958. Papers on constitutional and legal limits, religion in the history of American ideas, religion in elementary and secondary school history curriculums, etc.

Beach, Fred Francis, and Robert T. Will. *The State and Nonpublic Schools*. Washington, D.C.: U.S. Government Printing Office, 1958. An outline, with statistical data, of the relationship between the U.S. and nonpublic schools.

Brickman, William W. "Church, State and School." *School and Society*, vol. 85 (April 13, 1957), pp. 122-127. A careful review of literature for the previous five years, concluding that we need the private as well as the public school and should give public support to it.

Burr, Nelson R. "Religion and Education," in James Ward Smith and A. Leland Jamison, eds., *A Critical Bibliography of Religion in America* (Religion in American Life, Vol. 4). Princeton, N.J.: Princeton University Press, 1961, pp. 654-677.

Drouin, Edmond G. *The School Question, a Bibliography on Church-State Relationships in American Education, 1940-1960*. Washington, D.C.: The Catholic University of America Press, 1963. Includes such aspects of religion in public education as the Bible, released time, religious garb, and compulsory flag salute, as well as public aid to church-related schools.

Fellman, David, ed. *The Supreme Court and Education (Classics in Education, No. 4)*. New York: Teachers College, Columbia University, 1960. Statements from decisions of the U.S. Supreme Court.

Ford, Paul Leicester, ed. *Pamphlets on the Constitution of the United States, Published during Its Discussion by the People, 1787-1788*. New York: Da Capo Press, 1968. Essays by some Founders on some of the leading principles of the Federal Constitution.

Howe, Mark De Wolfe, compiler. *Cases on Church and State in the United States*. Cambridge, Mass.: Harvard University Press, 1952. Presents and comments upon decisions pertaining to disestablishment of churches, church as corporation, ecclesiastical adjudications, police powers, and education.

Jefferson, Thomas. "A Bill for Establishing Religious Freedom," in Julian P. Boyd, ed., *The Papers of Thomas Jefferson*. Princeton, N.J.: Princeton University Press, 1950———, Vol. II, pp. 545-547. An important primary source document for the foundations of church-state relations in the United States.

McCluskey, Neil G., ed. *Catholic Education in America. A Documentary History*. New York: Classics in Education No. 21, Teachers College, Columbia University, 1964. Some documents, many of which pertain to church-state relationships in education.

McGrath, John J. *Church and State in American Law*. Milwaukee: The Bruce Publishing Co., 1962. Cases and materials on churches, private schools and charities, public schools and religious freedom, freedom to proselytize, and freedom to act.

Madison, James. "A Memorial and Remonstrate," in *The Papers of James Madison,* edited by William F. Hutchinson (and others). Chicago and London: University of Chicago Press, 1962+, vol. 8 (1973), pp. 298-304. An essential document for understanding church-state relationships in the U.S., with valuable editorial and critical notes on pp. 295-298.

Mode, Peter G. *Sourcebook and Bibliographical Guide for American Church History.* Menasha, Wis.: George Banta Publishing Co., 1921. Annotated bibliography on the major denominations from the Colonial period to the time of writing, classified chronologically.

Swindler, William Finley, compiler. *Sources and Documents of United States Constitutions.* Dobbs Ferry, N.Y.: Oceana Publications, 1973————. To be 10 vols., of which vols. 1 and 2 are published, this excellent work will eventually supersede Francis W. Thorpe's 7-vol. *Federal and State Constitutions* . . . (Washington, D.C.: Government Printing Office, 1909).

C. MATERIALS ON THE SUBJECT

1. Books

Antieau, Chester James, Phillip Mark Carroll, and Thomas Carroll Burke. *Religion under the State Constitutions.* A publication of the Institute for Church-State Law, Georgetown University. Brooklyn, N.Y.: Central Book Co., 1965. State constitutional clauses banning aid to church-related educational institutions, limiting the free exercise of religion, banning denial of civil rights because of religious beliefs, and providing for church tax exemptions.

Antieau, Chester James, Arthur T. Downey, and Edward C. Roberts. *Freedom from Federal Establishment.* Milwaukee, Wis.: The Bruce Publishing Company, 1964. Formation and early history of the First Amendment religion clauses.

Blanshard, Paul. *Communism, Democracy, and Catholic Power.* Boston: Beacon Press, 1951. The anti-Catholic position for which Blanshard is famous.

Blum, Virgil Clarence. *Freedom of Choice in Education.* Rev. ed. Glen Rock, N.J.: Paulist Press, 1963. Freedom of choice in education benefits all, encourages competition, and is fundamental to true liberty.

Blum, Virgil Clarence. *Freedom in Education.* Garden City, N.Y.: Doubleday and Company, 1965. Proposes federal aid for all children.

Brady, Joseph H. *Confusion Twice Confounded: The First Amendment and the Supreme Court.* South Orange, N.J.: Seton Hall University Press, 1954. Reviews the Everson and McCollum decisions; concludes that the Supreme Court justices look for guidance not to the Constitution or any other legal source, but to their own prepossessions.

Brickman, William W., and Stanley Lehrer, eds. *Religion, Government, and Education.* New York: Society for the Advancement of Education, 1961. Articles on such subjects as Constitutional and Legal Aspects of the Church-State-School Problem, Religious Celebrations in School, The Debate Over Public Aid to Religious Schools.

Brown, Brendan Francis. "Churches, Law Governing (U.S.)." *The New Catholic Encycylopedia.* New York: McGraw-Hill, 1967, vol. 3, pp. 864-868. Covers nonestablishment, incorporation of churches, moral personality of churches, spiritual disputes, and property rights.

Butts, R. Freeman. *The American Tradition in Religion and Education* (Beacon Press Studies in Freedom and Power, Vol. 5). Boston: Beacon Press, 1950. Discusses the historical context and opts for complete separation of church and state in education.

Callahan, Daniel, ed. *Federal Aid and Catholic Schools.* Baltimore and Dublin: Helicon Press, 1964. Presents Catholic, Protestant, and Jewish viewpoints, and the approaches used in England, Italy, Canada, Germany, and Austria.

"Church and State in the U.S. (Legal History.") *The New Catholic Encyclopedia.* New York: McGraw-Hill, 1967, vol. 3, pp. 742-758. This composite article outlines the subject in the Colonial period, through disestablishment, the period of bitter conflict, and the present search for a solution.

Cobb, Sanford H. *The Rise of Religious Liberty in America.* New York: The Macmillan Co., 1902. Historical development, mainly of the Colonial period but extending through the national, through which United States civil law came to entire liberty of conscience and of worship.

Columbia University Bicentennial Conference. *National Policies for Education, Health and Social Services.* Garden City, N.Y.: Doubleday, 1955. Contains articles on religion in American life, religion and general education, constitutions and schools, etc.

Connors, Edward M. *Church-State Relationships in Education in the State of New York.* Washington, D.C.: The Catholic University of America Press, 1951. A good example of studies on church-state relationships in education in the various states originating as a doctoral dissertation at The Catholic University of America.

Constitutional Problems in Church-State Relations. A Symposium. New York: Da Capo Press, 1971. Unsigned papers originally published in the *Northwestern University Law Review,* vol. 61 (November-December, 1966), pp. 759-839.

Costanzo, Joseph F. *This Nation Under God: Church, State and Schools in America.* New York: Herder and Herder, 1963. On religious liberty in education and federal aid.

Creedon, Lawrence P., and William D. Falcon. *United for Separation; An Analysis of POAU Assaults on Catholicism.* Milwaukee, Wis.: Bruce, 1959. History, leaders, aims, contradictions, and random case histories of Protestants and Other Americans United for the Separation of Church and State.

Curran, Francis Xavier. *The Churches and the Schools, American Protestantism and Popular Elementary Education.* Chicago: Loyola University Press, 1944. Excellent general study showing Protestant support of the parochial school idea.

Dierenfield, Richard B. *Religion in American Public Schools.* Washington, D.C.: Public Affairs Press, 1962. A good general study of the subject of the title.

Drinan, Robert F. "Can Public Funds be Constitutionally Granted to Private Schools." *Catholic Education: A Book of Readings,* ed. by Walter B. Kolesnik and Edward J. Power. New York: McGraw-Hill Book Co., 1965, pp. 119-132. Summary of a legal viewpoint that warrants public funds being constitutionally granted to private schools.

Drinan, Robert F. "Federal Aid to Education." *The New Catholic Encyclopedia.* New York: McGraw-Hill, 1967, vol. 5, pp. 870-874. An outline history, presenting also the political assumptions, philosophical assumptions, and proposed accommodations for federal aid.

Drinan, Robert F. *Religion, the Courts, and Public Policy.* New York: McGraw-Hill, 1963. After delineating areas of church-state cooperation, treats religion in public education, the church-related school, and federal aid and other benefits to private school.

Dunn, William Kailer. *What Happened to Religious Education? The Decline of Religious Teaching in the Public Elementary School, 1776-1881.* Baltimore: Johns Hopkins Press, 1958. Tracing the history of religion in the schools from the Revolution to the Civil War, indicates early importance attributed to religious instruction in education.

Educational Policies Commission (National Education Association of the United States, and American Association of School Administrators). *Moral and Spiritual Values in the Public Schools.* Washington D.C.: National Education Association, 1951. The American public school respects religious beliefs and should cooperate in teaching those values which the American people are agreed upon, like moral responsibility, devotion to truth, brotherhood, the pursuit of happiness, and spiritual enrichment.

Ehlers, Henry, and Gordon C. Lee, eds. *Crucial Issues in Education: An Anthology*. New York: Henry Holt, 1955, pp. 118-178. Bibliography with each unit. Under freedom in education, treats censorship and loyalty; under religion and morals, some implications of church-state separation, and values; under the equalization of educational opportunity, segregation and federal support; also goals, and the gofted; 5tj ed;. 1973.

Emerson, Thomas Irwin, and David Haber, eds. "Organized Religion and Education." *Political and Civil Rights in the United States; A Collection of Legal and Related Materials*. 3rd ed. Buffalo, N.Y.: Dennis & Co., 1967. Summary material and background on aid to education, released time, bible reading, flag salute, etc.

Erickson, Donald A., ed. *Public Controls for Nonpublic Schools*. Chicago: University of Chicago Press, 1969. Essays in such areas as the Amish, sectarian Protestantism, the legal framework for state regulation of nonpublic schools, and a Roman Catholic viewpoint.

Fund for the Republic. *Religion and the Schools*. New York: The Fund, 1959. Presents views for separation of religion from public schooling and for denial of public financial support for church-related schools.

Gabel, Richard James. *Public Funds for Church and Private Schools*. Washington, D.C.: The Catholic University of America Press, 1937. This massive doctoral dissertation carefully traces the history of the subject from Colonial times to the time of writing.

Greene, Evarts Boutell. *Religion and the State: The Making and Testing of an American Tradition*. New York: New York University Press, 1941. An even interpretation between the opposing views of the First Amendment.

Hauser, Conrad Augustine. *Teaching Religion in the Public Schools*. New York: Round Table Press, 1942. Religion can and must be taught in public schools, and demands sectarian cooperation.

Healey, Robert M. *Jefferson on Religion in Public Education*. New Haven: Yale University Press, 1962. Jefferson's positions and what they would be on such current controversies as man, sectarianism, religious freedom, and religion in education.

Herbert, Will. "Religion and Education in America," in James Ward Smith and A. Leland Jamison, eds. *Religious Perspectives in American Culture* (Religion in American Life, Vol. 2). Princeton, N.J.: Princeton University Press, 1961, pp. 11-51. Educators, religious leaders, and concerned laymen should all cope with the problems involved between religion and education.

Howe, Mark De Wolfe. *The Garden and the Wilderness: Religion and Government in American Constitutional History*. Chicago: University of

Chicago Press, 1965. Scholarly challenge to the U.S. Supreme Court's use of history in its decisions; see also his article in the *Buffalo Law Review*, vol. 8 (Winter, 1959), pp. 242-250.

Hurley, Mark J. *Church-State Relationships in Education in California.* Washington, D.C.: The Catholic University of America Press, 1948. Another of the works originating in dissertations at The Catholic University of America on church-state relationships in education in the various states.

Kauper, Paul G. *Civil Liberties and the Constitution.* Ann Arbor, Mich.: University of Michigan Press, 1962. Treats religious education and aid to parochial schools in addition to other civil liberties.

Kerwin, Jerome G. *Catholic Viewpoint on Church and State.* Garden City, N.Y.: Hanover House, 1960. Catholics' reflections and non-Catholics' fears and resentments during the development of the Catholic viewpoint on church and state.

Kurland, Philip B. *Religion and the Law of Church and State and the Supreme Court.* Chicago: Aldine Publishing Co., 1962. A brief historical overview of "authorities in search of a doctrine," that illustrates the Supreme Court's lack of consistency, concluding with a suggested principle for attaining the First Amendment's objectives.

La Noue, George R., ed. *Educational Vouchers: Concepts and Controversies.* New York: Teachers College Press, Columbia University, 1972. Essays on various aspects of the unregulated and regulated voucher and the U.S. congressional response.

Loughery, M. Bernard Francis. *Parental Rights in American Educational Law, Their Bases and Implementation.* 2nd ed. Washington, D.C.: The Catholic University of America Press, 1957. Originally a Ph.D. dissertation, discusses the nature of the principle of parental rights, factors in American educational law affecting its exercise, effects of judicial interpretation, etc.

Lowell, C. S. *The Great Church-State Fraud.* New York: Robert B. Luce, 1973. So one-sided against federal aid to church schools that in this complex issue he implies an impugning of either the intelligence or the good faith of his opponents.

McCluskey, Neil G. *Catholic Viewpoint on Education.* Garden City, N.Y.: Image Books, Doubleday & Co., 1962. Popular presentation of historical background, Catholic schools in theory and practice, parental rights, governmental aid, and some proposals.

McCluskey, Neil Gerard. *Public Schools and Moral Education: The Influence of Horace Mann, William Torrey Harris and John Dewey.* New

York: Columbia University Press, 1958. Unless present patterns are changed, the American public school will become increasingly secular.

McCormick, Leo J. *Church-State Relationships in Education in Maryland.* Washington, D.C.: The Catholic University of America Press, 1942. An important state treated in one of the series originating in doctoral dissertations at The Catholic University of America.

McGarry, Daniel D., and Leo Ward, eds. *Educational Freedom and the Case for Government Aid to Students in Independent Schools.* Milwaukee: Bruce Publishing Co., 1966. Articles on such subjects as Historical Background for Freedom in American Education, Pluralism in Education in a Free Society, International Panorama, and Bibliography.

McGrath, John J. *Catholic Institutions in the United States: Canonical and Civil Law Status.* Washington, D.C.: The Catholic University of American Press, 1968. Treating persons in law, property of institutions, and institutions' auspices, arrives at a novel conclusion of "cooperative separateness."

McLaughlin, Raymond. *A History of State Legislation Affecting Private Elementary and Secondary Schools in the United States, 1870-1945.* Washington, D.C.: The Catholic University of America Press, 1946. Constitutional provisions and state laws affecting private elementary and secondary schools in force in 1945.

Melby, Ernest Oscar, and Morton Puner, eds. *Freedom and Public Education.* New York: Praeger, 1953. An anthology, some selections of which discuss aspects of church-state-school relationships, with "selected references" at the end of each chapter.

Moehlman, Conrad Henry. *School and Church: The American Way; An Historical Approach to the Problem of Religious Instruction in Public Education.* New York: Harper, 1944. Proposes that Protestants should not abandon religious education to day schools and should opt for confining it to Sunday school.

Moehlman, Conrad Henry. *The Wall of Separation between Church and State.* Boston: Beacon Press, 1951. An historical study opposing recent criticism, particularly Roman Catholic, of Supreme Court interpretations of the religious clause of the First Amendment.

Morgan, Richard E. *The Politics of Religious Conflict; Church and State in America.* New York: Pegasus, 1968. A study of the relationship between church and state in the U.S., concentrating on the tension factors, groups, conflict areas, and prospects.

Morgan, Richard E. *The Supreme Court and Religion.* New York: Free Press, 1972. Short description of important area of the U.S. constitution and the difficult setting in which the Supreme Court works. Supplements his book with "The Establishment Clause and Sectarian Schools: A Final Installment?" *The Supreme Court Review* (1973), pp. 57-97.

Murray, John Courtney. *We Hold These Truths; Catholic Reflections on the American Proposition*. New York: Sheed and Ward, 1960. "Catholic reflections on the American proposition" in such areas as pluralism, consensus, the school question, censorship, religious freedom, war, and moral values.

Oaks, Dallin H., ed. *The Wall between Church and State*. Chicago: University of Chicago Press, 1963. Articles on both sides of problems of church and state, public aid to parochial schools, tax exemptions for religious activities, and school prayer cases.

O'Neill, James Milton. *Catholicism and American Freedom*. New York: Harper, 1952. In reply to Paul Blanshard, presents the historical record, and the Catholic belief and practice on issues like the separation of church and state, democracy, religious freedom, and Catholic education.

O'Neill, James Milton. *Religion and Education Under the Constitution*. New York: Harper, 1949. Historical overview of the First Amendment and Jefferson's ideas, Madison's views, Congress, the Supreme Court, several states, and the Fourteenth Amendment.

Pfeffer, Leo. *Church, State and Freedom*. rev. ed. Boston: Beacon Press, 1967. The evolution of the First Amendment principle of freedom of religion and applications against Catholic concepts to specific items in the U.S., especially education.

Phenix, Philip Henry. "Religion in American Public Education," in George Z. F. Bereday and Luigi Volpicelli (eds.), *Public Education in America: A New Interpretation of Purpose and Practice*, pp. 91-99. New York: Harper, 1958. The public school program has been severed from some of the deepest springs of human life, and we should be mature enough to use religion to enrich it.

Rathkopf, Charles A., and Arden H. Rathkopf. *The Law of Zoning and Planning*. 2 vols. + supplements. New York: Clark Broadman & Co.; Albany, N.Y.: Banks & Co., 3rd ed., 1959. Vol. I, pp. 259-267, contains a chapter on "Churches, Convents, Schools Conducted by Churches, Camp Meetings."

Reed, George E. "Freedom of Religion, U.S. Law of," *The New Catholic Encyclopedia*. New York: McGraw-Hill, 1967, vol. 6, pp. 114-122. Genesis of the religion clauses in the First Amendment and their impact on the new nation.

Regan, Richard J. *American Pluralism and the Catholic Conscience*. New

York: The Macmillan Co., 1963. The Catholic conscience on political tolerance, American democracy, parochial schools, religion and the public schools, natural law, birth control, censorship, and other items.

Reilly, Daniel F. *The School Controversy (1891-1893).* Washington, D.C.: The Catholic University of America Press, 1943. Rights of church, state, and family. Primary sources: Bouquillon, Tomas. *Education: To Whom Does It Belong?* Baltimore: John Murphy & Col, 1891; and Holaind, René I. *The Parent First: An Answer to Dr. Bouquillon's Query.* New York: Benziger Brothers, 1891.

Schachner, Nathan. *Church, State and Education.* New York: American Jewish Committee, 1947. Reprinted from *American Jewish Yearbook,* vol. 49 (1947-1948), pp. 1-48. On issues relating to religion in public education and aid to students in church-related schools, favors complete separation of church and state.

Sizer, Theodore R., ed. *Religion and Public Education.* Boston: Houghton Mifflin, 1967. Experts present varied positions on teaching *about* religion, theological perspectives on public education, and the concept of the religiously neutral school.

Smith, Elwyn A., ed. *Church-State Relations in Ecumenical Perspective.* Pittsburgh: Duquesne University Press, 1966. Varied positions by famous authors on secularity and ecumenism, Jewish commitments, biblical concepts, natural law, etc.

Smith, Elwyn A., ed. *The Religion of the Republic.* Philadelphia: Fortress Press, 1971. Among the varied essays is one on "Is the Public School Religious or Secular?" pp. 22-24.

Smith, Elwyn A. *Religious Liberty in the United States.* Philadelphia: Fortress Press, 1972. The development of church-state thought since the Revolutionary era, with a conclusion on the meaning of church-state separation.

Smith, Seymour A. *Religious Cooperation in State Universities: An Historical Sketch.* University of Michigan, 1957. After the Protestant era, the dawn of a new day and a growing maturity of a complex pattern of religious cooperation.

Sorgen, Michael S., and others. *State, School, and Family.* New York: M. Bender, 1973. Cases and comments on government and education, Chapter 15 dealing with nonpublic education and Chapter 16 with vouchers and other innovations.

Spurlock, Clark. *Education and the Supreme Court.* Urbana, Ill.: University of Illinois Press, 1955. Covers 39 cases from 1789 to 1953, including almost all directly concerned with education and others on issues affecting it.

Stokes, Anson Phelps. *Church and State in the United States.* 3 vols. New York: Harper, 1950. Bibliography: Vol. III, pp. 769-836. Education is given special treatment in Vol. I, Chapter 12, and Vol. II, Chapter 19.

Thayer, Vivian Trow. *The Attack upon the American Secular School.* Boston: Beacon Press, 1951. The American secular school answers the needs of our time to the extent that its attackers should be put down, and no public assistance given religious schools.

Torpey, William George. *Judicial Doctrines of Religious Rights in America.* Chapel Hill, N.C.: University of North Carolina Press, 1948. Covers many areas, including "Educational Practices Involving the Right of Religious Freedom" (Chapter 9, pp. 233-276).

Ward, Leo R. *Federal Aid to Private Schools.* Westminster, Md.: Newman Publishing Co., 1964. Presents an historical overview and a philosophical analysis of what is being done and what can be done.

Ward, Leo R. *Religion in All the Schools.* Notre Dame, Ind.: Fides, 1960. The "wall of separation" does not overcome the right of religious literacy in pluralistic society.

Witkowiak, Stanislau B. *Limitations Imposed Upon the Rights and Powers of Respective States over Education by the United States Supreme Court* (Washington, D.C.: The Catholic University of America Press, 1942). This Ph.D. dissertation concludes that the Supreme Court has maintained a high regard for the rights of the states, but limited by the rights of the child, parent, teacher, and private school.

Wolf, Donald J., ed. *Toward Consensus: Catholic-Protestant Interpretations of Church and State.* Garden City, N.Y.: Doubleday Anchor Books, 1968. Presentations on church-state relations by important Catholic and Protestant writers and by the Second Vatican Council and the World Council of Churches.

2. Recent Periodical Literature

Areen, Judith. "Educational Vouchers." *Harvard Civil Rights-Civil Liberties Law Review,* vol. 6 (May, 1971), pp. 466-504. Examines the constitutional and public policy questions surrounding the major voucher plans—including expansion of equal educational opportunity, aid to parochial schools, and maintenance of educational quality.

Augustin, Morris. "The New World of Catholic Church-State Relations." *American Ecclesiastical Review,* vol. 161 (July, 1969), pp. 1-17. A summary of the current status, an appraisal of post-Vatican II Catholic statements, and a rational presentation of alternatives in the school question.

Ball, William B., and Leo Pfeffer. "Congress Shall Make No Law ... " *Saturday Review* (January 21, 1967), pp. 58-60, 77, 80. Two opposing views on federal aid to church-related education: "Church and State: The Absolutist Crusade," by Ball, and "What Price Federal Aid," by Pfeffer.

Brickman, William W. "The School and the Church-State Question." *School and Society,* vol. 71 (May 6, 1950), pp. 273-282. It would be difficult to prove that the church was ever historically separated from the public schools, and payments to parochial schools do not endanger the separation of church and state.

Brickman, William W. "The Supreme Court and the Sectarian School." *Intellect,* vol. 102 (November, 1973), pp. 82-84. It is in the interest of the entire nation to perpetuate a dual educational system, public and nonpublic.

Brindel, Paul. "Zoning Out Religious Institutions." *Notre Dame Lawyer,* vol. 32 (August, 1957), pp. 627-641. If our democratic system is to realize its proclaimed values, zoning ordinances for private educational and religious facilities must be designed and applied accordingly.

Butler, William J. "The Effect of State Aid to Church Schools on Public Education." *Journal of Church and State,* vol. 6 (Winter, 1964), pp. 74-84. Aid would increase the number of denominations with parochial schools and thus fragment the nation.

Butts, Robert Freeman. "Church and State in American Education." *Teachers College Record,* vol. 52 (December, 1950), pp. 145-157. If we substitute some form of "cooperation" for neutrality between church and state in education, we are returning to some form of establishment of religion.

Butts, Robert Freeman. "James Madison, the Bill of Rights and Education." *Teachers College Record,* vol. 60 (December, 1958), pp. 121-128. The education profession should apply Madison's view of the Bill of Rights to education.

Carey, Hugh L. "The Child Benefit System in Operation—Federal Style." *Catholic Lawyer,* vol. 12 (Summer, 1966), pp. 185-192 and 266. Opts for child-benefit government aid to raise educational quality and to bring equality of educational opportunity to every child.

Choper, Jesse H. "The Establishment Clause and Aid to Parochial Schools." *California Law Review,* vol. 56 (April, 1968), pp. 260-341. The First Amendment's "establishment clause" does not preclude aid.

"Church-related Schools." *The New Republic,* vol. 148 (March 2, 1963), pp. 4-5 and continued in same vol. (March 23, 1963), pp. 3-5, and (May 11, 1963), pp. 4-6. The editors reverse their stand against aid to church-related schools to "a more serviceable approach" of aid for secular ends without worry if this incidentally helps a church.

"Church-State–Religious Institutions and Values: A Legal Survey–1964-66." *Notre Dame Lawyer,* vol. 41 (June, 1966), pp. 681-785. Analysis of the U.S. church-state relationship in many areas, including education (pp. 704-719).

Coan, Robert J. "Bible Reading in the Public Schools." *Albany Law Review,* vol. 22 (January, 1958), pp. 156-173. Gives reasons in separation of church and state for excluding Bible reading from the public schools.

Costanzo, Joseph F. "Thomas Jefferson, Religious Education and Public Law." *Journal of Public Law,* vol. 8 (Spring, 1959), pp. 81-108. Jefferson, easily misunderstood, must be quoted correctly. The "wall" that protects the free exercise of religion must be as high as that which keeps governmental powers from preferential treatment of religion.

Donahue, Charles. "Freedom and Education: The Pluralist Background." *Thought,* vol. 27 (Winter, 1952-53), pp. 542-60. It is strange that so many of the proponents of freedom confuse their cause by defending monistic secularism in education.

Drinan, Robert F., and Rolfe Lanier Hunt. "Should Public Funds Aid Parochial Schools?" *Parents' Magazine,* vol. 38 (November, 1963), pp. 70f, 118, 120, 122. A debate.

"Educational Vouchers–Challenge to the Wall of Separation?" *Valparaiso University Law Review,* vol. 5 (Spring, 1971), pp. 569-602. Unsigned article that considers vouchers unconstitutional.

Erickson, Donald A. "Public Funds for Private Schools." *Saturday Review* (September 21, 1968), pp. 66-68 and 78-79. By channeling support to private schools, we may provide the shock necessary to kindle needed reforms in public schools.

"Expanding Concepts of Religious Freedom." *Wisconsin Law Review* (Spring, 1966), pp. 215-330. Articles by Philip B. Kurland, Marc Galanter, Wilber G. Katz, and Harold P. Southerland on society's perplexing problem of religious freedom.

"Federal Aid to Religous Schools." *Notre Dame Lawyer,* vol. 37 (March, 1962), pp. 285-322. Two articles: one by Paul M. Butler and Alfred L. Scanlon on the wall of separation, the other a negative answer to federal funds for parochial schools by Leo Pfeffer.

"The First Amendment and Federal Aid to Church-Related Schools."

Georgetown Law Journal, vol. 50 (Winter, 1961), pp. 351-455. Studies made by the Department of Health, Education, and Welfare on the impact of the First Amendment upon federal aid to education and by the National Catholic Welfare Conference on the constitutionality of the inclusion of church-related schools in federal aid.

Freund, Paul A. "Public Aid to Parochial Schools." *Harvard Law Review,* vol. 82 (June, 1969), pp. 1680-1692. An interpretation not favorable to aid, cited in *Lemon* v. *Kurtzman* (1971).

Gabel, Richard James. "Religion After the Adoption of the Federal and State Constitutions." *Catholic Educational Review,* vol. 38 (September, 1940), pp. 385-99. A march toward secularism in the schools has for various historical reasons proceeded unhappily through U.S. history, and true religious liberty in education today requires greatness of vision.

Gianella, Donald A. "Religious Liberty, Nonestablishment, and Doctrinal Development." *Harvard Law Review,* vols. 80 (May, 1967), pp. 1381-1431, and 81 (January, 1968), pp. 513-590. Favors a broader concept of religious freedom than now exists.

Griswold, Erwin N. "Absolute is in the Dark—A Discussion of the Approach of the Supreme Court to Constitutional Questions." *Utah Law Review,* vol. 8 (Summer, 1963), pp. 167-182. Challenges the Supreme Court's absolutist interpretations of the First Amendment with respect to religion and public education.

Handlin, Oscar, and William L. Miller. "Two Views on Aid to Catholic Schools." *Catholic World,* vol. 193 (July, 1961), pp. 216-224. Discussion: vol. 193 (September, 1961), pp. 338-339; vol. 194 (November, 1961), pp. 130-131. A debate.

Hardon, John Augustine. "Cooperation of Church and State: I) In American Legislation, II) In the Supreme Court, III) In American Education." *Homiletic and Pastoral Review,* 57: 309-319 (Jan.), 419-427 (Feb.), 523-531 (March, 1957). Non-Catholics' role in establishing cooperation, the Supreme Court's classic decisions to guard freedom of conscience, and the most important and delicate area of cooperation in education.

Harrison, Joseph W. "The Bible, the Constitution and Public Education." *Tennessee Law Review,* vol. 29 (Spring, 1962), pp. 363-418. Because of the difficulties involved, children's religious instruction should be left to the church or the parents.

Henle, R. J. "American Principles and Religious Schools." *Saint Louis University Law Journal,* vol. 3 (Spring, 1955), pp. 237-51. Whether various religious groups want state aid to their schools or not, it is essential to apply a fine balance of principles.

Herberg, Will. "The Sectarian Conflict over Church and State; A Divisive Threat to our Democracy?" *Commentary,* vol. 14 (Nov., 1952), pp. 450-462.

Herrick, David J. "Religious Freedom and Compulsory Education: The Plight of the Amish." *South Dakota Law Review,* vol. 17 (Winter, 1972), pp. 251-263. Attempts to define the limits of the state's police power when confronted with a religious issue.

Jacobson, Philip. "The Nonsectarian Public Parochial School." *Christian Century,* vol. 86 (June 4, 1969), pp. 769-774. If public schools are to be given the chance to justify U.S. faith in them, there must be concern to maintain the separation of church and state. Neil G. McCluskey presents the Catholic view in the succeeding article (pp. 775-779), "Child Support or Wall of Separation?"

"The Jewish Forum's 45th Anniversary Supplement on 'Federal Aid to Parochial Schools'—Should Jews Support It? . . . " *Jewish Forum,* vol. 45 (May-June, 1962), pp. 23-39. The periodical "reverses its 44-year-old position of opposing federal aid to parochial schools" (editorial, same issue, p. 7).

Katz, Wilber G., and Harold F. Southerland. "Religious Pluralism and the Supreme Court." *Daedalus,* vol. 96 (Winter, 1967), pp. 180-192. Includes a discussion of education in the context of the relations between government and religion.

Kauper, Paul G. "Everson v. Board of Education: A Product of the Judicial will." *Arizona Law Review,* vol. 15 (1973), pp. 307-326. Kauper's best statement in challenging the Supreme Court's interpretation of the First Amendment. See also his articles in *Alabama Law Review,* vol. 19 (Spring, 1967), pp. 275-297, and *Michigan Law Review,* vol. 60 (November, 1961), pp. 1-40.

Kelley, Dean M. "Principles and Policies Which Should Govern Working Relations of Church and State in Education." *Journal of Church and State,* vol. 16 (Winter, 1974), pp. 101-119. The theoretical principles for both church and state to exercise for the welfare of both.

Kenealy, William J. "Equal Justice Under Law––Tax Aid to Education." *Catholic Lawyer,* vol. 7 (Summer, 1961), pp. 183-202. Treats federal aid under the aspects of general welfare, parental freedom, equal protection, constitutionality, and other considerations.

Kizer, George A. "Religion and Education: Cooperation or Conflict?" *School and Society,* vol. 99 (March, 1971), pp. 152-156. Leaders in both religion and education should make honest and wise choices today to avoid weakening both religion and education.

Kurland, Philip B. "The Supreme Court, Compulsory Education, and the First Amendment's Religion Clauses." *West Virginia Law Review,* vol. 75 (April, 1973), pp. 213-245. Applauds the *Yoder* decision on humanitarian grounds.

La Noue, George R. "Child Benefit Theory Revisited: Textbooks, Transportation and Medical Care." *Journal of Public Law,* vol. 13, n. 1 (1964), pp. 76-94. Opposes the "child benefit" theory.

Lippmann, Walter. "Walter Lippmann Interviewed by Charles Collingwood." *The New Republic,* vol. 148 (May 18, 1963), pp. 15-18. A general view on current affairs in which Lippmann asserts that it is not beyond the wit of man to find a way of aiding all schools, even parochial, without getting involved in the question of the teaching of religion.

McCluskey, Neil G., and Leo Pfeffer. "Federal Aid for Private and Parochial Schools?" *Current History,* vol. 41 (August, 1961), pp. 70-81. A debate.

McDevitt, John. "Aspects of Canon and Civil Law Relative to Parochial Schools." *The Jurist,* vol. 14 (October, 1954), pp. 481-503. Contrasts and conflicts between the Canon Law of the Roman Catholic Church and United States civil law, mostly as interpreted by the U.S. Supreme Court.

McInnes, William C. "Win One, Lose One: The Supreme Court." *America,* vol. 125 (September 18, 1971), pp. 170-173. *Tilton, Lemon,* and *DiCenso* cases present a new direction and beginning.

McMahon, Paul B. "State Aid to Education and the Doctrine of Separation of Church and State." *Georgetown Law Journal,* vol. 36 (May, 1948), pp. 631-647. The "establishment of religion" clause of the First Amendment legally permits aid to religion equally given, and the "free exercise" clause does not prohibit such aid when not in derogation of the rights of any individual.

Mullaney, Thomas R. "Tax Credits and Parochial Schools." *Commonweal,* vol 98 (April 27, 1973), pp. 185-188. No less than twenty-two tax-credit bills were introduced in the new Congress, and Citizéns Relief for Education by Income Tax (CREDIT) continues to try to influence Congress in this direction to make Catholic education viable.

Murray, John Courtney. "Reflections on the Religiously Pluralistic Society." *Catholic Mind,* vol. 57 (May-June, 1959), pp. 196-288. An anthology of articles by Murray, such as "Church, State and Religious Liberty," "Church, State and Political Freedom," and "The Catholic University in a Pluralistic Society."

National Catholic Educational Association. "The Right to Educate—the Role of Parents, Church, State." *National Catholic Educational*

Proceedings, vol. 55 (August, 1958), pp. 1-416. Addresses on such subjects as theological aspects of church-state relations, the correlative duty to the right to educate, the importance of religion, etc.

"No Law But Our Own Prepossessions." *American Bar Association Journal,* vol. 48 (October, 1962), pp. 939-941. Originally published, vol. 34 (June, 1948), pp. 482-485. Editorial challenging "wall of separation" concept, originally published after the McCollum decision and reprinted after *Engel* v. *Vitale.*

O'Neill, Michael. "Giving Americans a Choice: Alternatives to Public Education." *America,* vol. 122 (January 24, 1970), pp. 66-70. Reply: Ruth E. Brady, vol. 122 (April 4, 1970), p. 360. Backers of Catholic schools are in a position to lead a campaign for a radically different method of funding U.S. elementary and secondary education.

Pfeffer, Leo. "The Supremacy of Free Exercise." *Georgetown Law Journal,* vol. 61 (May, 1973), 1115-1142. Temperate statement supporting strict church-state separation.

Pfeffer, Leo, and James Milton O'Neill. "The Meaning of the Establishment Clause—A Debate: No Law Respecting an Establishment of Religion [Leo Pfeffer], Nonpreferential Aid to Religion is not an Establishment of Religion [J. M. O'Neill]." *Buffalo Law Review,* vol. 2 (Spring, 1953), pp. 225-78.

Prance, Norman R. "The Amish and Compulsory School Attendance: Recent Developments." *Wisconsin Law Review,* 1971, no. 3, pp. 832-853. Written before the *Yoder* decision in which the Amish prevailed over compulsory education laws, giving good background information.

Punke, Harold Herman. "Religious Issues in American Public Education." *Law and Contemporary Problems,* vol. 20 (Winter, 1955), pp. 138-168. Treats public and sectarian uses of property, objections to school regulations, retirement credit for parochial school experience, released time, and public funds for parochial schools.

Regan, Richard J. "The Dilemma of Religious Instruction and the Public Schools." *Catholic Lawyer,* vol. 10 (Winter, 1964), pp. 42-54, 82. After the Schempp case (1963), studies options of public-school students in released-time religion classes and of those who are not so enrolled.

"Religion and Education." *Progressive Education* (Special Issue), vol. 33 (September, 1956), pp. 129-160. Articles on such issues as separation of church and state, the relation between religion and education, and both sides of the issue of private and church-related schools in American eduation.

"Religion in Public Education," Special Feature. *The Living Light,* vol.

10, no. 3 (Fall, 1973), pp. 414-467. Articles on the historical "Evolution of an Idea," "Toward the Implementation of an Idea," "The Pennsylvania Model," and "The English Experience."

"Religion and the State." *Law and Contemporary Problems,* vol. 14 (Winter, 1949), pp. 1-169. Articles on the Supreme Court as national school board, foundations of the *Everson* and *McCollum* decisions, separation and cooperation of church and state, religious education, federal aid, and religious institutions in tax and labor legislation.

"The Right to Educate: A Symposium." *Catholic Lawyer,* vol. 4 (Summer, 1958), pp. 196-243. Articles on the roles of parent, church, and state, on the status of the private school in law, and on the Catholic obligation to educate.

Ruiz-Gimenez Cortez, D. Joaquin. "Religious Liberty—the Rights of Parents in the Education of their Children." *Catholic Lawyer,* vol. 11 (Autumn, 1965), pp. 285-312. Countries must facilitate by their legislation on the exercise of the right of religious liberty, particularly for families educating their children.

Ruxin, Paul T. "The Right Not To Be Modern Men: The Amish and Compulsory Education." *Virginia Law Review,* vol. 53 (May, 1967), pp. 925-952. Courts and legislatures should give the Amishman and his children the right, within limits, to choose not be be modern men.

Sharff, Michael. "Religion and the Zoning Laws." *New York University Intramural Law Review,* vol. 15 (March, 1960), pp. 194-207. Separately considers substantial questions on the exclusion of churches and parochial and private schools from residential neighborhoods.

Sheffey, E. Summers. "The First Amendment and Distribution of Religious Literature in the Public Schools." *Virginia Law Review,* vol. 41 (October, 1955), pp. 789-807. It seems that the distribution of sectarian literature in the public schools with the assistance of school personnel would be legally barred by the First Amendment.

Siegel, Seymour. "Church and State: A Reassessment." *Catholic Mind,* vol. 69 (April, 1971), pp. 30-34. A Jew argues that, in order to guarantee the free exercise of religion, preserve religious values, and encourage educational pluralism, the Jewish community should reverse its traditional stand and support governmental aid to nonpublic schools.

Stanmeyer, William A. "Free Exercise and the Wall: The Obsolescence of a Metaphor." *George Washington Law Review,* vol. 37 (December, 1968), pp. 223-243. The historical denouement of the "wall" metaphor (to be later superseded by the "entanglement" metaphor).

Stout, David William. "The Establishment of Religion under the

Constitution." *Kentucky Law Journal,* vol. 37 (March, 1949), pp. 220-239. Perhaps the First Amendment should be replaced or clarified by another.

Sullivan, Michael M., and Stephen D. Willett. "Public Aid to Private Education." *The Catholic University of America Law Review,* vol. 20 (Spring, 1971), pp. 528-540. Examines public aid with reference to the *DiCenso, Lemon,* and *Tilton* decisions, and the First Amendment.

Taylor, T. Raber. "Federal Aid for Children and Teachers in All Schools." *Catholic Lawyer,* vol. 12 (Summer, 1966), pp. 193-202. Advocates raising the amounts of government money given each child under the child-benefit theory.

Van Alstyne, William W. "Constitutional Separation of Church and State: The Quest for a Coherent Position." *American Political Science Review,* vol. 57 (December, 1963), pp. 865-882. An historical search for perspectives.

Whelan, Charles M. "Supreme Court Cases: Questions and Answers." *America,* vol. 124 (April 10, 1971), pp. 372-375. See also other articles in the same periodical by this constitutional lawyer: vol. 124 (May 29, 1971), pp. 568-570; vol. 125 (July 10, 1971), pp. 8-11 and (July 24, 1971), pp. 32f; vol. 126 (February 26, 1972), pp. 195-198; vol. 128 (April 21, 1973), p. 353; vol. 129 (July 7, 1973), pp. 6-8.

Yanitelli, Victor R. "A Church-State Anthology, the Work of Father Murray." *Thought,* vol. 27 (Spring, 1952), pp. 6-42. Tribute to John Courtney Murray, an original and courageous thinker in U.S. church-state relationships.

XIII. THE FEDERAL GOVERNMENT AND EDUCATION

A. BACKGROUND

1. General References

Adams, Charles F., and others. "Financing Education: Who Benefits? Who Pays?" *Proceedings of the NEA Committee on Educational Finance, National Conference on School Finance* (15th, New York, N.Y., March 26-28, 1972). Contains papers that discuss (1) the role of the federal government in educational finance; (2) some proposals for full state funding of schools; (3) implications for educational finance of recent state court decisions; (4) state plans for financing public schools; and (5) issues in school finance such as property tax reform and school bond markets.

Alexander, Kern, Roe L. Johns, and Richard Rossmiller, eds. *Dimensions of Educational Need, Vol. 1.* Gainesville, Florida: National Educational Finance Project, 1969. Provides framework for research into school finance by the National Education Finance Project.

Allen, Hollis P. *The Federal Government and Education.* New York: McGraw-Hill, 1950. A thorough report regarding education for the Hoover Commission task force on public welfare.

Allen, James E., Jr. *Federalism in Education—The Role of the Federal Government.* Paper presented at the Annual Meeting of the Education Commission of the States (Denver, July 8, 1969). Focuses on ways in which federal financial support should be broadly allocated.

Bendiner, Robert. *Obstacle Course on Capital Hill.* New York: McGraw-Hill, 1964. Examination of present functioning of Congress of the U.S. including the issue of federal aid to elementary and secondary schools.

Benson, Charles S. *The Economics of Public Education.* Boston: Houghton Mifflin, 1961. School finance viewed as a sub-area of public finance.

Berke, Joel S., and Michael W. Kirst. *Federal Aid to Education.* Lexington, Mass.: D. C. Heath, 1972. Shows the process of decision making in the federal establishment and makes recommendations.

Conant, James B. *Shaping Educational Policy.* New York: McGraw-Hill, 1964. Educational policy for the public schools and higher education with specifics on New York and California, resulting from a study made by a Carnegie grant.

Corey, Arthur F. "Financial Implications of Issues and Trends in Education." *Phi Delta Kappan,* vol. XLII, no. 1 (October, 1960), pp. 3-7. A look at the issues of the defensible limits of public education, the cost of public schools, and who should pay for public education and how.

Diamond, R. A., and E. Witt, eds. *Education for a Nation.* Washington, D.C.: Congressional Quarterly Inc., 1972. Covers such areas as school finance, Congress and the Office of Education, and Federal Education Programs with projections from 1958-1979.

Educational Policies Commission. *Educational Responsibilities of the Federal Government.* Washington, D.C. National Education Association, 1964. Federal educational policies contrasted to federal responsibilities.

Educational Policies Commission. *National Policy and the Financing of the Public Schools.* Washington, D.C.: National Education Association, 1959. Reviews impact of education on the nation, evaluates present financial base that public schools operate on, and discusses the implications of these matters regarding national policy.

Fellman, David, ed. *The Supreme Court and Education.* New York: Teachers College, Columbia University, 1960. Series of Supreme Court cases regarding education and religion, education and racial segregation, and academic freedom.

Ford, Gerald R. "Future Role and Direction of Federal Support for Public Education." *Community Education Journal,* vol. 4, no. 1 (Jan./Feb., 1974), pp. 20-21, 62. Describes role of federal government for the future in public education as being supportive of the local school board.

Fullam, Marie G., and Kenneth A. Simon. *Projections of Educational Statistics to 1973-74.* Washington, D.C.: U.S. Government Printing Office, 1964. Makes projections in areas of enrollments, graduates, teachers, and expenditures for elementary and secondary schools and institutions of higher education.

Grant, W. Vance, and Kenneth A. Simon. *Digest of Educational Statistics.* Washington, D.C.: U.S. Government Printing Office, 1965. Includes data of current, national interest and value with statistics regarding all levels of education and federal programs of education.

Gruber, Frederick C., ed. *Education and the State*. Philadelphia: University of Pennsylvania Press, 1960. Includes articles by Edward Brice, Roy Nichols, William Kvaraceus, and James Russell dealing with the relationship of public education and democracy.

Guthrie, James W. "City Schools in a Federal Vise: The Political Dynamics of Federal Aid to Urban Schools." *Education in an Urban Society,* vol. 2, no. 2 (February, 1970), pp. 199-218. Analyzes the recent role of the federal government in public education in view of the reported rural bias of the Congress and the urban bias of the Executive.

Harris, Seymour E. *How Shall We Pay for Education?* New York: Harper, 1948. Analysis of current financial problems in education.

Hartman, Robert W., and Robert D. Reischauer. *Reforming School Finance*. Washington, D.C.: Brookings Institute, 1973. A study of the provision for finance to elementary and secondary education.

Howe, Harold II. *The People Who Serve Education*. Washington, D.C.: U.S. Government Printing Office, 1969. Discusses the state of the education professions with emphasis on issues and developments changing the professions.

Johns, Roe L., and Edgar L. Morphet. *The Economics and Financing of Education*. Englewood Cliffs, N.J.: Prentice-Hall, Inc., 1969. A systems approach in analyzing educational finance policies as they affect the social system.

Lindman, Erick L. *The Federal Government and Public Schools*. Washington, D.C.: American Association of School Administrators, 1965. Deals with the relationship among local, state, and federal governments as they effect educational policy.

Lindman, Erick L., and others. *Federal Policy and the Public Schools, A Series of Nine Essays Focusing on Questions and Issues Around Which Policy Evolves*. Washington, D.C.: American Association of School Administrators, 1967. Each essay is concerned with the general topic "Federal Policy and the Public School" and focuses on questions and issues around which national policy evolves.

Munger, Frank J., and Richard F. Fenno, Jr. *National Politics and Federal Aid to Education*. Syracuse, New York: Syracuse University Press, 1962. Deals with political factors that affect federal aid to elementary and secondary education.

Pell, Claiborne, and Albert H. Quie. "Two Congressmen Look at American Education." *Childhood Education,* vol. 46 (September, 1969), pp. 17-21. Two separate accounts dealing with current problems in education, including the role of the federal government in solving them.

Pierce, Truman M. *Federal, State and Local Government in Education.* New York: The Center for Applied Research in Education, Inc., 1964. Examines widening role of government in American education, reviewing the origin and development of educational services offered by different governmental branches.

Quattlebaum, Charles A. *Federal Aid to Elementary Education.* Chicago: Public Administration Service, 1948. Analytic study of the financial problems of the American educational system and recommendations of Congress and advisory commissions for solving the difficulties.

Saunders, Charles B., Jr. "Fewer Dollars, Shrinking Enrollments, Fixed Cost: New Financial Dilemma." Presented at American Association of School Administrators Annual Convention (106th, Atlantic City, New Jersey, February 22-26, 1974). Author analyzes what should be the proper role of the federal government in the financing of public elementary and secondary education.

Soloman, Jack, Jr. *Complete Handbook on Federal Aid to Education.* Lincolnwood, Illinois: National Textbook Corporation, 1961. Organized into a concise section of background and discussion followed by debate of federal aid issues.

Sutherland, Arthur E. "The Supreme Court and the Public School." *Harvard Educational Review,* vol. 24 (Spring, 1954), pp. 71-85. Discussion of the relationship between the U.S. Supreme Court and education in the public schools.

Tiedt, Sidney W. *The Role of the Federal Government in Education.* New York: Oxford University Press, 1966. Covers the subject in general terms, with special emphasis on such issues as Church-State and arguments for and against federal aid.

2. Historical Development

American Association of School Administrators. *The Federal Interest in Education.* Washington, D.C.: American Association of School Administrators, n.d. Address at the Northern New England Drive-In Conference, April 13, 1967, dealing with changes taking place in intergovernmental relations in education with an historical perspective.

Barnard, Harry V., and John H. Best. "Growing Involvement in American Education, 1918-1945." *Current History,* vol. 62, no. 370 (June, 1972), pp. 290+. Cites examples of expansion of federal education activities during national crisis periods.

Johns, Roe L. *Full State Funding of Education:* Pittsburgh: University of Pittsburgh Press, 1973. School finance traced throughout history including theorist contributions, the impact of court decisions, and findings and recommendations of the National Educational Finance Project.

Lee, Gordon C. *The Struggle for Federal Aid.* New York: Teachers College, Columbia University Bureau of Publications, 1949. Historical analysis of attempts made to enact legislation for federal aid to education between 1870 and 1890.

National Education Association. Division of Federal Relations. *It's Older than the Constitution.* Washington, D.C.: National Education Association, October, 1964. Historical overview of landmarks in educational legislation.

Norton, John K., Comp. *Dimensions in School Finance.* Washington, D.C.: National Education Association, 1966. Traces major trends in local, state, and federal school finance programs during the past decade and assesses the current situation in the field.

Office of Education Centennial Information Committee. *OEO–Highlighting the Progress of American Education.* Washington, D.C.: U.S. Government Printing Office, 1967. A look at major educational developments throughout American history with vignettes suggesting the attitude of the past and forecasts as to future developments.

Taylor, Arthuryne J. "Federal Financing of Education, 1945-1972." *Current History*, vol. 62, no. 370 (June, 1972), pp. 298+. An overview of federal funding for education during the post-World War II years.

B. FEDERAL ORGANIZATIONS

Bailey, Stephen K. *The Office of Education and the Education Act of 1965.* Indianapolis, Indiana: The Bobbs-Merrill Company, Inc., 1966. A look at the changing relationship between the federal government and primary and secondary education, along with the implications thereof.

Department of Health, Education and Welfare. Office of Education. *HANDBOOK Office of Education.* Washington, D.C.: U.S. Government Printing Office, 1963. Includes a brief discussion of career opportunities in the Office of Education, along with an explanation of its organization and activities.

–––– "Gardner Hews Out the Great Society." *Newsweek* (February, 1966), pp. 22+. Discusses the arrival of John W. Gardner as head of the HEW Department and gives an overview of HEW's activities.

Green, Edith. "Education: Our Largest Enterprise." *College Management,* vol. 5 (March, 1970), pp. 4-5. Discusses the need for developing a cabinet-level Department of Education and Manpower Training.

Green, Edith. "Education's Federal Grab Bag." *Phi Delta Kappan,* vol. LIV, no. 2 (October, 1972), pp. 83-6. Accuses USOE and HEW of poor management and cites examples to support the charge.

Kelley, Clarice Y. *Where It's Happening.* Garden City, New York: Doubleday & Company, Inc., 1968. Presents information regarding projects funded by the U.S. Office of Education.

Kursh, Harry. *The United States Office of Education; A Century of Service.* New York: Chilton, 1965. Explanation of why the Office of Education was created and how it operates.

Marland, Sidney P., Jr. "A Responsible Stewardship." *Phi Delta Kappan,* vol. LIV, no. 2 (October, 1972), pp. 87-8. Defends mismanagement of USOE through its management-improvement efforts and reforming of contract/grant procedures.

Stiles, Lindley J. "The Cooperative Research Program, Contributions and Next Steps." *Phi Delta Kappan,* vol. XLIII, no. 6 (March, 1962), pp. 231-236. Reviews accomplishments of USOE Cooperative Research Program including suggestions for action.

———— "$10.2 Billion—How to Spend It." *Newsweek* (February 28, 1966), p. 29. Chronicles the breakdown in spending of $10.2 billion the Department of HEW will spend in fiscal year 1967.

U.S. Department of Health, Education and Welfare, Office of Education. *A Federal Education Agency for the Future.* Washington, D.C.: U.S. Government Printing Office, 1961. Offers a report of the Committee on the Mission and Organization of the Office of Education.

C. ARGUMENTS

1. Pro-Federal Aid to Education

American Association of School Administrators. *Federal Financial Relationships to Education.* Washington, D.C.: National Education Association, 1967. Discusses need for an increase of general aid to provide unearmarked funds.

Berke, Joel S. "Full Federal Funding: Educational Nightmare." *Current History,* vol. 63 (August, 1972), pp. 80-1+. Discusses federal government's failure to provide sufficient funding for education.

Berke, Joel S., and Michael Kirst. "How the Federal Government Can

Encourage State School Finance Reform." *Phi Delta Kappan,* vol. LV, no. 4 (December, 1973), pp. 241-4. A recommendation that federal aid be given to states to equalize expenditures and educational opportunities.

Carpenter, W. W. "Pupil Migration and Federal Support." *Phi Delta Kappan,* vol. XLI, no. 8 (May, 1960), pp. 362-363. Presents effects of migration on pupil progress along with an argument in support of federal aid to education.

Cordasco, Francesco. "The Federal Challege and Peril to the American School." *School & Society,* vol. 94 (Summer, 1966), pp. 263-265. A review of federal educational statutes, noting that they are "critically an attestation of the forfeiture of the prerogatives of American educational leadership."

DeWitt, Nicholas. "Investment in Education & Economic Development." *Phi Delta Kappan,* vol. XLVII, no. 4 (December, 1965), pp. 197-199. Focuses on the need for educational allocations as a positive productive investment needed for economic growth.

Fulbright, J. William. "Education and Public Policy." *National Association of Secondary-School Principals' Bulletin,* vol. 49 (March, 1965), pp. 3-13. Discussion of the needs of education to meet qualitative and creative growth of citizens' private lives.

Humphrey, Hubert H. "International Scene: Our Commitments and Responsibilities." *National Association of Secondary-School Principals' Bulletin,* vol. 50 (April, 1966), pp. 57-70. Suggests that investment in education should be given urgent national priority and cites examples of this being done by the U.S. at home and abroad.

Mort, Paul R. *Federal Support for Public Education.* New York: Teachers College, Columbia University Bureau of Publications, 1936. Presents information resulting from research on state educational needs and suggests a plan for federal support to education.

National Association of Manufacturers. Government Economy Committee. *Does Public Education Need Federal Aid?* New York: National Association of Manufacturers, 1956. Reviews the case of federal aid to education including specific references to the findings of the Commission on Intergovernmental Relations and the White House Conference on Education.

National Education Association. Division of Federal Relations. *Questions and Answers.* Washington, D.C.: National Education Association, n.d. Discusses federal support for education and implications thereof.

National Education Association, Research Division. "Federal Aid to Education: Teacher Opinion Poll." *Today's Education,* vol. 58 (January,

1969), p. 8. Gives statistics of nation-wide poll questioning teachers about federal aid.

Shermis, Sherwin S. "The Semantics of Federal Aid and Federal Control." *Phi Delta Kappan,* vol. XLIII, no. 1 (October, 1961), pp. 35-7. Presents background of information regarding fear of federal control that has caused important aspects of the need for federal aid to be overlooked.

Sufrin, Sidney C. *Issues in Federal Aid to Education.* Syracuse, N.Y.: Syracuse University press, 1962. Examines and evaluates issues dealing with general federal aid and asserts that federal interest in education should go beyond supplying of funds.

Williams, Harrison A. "Competing for the Federal Dollar." *Compact,* vol. 5, no. 2 (April, 1971), pp. 5-6. Education should be a top priority of the federal government and as such should receive much more federal financial support.

2. Con-Federal Aid to Education

Marinaccio, Anthony. "We Reject Federal Aid." *Nation's Business,* vol. 49, no. 9 (September, 1961), p. 34. Cites belief that federal aid would lead to federal control.

McMurrin, Sterling M. "Federal Aid Could be Disastrous." *Nation's Business,* vol. 50, no. 10 (October, 1962), p. 64.

Weinstein, Bernard L., and Kern Alexander. "Defining a Responsible Federal Role in School Financing." *Planning and Changing,* vol. 4, no. 4 (Winter, 1974), pp. 233-236. States that a strong case can be made against increased federal aid to education from intergovernmental and fiscal perspectives.

D. THE KENNEDY-JOHNSON YEARS

1. General Legislation

Baker, John H. *The Impact of Federal Aid to Primary and Secondary Education on Selected Southern California School Districts.* Claremont, Calif.: Institute for Studies in Federalism of Claremont Men's College, 1966. Studies impact of federal aid on specific school districts and provides statistics for funds needed and received.

Bloom, A. M. "Johnson Program Deserves Profession's Support." *American School & University,* vol. 37 (March, 1965), p. 7. Commendation of President Johnson's comprehensive program of federal aid that attempts to end fear of federal control and church-state controversy.

Boutwell, William D. "What's Happening in Education? President Johnson's Education Message to Congress." *P.T.A. Magazine,* vol. 59 (March, 1965), pp. 17-18. A look at President Johnson's all-inclusive plan for federal support of education.

Boutwell, William D. "What's Happening in Education? Quie Controversy." *P.T.A. Magazine,* vol. 61 (June, 1967), pp. 11-13. Discusses federal funding prospects for 1968.

Brademas, John. "Head Start: Do Not Pass Go; Do Not Collect $200 Million." *Grade Teacher,* vol. 85 (April, 1968), pp. 29+. Congressman John Brademas presents effects of cuts in the Head Start and Follow Through programs.

Cohen, Wilbur J. "Education Legislation 1963-68: Various Vantage Points." *Educational Researcher,* vol. 1, no. 3 (March, 1972), pp. 4-10. Discussion of Johnson Task Force Reports with commentary on other educative legislation from 1963-1968.

Committee on Education and Labor. *Legislation Concerning Education and Training.* Washington, D.C.: U.S. Government Printing Office, 1965. Reports education legislation enactments from April 24, 1961 to June 8, 1965.

Flanigan, Jean M. "Is There a Taxpayers' Revolt?" *Phi Delta Kappan,* vol. XLIX, no. 2 (October, 1967), pp. 88-91. States data on local, state, and federal revenues for public schools from school year 1955-56 through 1966-7.

Hanlon, Joseph. "The Proposed School Assistance Act." *Phi Delta Kappan,* vol. XLVII, no. 7 (April, 1961), pp. 292-295. Presents good and bad effects of President Kennedy's education proposals.

———— "Here's Scoreboard on Available Federal Aid for Schools." *Nation's Schools,* vol. 75 (February, 1965), p. 21. Outlines legislation that makes moneys available for education in 1965 and designates who qualifies.

Humphrey, Hubert H. "Candidates for the Presidency Answer Questions on—The Federal Government's Role in Support of Education." *Phi Delta Kappan,* vol. XLI, no. 7 (April, 1960), pp. 297-298. Humphrey is questioned about his views on the role of the federal government in public education.

Kennedy, Robert, Eugene McCarthy, and Charles H. Percy. "Presidential Aspirants on Federal Education Policy." *Phi Delta Kappan,* vol. XLIX, no. 10 (June, 1968), pp. 580-2. Consists of replies by Kennedy, McCarthy, and Percy in answer to questions regarding federal education policy.

Keppel, Francis. "Many Issues of Education." *Pennsylvania School Journal,* vol. 114 (September, 1965), p. 9. Contains an address by the U.S. Commissioner of Education to the 1965 White House Conference on Education.

Keyserling, Leon H. "Sharing Revenue with the States." *The New Republic* (March 25, 1967), pp. 14-18. Analysis of national economic policies over the last six years and their relationship to the proposal to share federal revenues with the states.

Land, William G. "Tactics and Strategy of Federal Education Efforts." *Phi Delta Kappan,* vol. XLVI, no. 5 (January, 1965), pp. 211-212. Outlines education-related developments in Washington, D.C. including recommendations of the task force on education sponsored by the Carnegie Corporation and President Johnson's October 25, 1965 speech containing his credo on education.

Land, William G. "The Temper of Our Times: Washington Report." *Phi Delta Kappan,* vol. XLIX, no. 8 (April, 1968), pp. 445-446. Education losing priority on Administrative totem pole according to President Johnson's education message.

Legislative Reference Service of the Library of Congress. *Catalog of Federal Aids to State and Local Governments.* Washington, D.C.: U.S. Government Printing Office, 1964. Lists and describes available federal aid for state and local governments in the fiscal year 1964 or later.

Minear, Leon P. "Some Unsolved Problems of Federal Aid to Education." *School and Society,* vol. 96, no. 2304 (March 2, 1968), pp. 135-7. Outlines specific problems arising as federal involvement in education widens.

National Education Association. *Education and the Eighty-Eighth Congress.* Washington, D.C.: The Association, n.d. Outlines education legislation of general interest enacted by the 88th Congress.

National Education Association Legislative Commission. *Federal Legislative Policy.* Washington, D.C.: National Education Association, n.d. Outlines platform and resolutions of the NEA convention on July 3, 1964.

Quattlebaum, Charles A. "Enactments by the 89th Congress Relevant to Education and Training Below College Grade, 1965-66." *School and Society,* vol. 95, no. 2294 (October 14, 1967), pp. 360-363. Brief review of major Congressional education enactments of the 89th Congress in 1965, with the exclusion of appropriation acts.

Thomas, Norman C. "Policy Formulation for Education: The Johnson Administration." *Educational Researcher,* vol. 2, no. 5 (May, 1973), pp.

4+. Uses systems approach in looking at the formulation of national education policy.

U.S. Department of Health, Education, and Welfare. Office of Education. *Progress in Education*. Washington, D.C.: U.S. Government Printing Office, 1969. 1968 annual report summarizing research projects and programs directed by the Office of Education.

U.S. Department of Health, Education, and Welfare. Office of Education. *Progress of Public Education in the United States of America 1966-1967*. Washington, D.C.: U.S. Government Printing Office, 1967. Provides statistics on educational attainment and funds contributed by federal, state, and local governments.

U.S. Department of Health, Education, and Welfare. Office of Information of the Office of Education. *Milestones in Education*. Washington, D.C.: U.S. Government Printing Office, 1964. Focuses on legislation enacted by the 88th Congress to strengthen education.

U.S. House of Representatives. Committee on Education and Labor. *A Compendium of Statutes Administered by, Delegating Authority to, or Under Which Authority has been Delegated to the U.S. Office of Education, Department of Health, Education, and Welfare*. Washington, D.C.: U.S. Government Printing Office, 1965. Offers legislative histories along with subsequent amendments in presenting federal education statutes that the Office of Education is concerned with.

U.S. House of Representatives. Special Subcommittee on Education of the Committee on Education and Labor. *U.S. Office of Education*. Washington, D.C.: U.S. Government Printing Office, 1967. Presents hearings held in 1966 by the Second Session of the 89th Congress on the Study of the USOE.

U.S. Senate. Committee on Labor and Public Welfare. *Enactments by the 88th Congress Concerning Education and Training, 1963-1964*. Washington, D.C.: U.S. Government Printing Office, 1964. A comprehensive account of enactments by the 88th Congress regarding education and training.

U.S. Senate. Committee on Labor and Public Welfare. *White House Conference on Education, A Milestone for Educational Progress*. Washington, D.C.: U.S. Government Printing Office, 1965. An account of Johnson's July 20-21, 1965 White House Conference on Education.

———— "Washington Report." *Phi Delta Kappan*, vol. L, no. 5 (January, 1969), pp. 302-303. Contains comments by former members of the Johnson Administration, Samuel Halperin and Harold Howe II, regarding inadequacies at federal, state, and professional organization levels; discusses small number of schools to benefit from bilingual and dropout aid.

2. Impact Laws 815, 874

———— "Figures on Federal Aid." *School and Society*, vol. 94, no. 2276 (April 2, 1966), p. 174. Statistical data presented on federal aid that has been authorized by Public Laws 815 and 874.

Labovitz, I. M. *Aid for Federally Affected Public Schools*. Syracuse, New York: Syracuse University Press, 1963. Facts presented on the origin, development, and operation of P.L. 815 and 874.

———— "School Assistance in Federally Affected Areas: Public Law 815 and Public Law 874." *School Life*, vol. 46, no. 6 (May, 1964), pp. 8-9. Provides tables of information dealing with accomplishments of Public Law 815 and Public Law 874.

3. The National Defense Education Act

Bradford, Bruce E. *Impact of Title III of the National Defense Education Act on Teaching of Science in Selected Connecticut High Schools*. Storrs, Conn.: University of Connecticut, 1965. Study showing a general impact in science education in Connecticut high schools, especially in the area of equipment received.

Cohen, Wilbur J., and Francis Keppel. *National Defense Education Act of 1958, as Amended*. Washington, D.C.: U.S. Government Printing Office, 1964. Consists of articles by Cohen and Keppel discussing NDEA programs, followed by an amended text of the NDEA.

4. The Vocational Education Act

Kliever, Douglas E. *Vocational Education Act of 1963, A Case Study in Legislation*. Washington, D.C.: American Vocational Association, 1965. Focuses on the development of the Vocational Education Act of 1963.

———— "The Vocational Education Act of 1963." *School Life*, vol. 46, no. 5 (March/April, 1964), pp. 3-12. Offers background and specifics of the Vocational Education Act of 1963.

5. The Elementary and Secondary Education Act

Alford, Albert L. "The Elementary and Secondary Education Act of 1965." *Phi Delta Kappan*, vol. XLVI, no. 10 (June, 1965), pp. 483-8. Examination of Public Law 89-10 with suggestions for action school administrators should be taking as they wait for funds provided by the Education Act.

Balyeat, Ralph, and Douglas Norman. "Whither ESEA III?" *Phi Delta*

Kappan, vol. LV, no. 3 (November, 1973), pp. 190-192. Discussion of Title III of the Elementary and Secondary Education Act of 1965 with an explanation for its downfall and suggestions to remedy existing problems.

Brickman, William W. "President Johnson's Educational Program for All Children." *School and Society,* vol. 93, no 2262 (Summer, 1965), p. 288. Brief description of the Morse-Perkins Bill with a discussion regarding the Title II provision on secular textbooks for parochial schools.

California State Department of Education. Division of Instruction. *The California Pace.* Sacramento, California: California State Department of Education, 1970. Narrative reports of 1968-69 projects funded by Title III of the Elementary and Secondary Education Act.

Cordasco, Francesco. "The Challenge of the Non-English Speaking Child in the American School." *School and Society,* vol. 96 (March 30, 1968), pp. 198-201. On the proposal for the enactment of the Bilingual Education Act (Title VII, ESEA), with historical background.

Grieder, Calvin. "Here's Hope: Time Can Untie Strings on Federal Funds." *Nation's Schools,* vol. 76 (October, 1965), p. 12. Grieder looks at the limitations of the Elementary and Secondary Education Act of 1965.

Guthrie, James W. "A Political Case History: Passage of the ESEA." *Phi Delta Kappan,* vol. XLIX, no. 6 (February, 1968), pp. 302-306. ESEA historically viewed as not executing usual aspects of general aid to education in theory or in action.

Hecht, Kathryn A. "Title I Federal Evaluation: The First Five Years." *Teacher's College Record* (September, 1973), pp. 67-78. Discusses evaluation of the first five years of Title I of the 1965 Elementary and Secondary Education Act.

Hughes, John F., and Anne O. Hughes. *Equal Education.* Bloomington, Indiana: Indiana University Press, 1972. Examination of federal aid to education with a thorough analysis of Title I of the Elementary and Secondary Education Act of 1965.

La Noue, George R. "The Title II Trap." *Phi Delta Kappan,* vol XLVII, no. 10 (June, 1966), pp. 558-565. A discussion of the problems involved for educators charged with the task of distributing ESEA Title II moneys, as seen by La Noue.

Meranto, Philip. *The Politics of Federal Aid to Education in 1965: A Study of Political Innovation.* Syracuse, N.Y.: Syracuse University Press, 1967. A study of events leading up the the passage of the Elementary and Secondary Education Act of 1965.

National Education Association. The Department of Rural Education. *PACE*. Washington, D.C.: The Association, 1966. Illustrates hypothetical examples of preparation and submission of a project proposal under Title III of Public Law 89-10.

U.S. Department of Health, Education, and Welfare. Office of Education. *American Education*. Washington, D.C.: U.S. Government Printing Office, April, 1965. Gives details and implications of the Elementary and Secondary Education Act of 1965.

U.S. House of Representatives. *H.R. 2362*. Washington, D.C.: U.S. Government Printing Office, 1965. Complete form of the "Elementary and Secondary Education Act of 1965."

6. The Higher Education Acts

Beckler, John. "The Disemboweling of Aid to Higher Education." *College Management,* vol. 8, no. 5 (May, 1973), pp. 14-18. A discussion of the 1972 Education Amendment.

———— "The Higher Education Facilities Act of 1963." *School Life,* vol. 46, no. 6 (May, 1964), pp. 13-22. Reports expenditures authorized by the Higher Education Facilities Act of 1963.

U.S. House of Representatives. *H.R. 9567*. Washington, D.C.: U.S. Government Printing Office, 1965. Presents the "Higher Education Act of 1965."

E. THE NIXON ADMINISTRATION

Commager, Henry Steele. "Only the National Government." *Today's Education,* vol. 62, no. 6 (Sept./Oct., 1973), pp. 47-8. Evaluation of the role of the federal government as compared to the way President Nixon sees it.

Elam, Stanley M. "Nixon's Cut-Rate Rhetoric is No Substitute for Money." *Phi Delta Kappan,* vol. LI, no. 9 (May, 1970), pp. 461-462. Nixon Administration's financial rhetoric causing delay in needed improvements in education.

Fischer, G. D. "NEA Charges President Nixon Reneged on Campaign Pledge to Nation's Teachers." *School and Society,* vol. 98, no. 2325 (April, 1970), pp. 199-200. Tells how Nixon cut vital education programs after his election.

———— "The Honeymoon is Over." *Phi Delta Kappan,* vol. L, no. 10 (June, 1969), p. 553. Focuses on the education cuts of the Nixon Administration.

James, H. T. "Big $$ Boost in Federal Aid Debunked as Myth." *Compact,* vol. 7 (May, 1973), pp. 29-31. Overview of continuing decline of federal aid including discussion of enrollment decline and state's obligation for funding.

Lessinger, Leon M. "Accountability for Results: A Basic Challenge for America's Schools." *American Education,* vol. 5, no. 6 (June/July, 1969), pp. 2-4. Suggests an educational redevelopment program to provide for accountability of the education process and its students.

Mallan, John P. "Washington. The Impounded Controversy." *Change,* vol. 5, no. 5 (June, 1973), pp. 10, 61. Discusses whether the President can impound or withhold funds appropriated by Congress for higher education.

Mandel, Richard, and Francis D. Murnaghan, Jr. "Trends and Musts in Federal Education Legislation." *Phi Delta Kappan,* vol. L, no. 10 (June, 1969), pp. 554-559. Focuses on forward-looking goals of urban city school board leaders with a strong indictment of federal mishandling of appropriation measures.

Marland, Sidney P., Jr., and R. Schwartz, ed. "USOE's Marland Asks Realignment of Federal Education Priorities." *Nation's Schools,* vol. 87 (April, 1971), pp. 37-40. Interview with U.S. Commissioner of Education, Sidney P. Marland, Jr., including views on revenue-sharing and aid to parochial schools.

Nathan, Richard P. "Nixon's Domestic Policy and Education." *Compact,* vol. 5, no. 2 (April, 1971), pp. 7-8. Revenue-sharing, the keystone of the responsible decentralization objective of the Nixon Administration, is both an economic and a political reform.

National School Public Relations Association. *Federal Aid: New Directions for Education in 1969-70.* Washington, D.C.: National School Public Relations Association. An overview of historic education legislation enacted by the 90th Congress.

Nixon, Richard M. "A Candidate for the Presidency Answers Questions on—The Federal Government's Role in Support of Education." *Phi Delta Kappan,* vol. XLI, no. 8 (May, 1960), p. 349. Nixon replies to Phi Delta Kappan questions on federal aid with excerpts from answers to questions posed by education groups in Detroit.

Nyquist, Ewald B. "Shattered Hopes for an Educational Partnership." *Compact,* vol. 7, no. 5 (Nov./Dec., 1973), p. 27. Focuses on the declining role of the federal government in education.

Pappadakis, Nick, and W. Fred Totten. "Financing the New Dimensions of Community Education." *Phi Delta Kappan,* vol. LIV, no. 3 (November, 1973), pp. 192-4. Offers suggestions for meeting the cost of new dimensions in community education.

———— *Progress Report of the President's Commission on School Finance.* Washington, D.C.: President's Commission on School Finance, March 22, 1971. Discusses weaknesses in the educational process that have led to the crises schools are facing.

Rice, A. H. "Let's Stop Playing Politics and Endorse Revenue-Sharing." *Nation's Schools,* vol. 87 (April, 1971), p. 14. Presents drawbacks of Nixon's revenue-sharing proposal and urges interested educational organizations to speak out on the matter.

Rivlin, Alice M. "Education, Politics, and Federal Aid." *The Progressive,* vol. 34, no. 10 (October, 1970), pp. 31-35. Education as an important issue in 1970 political campaign—Administrative vs. Democratic views regarding use of federal funds for education.

———— "Washington Report." *Phi Delta Kappan,* vol. L, no. 4 (December, 1968), pp. 241-242. Outlines 1969 Congressional appropriations for the various Title programs; discussion of the proposed Higher Education Amendment of 1968 and the Vocational Education Amendment of 1968.

———— "Washington Report." *Phi Delta Kappan,* vol. L, no. 9 (May, 1969), pp. 548-549. Discusses the Nixon Administration's plans for elementary and secondary education for the 1970's.

F. CONTEMPORARY ISSUES

1. Voucher Plan

   Jencks, Christopher. "Giving Parents Money for Schooling." *Phi Delta Kappan,* vol. LII, no. 1 (September, 1970), pp. 49-52. Analysis of possible effects of the voucher system.

   ———— "Voucher Plan; NEA Position." *Today's Education,* vol. 59, no. 6 (November, 1970), p. 80. Analysis of negative effects of the voucher system.

2. Church-State

   Barker, Ernest. *Church, State and Education.* Ann Arbor, Michigan: University of Michigan Press, 1957. Nine essays, originally published in 1930, discussing church, state and education matters.

   Blum, Virgil C. *Freedom in Education.* Garden City, New York: Doubleday & Company, Inc., 1965. A study of the relationship between church and state in education emphasizing the importance of individual pupil freedom.

   Brickman, William W., and Stanley Lehrer, eds. *Religion, Government, and Education.* New York: Society for the Advancement of Education, 1961. Discussion of church-state-school relations with special emphasis on the question of governmental aid for religious schools.

Butts, R. Freeman. *The American Tradition in Religion and Education*. Boston: Beacon Press, 1950. Historical overview of the principle of separation of church and state.

Clogg, Ambrose A. "Church Groups and Federal Aid to Education, 1933-1939." *History of Education Quarterly*, vol. IV, no. 3 (September, 1964), pp. 137-154. A brief history of the church-state issue.

Costanzo, Joseph F. *This Nation Under God*. New York: Herder and Herder, Inc., 1964. Historical overview of religious liberty in education and federal aid to education.

———— "The Court Decision—and the School Prayer Furor." *Newsweek* (July 9, 1962), pp. 43-45. Offers societal reactions to the 1962 U.S. Supreme Court decision forbidding prayer in New York public schools.

Duker, Sam. *The Public Schools and Religion: The Legal Context*. New York: Harper & Row, 1966. Presents, with little technical jargon, Supreme Court cases that deal with the church-state controversy.

Friedman, Murray, and Peter Binzen. "Politics and Parochiaid." *The New Republic* (January 23, 1971), pp. 12-15. Illustrates the need for public funding for private as well as public schools. Constitutionality of funding both is considered.

Fuller, Edgar. "Government Financing of Public and Private Education." *Phi Delta Kappan*, vol. XLVII, no. 7 (March, 1966) pp. 365-372. A look at governmental funding with an historical background of the issue and Court applications of the First Amendment.

Gibbs, James E., Jr., Carl J. Sokolowski, August W. Steinhilber, and William C. Strasser, Jr. *Dual Enrollment in Public and Nonpublic Schools*. Washington, D.C.: U.S. Government Printing Office, 1965. Examines the development and activities of dual enrollment programs in nine U.S. communities.

Gordis, Robert, William Gorman, F. Ernest Johnson, and Robert Lekachman. *Religion and the Schools*. New York: The Fund for the Republic, Inc., 1959. Discusses the roles of parochial schools in our society and religion in public schools.

Hock, Raymond A. "Next Stop, Fed.-Aid!" *Phi Delta Kappan*, vol. XLII, no. 8 (May, 1961), pp. 355-356. Fable regarding separation of church and state as it relates to education.

La Noue, George R. *Public Funds for Parochial Schools?* New York: National Council of the Churches of Christ in the U.S.A., 1963. The Protestant view of the role of the government in supporting religious schools, including the historical and legal background of the issue.

Loder, James E. *Religion and the Public Schools*. New York: National Board of Young Men's Christian Associations, 1965. Presents issues discussed during the winter of 1962-63 meetings by the New Jersey Committee for the Study of Religion in the Public Schools.

McGarry, Daniel, and Leo Ward. *Educational Freedom and the Case for Government Aid to Students in Independent Schools*. Milwaukee: The Bruce Publishing Company, 1966. Compilation of works by fifteen authors dealing with their concern for the right of independent schools to share in educational tax funds.

Morgan, Richard E. *The Politics of Religious Conflict*. Pegasus, New York: Western Publishing Co. Inc., 1968. Gives sources for the church-state controversy and suggests implications of the issue for the 1970's and 1980's.

National Education Association. Research Division. *Shared-Time Programs: An Exploratory Study*. Washington, D.C.: The Association, 1964. Report of a nation-wide study of shared-time programs.

Pfeffer, Leo. *Church, State and Freedom*. Boston: Beacon Press, 1953. Examination of the origin and implications of the relationship of church and state.

Sizer, Theodore, ed. *Religion and Public Education*. Boston: Houghton Mifflin Company, 1967. Compilation of essays dealing with the relationship between church and state.

Steinhilber, August W. "Supreme Court Decision on Government-Sponsored Prayer." *School Life*, vol. 44, no. 9 (July, 1962), pp. 8-9. Examines the Supreme Court case of Engel v. Vitale and lists other state rulings on religious observances in public schools.

———— "The Supreme Court—A Loss to Make Up For." *Time*, vol. 81, no. 26 (June 28, 1963), pp. 13-14. Points out reactions to court rulings on religious observances in public schools.

———— *Supreme Court of the United States Opinions, No. 468 & Nos. 142 & 119 (October Terms)*. Washington, D.C.: U.S. Government Printing Office, 1962. Consists of cases of Engel v. Vitale and Abington School District v. Schempp, concerning religious freedom in schools.

Tussman, Joseph, ed. *The Supreme Court on Church and State*. New York: Oxford University Press, 1962. Offers opinions of the court in cases dealing with the church-state issue.

U.S. Senate. Subcommittee on Constitutional Amendments of the Committee on the Judiciary. *School Prayer*. Washington, D.C. U.S. Government Printing Office, 1966. Proceedings from the 89th Congress,

Second Session, on Senate Joint Resolution 148, relating to prayer in public schools.

Ward, Leo R. *Federal Aid to Private Schools*. Westminster, Maryland: 1964. Discusses changing opinion of federal aid to private schools and obstacles involved in receiving aid.

Williams, J. Paul. "Church and State: Is the Wall of Separation Rising or Falling?" *School and Society,* vol. 93, no. 2256 (February 20, 1965), pp. 112-113. Focuses on the controversies involved in the tradition tenet of separation of church and state.

Wolterstorff, Nicholas. *Religion and the Schools*. Grand Rapids, Michigan: William B. Eerdmans Publishing Company, 1965. Discusses current religious and theological matters including sections on "The Pluralistic Society," "Religion and the Public School," and "The Place of the Non-Public Religious School in American Society."

3. Equality of Education

Alexander, Kern, Roe L. Johns, and Dewey H. Stollar, eds. *Status and Impact of Educational Finance Programs, Vol. 4*. Gainesville, Florida: National Educational Finance Project, 1971. Provides information dealing with status of educational financing in 1968-69 along with impact of state and federal finance programs on the equalization of educational opportunity.

Chamber of Commerce of the U.S. Education Department. *Education—An Investment in People*. Washington, D.C.: Chamber of Commerce of the U.S., 1964. Includes information on the correlation between levels of education and economic well-being, educational attainment in the U.S., and characteristics of American education.

McPherson, R. Bruce. "Will Classrooms and Schools Built with Federal Funds be Integrated?" *Phi Delta Kappan,* vol. XLVIII, no. 1 (September, 1966), pp. 11-15. Factual discussion directed at the ambivalent status of the federal government in subsidizing classroom construction for racially integrated and segregated schools.

Orfield, Gary. *The Reconstruction of Southern Education*. New York: John Wiley & Sons, Inc., 1969. Focuses on the political and administrative struggle concerning the future of education in the South since the passage of the 1964 Civil Rights Act.

———— "Report of the Board of Directors." *Liberal Education,* vol. 59, no. 1 (March, 1973), pp. 40-51. Report of the Board of Directors of the Association of American Colleges that covers federal aid to education, and the status of women in education.

Withrow, Frank B. "A Call to Action." *Rehabilitation Literature,* vol. 34, no. 6 (June, 1973), p. 167. Presented is a definition of equal education for all handicapped children and a summary of recommendations for the fiscal year 1973 by the National Advisory Committee on Handicapped Children.

4. Aid to Higher Education

American Assembly. *The Federal Government and Higher Education.* Englewood Cliffs, New Jersey: Prentice-Hall, 1960. Governmental policy making in regard to higher education, including an historical perspective.

Babbidge, Homer D., Jr., and Robert M. Rosenzweig. *The Federal Interest in Higher Education.* New York: McGraw-Hill, 1962. Vice-President of the American Council on Education and Assistant to the U.S. Commissioner of Education discuss the history of federal interest in higher education.

Cooper, William M., William G. Davis, Alphonse-Marie Parent, and Thomas R. McConnell. *Governments and the University.* Toronto, Canada: The Macmillan Co. of Canada Limited, 1966. Frank Gerstein lectures dealing with changes taking place in the relationship of governments to universities.

Dobbins, Charles G., ed. *Higher Education and the Federal Government: Programs and Problems.* Washington, D.C.: American Council on Education, 1963. Major addresses from the 1962 meeting of the American Council on Education.

Field, David W., and Raymond S. Moore. "The Higher Education Facilities Act." *Phi Delta Kappan,* vol XLVI, no. 6 (February, 1965), pp. 177-9. Explanation of the Higher Education Facilities Act of 1963 and its attempt to equalize financial assistance to American colleges and universities.

Gibson, Raymond C. *Block Grants for Higher Education.* Dubuque, Iowa: Wm. C. Brown Company, 1972. Suggests ideas for legislators to devise a sensible plan to support higher education.

Johnstone, D. Bruce. *Federal Support for Higher Education: Budget Alternatives and Implications.* New York: Ford Foundation, Jan., 1972. Attempts to draw together some of the criteria and information by which one might project the proper amount and form of federal financial support to higher education.

Morse, John F. *The Federal Government and Higher Education: Old Answers Breed New Questions.* Berkeley, Calif.: Center for Research and Development in Higher Education; Boulder, Colo.: Western Interstate Commission for Higher Education. Focuses on four basic propositions that lead to significant questions concerning government-university relations.

Ness, Frederick W. "Address of the President." *Liberal Education,* vol. 59, no. 1 (March, 1973), pp. 72-79. Comment on the position of higher education in national priorities.

O'Neil, Robert M. *The Courts, Government, and Higher Education.* New York: Committee for Economic Development, 1972. Forecasts direction of higher education during the 1970's.

Orlans, Harold. *The Effects of Federal Programs on Higher Education.* Washington, D.C.: The Brookings Institution, 1962. Report from a Brookings study designed to look at the effects of federally supported research programs upon the areas of science, social science, and the humanities at 36 colleges and universities.

Orwig, Mel D., ed. *Financing Higher Education: Alternatives for the Federal Government.* Iowa City, Iowa: The American College Testing Program, 1971. Examines economic, social, and institutional issues affecting financial support of undergraduate higher education.

Rivlin, Alice M. *The Role of the Federal Government in Financing Higher Education.* Washington, D.C.: Brookings Institution, 1961. Outlines governmental programs in financing higher education and depicts specific issues that need resolving.

Russell, John D. "Financing Higher Education in the Sixties." *Phi Delta Kappan,* vol. XLII, no. 1 (October, 1960), pp. 8-11. Deals with the development and possible solutions of financial demands in an expanding program of higher education.

Sasscer, Harrison. "Use of Public Funds by Private Institutions of Higher Education." *Phi Delta Kappan,* vol. XLV, no. 5 (February, 1964), pp. 242-246. Questions the manner in which private institutions should be held publicly accountable for receiving public funds.

State University of Iowa. Institute of Public Affairs. *Federal Programs Affecting Higher Education.* Iowa City, Iowa: State University of Iowa, Division of Special Services, 1962. Provides descriptions and administrative information on federal programs such as grants and loans for research, equipment, fellowships, scholarships, and other assistance programs.

Valien, Preston. "The Higher Education Amendments of 1968." *American Education,* vol. 4, no. 12 (December, 1968/January, 1969), pp. 10-11. Focuses on amendments to student assistance programs, other provisions of the Higher Education Act, National Defense Education Act, the Higher Education Facilities Act, and other miscellaneous amendments.

5. Federal-State: Local Relationships

Allen, James E., Jr. "New Impact for the Federal Partner." *Compact,* vol. 3, no. 4 (August, 1969), pp. 48-50. From the proceedings of the Annual Meeting of the Education Commission of the States (3rd, Denver, Colorado, July 7-9, 1969).

American Association of School Administrators. *The Federal Government and Public Schools.* Washington, D.C.: The Association, 1965. Document prepared by a special commission of educators examining developing relationships among local, state, and federal governments as they affect public schools.

Bolmeier, Edward C. *The School in the Legal Structure.* 2nd ed. Cincinnati: W. H. Anderson Co., 1973. Describes legal aspects of federal, state and local school relations.

Cameron, David R., and Richard I. Hofferbert. "The Impact of Federalism on Educational Spending: Patterns within and across Nations." International Political Science Association, Brussels (Belgium). 1973. Drawing on implications of recent studies in comparative urban research, they examine the extent to which the structure of inter-governmental relations affects the allocations of public funds.

Campbell, Roald F. "Federal-State Educational Relations." *Phi Delta Kappan,* vol. XLIX, no. 1 (September, 1967), pp. 16-20. Analysis of federal-state relations in education suggesting reduced power aspects and strengthening of interdependent relationship.

Hawkins, James E. "Federal-State Regional Commissions: A New Partnership." *Compact,* vol. 4 (April, 1970), pp. 18-19. Contains information on the development and operation of regional commission programs.

National Education Association. *National Conference on School Finance* (9th, Chicago, Illinois, April 3-5, 1966). Proceedings: Local-State-Federal Partnership in School Finance. Washington, D.C.: The Association, 1966. Consists of 24 papers dealing with local-state-federal partnerships in school finance.

Sasscer, Harrison, ed. *New Prospects for Achievement.* Washington, D.C.: American Council on Education, 1964. Presents major addresses from the June, 1963 Conference of the Commission on Federal Relations of the Council on Education.

6. International Education

Davis, James M. "The U.S. Government and International Education: A Doomed Program?" *Phi Delta Kappan,* vol. LI, no. 5 (January, 1970), pp.

235-238. The funding crisis in international education with an historical overview.

Read, Gerald. "The International Educational Act of 1966." *Phi Delta Kappan*, vol. XLVII, no. 8 (April, 1966), pp. 406-409. Outlines content and implications of educational legislation under consideration by the Johnson Administration.

XIV. THE EDUCATION OF WOMEN

A. GENERAL

1. Historical

Bass, Ann T. "The Development of Higher Education for Women in this Country." *Contemporary Education,* vol. 41 (1970), pp. 285-288. Historical analysis of women's education in the U.S. on the debate that accompanied women's educational progress from colonial times to the present. Questions whether the "avenues of emancipation" are really open to women throught U.S.

Bunkle, Phillida. "Sentimental Womanhood and Domestic Education, 1830-1870." *History of Education Quarterly,* vol. 14 (Spring, 1974), pp. 13-31. Asserts that a sexual ideology with profoundly anti-feminist implications developed in the northern United States during the forty years after 1830. The bourgeois ideal of sentimental womanhood defining women as spiritual, emotional and dependent was more prevalent than the ideology of feminism and reform.

Capen, Eliza P. "Zilpah Grant and the Art of Teaching: 1829." *New England Quarterly,* vol. 20 (1947), pp. 347-364. On Ipswich Female Academy in Massachusetts.

Conway, Jill. "Perspectives on the History of Women's Education in the United States." *History of Education Quarterly,* vol. 14 (Spring, 1974), pp. 1-12. Puts forth the thesis that developing programs of study designed to raise women's consciousness and bring them into American intellectual life tend to be historical and to subscribe to many of the unexamined assumptions of American educational history.

Cott, Nancy. *Root of Bitterness.* New York: E. P. Dutton, 1972. A collection of the documents of social history of American women from early colonial times to the beginning of the twentieth century.

Flexner, Eleanor. *Century of Struggle: The Women's Rights Movement in the United States.* Cambridge: Belknap Press of Harvard University, 1959. Scholarly history of women in U.S. Battle for equal rights from

1800-1920. Outlines the beginnings of higher education for women including pioneer work of Dr. Elizabeth Blackwell and astronomer Maria Mitchell.

Horowitz, Helen. "Varieties of Cultural Experiences in Jane Addams' Chicago." *History of Education Quarterly,* vol. 14 (Spring, 1974), pp. 69-86. Good analysis of forces at work in establishment of Hull House.

Kraditor, Aileen. *Up from the Pedestal: Selected Writings in the History of American Feminism.* Chicago: Quadrangle, 1968. History of women in the United States represented through a series of selected writings. Basic inequality is related to the fixed and rigid structure of the family in the United States. Included are documents of Willard, Beecher, Grimke, Stanton, and by Mary Bunting on the Radcliffe Institute for Independent Study instituted in 1961 for women who are older, married or unmarried and desire to do research or study in some specific field.

Lerner, Gerda. "The Lady and the Mill Girl. Changes in the Status of Women in the Age of Jackson." *Midcontinent American Studies Journal,* vol. 10 (1969), pp. 5-15. Overview of different periods of American history and the role of women.

Lougie, Carolyn C. "Noblesse, Domesticity, and Agrarian Reform: The Education of Girls by Fénélon and Saint Cyr." *History of Education Quarterly,* vol. 14 (Spring, 1974), pp. 87-114. Asserts that the education of girls is a key to understanding social conflict. Purpose is to study social conflict by studying education of girls in socio-political context, focusing on the significant theoretical and institutional achievements of the 17th century and the domestic education of French girls: Fénélon's *Treatise on the Education of Girls* (1687) and the Maison Royale de Saint Louis at Saint Cyr, founded by Madame de Maintenon in 1686.

Martin, Wendy. *The American Sisterhood.* New York: Harper and Row, 1972. An anthology of the writings of the feminist movement from colonial times to the present.

McGuigan, Dorothy Gies. *A Dangerous Experiment—100 Years of Women at the University of Michigan.* Ann Arbor, Michigan: University of Michigan Center for Continuing Education of Women, 1970. History of women at the University of Michigan since 1870 which reflects the change in admissions policies, attitudes regarding roles, careers, marriage, families and academic capability over the past 100 years.

Newcomer, Mabel. *A Century of Higher Education for American Women.* New York: Harper and Row, 1959. Education of women until 1870 was primarily professional education. Industrialization of the economy and the need for teachers were often reasons for colleges opening doors to women. Much work is needed in higher education to counteract discrimination and provide an education of high quality to women who will take their place in modern labor market.

O'Neill, William L. *Everyone was Brave: The Rise and Fall of Feminism in America.* Chicago: Quadrangle, 1969. Study of feminism from a historical perspective.

Rossi, Alice, ed. *Essays on Sex Equality by John Stuart Mill.* Chicago: University of Chicago Press, 1970. Selections include early essays on marriage and divorce (1832) by J. S. Mill and H. T. Mill, enfranchisement of women (1851) by H. T. Mill, the subjection of women (1869) by J. S. Mill.

Rossi, Alice, ed. *The Feminist Papers.* New York: Bantam, 1974. A comprehensive anthology of major feminist writings concerned with political, economic, sexual, educational and reproductive liberation.

Rowbotham, Sheila. *Women, Resistance and Revolution: A History of Women and Revolution in the Modern World.* New York: Random House, 1972. Narrative history of feminism. Explores the relationship between feminism and social revolution and the varied historical forms that the attempt to change the position of women has taken.

Sack, Saul. "The Higher Education of Women in Pennsylvania." *Pennsylvania Magazine of History and Biography,* vol. 83 (1959), pp. 29-73. Valuable history with notices of women's colleges, rise of coeducation.

Scott, Ann. "After Suffrage: Southern Women in the Twenties." *Journal of Southern History,* vol. 30 (1964), pp. 298-318. Historical account of the political and social welfare activities of women in the South after 1920. Often women would join with labor unions and progressive politicians. Their main success was in the area of the institution of child labor laws.

Scott, Ann. *The American Woman: Who was She?* Englewood Cliffs, N.J.: Prentice-Hall, 1971. A documentary history of American women which includes a chapter on education.

[United States Bureau of Education] *The Curriculum of the Women's College.* Bulletin 1918, No. 6. Washington: Government Printing Office, 1918. A detailed account of early 19th century curricula.

Wein, Roberta. "Women's Colleges and Domesticity 1875-1918." *History of Education Quarterly,* vol. 14 (Spring, 1974), pp. 31-48. Deals with the views of the president of Wellesley, Alice Freeman Palmer, and the president of Bryn Mawr, M. Carey Thomas, regarding the best kind of education for women and the eventual role of these women in society. Bryn Mawr represented a departure from traditional education of women and sought to instill traits of independence, competitiveness rather than passivity while Wellesley concentrated on combining strong academic program with the cultivation of genteel traits, grace and appreciation of the spiritual joys of wifehood and motherhood.

Woody, Thomas. *A History of Women's Education in United States*. 2 vols. New York: Octagon Press, 1966 [originally, 1929]. Historical, well documented study. Good resources for contemporary research into history of women's education.

B. WOMEN AND SCHOOLS

1. Sex Role Stereotyping in Education

Angrist, Shirley S. *The Study of Sex Roles*. Margaret Morrison Carnegie College Reprint #15. Pittsburgh: Carnegie Mellon University, 1967. Analyzes the research findings that women learn to operate on the basis of contingency orientation. Marriage is found to be the most important contingency in the U.S. Angrist contends that sex role is made up of four constituents: label, behavior, expectations and social location and that the changing sex role norms in society justify observing actual role involvement by actors as a complex phenomenon than as a series of individual roles.

Bem, Sandra L., and Daryl J. "Training the Woman to Know Her Place: The Power of a Nonconscious Ideology," in D. J. Bem, ed., *Beliefs, Attitudes and Human Affairs*. Belmont, California: Brooks-Cole, 1970. Critique of unconscious sexism which pervades American society and its effect in limiting women in full self-development of their potential via work opportunities.

Digman, J. M. "Principal Dimensions of Child Personality as Inferred from Teacher's Judgements." *Child Development*, vol. 34 (1963), pp. 43-60. Teachers tend to see the sexes in culturally stereotyped ways and they thus assign traits to each sex on that basis. Grades 1 and 2 were studied in this analysis.

Freeman, Jo. "Growing Up Girlish." *Transaction*, vol. 8 (November/December, 1970), pp. 36-43. Analysis of some prevalent sex role stereotyping of girls' behavior in American society.

Goldberg, Philip. "Are Women Prejudiced against Women?" *Transaction*, vol. 5 (April, 1968), pp. 28-30. In evaluating articles arbitrarily attributed to female and male authors, regardless of the actual sex of the author, college women consistently gave higher ratings to those purportedly written by men, even in cases where subject dealt with female interests.

Horner, Matina. "Women's Will to Fail!" *Psychology Today*, vol. 3 (March, 1969), pp. 36-38. Woman's motivation to achieve is shown to be detrimentally influenced by her need to appear "feminine."

Levy, Betty. "The School's Role in the Sex-Role Stereo-typing of Girls: A Feminist Review of the Literature." *Feminist Studies,* vol. 1 (Summer, 1972), pp. 5-23. Analysis of the current literature.

Maccoby, Eleanor E. "Role-taking in Childhood and its Consequences for Social Learning." *Child Development,* vol. 30 (1959), pp. 239-252. Analyzes the advantages of role-playing for social learning in the classroom.

Rosenkrantz, P., and S. Vogel, *et al.* "Sex-role Stereotypes and Self-Concepts in College Students." *Journal of Counseling and Clinical Psychology,* vol. 32 (1968), pp. 287-295. Higher valuation of male traits were found among college students.

Sexton, Patricia C. *The Feminized Male; Classrooms, White Collars and the Decline of Manliness.* New York: Random House, 1969. Analyzes the effect on boys of an educational system in which most of the elementary teachers are women. Feels that women teachers discourage the boys from acting manly in their rewarding of "feminine" traits as passivity, obedience, neatness, politeness, good grades, etc. Answer is to give women a chance to enter other professions than teaching and get more men into the classrooms on the elementary level.

2. Sexism in School Curricula

Ahlum, Carol, and Jackey Fralley. "The High School Classroom: Feminist Studies." *Today's Education* (December, 1972). A survey of the recent attempts to introduce women's study into the high school curriculum.

Barry, Kathleen. "View from the Doll Corner." *Women: A Journal of Liberation,* vol. 1 (Fall, 1969). Asserts that girls are treated differently in this society, in a way that limits their potential.

Davis, O. L., and J. Slobodian. "Teacher Behavior Towards Boys and Girls During First Grade Reading Instruction." *AERA Journal* (May, 1967), pp. 261-269. Observations of ten first grade teachers and students during Spring of 1965 did not support the hypothesis that female first grade teachers discriminate against boys and favor girls. Concludes that many more obervational studies of teacher behavior in relation to both sexes are needed.

Ehrlich, Carol. "The Male Sociologist's Burden: The Place of Women in Marriage and Family Texts." *Journal of Marriage and the Family* (August, 1971), pp. 427-87. Analysis of six college texts (1964 or later) revealed an abundance of value judgments and myth often presented as fact about marriages and family structure.

Flanagan, John C. "Quality Education for Girls." *Women's Education,* vol. 5 (1966), pp. 1-7. Today's education in the U.S. is not capable of educating girls to become fully self-realized as workers, mothers or informed citizens. Girls tend to be under-educated in the natural sciences and mathematics, and do not have access to as much financial aid for college education as boys.

Frazier, Nancy, and Myra Sadker. *Sexism in School and Society*. New York: Harper and Row, 1973. General introduction to question of sexism in the school. General discussion of the Women's movement, historical and contemporary; criticisms of the movement; the relationship between racism and sexism. The child nurture issue is handled from a number of perspectives, including child care facilities, working mothers, and the future of the nuclear family. The chapter on biological and psychological theories of differences is a creative interweaving of "various interpretations of factual information." Probes the effects of sexist toys, books and teachers on the development of young children.

Frisof, Jamie. "Textbooks and Channeling." *Women: A Journal of Liberation* (Fall, 1969). Analysis of selected social studies of textbooks used in grades 1-5. Pictures of males are prevalent and women are shown as dull and unimportant.

Gerber, Ellen. "The Changing Female Image: A Brief Commentary on Sport Competition for Women." *Journal of Health, Physical Education, Recreation* (October, 1971). Asserts that views are changing with regard to female participation in traditionally viewed "male" sports.

Harrison, Barbara. *Unlearning the Lie: Sexism in the School*. New York: Liveright, 1973. Account about people awakening to the roots and implications of sexism in their lives and schools. Illustrates role conflict between professional staff and parents.

Howe, Florence. Female Studies #2. [Collected by the Commission on the Status of Women of the Modern Language Association, 1970]. Collection of syllabi on the study of women, principally in literature, which have been experimented with in several colleges and universities throughout the United States.

Howe, Florence. "Liberated Chinese Primers." *Women: A Journal of Liberation* (Fall, 1970), pp. 33-34. Discussion of four children's books showing positive images of women.

Key, Mary Ritchie. "The Role of Male and Female in Children's books—Dispelling All Doubt." *Wilson Library Bulletin* (October, 1971), pp. 167-176. Survey of the recent studies on sexism in children's books.

Lewis, Susan. "Exploding the Fairy Princess and Other Myths." *Scholastic Teacher/Elementary Teacher's Edition* (November, 1971), p. 11. Annotated listing of recent non-sexist children's books.

Nilsen, Alleen R. "Women in Children's Literature." *College English* (May, 1971), pp. 918-926. Survey of the winners of the Caldecott Award for children's stories reveals that a number are concerned with males. Few stories were concerned with women or presented women in a positive light.

Stacey, P., *et al. And Jill Came Tumbling After: Sexism in American Education.* New York: Dell, 1974. Collection of analytical writings on the genesis of sexual sterotyping. Sexism in textbooks, teaching techniques, teachers' attitudes and expectations; sexual discrimination on the college level; sexism in the high school.

Torrance, E. Paul. "Changing Reactions of Preadolescent Girls to Tasks Requiring Creative Scientific Thinking." *The Journal of Genetic Psychology* (1963), pp. 217-223. Excellent article of special interest for science teachers and parents of girls.

Trilling, Diana. "The Image of Women in Contemporary Literature," in Robert J. Lifton, ed. *The Woman in America.* Boston: Houghton Mifflin, 1965. Literature of modern times tends to reflect the sickness of modern society and does not attempt to provide solutions. Treatment of women in the work of Norman Mailer manifests American society asserting itself, overly concerned with immediate sexual satisfaction and mechanisms to get it.

3. Women and Higher Education

Brown, Donald. "Value Change in College Women." *Journal of the National Association of Women Deans and Counselors* (June, 1962), pp. 148-55. Puts forth the thesis that changes in value occur when women meet value conflict concurrent with individual growth. Value change involves great anxiety due to socialization process regarding "femininity." Needed are more role models at college level who have equal status with men and who are successfully handling roles of scholar, wife, and mother.

Cless, Elizabeth L. "A Modest Proposal for the Educating of Women." *The American Scholar,* vol. 38 (1969), pp. 618-627. Attacking the fallacy of equality for women in the present male-oriented education structure, urges greater flexibilities in education to accommodate the variety of female life styles.

Cross, K. Patricia. *The Undergraduate Woman.* [Research Report #5] Washington: American Association for Higher Education, 1971. Synthesis of research presented to prompt educational institutions to end discrimination of women.

Epstein, Gilda, and Arline Bronzaft. "Female Freshmen View Their Roles as Women." *Journal of Marriage and the Family,* vol. 34 (November, 1972). Survey of public university freshmen women from lower middle class backgrounds revealed that many young women foresee dual role as career person and wife/mother.

Folger, John K., *et al. Human Resources and Higher Education*. [Staff Report of the Commission on Human Resources and Advanced Education] New York: Russell Sage Foundation, 1969. Maintains that women in the U.S. must have more opportunities to continue education, enter into retraining programs and have access to adult counseling.

Freedman, Mervin B. "Changes in Six Decades of Some Attitudes and Values Held by Educated Women." *Journal of Social Sciences* (1969), pp. 19-28. Studying Vassar alumnae from 1904-1956, reveals a close parallel between social change and psychological change processes. Older alumnae scored higher on tests of authoritarianism and ethnocentrism and the later graduates scored higher than 1940 graduates on the same measures. Suggests that the "tenor of the times" has more effect than anything on the attitudes of college students. Seniors tended to be less authoritarian than freshmen.

Furniss, W. Todd, and Patricia Graham. *Women in Higher Education. American Council on Education*. Washington: 1972. Contends discrimination against women exists and must be eliminated. Conscious and unconscious practices of men present greatest obstacle to women in their endeavors in higher education. Issues raised are academic ability, social barriers, role of women's colleges, feminism, black feminism.

Ginzberg, Eli, and Alice Yohalen. *Educated American Women: Self Portraits*. New York: Columbia University Press, 1966. Contains 26 histories of women who attended graduate or professional schools after World War II. The women recount how they managed their dual roles of career women and wives/mothers, with solutions adopted to meet the needs of their work and family life.

Husbands, Sandra A. "Women's Place in Higher Education." *School Review,* vol. 80 (February, 1972), pp. 261-73. Analysis of factors which force women to accept passive roles and to go into "feminine" areas of study.

Jencks, Christopher, and David Riesman. *The Academic Revolution*. New York: Doubleday, 1969. Reviews the rise of coeducational and women's colleges. Evaluates past and present relation of women's needs to the education that they receive and predicts a declining influence of women's colleges on educational trends.

Komarovsky, Mirra. *Women in the Modern World—Their Education and their Dilemmas*. Boston: Little Brown, 1953. Education designed for women is failing. Women continue to be trained to accept "traditional" views of their role in society.

Lewis, Edwin C. "Choice and Conflict for the College Woman." *Educational Digest,* vol. 35 (1969), pp. 52-54. For a woman to have the desire to combine the dual role of marriage and career, two things are essential in order for her to succeed: she must be motivated to face the responsibilities of each role, and she must have the cooperation and support of an understanding and courageous spouse.

Lewis, Edwin C. *Developing Women's Potential*. Ames, Iowa: Iowa State University Press, 1969. Failure of women to see an obligation to themselves and to society to develop their potential to the fullest and make productive use of their intelligence is a function of socialization process.

Opal, D. David, ed. *The Education of Women: Signs for the Future*. Washington: American Council on Education, 1959. Collection of articles on women, employment and higher education.

Schab, Fred. "Southern College Women." *Journal of the American Association of University Women*, vol. 60 (1967), pp. 142-44. Study conducted at the University of Georgia in 1966 revealed that most undergraduate women wanted to be married by the age of 25; and although they conceived of themselves having a career, they thought it best to give it up with the birth of their first child.

4. Continuing Education of Women

Blackwell, Gordon. "The College and the Continuing Education of Women." *Educational Record*, vol. 44 (January, 1963), pp. 33-39. There is an increasing demand for continuing education of women.

Bunting, Mary I. "Education." *A Woman's Work*. New York: Barnard College, 1967. Asserts that revision is needed in graduate and professional education for women. Included would be the establishment of financial aid policies that do not immediately disqualify part-time students, since many mature women can go to school only on a part-time basis. Further, women's colleges should seek financial aid to help promising graduates who need help in order to go on to advanced eduation.

Bunting, Mary I. The Radcliffe Institute for Independent Study. *The Educational Record*, vol. 42 (1961), pp. 279-286. Radcliffe Institute for Independent Study was established to aid women fulfill their potential. An Associate Scholar Program is for gifted women who wish to conduct independent projects on a part-time basis. Women in the program usually hold advanced degrees and are provided physical and financial access.

Clarenbach, Kathryn F. "Can Continuing Education Adapt?" *American Association of University Women Journal*, vol. 63 (1970), pp. 62-65. Notes some progress in continuing education of women. Priorities must be established that support the movement to include educational institutions in the Civil Rights Act of 1964, and encouragement of the employment of women as faculty and administrators should be at the top of the list.

Dennis, Lawrence, ed. *Education and a Woman's Life*. Washington:

American Council on Education, 1963. Report of the Itasca Conference on Continuing Education of Women held in Minnesota in 1962. Focuses on need for continuing education.

Dolan, Eleanor F. "Women's Continuing Education: Some National Resources." *Journal of the National Association of Women Deans and Counselors,* vol. 29 (1965), pp. 34-58. Efforts of the American Association of University Women and the establishment of special programs at various universities throughout the country in continuing education.

La Fevre, Carol. "The Mature Woman as Graduate Student." *School Review,* vol. 80 (February, 1972), pp. 281-297. Study of married doctoral candidates who have children and are still able to complete doctoral requirements.

Letchworth, George E. "Women Who Return to College: An Identity-Integrity Approach." *Journal of College Student Personnel,* vol. 11 (1970), pp. 103-106. An analysis of the "identity-integrity" model of motivation that older women have in returning to college after many years away from school.

Lubetkin, Barry, and Arvin I. Lubetkin. "Achievement Motivation in a Competitive Situation: The Older Female Graduate Student." *Journal of Clinical Psychology,* vol. 27 (1971), pp. 269-71. The older, more mature graduate students tend to exhibit a far greater achievement motivation than the younger undergraduate. Older women tend to have thrown off traditional views of "femininity" and are able to assert themselves in the academic sphere.

McGowan, Barbara, and Phyllis Liu. "Creativity and Mental Health of Self-Renewing Women." *Management and Evaluation in Guidance,* vol. 3 (1970), pp. 138-47. Found that many women returning to college and thinking about a career often have the following personality characteristics: high intelligence, creativity, relaxed, adventuresome and assertive.

Mitchell, Susan B. "Women Doctoral Recipients Evaluate Their Training." *The Educational Forum,* vol. 34 (1970), pp. 533-539. Found that 99% of the women who receive the doctoral degree enter the work force and are happy with their positions.

Randolph, Kathryn S. *The Mature Woman in Doctoral Programs.* Unpublished doctoral dissertation (Indiana University, 1965). Discrimination against women was found in admissions, financial aid, assistantships, attitudes and guidance.

Raushenbush, Esther. "Unfinished Business: Continuing Education for Women." *Educational Record,* vol. 42 (1961), pp. 261-269. Not enough continuing education programs available for women who are desirous of going back to school. Women should be encouraged to plan for careers realistically, developing the capabilities to reenter the labor force when they wish to.

C. WOMEN AND WORK

1. Career Determinants

Astin, Helen S. "Career Development of Girls during the High School Years." *Journal of Counseling Psychology*, vol. 16 (1968), pp. 536-40. Was designed to predict the career plans of 817 girls in their senior year of high school from their personal characteristics as 9th graders and from selected environmental characteristics of their high school.

Bailyn, Lotte. "Notes on the Role of Choice in the Psychology of Women," in Robert J. Lifton, ed., *The Woman in America*. Boston: Houghton Mifflin, 1965. Women, unlike men, have to choose their careers at the price of overcoming personal role conflict brought about by the socialization process.

Cook, Barbara. "Role Aspiration as Evidenced in Senior Women." Unpublished doctoral dissertation (Purdue University, 1967). Women who pursue careers tend for the most part to be (1) mostly single, (2) less conforming on religious beliefs, (3) more likely to have had working mothers, (4) and more committed to using their intellectual abilities in satisfying work.

Harmon, Leonore W. "The Childhood and Adolescent Career Plans of College Women." *Journal of Vocational Behavior*, vol. 1 (1971), pp. 45-56. By the time women get to college they have already narrowed their choice of careers to the more traditonal feminine careers—teaching, nursing, social work, etc., and have given up many of the career aspirations they held in their teenage.

Kaley, M. M. "Attitudes Toward the Dual Role of Married Professional Women." *American Psychologist*, vol. 26 (1971), pp. 301-306. Concluded that women have positive attitudes toward their dual role as career woman and wife, but that often husbands have negative attitudes.

Kenniston, Kenneth, and Ellen Kenniston. "An American Anachronism: The Image of Women and Work." *The American Scholar*, vol. 33 (Summer, 1964), pp. 355-75. Contends that American stereotypes of femininity are antithetical to strong career commitments in women.

Leon, Gloria R. "The Mother-Professional Model in Academia." *American Psychologist*, vol. 25 (1970), pp. 874-75. Makes a plea for more tenured part-time positions in higher education.

Schmidt, Merlin. "Personality Change in College Women." *Journal of College Student Personnel,* vol. 11 (1970), pp. 414-419. Concluded that in general after four years of college, women tend to be less dogmatic and have great interpersonal competence.

Turner, Ralph H. "Some Aspects of Women's Ambition." *American Journal of Sociology,* vol. 70 (1964), pp. 271-85. Unlike men, women tend to seek intrinsic benefits from their careers.

White, Kinnard. "Social Background Variables Related to Career Commitment of Women Teachers." *Personnel and Guidance Journal,* vol. 45 (1967), pp. 648-652. Found that social background experiences appear to affect the level of career commitment in young women employed as elementary school teachers.

White, Sulvia. "The Modern Women's Dilemma." *American Association of University Women Journal,* vol. 57 (1964), pp. 125-126. Calls for a change in society's attitudes toward women and their role, not only as homemakers and women, but as individuals who have the responsibility of fulfilling themselves with interesting and challenging work.

Woodring, Paul. "New Horizons for Educated Women." *Saturday Review* (July 19, 1969). Catalyst is the name of national non-profit organization established in 1962 to promote the part-time employment of educated women. Organization has cordinated its activities with colleges, public schools, industry, and government agencies.

2. Women in College and University Positions

Astin, Helen S. *The Woman Doctorate in America.* New York: The Russell Sage Foundation, 1969. Counter to the prevailing notion that women professionals do not make a strong commitment to their careers, found that most women doctorates make a strong commitment and are productive professionally. Among the women who receive their doctorate in 1957-58, 91% were employed, most of them in teaching on the college level. At least 1/3 felt that sex discrimination had hindered their professional development.

Bernard, Jessie. *Academic Women.* University Park: The Pennsylvania State University Press, 1964. Reveals low status of academic women. Women suffer discrimination in relation to promotions and administration positions in higher education.

Graham, Patricia. "Women in Academe." *Science,* vol. 169 (1970), pp. 1284-1290. Lack of feminine militancy affords the university the opportunity to remove a great deal of the sex discrimination that is now prevalent.

Harris, Ann S. "The Second Sex in Academe." *The American Association of University Professors Bulletin* (Fall, 1970), pp. 283-95. Discrimination against women in higher education is widespread.

Mooney, Joseph D. "Attrition Among Ph.D. Candidates: An Analysis of a Cohort of Recent Woodrow Wilson Fellows." *The Journal of Human Resources,* vol. 3 (1968), pp. 47-62. Sex, field of study, size of graduate school, academic achievement seem to have an impact on attrition.

Oltman, Ruth M. *Campus 1970–Where do Women Stand?* [Research Report of a Survey on Women in Academe] Washington: American Association of University Women, 1970. Women are underrepresented at every level in institutions of higher education, particularly public institutions. More representation of women exists in smaller women's colleges.

Pullen, Doris L. "The Educational Establishment: Wasted Women," in Mary L. Thompson, ed., *Voices of New Feminism.* Boston: Beacon Press, 1970. Women's colleges should lead the way as models of educational opportunities.

Robinson, Lora H. *The Status of Academic Women.* [ERIC Clearinghouse on Higher Education]. Washington: George Washington University, 1971. Concludes that women have very low status in higher education. Specific studies of women doctoral degree holders manifest the many obstacles that women have to overcome to pursue a career.

Roby, Pamela. "Structural and Internalized Barriers to Women in Higher Education," in Constantina S. Rothchild, ed., *Sociology of Women.* Boston: Ginn-Blaisdell, 1971. Discrimination in admissions is based on assumption that women will have a high rate of attrition.

Rossi, Alice, and Ann Calderwood, eds. *Academic Women on the Move.* New York: Russell Sage Fund, 1973. Series of articles studying the position of women in higher education.

Rossi, Alice. "Discrimination and Demography Restrict Opportunities for Academic Women." *College and University Bulletin* (February, 1970), pp. 74-78. Statistical review of status of women in higher education over the last 30 years with notice of future trends.

Rossi, Alice. "Job Discrimination and What Women Can Do About It." *Atlantic,* vol. 225 (1970), pp. 99-102. Discrimination against women in education is manifest in social rejection, and promotion of less competent men. As women become more aware of the various modes of discrimination, they can begin to use new laws to combat it.

Rossi, Alice S. "Status of Women in Graduate Departments of Sociology, 1968-1969." *The American Sociologist,* vol. 5 (1970), pp. 1-12. Found that the more prestigious the sociology department, the fewer women were part of the graduate faculty. At Berkeley, Chicago, Columbia, Harvard, and Michigan there does not exist one female full professor. High attrition rates and low career achievement cannot be attributed to lack of ability. In graduate school, women tend to be better students than males in the field of sociology but lack of role models and colleagues in higher education can explain the attrition.

Simon, Rita, *et al.* "Of Nepotism, Marriage and the Pursuit of an Academic Career." *Sociology of Education,* vol. 39 (1966), pp. 344-358. Women who complain of nepotism rules as anti-women tend to be more professionally productive than other women, married or single, and as productive as men. A change in the nepotism rules will not solve the problem of women Ph.D.'s as long as discrimination against women in higher education is allowed to continue.

Simon, Rita, *et al.* "The Woman Ph.D.: A Recent Profile." *Social Problems,* vol. 15 (Fall, 1967), pp. 221-236. Study conducted between 1958 and 1963 reveals that women who received their degree during this time are not likely to have been appointed to administrative posts and have not received equal salaries or promotions.

Simpson, Lawrence A. *A Study of Employing Agents' Attitudes Toward Academic Women in Higher Education.* Unpublished doctoral dissertation (Pennsylvania State University, 1968). Administrators discriminate against women when they choose between equally qualified candidates for faculty posts. It was found that age and experience had an influence on whether a woman was hired or not; degree and rank did not. Generally, those who discriminate against academic women manifest negative attitudes toward women in general.

3. Women in Other Careers

Bowers, John Z. "Women in Medicine: An International Study." *New England Journal of Medicine,* vol. 275 (August 18, 1966), pp. 362-365. Discrimination against women in medicine is more pronounced in the United States than in most other countries, according to findings of study of status of women in medicine in U.S., Europe, Australia, Asia, Africa south of the Sahara, and Latin America.

Epstein, Cynthia. *Woman's Place: Options and Limits in Professional Careers.* Berkeley: University of California Press, 1970. Beginning with a survey of cultural explanation of the modern woman in American society, the value systems, process of socialization, role-conflict, attempts to identify those social forces which tend to keep women in their place. Concentrating on the professions of law, medicine, science and teaching, attempts to identify those structures, behavior norms and tendencies which have to change.

Lopate, Carol. *Women in Medicine.* Baltimore: The Johns Hopkins Press,

1968. Suggests some of the things which might facilitate women's becoming successful doctors: flexible scheduling during the training years, child care facilities, child care tax deductions, and more financial aid.

Matthews, Margie R. "The Training and Practice of Women Physicians: A Case Study." *Journal of Medical Education,* vol. 45 (1970), pp. 1016-1024. Six per cent of physicians in this country are women. Role conflict, lack of innovative changes to suit realities of women's education are cited as possible causes.

Rossi, Alice. "Women in Science: Why so Few?" *Science,* vol. 148 (May 28, 1965), pp. 1196-1202. Concludes that women in science over the period 1950-1960 are more likely not to have an advanced degree, less likely to be married. They earn less money than men and work fewer hours per week. Rate of increase of women employed during this time period in science and engineering was 209% compared to rate among men of 428%.

XV. BIOGRAPHIES OF AMERICAN EDUCATORS

A. BIBLIOGRAPHIES

Biography Index: A Cumulative Index to Biographical Material in Books and Magazines [quarterly] 1947 +

Comprehensive Dissertation Index, 1861-1972. Ann Arbor: Xerox, 1973. Convenient entree to *Dissertation Abstracts* (below) and some additional entries. A search should start with "Education," vol. xx-xxiv, by name of biographee.

Dissertation Abstracts International, formerly Dissertation Abstracts. Listing of most completed dissertations, within months after their submission, periodically cumulated.

Finkelstein, Barbara J. "Schooling and Schoolteachers: Selected Bibliography of Autobiographies in the Nineteenth Century." *History of Education Quarterly,* vol. 14 (1974), pp. 293-300. Suggests some additional sources, especially under "Recollections of Teaching" heading.

Freidel, Frank, ed. *Harvard Guide to American History,* revised ed. 2 vols. Cambridge: Harvard University Press, 1974. Further reference and bibliographical sources are to be found in vol. 1, pp. 154-5. Individual biographies, by subject, are in vol. 1, pp. 156-273. The previous edition is still useful: Oscar Handlin, *et al., Harvard Guide to American History* (Cambridge: Harvard University Press, 1954; New York: Atheneum, 1970).

Kaplan, Louis. *A Bibliography of American Autobiographies.* Madison: University of Wisconsin Press, 1961. About 6000 generally booklength entries before 1946, by author with identifying note. Cross index. Emphasis on the American West.

Lillard, Richard G. *American Life in Autobiography, a Descriptive Guide.* Stanford: Stanford University Press, 1956. More than 400 titles, U.S., 1900 +. Classification by occupation, paragraph description of each autobiography.

Lopez, Manuel D. "A Guide to the Inderdisciplinary Literature of the

History of Childhood." *History of Childhood Quarterly,* vol. 1 (1974), pp. 463-494. Essentially, a bibliography of bibliographies, both of biographies and for biographers (of somewhat Freudian leanings). A logical starting point.

O'Neill, Edward H. *Biography by Americans, 1658-1936.* Philadelphia: University of Pennsylvania Press, 1936. About 7000 biographies, listed by name of subject. No elaboration or identification of subjects. Autobiographies, diaries, and journals are excluded.

Parker, Franklin. "Biographies of Educators: A Partial Bibliography of 153 Doctoral Dissertations." *Peabody Journal of Education,* vol. 40 (1962), pp. 142-149; *Paedagogica Historica,* vol. 2 (1962), pp. 389-393. A convenient first checklist for dissertations.

B. GENERAL SOURCES

Barnard, Henry, ed. *American Journal of Education,* 32 vols. Includes a number of biographical articles. For information on indexes, see Francesco Cordasco, "Henry Barnard's *American Journal of Education,*" *History of Education Quarterly,* vol. 11 (Fall, 1971), pp. 328-332.

Barnard, Henry. *Memoirs of Teachers and Educators.* New York: Brownell, 1859, 1861; New York: Arno Press, 1969. Thirty educators' brief biographies, some of which are still informative. Most of the memoirs also appeared in *American Journal of Education.*

Clifton, John L. *Ten Famous American Educators.* Columbus, Ohio: Adams, 1933. Mann, H. Barnard, McGuffey, Webster, Harris, Harper, W. James, Eliot, Willard, Harvey.

Curti, Merle. *The Social Ideas of American Educators.* New York: Scribner's, 1935. Rev. ed., Totowa, N.J. Littlefield, Adams, 1966. Dated but still penetrating analyses of social philosophies, with background biographical information: Mann, H. Barnard, B. T. Washington, Harris, J. L. Spaulding, Parker, Hall, W. James, Thorndike, Dewey.

Fenner, Mildred Sandison, and Elinor C. Fishburn. *Pioneer American Educators.* Washington: National Education Association, 1944; Port Washington, N.Y.: Kennikat, 1968. Rudimental biographical sketches of 20 American educators. Almost undocumented.

Fleming, Alice. *Great Woman Educators.* Philadelphia: Lippincott, 1965. Biographical sketches of 10 woman educators. Undocumented. Possibly a useful primer.

James, Edward T., Janet Wilson James, and Paul S. Boyer, eds. *Notable American Women, 1607-1950.* 3 vols. Cambridge: Harvard University Press, 1971. Intended as a supplement of *Dictionary of American Biography* (below) in which about 95% of entries are men.

Johnson, Allen, and Dumas Malone, eds. *Dictionary of American Biography*. 20 vols. New York: Scribner's, 1928-1937. Supplements, 1944-1958. Standard source; brief biographies with bibliographies.

National Cyclopedia of American Biography. New York; Clifton, N.J., 1893-1973. 54 vols. + current supplements. More inclusive than *Dictionary of American Biography*, sometimes less reliable.

Willard, Frances E[mily], and Mary A. Livermore. *A Woman of the Century*. Buffalo, N.Y.: Moulton, 1893. Sketches of about 1500 women, most of them living in 1893. Usually fulsome, uncritical, but includes some women educators for whom biographical information is not readily available elsewhere. There are other older national and regional compilations of biographies which may be useful.

C. INDIVIDUAL BOOKLENGTH BIOGRAPHIES

These include diaries, journals, autobiographies, and biographies by historians and other writers. Distinctions as to form and source are arbitrary and not helpful. "Diaries" are sometimes altered later by their authors, and become in fact journals. Some biographies, for instance the one by J. W. Linn, have been written during the lifetime of and under the direction of the subject. It can at most be hoped that a biography will be balanced, and that the autobiographer will be frank. Factually they should be correct, but even the most dutiful factualist selects his facts, and is not "objective." There is no hallmark of a "satisfactory" biography. The user must decide that, on the basis of his own criticism, his projected use of the biography, and the alternatives available. Biographies of some masters, teachers, and relatively obscure administrators have been included, as more nearly typical of the "educator." Some biographies of "great men" have been omitted. (It is said that there have been a dozen biographies of Horace Mann.) Many dissertations and theses are biographical in form, and biographical articles appear perennially in local and state historical journals. Some are still in manuscript, although locating them is difficult.

Abbott, Mather A. *Bott, the Story of a Schoolmaster*. New York: Husted, 1936.

Addams, Jane. *Twenty Years at Hull House*. New York: Macmillan, 1910. [repr., 1959.] Addams (1860-1935) established in Chicago the first settlement house, in which education was to be one of the most important ways of helping. Genial, personal, realistic.

————————. *The Second Twenty Years at Hull House*. New York: Macmillan, 1930. An extension, somewhat less personal, more concerned with social analysis and criticism. The two autobiographical segments were republished (1935) as *Forty Years at Hull House*.

Alcott, W[illiam] A[ndrus]. *Confessions of a School Master*. Andover, Mass.: Gould, Newman and Saxton, 1839; Philadelphia: Lantz, 1856; New York: Arno, 1969. Written largely for didactic purposes, still an excellent description of day-to-day teaching in the district school *ca.* 1830, and a biography of more than a decade. See Barnard, *Memoirs*.

Alderman, Edwin A., and Armistead C. Gordon. *J. S. M. Curry*. New York: Macmillan, 1911. Curry (1825-1903) was a U.S. and confederacy congressman, and Confederate soldier. He was general agent of the Peabody Fund for the reconstruction of schools in the South, and trustee of the Slater Fund for the education of Negroes. A memorial volume, but not as over-laudatory as many.

Allen, Gay. *William James*. New York: Viking, 1967. An insightful portrait of the philosopher's personality.

Ashburton, Frank D. *Peabody of Groton: A Portrait*. New York: Coward McCann, 1944. Endicott Peabody (b. 1857) was educated at an English public school and at Cambridge. Having been ordained in the Episcopal Church, he founded (1884) Groton, a private and elitist prep academy. He was rector there for 56 years. Contains much correspondence, etc.

Ayres, Anne. *The Life and Work of William Augustus Muhlenberg*. New York: Harper, 1880. Although Muhlenberg was primarily an Episcopalian churchman, he was superintendent-in-fact of the Lancaster, Pa. schools, where the monitorial method was introduced, and established in 1828 an important academy preparatory school.

Bascom, John. *Things Learned by Living*. New York: Putnam's, 1913. Bascom (1827-1911) wrote prolifically on sociology, psychology, and aesthetics, and was president of the University of Wisconsin. 'Life of the university president' is a frequent basis for biography of an educator.

Baylor, Ruth M. *Elizabeth Palmer Peabody*. Philadelphia: University of Pennsylvania Press, 1965. Elizabeth Peabody (1804-1894) was an important early advocate of the kindergarten, and of many other good causes. A systematic book, in part topically organized.

Blair, Anna Lou. *Henry Barnard, School Administrator*. Minneapolis: Educational, 1938. Superintendent of schools in Connecticut and Rhode Island, Barnard was editor of *Connecticut Common School Journal* and *American Journal of Education* (q.v.). Next to Horace Mann he is seen as most important in the "common school revival."

Boucher, Jonathan. *Reminiscences of an American Loyalist, 1738-1789*. Boston: Houghton Mifflin, 1925. A Church of England priest in Virginia and Maryland, Boucher had kept school in England, and came to Virginia as a school master. Later ordained, he continued as a master. A somewhat bowdlerized autobiography of an ambitious, self-serving, and engaging man.

Bradford, Mary D. *Memoirs of Mary D. Bradford: Autobiographical and Historical Reminiscences of Education in Wisconsin, through Progressive Service from Rural School Teacher to City Superintendent.* Evansville: Antes, 1932.

Bragdon, Henry W. *Woodrow Wilson: The Academic Years.* Cambridge: Harvard University Press, 1967. Wilson as student; as professor at Bryn Mawr, Princeton; and as president of Princeton. Scholarly, comprehensive, critical.

Brookes, George S. *Friend Anthony Benezet.* Philadelphia: University of Pennsylvania Press, 1937. Benezet (1713-1784) was a Philadelphia school master and teacher of free blacks, early Abolitionist, public benefactor. A conventional scholarly biography.

B[rown], M[ary] E., and H. G. Brown. *The Story of John Adams, a New England Schoolmaster.* New York: Scribner's, 1900. Adams (1772-1863) was principal of Phillips Andover Academy, 1810-1833, and principal of academies at Eldbridge, N.Y., and Jacksonville, Ill. From 1842 to 1845 he was a missionary for the American Sunday School Union. A pious book.

Brumbaugh, Martin Grove. *The Life and Work of Christopher Dock.* Philadelphia: Lippincott, 1908. A venerated and near-legendary Pennsylvania German school master (d. 1770), also author of a treatise on how to teach. Substantial collateral material included; this biography still useful.

Burns, Edward McNall. *David Starr Jordan: Prophet of Freedom.* Stanford: Stanford University Press, 1953. Jordan (1851-1931) was first president of Stanford. A history and exposition of Jordan's social and educational thoughts.

Butler, Nicholas Murray. *Across the Busy Years.* 2 vols. New York: Scribner's, 1939. Autobiography of longtime president of Columbia. The first part of Volume I is an interesting description of boyhood, student life at Columbia, and the establishment of Teachers College.

Byers, Tracy. *Martha Berry.* New York: Putnam's, 1932. In 1902 Miss Berry established in Georgia an agricultural school for poor whites. The school was still in operation in 1932. The writer was enraptured: The reader is unlikely to be.

Cade, John B. *The Man Christened Josiah Clark.* New York: American Press, 1966. Joseph Samuel Clark (1871-1944), a black native of Louisiana, first taught in 1890, and was president of Southern University (Louisiana), 1913-1938. Wholly uncritical, based largely on interviews, is one of the few biographies of black educators.

Caldwell, Charles. *A Discourse on the Genius and Character of the Rev. Horace Holley, LL. D.* Boston: Hillard, Gray, Little, and Wilkins, 1828. Holley (1781-1827) transformed Transylvania University (Lexington,

Kentucky) during his presidency from an academy in-fact to an approximation of a university, adding a medical and a law school. Ousted by political pressure, he had planned a similar university at New Orleans before he died at sea. *Discourse* is partly Kentucky political polemic, part biography.

Campbell, Jack K. *Colonel Francis W. Parker, the Children's Crusader.* New York: Teachers College, Columbia University. 1967. Parker, a Civil War soldier who died in 1902, was a romantic in education, by some definitions an early Progressive. He originated the "Quincy Plan" and was principal of a normal school and experimental schools in Chicago. Fully documented, sometimes limited sources ingeniously used.

Carriel, Mary Turner. *The Life of Jonathan Baldwin Turner.* Urbana: University of Illinois Press, 1961. A book of uneven quality. Turner was from Massachusetts, graduated from Yale, and saw himself as a missionary, was a strong temperance and antislavery man. Professor at Illinois College, Jacksonville, Ill., 1833-1847. He introduced the Osage orange as a hedgerow plant, and was important in the founding of the University of Illinois and the passing of the Morrill Act.

Chase, Mary Ellen. *A Goodly Fellowship.* Macmillan, 1939. Autobiography, early 20th century, teaching in one-room schols in Maine, boarding schools, and at Smith College, and lecturing. Readable, sometimes opinionated.

Cogswell, Joseph Green. *Life of Joseph Green Cogswell as Sketched in His Letters.* Anna Eliot Ticknor, ed. Cambridge: Riverside, 1874. Bancroft was Cogswell's (1786-1871) co-master at Round Hill.

Colesworthy, D[aniel] C[lement]. *John Tileston's School.* Boston: Antiquitarian, 1887. Colesworthy was a longtime (*ca.* 1749-1819) Boston writing school master, trained by apprenticeship. Shorter sketches of other masters are included. Interesting, probably not wholly accurate.

Conant, James Bryant. *My Several Lives.* New York: Harper & Row, 1970. Conant's (1893-   ) account of his life as chemist and Harvard professor, president of Harvard, as scientist in World War II, as Commissioner and Ambassador to Germany, touching on his "self-appointed" investigation of the public schools, which was to be more fully described in a subsequent book.

Cooley, Timothy Mather. *Sketches of the Life and Character of the Rev. Lemuel Haynes.* New York: Harper, 1837. Connecticut born Negro, a school master during the Revolutionary War era, while preparing for the ministry. A book leaning toward sanctity.

Cornwell, John Jacob. *A Mountain Trail: To the Schoolroom, the Editor's Chair, the Lawyer's Office, and the Governorship of West Virginia.* Philadelphia: Dorrance, 1939.

Covello, Leonard. *The Heart is the Teacher*. New York: McGraw-Hill, 1958. (repr. as *The Teacher in the Urban Community* . . . Totowa, N.J.: Littlefield, Adams, 1970). Covello was teacher and principal in New York City schools for immigrant pupils, except for a recess for intelligence work in World War I. The book is written straightforwardly.

Crawford, Benjamin Franklin. *William Holmes McGuffey*. Delaware, Ohio: Carnegie Church Press, 1963. McGuffey was original compiler of the famous *Readers*. This is a brief and elementary biography, wholly admiring.

Cunningham, Charles E. *Timothy Dwight*. New York: Macmillan, 1942. Latter-day New England divine, academy master, president of Yale, 1795-1817. Dwight's personality was difficult to recapture. Much background material, interesting reading.

Denison, J. H. *Mark Hopkins*. New York: Scribner's, 1935. Hopkins was the dedicated longtime (1836-1872) president of Williams College. A book handicapped by lack of sources available to the author.

Drost, Walter H. *David Snedden and Education for Social Efficiency*. Madison: University of Wisconsin Press, 1967. Snedden (b. 1868) was professor of administration at Teachers College, Columbia, and Massachusetts Commissioner of Education. A careful treatment of a conservative utilitarian sociologist of education.

Du Bois, W[illiam] E[dward] Burghardt. *Dusk of Dawn*. New York: Harcourt, 1940. Du Bois (1868-1963), black sociologist and intellectual, was longtime supporter of NAACP and antagonist of B. T. Washington's conciliatory approach. At the time of his death in Africa he was a far-left extremist. A personal and intellectual biography.

Dunn, Esther Cloudman. *Pursuit of Understanding*. New York: Macmillian, 1945. "Not literally autobiographic . . . typical" recollections of attending school, teaching high school, teaching in college in the early 20th century. Sometimes evocative.

Duntin, Larkin, ed. *A Memorial to the Life and Services of John D. Philbrick*. Boston: New England, 1888. Philbrick (1818-1886) began his career as educator in 1842, served in a variety of positions, including superintendent of schools in Boston and Connecticut. He is credited with "grading" schools.

Durfee, Calvin. *Sketch of Ebenezer Fitch, D.D.* Boston: Massachusetts Sabbath School Society, 1865. Fitch was a Yale tutor, 1780-83 and 1786-91. He was first president of Williams College, 1793-1815 and thereafter a church minister in New Jersey. A book steeped in sanctity.

Dykhuizen, George. *The Life and Mind of John Dewey*. Carbondale, Ill.: Southern Illinois University Press, 1973. Copious, carefully researched, sympathetic.

Emerson, George B[arrell]. *Reminiscences of an Old Teacher*. Boston: Mudge, 1878. Emerson (1797-1881) taught 1817-1855, was co-author of *The School and Schoolmaster*, 1842, an important treatise on pedagogy, and spoke and wrote in behalf of school reform.

Emerson, Ralph. *The Life of Rev. John Emerson*. Boston: Crocker and Brewster, 1834. J. Emerson (1777-1833) was first a Baptist minister, second the founder of a seminary for "females" in Byfield, Mass., in 1818. Mary Lyon and Zilpah Grant were his students, the latter his assistant. Emerson's general influence on the education of girls may have been of considerable importance. Primarily correspondence, occasional passages by his brother.

Erskine, John. *My Life as a Teacher*. Philadelphia: Lippincott, 1948. Memoirs of a professor (*ca*. 1903-1947) at Amherst, Columbia, with A.E.F. University in France in 1918, and as lecturer. Urbane, sometimes insightful.

Farish, Hunter Dickinson, ed. *Journal and Letters of Philip Vickers Fithian, 1773-74*. Charlottesville: University of Virginia Press, 1957. Fithian's much annotated journal is the most complete picture of the tutor to the Southern aristocracy. Norton, Lewis, *Robert Carter of Nomoni Hall: A Virginia Planter* (Williamsburg, Va.. Colonial Williamsburg, 1941) provides a useful background.

Ferris, David Frederic. *Judge Marvin and the Founding of the California Public School System*. Berkeley: University of California Press, 1962. Marvin (1815-1857), noted as a law bibliographer, spent seven years in California, as county judge, real estate speculator, journalist, Indian fighter and as the first California superintendent of schools. He framed and lobbied for some key California school laws. A succinct annotated bibliography.

Flexner, Abraham. *Daniel Coit Gilman*. New York: Harcourt, Brace, 1946. Gilman (1831-1909) became a staff member at Yale, *ca*. 1856, and was superintendent of the New Haven schools. He was president of University of California (Berkeley) and of Johns Hopkins, pathbreaking graduate university, 1875-1901. A succinct account of Gilman's professional activities, emphasizing the organization of Johns Hopkins University.

Flexner, Abraham. *I Remember: The Autobiography of Abraham Flexner*. New York: Simon, 1940. Flexner, 1866-1959, operated a private school, was later important as medical school critic and school reformer.

Ford, Emily Ellsworth Fowler. *Notes on the Life of Noah Webster*, ed. by Emily E. F. Skell. 2 vols. New York: n. pub., 1912. Webster (1758-1843) was the compiler of the "Blue Back Spellers" and of Webster's Dictionary. He was an ardent nationalist and Federalist. A thorough-going, carefully documented book, including letters and long sections of diaries.

Frankel, Ruth L. *Henry M. Leipziger: Educator and Idealist*. New York: Macmillan, 1933. Leipziger (1853-1917) was a New York City educational reformer, a manual training high school principal, supporter of free libraries, and director of the schools' free lecture program. A shallow, lauding book.

Franklin, Fabian. *The Life of Daniel Coit Gilman*. New York: Dodd, Mead, 1910. Gilman (1831-1909) became a staff member at Yale *ca.* 1856 and was superintendent of the New Haven schools. He was president of University of California, Berkeley, and of Johns Hopkins, pathbreaking graduate university, 1875-1901. The biography is of his professional life; its essence and Gilman's personality may have escaped.

Freidel, Frank Burt. *Francis Lieber*. Baton Rouge: Louisiana State University Press, 1947. Lieber (1798-1872), after fighting in the Waterloo campaign, attending universities in Germany, and going to Greece to aid the Revolution, came to the United States in 1827. He was a gymnastics instructor, encyclopedist, penal reformer, longtime professor at University of South Carolina and Columbia, and a Civil War publicist. A scholarly biography.

Fulton, John. *Memoirs of Frederick A. P. Barnard*. New York: Macmillan, 1896. Barnard (1809-1899) taught in several schools and was president of the University of Mississippi before he became president of Columbia University in 1864. His earlier career is described in greater detail. An interesting and informative book.

Gallaudet, Edward Miner. *The Life of Thomas Hopkins Gallaudet*. New York: Holt, 1888, 1910. Gallaudet (1787-1851) was a path-breaker in the instruction of the deaf, and in the use of sign language for that purpose. A patrifilial book.

Garland, Mary J. *A Sketch of the Life of Elizabeth Palmer Peabody*. Boston: Todd, n.d.

Gatewood, Willard B., Jr. *Eugene Clyde Brooks*. Durham, No. Carolina: Duke University Press, 1960. Brooks (1871-1947) was teacher; principal; Goldsboro, No. Carolina city superintendent; superintendent of schools of No. Carolina; and president of No. Carolina State College, 1924-33. A careful, unpretentious book.

Gegenheimer, Frank Albert. *William Smith: Educator and Churchman, 1727-1803*. Philadelphia: University of Pennsylvania Press, 1943. Philadelphian, Episcopalian. Involved with academy and college.

Giffin, William Milford. *School Days in the Fifties; a True Story with Some Untrue Names of Persons and Places. With an Appendix containing an autobiographical sketch of Francis Wayland Parker*. Chicago: Flanagan, 1906. Giffin was Parker's colleague in Chicago.

Gildersleeve, Virginia C. *Many a Good Crusade*. New York: Macmillan, 1954. Professor of English (b. 1877), dean of Barnard College, Columbia University, describes, sometimes with too much satisfaction, her academic career and contributions to the League of Nations, the WAVES, and other good causes.

Gillespie, Neal C. *The Collapse of Orthodoxy: The Intellectual Ordeal of George Frederick Holmes.* Charlottesville: University of Virginia Press, 1972. Holmes (1820-1897), professor at University of Virginia, and elsewhere earlier, treated as representative Christian intellectual in the South.

Goode, William J., *et al.*, eds. *Willard Waller: On the Family, Education, and War.* Chicago: University of Chicago Press, 1970. Includes a long, insightful biographical essay on one of the most important American sociologists of education.

Goodrich, S[amuel] G[riswold]. *Recollections of a Lifetime, or Men and Things I Have Seen.* 2 vols. New York: Miller, Orton, and Mulligan, 1856; Detroit: Gale, 1967. Goodrich (1793-1860), sometimes as "Peter Parley," wrote numerous elementary texts and children's books. One of the most readable and carefully annotated autobiographies. There is at least one other autobiographical work.

Goodspeed, Thomas W. *William R. Harper, First President of the University of Chicago.* Chicago: University of Chicago Press, 1928. Harper (1856-1906) was at 34 the first president of University of Chicago, a "great university from the beginning." An informal and perhaps not overly insightful biography by a friend, who was also advisor to John D. Rockefeller, Sr., who was University of Chicago's chief benefactor.

Gordon, Armistead C. *Memories and Memorials of William Gordon McCabe.* 2 vols. Richmond: Old Dominion, 1925. Plantation tutor, master of University (prep) School in Petersburg and Richmond, 1865-1908, McCabe (*ca.* 1841-1920) was a man of high reputation as author and scholar. A discursive, informative memorial.

Gordon, Julia Weber. *My Country School Diary.* New York: Harper, 1946. New York: Delta, 1970. A day-to-day account by an exemplary teacher in a one-room school in New Jersey, 1936-1940. The later edition has an enthusiastic introduction by John Holt.

Gould, Elizabeth Porter. *Ezekiel Cheever: Schoolmaster.* Boston: Palmer, 1904. Cheever (1614-1708) was longtime grammar school master in New Haven, Ipswich, Charlestown, and Boston. Probably the least unsatisfactory of several brief biographies, but not much better than Barnard's *Memoirs*.

Grant, Daniel T. *When the Melon is Ripe: An Autobiography of a Georgia Negro High School Principal and Minister.* New York: Exposition, 1955.

Griscom, John M. *Memoir of John Griscom, LL.D.* New York: Carter, 1859. Griscom's career, starting as a master of a private school in 1790 and ending as superintendent in 1851, included the principalship of a Lancastrian "High

School" in New York City and an academy, and a professorship of chemistry. Based on an autobiography; still interesting.

Guilford, Linda Thayer. *Use of a Life. Memorials.* New York: American Tract Society, 1885. Biography of Zilpah P. Grant Banister (1794-1884), an assistant in J. Emerson's school, later principal of Ipswich (Mass.) Seminary for females, and an early advocate and practitioner of girls' education. Mary Lyon was her assistant in Ipswich. Miss Grant retired in 1839.

Hackensmith, Charles W. *Biography of Joseph Neef, Educator in the Ohio Valley, 1809-1854.* New York: Carlton, 1973. Neef introduced Pestalozzian educational theory into the United States at the beginning of the 19th century, later taught in New Harmony, Ind. Technically competent, scholarly.

Hall, G. Stanley. *Life and Confessions of a Psychologist.* New York: Appleton, 1923. Forthright autobiography of early U.S. psychologist, researcher in education, college president.

Hall, Howard Judson. *Benjamin Tompson, 1642-1714: First Native-Born Poet of America.* Boston: Houghton Mifflin, 1924. A Massachusetts career teacher but not a successful one. Primarily of interest to Hall because of his literary efforts.

Hall, Isaac Freeman. *In School from Three to Eighty: Pictures of American Life, 1825-1925.* Pittsfield, Mass.: Eagle, 1927.

Manus, Paul H. *Adventuring in Education.* Cambridge: Harvard University Press, 1937. Autobiography of the first education professor at Harvard, 1891-1921. Manus (b. 1855) had previously held a variety of positions in Colorado. An intersting perspective.

Heffron, Ida Cassa. *Francis Wayland Parker.* Los Angeles: Deach, 1934. Written by an admiring former member of the staff at Parker's Chicago normal school. Idolizing, but descriptive of Parker's methods and beliefs.

[Hillard, George S., ed.]. *Life, Letters and Journals of George Ticknor.* 2 vols. Boston: Osgood, 1876. Ticknor (1791-1871) was one of the first Americans to study at a German univeristy. He was, as a faculty member, unsuccessful in reform attempts at Harvard. He was a scholar in the history of Spanish literature, and a proper Boston Brahmin. This book is primarily a collection of primary sources.

Hinsdale, B. A. *Horace Mann.* Scribner's, 1900. Mann (1796-1859) was first Massachusetts superintendent of schools, appointed in 1837. In his *Reports* and speeches, he served as spokesman for the common schools. At the time of his death he was president of Antioch College. He has probably been more often the subject of biographers than any other American educator. Hinsdale's is the first learned one, and rather fragile.

Holbrook, Alfred. *Reminiscences of the Happy Life of a Teacher.* Cincinnati: Elm St., 1885.

Holt, Rackham. *Mary McLeod Bethune.* Garden City, N.Y.: Doubleday, 1964. Bethune (1875-1955) taught in the South 1895-1903, in 1904 founded Bethune-Cookman College, Daytona Beach, Fla., and was president there 1932-42, 1946-47. She was active in reform and philanthropic organizations. An anecdotal book; there are at least two other biographies.

Horner, Harlan Hoyt. *The Life and Work of Andrew Sloan Draper.* [Champaign] : University of Illinois Press, 1934. Draper, 1848-1913, after practicing law and being active in politics, was New York superintendent of schools; superintendent of instruction, Cleveland; President of the University of Illinois; and New York commissioner of schools. A memorial biography, but measured in praise, well documented.

Howard, Oliver Otis. *Autobiography of Oliver Otis Howard.* 2 vols. New York: Baker & Taylor, 1907. Howard was a Civil War general and hero, director of the Freedman's Bureau, and founder of Howard University. The autobiography is verbose. None of the biographies of Howard seems satisfactory.

Howe, M. A. deWolfe. *The Life and Letters of George Bancroft.* 2 vols. New York: Scribner's, 1908. Bancroft (1800-1891), best known as historian and public official, was co-founder of "Round Hill," prototype for Eastern preparatory boarding schools, and as Secretary of Navy, founder of Annapolis Naval Academy. Biography mostly by excerpts from Bancroft's letters.

Hubbard, Jeremiah. *A Teacher's Ups and Downs from 1858-1879.* Richmond, Ind.: Palladium, 1879.

James, Henry. *Charles W. Eliot, President of Harvard University, 1869-1909.* 2 vols. Boston: Houghton Mifflin, 1930. Eliot (1834-1926) was educated at Harvard and taught there and at M.I.T. before becoming president of Harvard. A substantial biography, neither the first nor the last. Informative, sometimes critical.

Johnson, Henry. *The Other Side of Main Street: A History of a Teacher from Sauk Centre.* New York: Columbia University Press, 1943. Johnson, born in Sweden in 1867, spent his boyhood in Sauk Centre, Minn. He was a journalist, druggist, teacher, student at University of Minnesota, normal school teacher, and after 1906 a faculty member at Teachers College, Columbia. An urbane book.

Johnston, Henry Phelps. *Nathan Hale, 1776: Biography and Memorials.* New Haven: Yale University Press, 1914. Hale was a school and academy master during the few years from his graduation from Yale and the Revolution. Fulsomely written, as well documented as the case will allow.

Joncich, Geraldine. *The Sane Positivist; . . . Edward L. Thorndike.* Middletown, Conn.: Wesleyan University Press, 1968. Thorndike (1874-1949) was important as the formulator of the psychological "Law of Effect," for his experimental work, and for the introduction of inferential statistics in education. A painstaking, detailed personal biography.

Jordan, David Starr. *The Days of a Man.* 2 vols. Yonkers-on-Hudson: World, 1922. An autobiography. Jordan was also an important biologist and a man of wide interests. Sometimes meandering, often overkind.

Kennedy, Millard Fillmore, and Alvin F. Harlow. *Schoolmaster of Yesterday: A Three Generation History.* New York: Whittlesley, 1940. Informal history of Thomas, Benjamin, and Millard Fillmore Kennedy, who taught 1820-1919, most of that time in south central Indiana district schools. Popularized autobiography; descriptions of Thomas and Benjamin's lives must be read with still greater circumspection. Interesting if conjectural details.

Kingsbury, Alice E. *In Old Waterbury: The Memoirs of Alice E. Kingsbury.* Waterbury, Conn.: Mattatuck Historical Society, 1942.

Knowlton, William Smith. *The Old Schoolmaster.* Augusta, Me.: Burleigh & Flint, 1905. Pupils and teaching in latter 19th century Maine. Knowlton was schoolmaster, academy principal, county supervisor, and state superintendent of schools.

Krüsi, Hermann. *Recollections of My Life.* Elizabeth Sheldon Alling, ed. New York: Grafton, 1907. Krüsi (1817-1903), born and trained in Germany, a disciple of Pestalozzi, taught at Oswego (N.Y.) State Normal and Training School, 1862-1867. The autobiography is sometimes mundane.

Lancaster, Joseph. *Epitome of the Chief Events . . . in the Life . . . Written by Himself.* New Haven: author, 1838. Lancaster was one of the originators of the monitorial or Lancastrian schools, and popularized them in the United States.

Lansing, Marion. *Mary Lyon Through Her Letters.* Boston: Books, 1937. Lyon (1797-1849), who had begun to teach when she was 17, was a student and assistant of J. Emerson, and taught with Z. Grant Banister. She established Mt. Holyoke Female Seminary in 1836 and was principal there until her death. Detailed, discursive; there are at least two other biographies of Lyon.

Larson, Laurence M. *The Log Book of a Young Immigrant.* Northfield, Minn.: Norwegian-American Historical Association, 1939. Larson, b. 1868 in Norway, spent his boyhood in northwest Iowa. He taught in district schools, was an academy principal and a high school teacher, 1886-1907, attending with some interruptions Drake University and University of Wisconsin, and later was a faculty member at University of Illinois. An autobiography in

Americanization.

Learned, Marion Dexter. *The Life of Francis Daniel Pastorius*. Philadelphia: Campbell, 1908. Pastorius (1651-1720) was a pietistic German university graduate who taught in Philadelphia and Germantown *ca.* 1700. His papers are existent, and heavily drawn upon.

Levermore, Charles Herbert. *Samuel Train Dutton*. New York: Macmillan, 1922. Dutton was superintendent of schools, 1873-1900, in South Norwalk, Conn., New Haven, and Brookline, Mass.; and professor, Teachers College, 1900-1914. He was also interested in peace and international organizations. An adequate biography.

Leidecker, Kurt F. *Yankee Teacher: The Life of William Torrey Harris*. New York: Philosophical, 1946. Harris (1835-1906) was St. Louis superintendent, philosopher, and U.S. Commissioner of Education. This is the standard source; a more pointed analysis might be hoped for. See also Curti.

Linn, James Weber. *Jane Addams*. New York: Appleton-Century, 1935. Written by her nephew and literary executor, in a tone much like that of Addams' autobiography, but clearer in chronology and narration.

Lutes, Della Thompson. *Country Schoolma'am*. Boston: Little, 1941. A description of a year in the life of a new teacher in the Old Northwest. Lutes wrote other semi-autobiographical books.

McCabe, William Gordon. *Virginia Schools Before and After the Revolution . . . with a Sketch of Frederick William Coleman, M.A.; and Lewis Minor Coleman, M.A.* Charlottesville: Chronicle Steam, 1890. F. W. Coleman was operator of a log cabin academy well known for the success of its students and informal ways.

McCallum, James Dow. *Eleazar Wheelock, Founder of Dartmouth College*. Hanover, N.H.: Dartmouth College Press, 1939. Wheelock (1711-1779) was pastor, farmer, Christianizer of Indians, founder (1769) and president of Dartmouth.

McCosh, James. *The Life of James McCosh, a Record Chiefly Autobiographical.* William D. Slane, ed. New York: Scribner's, 1896. McCosh (1811-1894) was Scotch born, a Presbyterian minister, a professor in Belfast, and president of Princeton, 1868-1888. His book reports his primary interests in the ministry and in the philosophy of religion.

McCuskey, Dorothy. *Bronson Alcott, Teacher*. New York: Macmillan, 1940. Amos Bronson Alcott (1799-1888) was an idealistic teacher and traveling philosopher. A usable, if not great, biography, based on Alcott's manuscripts and printed materials.

McManis, J. T. *Ella Flagg Young and a Half-Century of the Chicago Public*

Schools. Chicago: McClurg, 1916. Mrs. Young, b. 1845, was teacher, principal, district superintendent, and, 1899-1915, superintendent in Chicago. She was a reform president of the NEA, a staff member in Dewey's laboratory school, and a strong supporter of "women's rights" and the Chicago Federation of Teachers. The book, generally laudatory and restrained, was written during her lifetime.

Magill, Edward Hicks. *Sixty-Five Years in the Life of a Teacher, 1841-1906.* Boston: Houghton Mifflin, 1907. Magill, as the name suggests, was a Friend. He was born (1825) in Pennsylvania, started to teach school at 16, and graduated from Brown in 1852. He became a faculty member at Swarthmore in 1869 and was president 1871-1890. Straightforward.

Mann, Mary Tyler Peabody. *The Life of Horace Mann.* Boston: Walker, Full, 1865. Often reprinted, in some editions as the first of 3 or 5 vols. of *The Life and Works of Horace Mann.*

Messerli, Jonathan. *Horace Mann: A Biography.* New York: Knopf, 1972. Not unduly admiring; Mann in his social context. The most recent of the Mann biographies.

Miller, Andrew James. *Old School Days: A Memoir of Boyhood, from Earliest Youth to Manhood, Including the Era of the Rebellion.* New York: Abbey, 1900.

Minnich, Harvey C. *William Holmes McGuffey.* New York: American, 1936. The most satisfactory of several biographies of McGuffey, here portrayed in perhaps somewhat greater than life size.

Morse, James King. *Jedidiah Morse.* Columbia University Press, 1939. Jedidiah Morse was author of early (1789 +) and influential geography texts, and rather briefly an academy master. He is chiefly dealt with here as a participant in New England church disputations.

Motley, Dan E. *Life of Commissary James Blair, Founder of William and Mary College.* Johns Hopkins Studies in History and Political Science, ser. 19, v. 10. Baltimore: Johns Hopkins Press, 1901. Blair was Church of England overseer in Virginia in the late 18th and early 19th centuries, and instrumental in the founding of William and Mary.

Moton, Robert Russa. *Finding a Way Out: An Autobiography.* Garden City, N.Y.: Doubleday, Page, 1921. Moton was at Hampton as student, teacher, and administrator 1885-1915, and then succeeded B. T. Washington at Tuskegee.

Mowry, William Augustus. *Recollections of a New England Educator, 1838-1908.* New York: Silver, Burdett, 1908. Mowry was a careerlong New England teacher, education journalist, school administrator. His autobiography is concrete and specific in detail.

Murray, James O. *Francis Wayland*. Boston: Houghton Mifflin, 1891. Wayland (1796-1865) was president of Brown University, 1841-55, and is often seen as an important innovator and reformer in higher education. This biography, careful if somewhat primitive, recounts these activities, but emphasizes Wayland's work as a Baptist minister.

Nathan, Beatrice Stephens. *Tales of a Teacher*. Chicago: Regnery, 1956. Colorful autobiographical sketches, most of them of teaching in California mountain, small town, and larger city schools, 1915-1946.

Norton, Minerva Brace. *A True Teacher: Mary Mortimer*. New York: Revell, 1894. Mortimer (1816-1877) was a colleague of Catherine Beecher and principal of a seminary for girls in Milwaukee. Biography made up of letters and students' recollections.

Nye, Russell B. *George Bancroft, Brahmin Rebel*. New York: Knopf, 1944. A competent biography.

Palmer, Anna Campbell (pseud., Mrs. George Archibald). *Joel Dorman Steele, Teacher and Author*. New York: Barnes, 1900. Upstate New Yorker, 1836-1886, academy "professor," author or coauthor of 18 texts, plus many revisions. A 19th century memorial volume on a devout, gentle, compulsive man, working himself to death but earning a substantial fortune in royalties.

Patri, Angelo. *A Schoolmaster of the Great City*. New York: Macmillan, 1928. Professional biography of teacher and reformer in New York City in the early 20th century. Intended to be didactic and inspirational; perhaps useful for descriptions of schools and pupils at the place and time.

Pelton, John Cotter. *Life's Sunbeams and Shadows: Poems and Prose, with an Appendix including biographical and historical notes in prose*. San Francisco: Bancroft, 1893. Pelton, born in Maine, was San Francisco's first public school teacher, 1849, and superintendent, 1850. The autobiography is an appendix to his collected verse.

Perry, Ralph Barton. *The Thought and Character of William James*. Cambridge: Harvard University Press, 1935. An important contribution, emphasizing James' thought and philosophy. Ideally supplemented by Allen's biography.

Perry, Thomas Sargent. *Life and Letters of Francis Lieber*. London: Trübner, 1882. Usable as a primary source.

Phelps, William Lyon. *Autobiography with Letters*. New York: Oxford University Press, 1939. Phelps (b. 1865) attended Yale and was a member of the English department there, 1892-1932. At least in part insightful recollections of the life of an Ivy League student and professor, with many digressions.

Poret, George Cleveland. *The Contributions of William Howard Payne to Public Education*. Peabody Contributions to Education No. 81. Nashville: Peabody College Press, 1930. Payne was the first professor of education at University of Michigan, presumptively first in the U.S., and chancellor of Peabody Teachers College.

Punchard, Benjamin Hanover. *Memoir of Benjamin Hanover Punchard, the Founder of the Punchard Free School*. Andover, Mass.: Draper, 1857.

Rice, Jessie Pearl. *J. S. M. Curry*. New York: King's Crown, 1949. Curry seen in a wider social context. Carefully annotated.

Rich, Arthur Lowndes. *Lowell Mason*. Chapel Hill: University of North Carolina Press, 1956. Mason (1792-1872) introduced the teaching of music in public schools. Church music editor, church musician, hymnist, early convert to Pestalozzian teaching, he became supervisor of music in Boston in 1838. The biography, topical in part, occasionally discursive, is meticulously annotated.

Riley, Edward Miles, ed. *The Journal of John Harrower*. Williamsburg: Colonial Williamsburg, 1963. Indentured servant as tutor, 1773-1776, with biographical sketch. Fragmentary, but informative.

Roberts, John Stacey. *William T. Harris*. Washington: National Education Association, 1924. Detailed exposition of Harris's philosophical and intellectual views.

Rodgers, Henry Denny, III. *Liberty Hyde Bailey*. Princeton: Princeton University Press, 1949. Bailey (1858-1953) was an innovator in vocational instruction in agriculture, and an agriculturalist and horticulturist.

Rogers, Walter P. *Andrew P. White and the Modern University*. Utica: Cornell University Press, 1942. White (1832-1918) was first president and co-founder of Cornell; White as a part of Cornell's history, written against a broad background of higher education.

Roselle, Daniel. *Samuel Griswold Goodrich, Creator of Peter Parley*. Albany: State University of New York Press, 1968. Professional, appropriately annotated.

Ross, Dorothy. *G. Stanley Hall, the Psychologist as Prophet*. Chicago: University of Chicago Press, 1972. A Freudian interpretation of an early enthusiast of Freud. Scholarly, well annotated.

Ross, Edward Alsworth. *Seventy Years of It: An Autobiography*. Appleton, 1936. Originator of "social control," an important sociologist of education, an apt autobiographer (1866-1951).

Rouse, Parke, Jr. *James Blair of Virginia*. Chapel Hill: University of North

Carolina Press, 1971. A competently written biography of an interesting figure.

Rudwick, Elliott M. *W. E. B. Du Bois: A Study in Minority Leadership.* Philadelphia: University of Pennsylvania Press, 1960. Repub. with new introduction as *W. E. B. Du Bois: Propagandist of the Negro Protest.* New York: Atheneum, 1969. Somewhat episodic, one of several semi-biographical treatments of Du Bois.

Salmon, David. *Joseph Lancaster.* London: Longmans, Green, 1904.

Sears, Jesse B., and A. D. Henderson. *Cubberley of Stanford.* Palo Alto: Stanford University Press, 1957. Elwood P. Cubberley, dean of education at Stanford, was influential in the school efficiency and survey movements, and as a historian of education. This biography is often over-accepting, unquestioning.

Sheldon, Edward Austin. *Autobiography of Edward Austin Sheldon.* Mary Sheldon Barnes, ed. New York: Ives-Butler, 1911. Sheldon (1823-1897) was founder of the Oswego, N.Y. normal school, *ca.* 1860, and was important in introducing object lessons into schools and normal school training. An autobiographer (and educator) of contagious enthusiasm and zest.

Shepard, Odell. *Pedlar's Progress: The Life of Bronson Alcott.* Boston: Little, Brown, 1937. Alcott, the romantic, described by a romantic. There are several other biographical works on Alcott.

Shoemaker, E. C. *Noah Webster, Pioneer of Learning.* New York: Columbia University Press, 1936. Topically organized, primarily around the history of Webster's school books. Factually useful; dubious interpretations.

Spaulding, Frank E. *One School Administrator's Philosophy: Its Development.* New York: Exposition, 1952. Spaulding (b. 1866, New Hampshire) attended Amherst and studied in Germany. He was a school superintendent, 1895-1920, with the A.E.F. in World War I, and chairman, Department of Education, Yale. Refreshing, sometimes naively, forthright.

————. *School Superintendent in Action in Five Cities.* Rindge, N.H.: Smith, 1955. Further information on Spaulding's professional life, with exposition in pride of his part in the school efficiency movement.

Steiner, Bernard C. *Life of Henry Barnard.* Washington, D.C.: U.S. Government Printing Office, 1919.

Stuart, Jesse. *The Thread That Runs so True.* New York: Scribner's, 1949. Stuart, b. 1907, was a Kentucky school teacher, a principal, and superintendent. He writes with verve and imagination.

Studer, Gerald C. *Christopher Dock: Colonial Schoolmaster.* Scottdale, Pa.:

Herald, 1967. The most recent and most complete biography. Somewhat breathless in style.

Swett, John. *Public Education in California*. New York: American, 1911. New York: Arno, 1969. Swett was born in New Hampshire (1830), attended and taught in district schools and academies there. He went to California in 1852. He was school teacher, principal, state and San Francisco superintendent. The book is an unusual but not unsatisfactory combination of local history and autobiography.

Swift, Frederick Fay. *James Baxter*. Oneonta, N.Y.: Swift-Dorr, 1971. Baxter, an interesting personage and an educator of an unusual genre, operated the "Baxter University of Music," 1853-1883, in a small upstate New York town. A small book which might have been more satisfactory as a journal article.

Talbot, Edith Armstrong. *Samuel Chapman Armstrong*. New York: Doubleday, Page, 1904. Armstrong was founder and first president of Hampton Institute. Born in Hawaii (1839), son of missionary parents, he graduated from Williams and fought in the Civil War. A memorial volume, but more frank than most.

Templeton, Joseph Crittenden. *Chronicles of a Pedagogue*. Sebastopol, Cal.: Sebastopol Times, 1925.

Tenenbaum, Samuel. *William Heard Kilpatrick*. New York: Harper, 1951. Kilpatrick (1871-1965) was Teachers College, Columbia, faculty member, popularizer of instrumentalism and developer of the "activity method" in teaching. Uncritical, in some important ways noninformative.

Tevis, Julia Ann [Hieronymous]. *Sixty Years in a School Room: An Autobiography of Mrs. Julia A. Tevis*. Cincinnati: Western Methodist, 1878.

Tharp, Louise Hall. *The Peabody Sisters of Salem*. Boston: Little Brown, 1950. A family portrait of three sisters, Elizabeth Peabody, the wife of Horace Mann, and the wife of Nathaniel Hawthorne. Readable professional, not wholly scholarly, biography.

Tharp, Louise Hall. *Until Victory: Horace Mann and Mary Peabody*. Boston: Little, Brown, 1953. Horace Mann as hero, with wife (Mary Peabody). A successful literary biography, most readable, if not always penetrating, and even if over-romanticized.

Torrence, Frederick Ridgeley. *Story of John Hope*. New York: Macmillan, 1948. Hope (1868-1936) was president of Morehouse College.

Towne, Laura M. *Letters and Diary of Laura M. Towne, Written from the Sea Islands of South Carolina, 1852-1884*. Ed. by R. S. Holland. Cambridge: Riverside, 1912. New York: Negro Universities Press, 1969. Towne

(1825-1901) went to St. Helena Island to aid the Negroes in 1861 and stayed after the Civil War as school principal and relief principal. She died there in 1901. A useful source for black and social history; about herself Towne is enigmatic.

Turner, James William. *Half a Century in the School Room, or Personal Memoirs of Jas. William Turner.* Carrier Mills, Ill.: Turner, 1920.

Tyack, David. *George Ticknor and the Boston Brahmins.* Cambridge: Harvard University Press, 1967. A highly competent scholarly biography.

Vaux, Roberts. *Memoirs of the Life of Anthony Benezet.* Philadelphia: Alexander, 1817. New York: Franklin, 1969. Early fragmentary biography of Benezet.

Venable, W. H. *John Hancock, Ph.D.* Cincinnati: Ruggles, 1892. Hancock (1825-1891) taught in a country school, then in Cincinnati. Depending upon the fortunes of the Republican party, he was superintendent there and in other Ohio cities, and Ohio superintendent, 1889-1891. A memorial volume, not much documented, but with revealing passages.

Washington, Booker Taliaferro. *Up From Slavery: An Autobiography.* New York: Burt, 1901. [Many subsequent editions] This is probably the most appealing of the autobiographies of educators. Washington (1859?-1915), born a slave, attended Hampton Institute, and founded and was president of Tuskegee Institute. There are several autobiographical fragments also. Washington was a more complex personality than his autobiography suggested.

Washington, Lawrence Daniel. *Confessions of a Schoolmaster.* San Antonio: Naylor, 1939.

Wayland, Francis, and H. L. Wayland. *A Memoir of the Life and Labors of Francis Wayland, Late President of Brown University.* 2 vols. New York: Sheldon, 1867. Almost entirely a compilation of correspondence by or about Wayland.

White, Andrew D. *Autobiography of Andrew Dickson White.* 2 vols. New York: Century, 1905. White (1832-1918), first president of Cornell, was scholar, administrator, politician, and diplomat. Topically organized, clear and detailed.

Whitney, Frank P. *School and I: The Autobiography of an Ohio Schoolmaster.* Yellow Spring, Ohio: Antioch Press, 1957.

Winslow, Miron. *Memoir of Mrs. Harriet L. Winslow.* New York: American Tract Society, 1840. Harriet Winslow (1796-1833) was the wife of an early missionary to Ceylon, and went with him and worked there. She was at the same time sanctimonious and brave, biased and generous. Her biography, intended to serve as a tract, was written by her husband after her death in Ceylon.

XVI. FOREIGN INFLUENCES ON AMERICAN EDUCATION

A. GENERAL

Armytage, W. H. G. *The American Influence on English Education*. London: Routledge and Kegan Paul, 1967. Brief mention of Americans who brought back English educational ideas: Francis Gilmer, Ralph Waldo Emerson, Henry Barnard, Horace Mann, and Abraham Flexner. Bibliography.

Beale, Howard K. *A History of Freedom of Teaching in American Schools*. New York: Charles Scribner's Sons, 1941. Influence of the French Revolution and of England on USA academic freedom.

Bohn, Donald. " 'Artustry' or the Immaculate Misconception of the '70's." *History of Education Quarterly*, vol. 8 (Spring 1968), pp. 107-110. French influence on teaching drawing and later on teaching art in American schools.

Brauner, Charles J. *American Educational Theory*. Englewood Cliffs, N.J.: Prentice-Hall, Inc., 1964. Mentions influence on USA education of English monitorial method and of German Herbartianism.

Butts, R. Freeman. "Civilization-Building and the Modernization Process: A Framework for the Reinterpretation of the History of Education." *History of Education Quarterly*, vol. 7 (Summer, 1967), pp. 147-174. A sweeping view of history which shows impact on American education of Comte, Spencer, Hegel, and others.

Chambliss, Joseph James. *The Origins of American Philosophy of Education, Its Development as a Distinct Discipline, 1808-1913*. The Hague, Netherlands: Martinus Nijhoff, 1968. Tells briefly the influence on American educational philosphy of Joseph Neef, Friedrich Froebel, Francis Bacon, Herbert Spencer, and Joseph Payne.

Childs, John L., *et al.* "A Review Symposium: Lawrence A. Cremin's *The Genius of American Education.*" *History of Education Quarterly*, vol. 7 (Spring, 1967), pp. 102-133. Seven reviewers touch on Plato, Aristotle, Seneca, Grundtvig, and other Europeans and their influence on the educational ideas of Jefferson, William T. Harris, John Dewey, and others.

Cohen, Sol. "Sir Michael Sadler and the Sociopolitical Analysis of Education." *History of Education Quarterly,* vol. 7 (Fall, 1967), pp. 281-294. Mention of influence of Pestalozzi, Froebel, and Lancaster on American education.

Cordasco, Francesco. *A Brief History of Education.* Paterson, N.J.: Littlefield, Adams and Co., 1963. Very useful outline-type handbook indicating the long view and wide range of foreign influences on American Education. Rev. ed., 1970.

Good, H. G. *A History of American Education.* Second Edition. New York: The Macmillan Co., 1962. Presents European influences. A representative general textbook. 3rd ed., 1973.

Hinsdale, Burke A. "Notes on the History of Foreign Influence Upon Education in the United States," pp. 591-629. *Report of the Commissioner of Education for the Year 1897-98.* Washington, D.C.: Government Printing Office, 1899. Useful for preliminary study of foreign influences on American education.

Joncich, Geraldine M., ed. *Psychology and the Science of Education: Selected Writings of Edward L. Thorndike.* New York: Bureau of Publications, Teachers College, Columbia University, 1962. British psychologist Lloyd Morgan's lecture at Harvard turned student Thorndike toward experimenting with animal intelligence, which was a starting point of American behaviorism.

Monroe, Paul. *Founding of the American Public School System. A History of Education in the United States* . . . New York: The Macmillan Co., 1940. Shows English, Dutch, Scottish, French, and German influence.

Nakosteen, Mehdi. *The History and Philosophy of Education.* New York: The Ronald Press Co., 1965. May give disproportionate credit in stressing the great impact of Indian, Persian, Hebrew, and Islamic culture on Greece and the West and thence on USA education.

Noble, Stuart G. *A History of American Education.* New York: Rinehart and Co., 1954. A general textbook presentation of European influences.

Perry, Leslie R., ed. *Bertrand Russell, A. S. Neill, Homer Lane, W. H. Kilpatrick: Four Progressive Educators.* New York: The Macmillan Co., 1967. Uses extracts from the four educators' writings on such themes as freedom, the role of the teacher, and basic nature of pupils.

Pulliam, John. "Changing Attitudes Toward Free Public Schools in Illinois." *History of Education Quarterly,* vol. 7 (Summer, 1967), pp. 191-208. Brief mention of church-sponsored education accompanying German and Scandinavian immigrants.

Travers, Paul D. "John Orville Taylor: A Forgotten Educator." *History of Education Quarterly*, vol. 9 (Spring, 1969), pp. 57-63. Taylor wrote the introduction to Sarah Austin's partial translation of Victor Cousin's *Report on the State of Public Instruction in Prussia*, 1835, and in other ways popularized German educational ideas.

Weigle, Luther A. *American Idealism*. New Haven: Yale University Press, 1928. Spanish, French, and English educational influence.

B. INDIVIDUAL AND SPECIFIC INFLUENCES

1. Jane Addams

   Parker, Franklin. "Jane Addams—Lady Who Cared." *Tradition*, vol. 4 (August, 1961), pp. 43-47. Addams influenced by seeing slums in Europe.

2. Alfred Binet

   Spring, Joel H. "Psychologists and the War: The Meaning of Intelligence in the Alpha and Beta Tests." *History of Education Quarterly*, vol. 12 (Spring, 1972), pp. 3-15. Frenchman Alfred Binet's influences on the early I.Q. Movement in America.

3. James G. Carter

   Chambliss, Joseph James. "James G. Carter on Baconian Induction." *History of Education Quarterly*, vol. 3 (December, 1963), pp. 198-209. Carter's belief that a science of education was possible was based on Englishman Francis Bacon's inductive method.

4. Colonial and Early Republic

   Barnard, H. C. *Education and the French Revolution*. Cambridge: The University Press, 1969. Influence of French *philosophes* (Rousseau *et al.*) on educational ideas of Benjamin Franklin, Thomas Jefferson, and others.

   Belok, Michael V. "The Courtesy Tradition and Early Schoolbooks." *History of Education Quarterly*, vol. 8 (Fall, 1968) pp. 308-318. Books of courtesy (etiquette and manners), part of a tradition reaching back to Aristotle, Cicero, Erasmus, Peacham, and John Locke, were used to teach reading in colonial schools.

   Best, John Hardin, ed. *Benjamin Franklin on Education*. New York: Bureau of Publications, Teachers College, Columbia University, 1962. English and French Enlightenment influenced Franklin's educational thought.

   Cremin, Lawrence A. *American Education: The Colonial Experience 1607-1783*. New York: Harper & Row, Publishers, 1970. Systematic and detailed treatment of European influence on Colonial American thought and education. Good bibliographical essay.

Geobel, Edmund Joseph. *A Study of Catholic Secondary Education During the Colonial Period Up to the First Plenary Council of Baltimore 1852*. Washington, D.C.: The Catholic University of America, 1936. Influence of English, French, and Italian scholars and schoolmen.

Hansen, Allen Oscar. *Liberalism and American Education in the Eighteenth Century*. New York: The Macmillan Co., 1926. French, English, and other enlightened Europeans' influence on early American educational thinkers.

Kemp, William Webb. *The Support of Schools in Colonial New York by the Society for the Propagation of the Gospel*. New York: AMS Press, 1972. Influence of Anglican minister Thomas Bray, the Society for the Propagation of Christian Knowledge, and its overseas mission, the Society for the Propagation of the Gospel.

Knight, Edgar W., and Clifton L. Hall. *Readings in American Educational History*. New York: Appleton-Century-Crofts, Inc., 1951. English and Dutch influence during the Colonial period.

Kuritz, Hyman. "Benjamin Rush: His Theory of Republican Education." *History of Education Quarterly,* vol. 7 (Winter, 1967), pp. 432-451. Traces early American educational thought to Locke and to Scottish influence.

Messerli, Jonathan. "The Columbian Complex: The Impulse to National Consolidation." *History of Education Quarterly,* vol. 7 (Winter, 1967), pp. 417-431. Traces early American national educational plans to French thinkers: Chalotais, Diderot, Condorcet, and others.

Parker, Franklin. "Philip Vickers Fithian: Northern Tutor on a Southern Plantation." *Journal of the West,* vol. 4 (January, 1965), pp. 56-62. British and French influence on southern education.

Pilcher, George William, ed. *The Reverend Samuel Davies Abroad: The Diary of a Journey to England and Scotland, 1753-55*. Urbana: University of Illinois Press, 1967. Travel diary of a Presbyterian minister raising education funds in Britain.

Rudolph, Frederick, ed. *Essays on Education in the Early Republic*. Cambridge, Massachusetts: The Belknap Press of Harvard University Press, 1965. English and French influence on early American theoretical plans for an education system.

Seybolt, Robert Francis. *Apprenticeship & Apprenticeship Education in Colonial New England & New York*. New York: Teachers College,

Columbia University, 1917. Chapter 1, "The Apprenticeship System in England," shows English influence.

Seybolt, Robert Francis. *Private Schools of Colonial Boston*. Westport, Conn.: Greenwood Press, Publishers, 1935. Newspaper and diary accounts of Colonial teachers, many of them born in England.

Seybolt, Robert Francis. *Source Studies in American Colonial Education. The Private School*. New York: Arno Press & The New York Times, 1971. Mentions European-born teachers of French and German.

Silver, Harold, ed. *Robert Owen on Education*. Cambridge: The University Press, 1969. Introduction mentions influence on American education of ideas from Frenchmen J. J. Rousseau and Claude Adrien Helvetius to English thinkers William Godwin and Robert Owen.

Small, Walter Herbert. *Early New England Schools*. New York: Arno Press & The New York Times, 1969. Early New England schools reflected mainly English influence.

Thayer, V. T. *Formative Ideas in American Education*. New York: Dodd, Mead and Co., 1965. Locke's influence on early American thought and education.

Urofsky, Melvin I. "Reforms and Response: The Yale Report of 1828." *History of Education Quarterly*, vol. 5 (March, 1965), pp. 53-67. Aristotelian and Thomistic influence on early American education.

5. Friedrich Froebel

Lawrence, Evelyn. *Friedrich Froebel and English Education*. Schocken Press, 1969. Essays about Froebel's influence on British primary education, which has, in turn, influenced recent USA open education.

Lazerson, Marvin. "Urban Reform and the Schools: Kindergartens in Massachusetts, 1870-1915." *History of Education Quarterly*, vol. 11 (Summer, 1971), pp. 115-142. Elizabeth Palmer Peabody's contact with Mrs. Carl Schurz and Peabody's European tour to observe Froebelian kindergartens.

6. William T. Harris

Anderson, Paul R. *Platonism in the Midwest*. New York: Temple University Publications, 1963. Plato, Hegel, and other idealists' influence on William Torrey Harris and other Midwestern American educators.

7. Johann F. Herbart

Dunkel, Harold B. "Herbart's Pedagogical Seminar." *History of Education*

Quarterly, vol. 7 (Spring, 1967), pp. 93-101. Herbart's influence on his assistant, Taute, and his later influence on Ziller and Rein—who in turn influenced Americans Charles DeGarmo and the McMurry brothers.

McMurry, Charles. *The Elements of General Method: Based on the Principles of Herbart.* Bloomington, Ill.: Public School Publishing Co., *1892. Herbart's influence spread by leading American interpreter.*

Moulton, Gerald L. Part I, "The American Herbartian: A Portrait from His Yearbooks." *History of Education Quarterly,* vol. 3 (September, 1963), pp. 134-142; Part II, vol. 3 (December, 1963), pp. 187-197. Kant's influence on Herbart and Herbart's education ideas as interpreted in the *Yearbooks* of the National Herbart Society.

Robarts, James R. "The Quest for a Science of Education." *History of Education Quarterly,* vol. 8 (Winter, 1968), pp. 431-446. Herbartianism and German experimental psychology held promise for a science of education in America. This quest has never been satisfied and continues today in the USA.

Sequel, Mary Louise. *The Curriculum Field: Its Formative Years.* New York: Teachers College Press, 1966. Among major curriculum movements, Herbartian influence is mentioned via Charles and Frank McMurry.

Strickland, Charles E. "The Child, the Community, and Clio: The Uses of Cultural History in Elementary School Experiments of the Eighteen-Nineties." *History of Education Quarterly,* vol. 7 (Winter, 1967), pp. 474-492. Mentions influence of the Herbartians and of Rousseau.

8. Higher Education

Barnes, Sherman B. "The Entry of Science and History in the College Curriculum, 1865-1914." *History of Education Quarterly,* vol. 4 (March, 1964), pp. 44-58. American acceptance of science and history as important school subjects through the ideas of Hegel, Comte, Kant, Spencer, and other Europeans.

Brickman, Willam W., and Stanley Lehrer, eds. *A Century of Higher Education: Classical Citadel to Collegiate Colossum.* New York: Society for the Advancement of Education, Inc., 1963. Willis Rudy's opening article examines the adaptation of European educational models in America.

Carrell, Wiliam D. "American College Professors: 1750-1800." *History of Education Quarterly,* vol. 8 (Fall, 1968), pp. 289-305. American professors held memberships in professional societies of London, Edinburgh, Paris, Utrecht, Rome, Göttingen, Mannheim.

Cohen, Sheldon S. "Benjamin Trumbull, the Years at Yale 1755-1759." *History of Education Quarterly,* vol. 6 (Winter, 1966), pp. 33-48. English Whig and European Calvinist influences on Yale.

Cordasco, Francesco. *Daniel Coit Gilman and the Protean Ph.D.: The Shaping of American Graduate Education.* Leiden, The Netherlands: E. J. Brill, Publisher, 1960. Rejects the influence of the German *Wissenschaftslehre* tradition on American graduate education.

Dulles, Foster Rhea. *Americans Abroad: The Centuries of European Travel.* Ann Arbor: University of Michigan Press, 1964. American scholars and university presidents who studies in Europe (mainly Germany) and brought back influential ideas: James B. Angell, Charles W. Eliot, Arthur Twining Hadley, John Grier Hibben, Andrew D. White, Daniel Coit Gilman, Basil Gildersleeve, William Graham Sumner, Herbert Baxter Adams, and others.

Flexner, Abraham. *I Remember.* New York: Simon and Schuster, 1940. Foundation executive Flexner's incisive comment on European models influenced USA higher education, particularly medical education. He helped bring Albert Einstein permanently to the USA.

Flexner, Abraham. *Universities: American, English and German.* New York: Oxford University Press, 1930. Critically compares and shows the influence of English and German universities on American universities. Mentions influence of Rousseau, Froebel, and Pestalozzi.

Florer, John H. "Major Issues in the Congressional Debate of the Morrill Act of 1862." *History of Education Quarterly,* vol. 8 (Winter, 1968), pp. 459-478. Congressman Morrill's argument for land grant colleges included his belief that the greater number of agricultural schools in Russia and France had put them ahead of the USA in development.

Ford, Charles E. "Botany Texts: A Survey of the Development in American Higher Education, 1643-1906." *History of Education Quarterly,* vol. 4 (March, 1964), pp. 59-71. British and French influence on American botany textbooks.

Fraser, Stewart, ed. *The Evils of a Foreign Education or Birdseye Northrop on Education Abroad.* Nashville: International Center, George Peabody College for Teachers, 1966. Mentions popularity of graduate study in Germany. Also comments on Americans studying in France and England.

Hans, Nicholas. "The Project of Transferring the University of Geneva to America." *History of Education Quarterly,* vol. 8 (Summer, 1968), pp. 246-251. English and French plan.

Herbst, Jurgen. *The German Historical School in American Scholarship: A*

Study in the Transfer of Culture. Ithaca: Cornell University Press, 1965. American students brought from German universities seminars, journals, and scholarship which influenced USA higher education.

Hofstadter, Richard, and Walter P. Metzger. *The Development of Academic Freedom in the United States*. New York: Columbia University Press, 1955. Concept of academic freedom in American higher education traced from German, French, and English influence.

Horn, D. B. *A Short History of the University of Edinburgh, 1556-1889*. Edinburgh: Edinburgh University Press, 1967. The University of Edinburgh's influences on the colonial colleges, on the College of New Jersey (later Princeton) via John Witherspoon, and on medical education at the College of Philadelphia and at King's College.

Kohlbrenner, Bernard J. "Religion and Higher Education: An Historical Perspective." *History of Education Quarterly*, vol. 1 (June, 1961), pp. 45-56. British and German influence on American higher education.

Kraus, Joe W. "The Development of a Curriculum in the Early American Colleges." *History of Education Quarterly*, vol. 1 (June, 1961), pp. 64-76. British influence on curriculum and administration of early American colleges.

Lazerson, Marvin. "F. A. P. Barnard and Columbia College: Prologue to a University." *History of Education Quarterly*, vol. 6 (Winter, 1966), pp. 49-64. German and British influences on Barnard's administration at Columbia.

Nash, Paul. "Innocents Abroad: American Students at British Universities in the Early Nineteenth Century." *History of Education Quarterly*, vol. 1 (June, 1961), pp. 32-44. British influence on such USA scholars as Benjamin Silliman, John Shaw, William Gibson, Valentine Mott, and others.

Parker, Franklin. "Abraham Flexner (1886-1959) and Medical Education." *Journal of Medical Education*, vol. 36 (June, 1961). Influenced by European university medical education.

Paulston, Roland G. "French Influence in American Institutions of Higher Learning, 1784-1825." *History of Education Quarterly*, vol. 8 (Summer, 1968), pp. 229-245. Influence of Frenchmen Marquis de Condorcet, Chevalier Quesnay de Beaurepaire, and others. French influence on the founding of the University of the State of New York and the University of Michigan.

Payton, Phillip W. "Origins of the Terms 'Major' and 'Minor' in American Higher Education." *History of Education Quarterly*, vol. 1 (June, 1961), pp. 57-63. German influence on American higher education.

Peterson, George E. *The New England College in the Age of the University*. Amherst: Amherst College Press, 1964. One thesis explored is that Darwinism coupled with other nineteenth century developments discouraged small colleges and hastened the rise of universities in the USA.

Ryan, Will Carson. *Studies in Early Graduate Education*. New York: Carnegie Foundation for the Advancement of Teaching, 1931. Mentions briefly the German universities as a model for graduate education at Johns Hopkins University, Clark University, and the University of Chicago.

Sack, Saul. *History of Higher Education in Pennsylvania*. Harrisburg: Pennsylvania Historical and Museum Commission, 1963. 2 vols. Meticulously detailed account of British, German, and other European influences on higher education in Pennsylvania.

Sloan, Douglas. *The Scottish Enlightenment and the American College Ideal*. New York: Teachers College Press, 1971. Impact of the Scottish Enlightenment and universities on American higher education, 1740-1810, especially on Princeton University Presidents John Witherspoon and Samuel Stanhope Smith and on Francis Alison of Philadelphia and Benjamin Rush of the College of Philadelphia.

Thwing, Charles F. *A History of Higher Education in America*. New York: D. Appleton & Co., 1906. French, German, English, and Scottish influence treated in considerable detail.

Walsh, James J. *Education of the Founding Fathers of the Republic: Scholasticism in the Colonial Colleges . . .* New York: Fordham University Press, 1935. Medieval (scholastic), renaissance, and Reformation influence on early American leaders and particularly on USA higher education.

9. Thomas Jefferson

Kaplan, Lawrence S. *Jefferson and France, An Essay on Politics and Political Ideas*. New Haven: Yale University Press, 1967. While enrolled at the College of William and Mary, Jefferson studied classical writings of Greece, Rome, and the French Enlightenment. As Virginia's governor, he introduced French into his alma mater's curriculum.

10. Horace Mann and Henry Barnard

Barnard, Henry. *National Education in Europe, Being an Account of the Organization, Administration, Instruction, and Statistics of Free Schools of Different Grades in the Principal States*. 2nd ed. New York: Charles B. Norton, 1854. School observations from Barnard's European tour of 1835-36: Germany (with an extract from Horace Mann's seventh annual report), Prussia, Switzerland, France, England, and 16 other national school systems.

Brubacher, John S., ed. *Henry Barnard on Education*. New York: Russell & Russell, 1965. English, French, and other European educators and school systems mentioned.

Cremin, Lawrence A. *The Republic and the School*. New York: Bureau of Publications, Teachers College, Columbia University, 1957. Calls Mann a child of the enlightenment. Readings from Mann's reports including the seventh report on European schools.

Jenkins, Ralph C., and Gertrude Chandler Warner. *Henry Barnard, An Introduction*. Hartford: Connecticut State Teachers Association, 1937. Barnard as delegate to International Exhibition, London, 1854. Saw kindergarten in operation and observed Pestalozzian and Froebelian teaching methods.

11. Monitorial Schools: Joseph Lancaster and Andrew Bell

Kaestle, Carl F. *Joseph Lancaster and the Monitorial School Movement: A Documentary History*. New York: Teachers College Press, Columbia University, 1973. Valuable sourcebook, with introduction and bibliographical essay. See also, Joseph Lancaster, *Improvements in Education As It Respects the Industrious Classes of the Community. 3rd Edition with Additions* [1805]. With An Introduction by Francesco Cordasco. Clifton, N.J.: Augustus M. Kelley, 1973.

Lannie, Vincent P., and Bernard C. Diethorn. "For the Honor and Glory of God: The Philadelphia Bible Riots of 1840." *History of Education Quarterly*, vol. 8 (Spring, 1968), pp. 44-106. Mentions English Lancastrian system as conducted in Philadelphia.

Reigart, John Franklin. *The Lancastrian System of Instruction in the Schools of New York City*. New York: Arno Press and The New York Times, 1969. [Originally, 1916] Brief account of origin of monitorial schools in England under Anglican Andrew Bell and particularly the Quaker educator Joseph Lancaster. Bibliography.

12. Maria Montessori

Hainstock, Elizabeth G. *Teaching Montessori in the Home: The School Years*. New York: Random House, 1971. How mathematics and language learning can be aided by supplementing the child's school instruction with Montessori methods at home.

Lillard, Paula Polk. *Montessori, A Modern Approach*. New York: Schocken Books, 1972. Puts Montessori into historical and philosophical perspective, explains the Montessori method, and appeals for its application in American schools. Notes, bibliography.

Montessori, Maria. *From Childhood to Adolescence, Including Erdkinder and The Function of the University.* New York: Schocken Books, 1973. The publisher's introductory note compares Montessori to Jerome Bruner, A. S. Neill, and Jean Piaget.

Montessori, Maria. *Dr. Montessori's Own Handbook.* New York: Schocken Books, 1965. At the urging of S. S. McClure, Montessori visited the USA, dedicated her handbook to Helen Keller and Anne Sullivan, and wrote it "in response to requests from thousands of American parents and teachers."

National Association for the Education of Young Children, Publications Committee, ed. *Montessori in Perspective.* Washington: National Association for the Education of Young Children, 1966. Seven essays put Montessori into historical perspective and present advantages and disadvantages of the Montessori method. 18 references.

Orem, Reginald C. *Montessori Today.* New York: G. P. Putnam's Sons, 1971. A well-rounded exposition on Montessorian education with guidelines for setting up a Montessori school. Annotated bibliography.

Standing, E. Mortimer. *The Montessori Method: A Revolution in Education.* Fresno: The Academy Library Guild, 1962. This Montessorian disciple analyzes: Parts One—Montessori Principles; Two—Montessori Illustrated; Three—Montessori in Action; Four—Montessori in America. Bibliography.

Stevens, Ellen Yale. *A Guide to the Montessori Method.* 2nd ed. New York: Frederick A. Stokes Co., 1913. The author, a pupil of John Dewey, describes the psychological basis of Montessori's methods.

13. A. S. Neill

Hart, Harold H., ed. *Summerhill: For & Against.* New York: Hart Publishing Co., Inc., 1970. Fifteen observers—among them Max Rafferty, Fred Hechinger, John Holt, Bruno Bettelheim, Sylvia Ashton-Warner, Paul Goodman, and Erich Fromm—react to Summerhill.

14. Open Education

"Americanizing the Open School." *Nation's Schools,* vol. 90 (September, 1972), pp. 45-49. Citing British influence, the article tells of diverse types and uses of space as American schools shift to open education.

Barth, Roland S. *Open Education and the American School.* New York: Agathon Press, 1972. Introduction traces sources of USA open education to British primary schools (especially Leicestershire plan) and to such figures as Freud, Erikson, Froebel, and Dewey. Chapter notes; good 249-item annotated bibliography.

Boyce, E. R. *Play in the Infants' School*. New York: Agathon Press, 1972. Introduction by Lillian Weber, leading USA advocate of open education along British primary school lines.

Cazden, Courtney B. *Infant Schools*. Newton, Mass.: Education Development Center, 1969. Interview with the director of London's Gordonbrock Infant School.

Featherstone, Joseph. "How Children Learn." *The New Republic*, vol. 157 (September 2, 1967), pp. 17-21. Second of three early widely circulated articles on British primary education which spurred USA open education.

Featherstone, Joseph. *Informal Schools in Britain Today: An Introduction*. New York: Citation Press, 1971. First of a series of booklets on British primary schools funded by the Ford Foundation. Chapter 7, "Relevance to the American Setting."

Featherstone, Joseph. "Open Schools I: The British and US." *The New Republic*, vol. 165 (September 11, 1971), pp. 20-25. Compares informal education in British and USA schools and the priority given in USA schools to administration and management at the expense of good teaching.

Featherstone, Joseph. "Open Schools II: Tempering a Fad." *The New Republic*, vol. 165 (September 25, 1971), pp. 17-21. Cautionary article. British informal education copied in USA open education has attracted adults who are angry at authority and who do not serve the real cause and needs of children.

Featherstone, Joseph. "Reading and Writing in British Junior Schools: Experiments in Learning." *The New Republic*, vol. 159 (December 14, 1968), pp. 23-25. Reading and writing are learned better in the best English junior schools when the teacher's interest in the context of the child's writing creates a bond of mutual trust.

Featherstone, Joseph. "Schools for Learning." *The New Republic*, vol. 159 (December, 1968), pp. 17-20. Teaching mathematics in British junior schools.

Featherstone, Joseph. *Schools Where Children Learn*. New York: Liveright, 1971. Author's articles which appeared in *The New Republic* and were among the earliest important descriptions of British primary schools. Helped inspire USA open education movement.

Featherstone, Joseph. "Teaching Children to Think." *The New Republic*, vol. 157 (September 9, 1967), pp. 15-19. Third of three widely circulated articles on British primary education which spurred USA open education.

Featherstone, Joseph. "What's Happening in British Classroooms." *The New Republic,* vol. 157 (August 19, 1969), pp. 17-21. First of three early widely circulated articles on British primary education which spurred USA open education.

Featherstone, Joseph. "Why So Few Good Schools." *The New Republic,* vol. 160 (January 1969), pp. 18-21. Teaching the expressive arts in British junior schools.

Gross, Beatrice and Ronald. "A Little Bit of Chaos." *Saturday Review,* vol. 53 (May 16, 1970), pp. 71-73, 84-85. Co-editors of *Radical School Reform* cite British models in an overview of USA open education.

Gross, Ronald and Beatrice, eds. *Radical School Reform.* New York: Simon & Schuster, 1969. Anthology includes Paul Goodman, Edgar Friedenberg, Herbert Kohl, Jonathan Kozol, John Holt, and Joseph Featherstone's "The British Infant Schools."

Hassett, Joseph D., and Arline Weisberg. *Open Education: Alternatives Within a Tradition.* Englewood Cliffs: Prentice-Hall, Inc., 1972. Book grew out of a workshop led by teachers from England's Nuffield Foundation Junior Science Program.

Hertzberg, Alvin, and Edward Stone. *Schools Are for Children.* New York: Schocken Books, 1972. Two USA elementary school principals' enthusiastic observations of informal British primary schools. "What to do" sections on the arts, mathematics, language, social studies, science.

Howes, Virgil M. *Informal Teaching in the Open Classroom.* New York: Macmillan Publishing Co., Inc., 1974. How to organize and manage the open classroom based in part on seven English and five U.S. schools as models.

Hull, William P. *Leicestershire Revisited: Occasional Paper No. 1.* Newton, Mass.: Education Development Center, 1970. Impressions of 1964 visit to Leicestershire (England) schools with contrasts to USA elementary schools.

I/D/E/A. *The British Infant School: Report of an International Seminar.* Melbourne, Fla.: I/D/E/A, 1969. Conference report with statements by E. Marianne Parry, inspector of infant and nursery schools in Bristol (England), and by Lady Bridget Plowden, chairman of the Central Advisory Council for Education (England).

Informal Schools in Britain Today. New York: Citation Press, 1971. Twenty-three booklets produced by Anglo-American Primary Education Project and the Ford Foundation. Authors are British and American teachers and observers of informal education, including British primary education. They deal with many school subjects.

Murrow, Casey, and Liza. *Children Come First: The Inspired Work of English Primary Schools*. New York: American Heritage Press, 1971. Informal practices in the better British primary schools recommended for USA teachers.

Nyquist, Ewald B. *The British Primary School Approach to Education: Time for Reform in Elementary Schools*. Albany, N.Y.: Office of the Commissioner of Education, 1970. Speech by the Commissioner of Education of New York State advocating British-type educational reforms.

Nyquist, Ewald B., and Gene R. Hawes, eds. *Open Education, A Sourcebook for Parents & Teachers*. New York: Bantam Books, 1972. Thirty articles, several of which indicate British primary education's influence on USA open education.

Pilcher, Paul S. "Open Education: In Britain and the U.S.A." *Educational Leadership*, vol. 30 (November, 1972), pp. 137-140. Points out that "integrated day" or "open classroom" is an indigenous and peculiarly British creation which arose to solve British school problems. Contrasts British-USA education in terms of open education.

Plowden, Lady Bridget, *et al. Children and Their Primary Schools: Report of the Central Advisory Council for Education*. London: Her Majesty's Stationery Office, 1966. 2 vols. Significant "Plowden Report" on the rationale and practices of modern British primary schools. Vol. II contains statistical tables.

Rathbone, Charles, ed. *Open Education: The Informal Classroom*. New York: Citation Press, 1971. Readings examining the practices and principles of the British infant schools and American counterparts.

Rogers, Vincent R. "English and American Primary Schools." *Phi Delta Kappan*, vol. 51 (October, 1969), pp. 71-75. Author asks three questions: What is so unusual about British primary schools? Why have similar ideas failed to take root in this country? What are the major drawbacks of this sort of schooling?

Rogers, Vincent R. "The Social Studies Revolution Begins in Britain." *Phi Delta Kappan*, vol. 50 (November, 1968), pp. 162-165. Reviews forces influencing secondary social studies curriculum in England and discusses the role of USA "neo-progressive" child-centered educationists.

Rogers, Vincent R., ed. *Teaching in the British Primary School*. New York: Macmillan Co., 1970. This collection of essays, most of them by British practitioners, is edited by a prominent American educator.

Rogers, Vincent R. "Three Lessons We Should Learn from British Education." *Phi Delta Kappan*, vol. 50 (January, 1969), pp. 295-296. In reviewing James Koerner's *Reform in Education: England and the United States,* Rogers writes: "If there is any bastion of relatively free, child-centered, experience-based learning left in the world, it is surely the English primary school."

Schlesinger, Joy. *Leicestershire Report: The Classroom Environment.* Cambridge, Mass.: Harvard Graduate School of Education, 1965. One of the earliest USA reports on several Leicestershire (England) open education classrooms.

Silberman, Charles E. *Crisis in the Classroom.* New York: Random House, 1970. Takes a careful, enthusiastic look at the British infant school model. Widely read Carnegie Corporation-backed book.

Silberman, Charles E., ed. *The Open Classroom Reader.* New York: Random House, 1973. Chapter 1, "Portraits of English Infant Schools," contains four articles. Other articles also trace USA open education to British primary school influence.

Villet, Barbara. "The Children Want Classrooms Alive with Chaos." *Life,* vol. 66 (April 11, 1969), pp. 50-52, 56. Illustrated article on American counterparts of the British infant schools.

Weber, Lillian. *The English Infant School and Informal Education.* Englewood Cliffs, N.J.: Prentice-Hall, 1971. Detailed study of experimental British infant schools by chief USA advocate of open education.

Youmans, Edward. *Education for Initiative and Responsibility.* Boston: National Association of Independent Schools, 1967. Commentary on a visit to experimental schools of Leicestershire, England. Appendix III lists curriculum materials and equipment for open education, with addresses of manufacturers.

15. Francis W. Parker

Parker, Franklin. "Francis W. Parker and Public Education in Chicago: The Stormy Career of a Great Educational Reformer." *Chicago Schools Journal,* vol. 42 (April, 1961), pp. 305-312. Influenced by a visit and study in Germany.

Parker, Franklin. "Francis Wayland Parker, 1837-1902." *Paedagogica Historica,* vol. 1 (1961), pp. 120-133. Influenced by visit to and study in Germany.

Tostberg, Robert E. "Colonel Parker's Quest for 'A School in which All Good Things Come Together.' " *History of Education Quarterly,* vol. 6 (Summer, 1966), pp. 22-42. Dewey called Parker, who studied in Germany, the father of American progressive education.

16. George Peabody

Parker, Franklin. *George Peabody, A Biography*. Nashville, Tenn.: Vanderbilt University Press, 1971. American philanthropist and founder of the Peabody Education Fund for the defeated southern states, the Peabody Institute of Baltimore, three museums and many libraries knew of Lord Shaftesbury's work with the Ragged Schools.

17. Johann H. Pestalozzi and Pestalozzianism

Black, Hugh C. "Pestalozzi and the Education of the Disadvantaged." *The Educational Forum*, vol. 33 (May, 1969), pp. 511-521. Recollections by a daughter of Pestalozzi's student and later fellow teacher are related to recent problems of USA education of disadvantaged.

Boram, Willam A. "William Maclure: Response." *History of Education Quarterly*, vol. 3 (March, 1963), pp. 77-80. "Maclure contributed to the meaningful progression of Pestalozzi's ideas from eighteenth centruy inception to twentieth century refinement."

Burgess, Charles. "William Maclure and Education for a Good Society." *History of Education Quarterly*, vol. 3 (March, 1963), pp. 58-76. Maclure as a carrier of educational ideas from Plato, Jonathan Swift, Locke, Helvetius, Rousseau, Pestalozzi, Robert Owen, Robert Dale Owen, and Joseph Neef.

Dearborn, Ned Harland. *The Oswego Movement in American Education*. New York: Arno Press, 1969. Educational principles of Pestalozzi as propagated in the USA in the Oswego Normal School (New York), under Director Edward A. Sheldon, by Herman Krusi, Jr., and Miss Margaret E. M. Jones.

Gutek, Gerald Lee. "An Examination of Joseph Neef's Theory of Ethical Education." *History of Education Quarterly*, vol. 9 (Summer, 1969), pp. 187-201. Influence of Pestalozzianism; Joseph Neef's work in New Harmony, Indiana; William Maclure; French revolutionary thinkers.

Monroe, Will S. *History of the Pestalozzian Movement in the United States*. New York: Arno Press & The New York Times, 1969. Pestalozzi's influence seen through the work of William Maclure, Joseph Neef, and Herman Krüsi.   Chapter XI is a bibliography of the Pestalozzian movement in the USA.

Rogers, Dorothy. *Oswego: Fountainhead of Teacher Education: A Century in the Sheldon Tradition*. New York: Appleton-Century-Crofts, 1961. Traces Pestalozzian ideas via Sheldon to Oswego and thence to other normal schools.

18. Jean Piaget

Bott, R., *et al. The Teaching of Young Children: Some Applications of Piaget's Learning Theory*. New York: Schocken Books, 1970. Gives examples, not methods, of ways for teachers to apply Piaget's theories in teaching eight subjects, among them science, art, and literature.

Brearley, Molly. *The Teaching of Young Children*. New York: Schocken Books, 1970. Draws many connections between Piaget's theories and informal education practices.

Bruner, Jerome S., *et al. Studies in Cognitive Growth: A Collaboration at the Center for Cognitive Studies*. New York: John Wiley & Sons, Inc., 1966. Dedicated to Jean Piaget. Contains 14 chapters, six of which Bruner wrote or coauthored.

Elkind, David. *Children and Adolescents: Interpretive Essays on Jean Piaget*. New York: Oxford University Press, 1970. Piaget's influence seen in the context of the 1950's and the need for new psychological understanding to help meet the post-Sputnik crisis in education. Bibliography.

Furth, Hans G. *Piaget for Teachers*. Englewood Cliffs, N.J.: Prentice-Hall, 1970. Catholic University of America professor interprets "what Piaget's discoveries can mean to our schools."

Gorman, Richard M. *Discovering Piaget, A Guide for Teachers*. Columbus, Ohio: Charles E. Merrill Publishing Co., 1972. "Introduction to Piaget's thoughts for use in an education or psychology course."

Kessen, William, and Clementina Kuhlman, eds. *Thought in the Young Child, Report of a Conference on Intellective Development with Particular Attention to the Work of Jean Piaget. Monographs of the Society for Research in Child Development*, vol. 72, no. 2 (1962), 175 pp. Nine papers plus discussion, comments, conclusions, and references.

Ripple, Richard, and Verne N. Rockcastle, eds. *Piaget Rediscovered, A Report of the Conference on Cognitive Studies and Curriculum Development, March 1964*. Ithaca: Cornell University, 1964. Papers of two conferences at which Piaget gave four lectures. Introduction on "Piaget Rediscovered."

Schwebel, Milton, and Jane Raph, eds. *Piaget in the Classroom*. New York: Basic Books, Inc., 1973. Eleven contributors at Rutgers Piaget Conference; Parts I, The Developing Mind; II, The Developing Child, and III, The Developing Teacher.

Society for Research in Child Development. *Cognitive Development in Children: Five Monographs of the Society for Research in Child*

Development. Chicago: The University of Chicago Press, 1970. Roger Brown in the Introduction points to Piaget as the great psychologist of cognitive development whom Americans "discovered" in the late 1950's. The first monograph, "Thought in the Young Child," is dominated by Piaget's influence.

Wadsworth, Barry J. *Piaget's Theory of Cognitive Development: An Introduction for Students of Psychology and Education*. New York: David McKay Co., Inc., 1971. Intended for undergraduates, the book presents the basic concepts of Jean Piaget's theory of cognitive development.

19. Herbert Spencer

Kazamias, Andreas M., ed. *Herbert Spencer on Education*. New York: Teachers College Press, 1966. A British reviewer of this book has pointed out that Spencer was more influential on American educators than on British education.

XVII. CONTEMPORARY ISSUES IN AMERICAN EDUCATION

A. ACCOUNTABILITY

Lessinger, Leon, and Associates. *Accountability: Systems Planning in Education.* Homewood, Illinois: ETC Publications, 1973. Each of several contributors has written chapters of explanation and support for various aspects of a systems approach to educational accountability, *e.g.*, "Accountability and Humanism: A Productive Educational Complementary," and "An Analysis of Costs and Effectiveness of an Individualized Subject Offering."

Lessinger, Leon M., and Ralph W. Tyler, eds. *Accountability in Education,* Worthington, Ohio: Charles A. Jones Publishing Co., 1971. Collection of essays dealing with variety of issues in accountability and explaining the theory, purposes and practices associated with it.

Murphy, Jerome T., and David K. Cohen. "Accountability in Education: The Michigan Experience." *The Public Interest,* vol. 36 (Summer, 1974), pp. 53-81. Reviews and analyzes the Michigan school accountability program, describing its unanticipated outcomes and general failure.

Ornstein, Allan C., ed. *Accountability for Teachers and School Administrators,* Belmont, Calif.: Fearon Publishers, 1973. Anthology of mostly previously published writings on accountability by Havighurst, Dyer, Fantini, Lessinger, Popham, Tyler, and others. Variety of aspects explored, *e.g.*, the concept itself, relationship to the teaching profession, proposals and methods, performance contracting, limitations, and potential for expansion.

Page, Ellis B. "How We All Failed at Performance Contracting." *Phi Delta Kappan,* vol. LIV (October, 1972), pp. 115-117. Describes the failure of Office of Economic Opportunity experiment with performance contracting. Results require re-examination of educational assumptions about teaching and learning.

Popham, W. James. "The New World of Accountability: In the Classroom." *The Bulletin of the National Association of Secondary School Principals,* vol. 56 (May, 1972), pp. 25-31. Advocates increased use of accountability in the classroom. Proposes criterion-referenced tests and instructional mini-lessons as the best ways to bring behavioral objectives to bear for improving teacher accountability.

Raths, James D. "Teaching Without Specific Objectives." *Educational Leadership,* vol. 28 (April, 1971), pp. 714-720. Opposes reliance on behavioral objectives as means to accountability. In favor of less restrictive evaluation procedures.

Simons, Herbert D. "Behavioral Objectives: A False Hope for Education." *The Elementary School Journal,* vol. 73 (January, 1973), pp. 174-181. Rejects the strong reliance on behavioral objectives. Advocates fail to understand the distinction between behavior (which can be measured) and knowledge, which lacks a theory of precise evaluation.

Wynne, Edward. *The Politics of School Accountability.* Berkeley, California: McCutchan Publishing Corp., 1972. Emphasis on producing accurate school information for the public. Analyzes historical effort and contemporary tensions surrounding this process.

B. ALTERNATIVES TO TRADITIONAL EDUCATION

Bremer, John. "Alternatives to Education." *Phi Delta Kappan,* vol. LIV (March, 1973), pp. 449-451. Supports the development of more alternatives and freedom for students in education so that students can experience real decision-making, which is crucial to real learning.

Broudy, Harry S. "Educational Alternatives—Why Not?" *Phi Delta Kappan,* vol. LIV (March, 1973), pp. 438-440. Philosophical analysis of alternative education movement which argues that useful alternatives must proceed from a clear idea of the school's role in society. Once this is done, creative diversity can replace random pluralism in the alternative school movement.

Center for New Schools. "Strengthening Alternate High Schools." *Harvard Educational Review,* vol. 42 (August, 1972), pp. 313-350. Presents case study of student involvement in decision-making at a Chicago alternative high school, followed by discussion of patterns of development common to alternative schools. Emphasis is on shared decision-making among staff, students and other significant groups.

Freire, Paulo. *Pedagogy of the Oppressed.* New York: Herder and Herder, 1971. Theory and rationale for revolutionary liberation of oppressed classes through radical educational practice. Emphasizes freedom, relevancy and quality for the learner. Written for Latin-American frame of reference.

Gartner, Alan, Colin Greer, and Frank Riessman, eds. *After Deschooling, What? Ivan Illich, et al.* New York: Harper and Row, 1973. Collection of essays reacting to Illich's deschooling idea, together with further speculation by Illich. Most previously published in *Social Policy.* Primarily sympathetic reactions to the topic.

Goodlad, John I. "The Child and His School in Transition." *The National Elementary School Principal*, vol. LII (January, 1973), pp. 28-34. Suggests that the future development of schools should provide more alternatives and flexibility through a two-step process of change. In the first step schools would be organized into multi-year phases with heterogeneous students. The "ultimate" school would operate 24 hours a day and capitalize more fully on technology.

Graubard, Allen. *Free the Children: Radical Reform and the Free School Movement*. New York: Pantheon Books, 1972. Examines theory and practice in wide range of types of free schools. Sees the need for a broad, radical political idealogy encompassing all of them.

Illich, Ivan. *Deschooling Society*. New York: Harper & Row, 1971. Calls for the "deschooling" of society as part of a larger cultural revolution. Schools should be replaced by voluntary learning networks and skills centers using a peer-matching system, so that education, as opposed to schooling, can be offered to the masses.

Kozol, Jonathan. *Free Schools*. Boston: Houghton Mifflin Co., 1972. Describes current problems and offers constructive criticism of the free school movement. Emphasizes need for basic education, meaningful free choice for students, and active confrontation with real social problems as the basis of the curriculum.

Saxe, Richard W., ed. *Opening the Schools: Alternative Ways of Learning*. Berkeley, Cal.: McCutchan Publishing, 1972. Explores alternatives for augmenting public school at secondary and higher levels. Primary emphasis on community learning experiences.

Singleton, Steven, David Boyer, and Paul Dorsey. "Xanadu: A Study of the Structure Crisis in an Alternative School." *Review of Educational Research*, vol. 42 (Fall, 1972), pp. 525-532. Analysis of problems of organizing and sustaining goals and activity at an alternative school. Generally critical view of alternative school movement.

C. CAREER EDUCATION

Bailey, Larry J., and Ronald W. Stadt. *Career Education: New Approaches to Human Development*. Bloomington, Illinois: McKnight & McKnight, 1973. Philosophy, development, rationale and future implications of career education.

Fitzgerald, T. H. "Career Education: An Error Whose Time Has Come." *School Review*, vol. 82 (November, 1973), pp. 91-105. Argues against the theory of the career education movement. "Career Education is a superficial philosophy of education because a primary orientation towards work is not an adequate response to the needs of education in a free but complex society."

Goldhammer, Keith, and Robert E. Taylor, eds. *Career Education: Perspectives and Promise*. Columbus, Ohio: Charles E. Merrill Publishing Co., 1972. Collection of essays, most not previously published, covering school-based models of career education from kindergarten through 12th grade. Many definitions of career education offered.

Hoyt, Kenneth B., Rupert N. Evans, Edward F. Mackin, and Garth L. Mangum. *Career Education: What It Is and How to Do It*. Olympus Publishing Co., 1972. Presents philosophical rationale and practical suggestions for implementing career education in the schools.

Marland, Sidney P., and James D. Koerner. *What Is Career Education?* Washington: Council for Basic Education, 1972. Marland explains the concept of career education, emphasizing early work experience and career development in schools. Koerner criticizes career education as detracting from the historic role of schools as conservators of the culture, and as an impractical idea. Comments from other participants, in this record of discussion.

Muirhead, Peter P. "Career Education: The First Steps Show Promise." *Phi Delta Kappan,* vol. LIV (February, 1973), pp. 370-372. Reports on efforts of Office of Education to stimulate interest and experimentation in career education concepts.

Nash, Robert J., and Russell M. Agne. "Career Education: Earning a Living or Living a Life?" *Phi Delta Kappan,* vol. LIV (February, 1973), pp. 373-377. Analyzes ideological premises underlying career education proposals, and identifies problems that may obscure other equally important aspects of human development, unless career education concepts are developed with caution.

Stevenson, John B. *An Introduction to Career Education*. Charles A. Jones Publishing Co., 1973. Explains career education concept, how it started, current practice and issues, practical applications, and future directions.

D. COMMUNITY CONTROL AND DECENTRALIZATION OF URBAN SCHOOLS

Altshuler, Alan A. *Community Control: The Black Demand for Participation in Large American Cities*. New York: Pegasus, 1970. General introduction to the theory, motivation and issues undergirding the community control movement.

Bard, Bernard. "Is Decentralization Working?" *Phi Delta Kappan,* vol. LIV (December, 1972), pp. 238-243. Claims that New York City decentralization has not resulted in any concrete improvements in educational quality for students.

Brownell, Samuel M. "Desirable Characteristics of Decentralized School

Systems." *Phi Delta Kappan,* vol. LIV (January, 1971), pp. 286-288. Describes characteristics of decentralized school system. Although advantages are cited, the need to maintain integrated schools and subdistricts is stressed.

Calvo, Robert C. "Issues and Problems in Decentralization." *Clearinghouse,* vol. 46 (May, 1972), pp. 540-552. Discusses meaning of decentralization, advantages and disadvantages, and political factors supporting and discouraging it.

Cordasco, Francesco, *et al.,* eds. *The School in the Social Order: A Sociological Introduction to Educational Understanding.* Scranton: International Textbook Co., 1970. Includes the text of *Reconnection for Learning: A Community School System for New York City* (1967) which was the report of the Mayor's Advisory Council on Decentralization of the New York City Schools.

Fantini, Mario, Marilyn Gittell, and Richard Magat. *Community Control and the Urban School.* New York: Praeger Publishers, 1970. Explanation and support for the concept of community control of city schools, with particular attention to the events surrounding the topic in New York City.

La Noue, George R., and Bruce L. R. Smith. *The Politics of School Decentralization.* Lexington, Mass.: Lexington Books, 1973. Study of political factors in the controversies, confrontations and issues on school decentralization, with special reference to five large cities.

Levin, Henry M., ed. *Community Control of Schools: Brookings Conference on the Community School, 1968.* Washington: The Brookings Institution, 1970. Collection of essays on community control from a Brookings Institution Conference. Topics include historic and philosophical background, black nationalism, community control alternatives, the Ocean Hill-Brownsville experiment, goals, and the implications of school competition.

Ornstein, Allan C. "Administrative/Community Organization of Metropolitan Schools." *Phi Delta Kappan,* vol. LIV (June, 1973), pp. 668-674. Reviews and analyzes data on decentralization and community control of schools. While administrative decentralization is moving ahead, community control is not.

Zimet, Melvin. *Decentralization and School Effectiveness.* New York: Teachers College Press, Columbia University, 1973. Study of the 1969 Decentralization Law in New York City. Describes the events and forces leading to the law, the early experience in District 7, and analyzes the effects. Provides recommendations for improvement.

E. COMPETENCY-BASED TEACHER EDUCATION

Davies, Ivor K. *Competency Based Learning: Technology, Management and*

Design. New York: McGraw-Hill Book Co., 1973. Reviews research on competency-based learning, and covers planning, organizing, leading, and controlling learning activities on a performance/competency model.

Fantini, Mario. "The Reform of Teacher Education: A Proposal from New York State." *Phi Delta Kappan,* vol. LIII (April, 1972), pp. 476-479, 482. Summarizes proposals for performance-based teacher preparation made by the New York State Fleischmann Commission. Included are recommendations for increased educational options, certification based on demonstrated teacher proficiency, and Teaching-Learning Centers for in-service as well as pre-service teacher improvement.

Flanders, Ned A. "The Changing Base of Performance-Based Teaching." *Phi Delta Kappan,* vol. LV (January, 1974), pp. 312-315. Present weak research base and continuing evaluation of CBTE means that the knowledge base is likely to change, producing new goals as well as new procedures.

Houston, W. Robert, and Robert B. Howsam, eds. *Competency-Based Teacher Education: Progress, Problems and Prospects.* Chicago: Science Research Associates, 1972. Authors brought together in this volume deal with five CBTE areas: objectives, curriculum design, evaluation, certification, and consortia.

McDonald, Frederick J. "The National Commission on Performance-Based Education." *Phi Delta Kappan,* vol. LV (January, 1973), pp. 296-298. Describes the work and goals of the National Commission to coordinate the C/PBTE movement, through the Educational Testing Service.

Rosner, Benjamin, and Patricia M. Kay. "Will the Promise of C/PBTE Be Fulfilled?" *Phi Delta Kappan,* vol. LV (January, 1974), pp. 290-295. Explains the concept and reviews the development of competency/performance-based teacher education. Whether or not the promise of C/PBTE (improving instructional quality) will be realized depends on willingness to arrive at a common definition and invest necessary time and resources in its development.

F. CONFLICTING COGNITIVE AND AFFECTIVE EMPHASES IN EDUCATION

Brown, George Isaac. *Human Teaching for Human Learning: an Introduction to Confluent Education.* New York: The Viking Press, Inc., 1971. An exposition, through theory and practical illustrations, of the idea of "confluent education." This concept is intended to blend together the affective (emotional) aspects of learning with the cognitive (intellectual) functions.

Carrison, Muriel P. "The Perils of Behavior Modification." *Phi Delta Kappan,* vol. LIV (May, 1973), pp. 593-595. Warns of dangers inherent in use of behavior modification, including unanticipated conditioning, uncontrolled personality modification, and detrimental effects on society from large numbers of persons educated through behavior modification.

Dennison, George. *The Lives of Children*. New York: Random House, Inc., 1969. Presents the affective educational viewpoint from the author's experiences while teaching at a Philadelphia free school for poor/minority students.

Ebel, Robert L. "What Are Schools For?" *Phi Delta Kappan,* vol. LIII (September, 1972), pp. 3-7. Argues that the focus of schooling should be on learning useful knowledge and building cognitive competence. Criticizes school concern for social adjustment, recreation, and similar non-intellective matters.

Hook, Sidney. *Education and the Taming of Power*. Open Court Publishing Co., 1974. Condemns the extremism of ultra-humanists such as Illich, Holt, Kozol, Dennison, Friedenberg, Goodman, and others who over-emphasize affective elements in education. Calls for a return to the balanced humanism of John Dewey.

Kagan, Jerome. "Understanding the Psychology of Mental Growth." *Grade Teacher Magazine,* vol. 83 (March, 1966), pp. 79, 123-130. Balanced view of what learning is and how it occurs. Stresses importance of both cognitive and affective components of learning.

Milhollan, Frank, and Bill E. Forisha. *From Skinner to Rogers: Contrasting Approaches to Education*. Lincoln, Nebraska: Professional Educators Publications, Inc., 1972. Reviews the philosophical and historical roots of behaviorist and humanistic psychology, using examinations of the psychological theories of B. F. Skinner and Carl Rogers to illustrate the contrasts and points of agreement between these two predominant influences in American educational psychology.

Neill, A. S. *Neill! Neill! Orange Peel!* New York: Hart Publishing Co., 1972. The autobiography of the recently deceased founder of Summerhill, the English school which has long served as the model for affective education. Neil stresses the importance of emotions in education, as he describes his own views and speculates on the future of affective education.

Skinner, B. F. "The Free and Happy Student." *Phi Delta Kappan,* vol. LIV (September, 1973), pp. 13-16. Criticizes affective orientation toward student freedom and choice within schools on the grounds that they are not qualified to make the best choices for future life needs; nor are they made "happier" by a permissiveness they do not want or need.

Thoresen, Carl E., ed. *Behavior Modification in Education*. Chicago: National Society for the Study of Education, 1973. Historical and contemporary perspectives on behavior modification development, analysis and synthesis with educational theory and descriptions of practice in educational and clinical settings.

G. CRITICISMS OF STANDARDIZED TESTING

Chandler, John T., and John Plakos. "Spanish-Speaking Students Classified as Educable Mentally Retarded." *Integrated Education,* vol. 7 (Nov.-Dec., 1969), pp. 28-33. Authors' research found that Spanish-speaking California students were classified as retarded on the basis of English language intelligence test. When retested with Spanish language WISC, most were found not to be retarded.

Ebel, Robert L. "The Social Consequences of Educational Testing" in Bruce Shertzer and Shelley C. Stone eds., *Introduction to Guidance.* Boston: Houghton Mifflin Co., 1970, pp. 226-234. Considers the negative effects of inappropriate use of testing and offers guidelines for proper use: emphasize tests to improve status, not to determine status; broaden achievements tested; share results openly; decrease test use to impose decisions and use it to improve personal decisions.

Rosenthal, Robert, and Lenore Jacobsen. *Pygmalion in the Classroom.* New York: Holt, Rinehart and Winston, 1968. Report of authors' study of the "self-fulfilling prophecy" effect of standardized intelligence test results on the academic performance of minority group students.

Samuda, Ronald. *The Intellectual Assessment of Minorities in the United States.* New York: Dodd, Mead & Co., 1975. Major theories, controversies, and research findings on the use of intellectual tests for minorities. Hereditarian and environmental points of view discussed along with the social and economic consequences, and guidelines for improved test use. Two appendices: annotated review of research and a compendium of assessment instruments.

Tittle, Carol K. "Women and Educational Testing." *Phi Delta Kappan,* vol. LV (October, 1973), pp. 118-119. Reports research documenting the preponderance of male language references in standardized achievement tests and the great amount of sex-role stereotypes used in these tests.

Wechsler, David. "The I.Q. as an Intelligence Test," in Harry L. Miller, ed., *Education for the Disadvantaged.* New York: The Free Press, 1967, pp. 72-79. Examines the theory of intelligence testing and its uses, viewing test itself as a relatively neutral instrument. Abuses result from inappropriate interpretation and use of test results.

H. DESEGREGATION AND BUSING

Foster, Gordon. "Desegregating Urban Schools: A Review of Techniques." *Harvard Educational Review,* vol. 43 (February, 1973), pp. 5-36. Reviews desegregation activity over recent years and evaluates advantages and disadvantages of various techniques of desegregation. Discusses economic, social and psychological constraints on desegregation, and argues for metropolitan approach to desegregation.

Green, Robert L., Eugenia Smith, and John H. Schweitzer. "Busing and the Multiracial Classroom." *Phi Delta Kappan,* vol. LIII (May, 1972), pp. 543-546. Contends that the public schools are the last hope for a workable multiracial society, and two-way busing is our last hope for averting school apartheid.

Harvey, James C., and Charles C. Holmes. "Busing and School Desegregation." *Phi Delta Kappan,* vol. LIII (May, 1972), pp. 540-542. Review of court cases since 1968 on the subject of desegregation and busing which led to Presidential opposition to court-ordered busing.

Holden, Anna. *The Bus Stops Here: A Study of School Desegregation in Three Cities.* New York: Schocken Books, 1974. Detailed study of desegregation in Charlottesville, Va., Providence, R.I., and Sacramento, Calif. Close attention to role of black community. Examines in-school climate and events as well as local politics. Summarizes with series of thirty conclusions.

Kirby, David J., T. Robert Harris, and Robert L. Crain. *Political Strategies in Northern School Desegregation.* Lexington, Mass.: Lexington Books, 1973. A "statistical social history" of efforts at school racial integration in 91 representative cities in the North and West, 1963-69.

Levine, Daniel U. "Integration in Metropolitan Schools: Issues and Prospects." *Phi Delta Kappan,* LIV (June, 1973), pp. 651-657. Sees current trends of metropolitan living patterns as reversing earlier progress in desegregation. Sees metropolitanism in education as a cure, but is not optimistic as to its probable implementation. Reviews court decisions on metropolitan school busing.

Levine, Daniel U., ed. *Models for Integrated Education.* Worthington, Ohio: Charles A. Jones Publishing Co., 1971. Contributors report, through case studies and essays from their personal experiences, on exemplary programs that have contributed to school integration.

Mills, Nicolaus. *The Great School Bus Controversy.* New York: Teachers College Press, Columbia University, 1973. Reprints of documents and papers covering most aspects of the issue of busing as a means of achieving racial school integration.

St. John, N. H. "Desegregation and Minority Group Performance." *Review of Educational Research,* vol. 40 (February, 1970), pp. 111-113. Review of research on the relationship of school racial composition to performance of minority students. Among major findings are that: following desegregation, students generally perform no worse, and usually better; powerful relationship between social class integration and achievement; relationship between integration and achievement conditioned by staff support and peer acceptance.

Weinberg, Meyer. *Desegregation Research: An Appraisal,* 2nd ed. Bloomington, Indiana: Phi Delta Kappa, 1970. Reports and analyzes the research conducted on the effects of desegregation through 1969. Concluding chapter summarizes major findings and research trends.

Wise, Michael B. "School Desegregation: The Court, the Congress, and the President." *School Review,* vol. 82 (February, 1974), pp. 159-182. Review of busing and other desegregation matters as influenced by the three branches of national government. Major legislation and court decisions are examined.

I. THE EDUCATION OF CULTURALLY, RACIALLY OR ETHNICALLY DIFFERENT STUDENTS

Alloway, David N., and Francesco Cordasco. *Minorities and the American City: A Sociological Primer for Educators.* New York: David McKay, 1970. A concise sociological primer attempting "to set the new minorities of American cities within an historically intelligible context." Deals with power, authority, and responsibility; ethnocentrism, class, and racial antagonisms; social reform movements; and the problem of leadership.

Ballard, Allen B. *The Education of Black Folks.* New York: Harper & Row, 1973. An overview of "the educational color line in America"; includes assessments of compensatory education (largely higher education), with discussions of socio-economic deprivation, Blacks, and educational opportunity.

Banks, James A. "Imperatives in Ethnic Minority Education." *Phi Delta Kappan,* vol. LIII (January, 1972), pp. 166-269. Recommends procedures and attitudes to remove racial and ethnic bias and oppression from the school. Advocates ethnic studies for all students, greater awareness by teachers of their racist assumptions and attitudes, and more attention to building good self-concepts in minority students.

Banks, James A., ed. *Teaching Ethnic Studies: Concepts and Strategies.* Washington: National Council for the Social Studies, 1973. Argues for bringing cultural pluralism into the classroom through ethnic studies. Various authors write to general issues as well as to particular issues of specific ethnic groups. Practical suggestions as well as theoretical statements.

Brickman, William W., and Stanley Lehrer, eds. *Education and the Many Faces of the Disadvantaged: Cultural and Historical Perspectives.* New York: John Wiley, 1972. Includes materials on Urban America; Black Americans; Spanish-speaking Americans; North American Indians; Immigrant and Refugee in America; Rural Poor; Middle Class as Culturally Deprived; Culturally Deprived Reader; Teacher and Federal Programs; the Disadvantaged in International Perspective.

Charnofsky, Stanley. *Educating the Powerless*. Belmont, Calif.: Wadsworth Publishing Co., 1971. Argues that before educational success can be experienced by culturally different students, they must begin to feel the power that comes from education supporting and reinforcing their values, cultural heritage, and group identity.

Coles, Robert. *Migrants, Sharecroppers, Mountaineers* (vol. II of *Children in Crisis* Series). Boston: Little Brown & Co.,1971. Intensive anthropological study of thirty rural families over six-month period, dealing not only with children, but also family and subculture. Highlights importance of kinship ties and Fundamentalist Christianity. Need to make education more directly relevant to their lives and more valuable as a resource to their progress and aspirations.

Cordasco, Francesco. "The Children of Immigrants in Schools: Historical Analogues of Educational Deprivation." *Journal of Negro Education*, vol. 42 (Winter, 1973), pp. 44-53. Largely concerned with New York City, *circa* 1880-1920, presenting "an overview of the American school in form and function as it presented itself to the immigrant child, and the response of the American school to the immigrant child."

Cordasco, Francesco, and David Alloway, eds. "Poverty in America: Economic Inequality, New Ideologies, and the Search for Educational Opportunity." *Journal of Human Relations* [Special Issue], vol. 20 (3rd Quarter, 1972), pp. 234-396. Articles on poverty contexts; minority responses to oppression; racial caste system; assimilation of Mexicans; educational neglect of Black, Puerto Rican, and Portuguese children.

Cordasco, Francesco, and Eugene Bucchioni. *The Puerto Rican Community and Its Children on the Mainland: A Sourcebook for Teachers, Social Workers and Other Professionals*. 2nd ed. Metuchen, N.J.: Scarecrow Press, 1972. Includes materials on Aspects of Puerto Rican Culture; the Puerto Rican Family; Puerto Rican Children in North American Schools; Conflict and Acculturation; with "Studies of Puerto Rican Children in American Schools," a bibliography of some 500 items.

Forbes, Jack D. "Segregation and Integration: The Multi-Ethnic or Uni-Ethnic School." *Phylon*, vol. 30 (1969), pp. 34-41. Cautions against trying to promote full ethnic integration as panacea for minority group achievement problems or as an assimilation device for minorities. Overzealousness can create more problems than it cures.

Fuchs, Estelle, and Robert J. Havighurst, *To Live on This Earth: American Indian Education*. Garden City, New York: Doubleday, 1972. Reports the results of the National Study of American Indian Education. Assembles data and analysis on historical background, Indian communities and their school systems, curricula for Indian youth, boarding schools, Indian attitudes toward education, the urban Indian, higher education and the Indian, and new approaches for their education.

Glazer, Nathan. "Ethnic Groups and Education: Towards the Tolerance of Differences." *Journal of Negro Education,* vol. 38 (Summer, 1969), pp. 187-195. Research indicates different groups differ in educational achievement regardless of their social and economic status and regardless of the educational system they are exposed to. Educational achievement should remain a positive value, but achievement standards and values should be tempered by cultural and ethnic differences.

Krug, Mark M. "White Ethnic Studies: Prospects and Pitfalls." *Phi Delta Kappan,* vol. LIII (January, 1972), pp. 322-324. Calls for more attention to the long-neglected ethnicity of varous "hyphenated" American groups in curriculum, texts and teacher attitudes. Rather than emphasizing the "melting pot" ideology, emphasis should be on capitalizing on the strengths of cultural pluralism.

Stent, Madelon D., William R. Hazard, and Harry N. Rivlin. *Cultural Pluralism in Education: A Mandate for Change.* New York: Appleton-Century-Crofts, 1973. Advocates cultural pluralism as a "co-existence" alternative to integration. Includes original contributions on related topics by representatives of minority groups.

J. EQUALITY OF EDUCATIONAL OPPORTUNITY

Coleman, James S., et al. *Equality of Educational Opportunity.* Washington: U.S. Government Printing Office, 1966. Analyzed data collected nation-wide on variety of variables designed to indicate the extent to which equal educational opportunity exists for the various segments of American society. Major findings were:
1. Minority-group students performed scholastically at substantially lower levels than most white students
2. Within regions of the U.S., there were no significant disparities in the quality of available school services.
3. Schools appeared to exert little influence upon achievement, which was independent of the student's social background.

Cordasco, Francesco. *The Equality of Educational Opportunity: A Bibliography of Selected References.* Totowa, N.J.: Rowman and Littlefield, 1973. Some 400 entries arranged under five main categories: Role of the School; Dropouts and Delinquency; Characteristics of the Disadvantaged Student; Teachers and Teacher Education; Programs and Materials. Also includes papers on the poor, particularly Puerto Ricans in urban settings.

Cordasco, Francesco, ed. *Toward Equal Educational Opportunity: The Report of the Select Committee on Equal Educational Opportunity, U.S. Senate.* New York: AMS Press, Inc., 1974. Deliberations of Senate Committee on school's role in promoting equality of educational opportunity. Among the issues discussed are the negative findings of the *Coleman Report,* the Jencks book, *Inequality,* the genetic primacy contentions of Jensen, the impact of busing and other integration practices, and the impact of school finance practices.

Crossland, Fred E. *Minority Access to College.* New York: Schocken Books, 1971. Presents and analyzes data on minority presence in higher education. Particular attention to black collegiate enrollment and status of black institutions. Discusses major barriers and efforts to reduce those barriers.

Guthrie, James W., and Thomas C. Thomas, "Policy Implications of the Coleman Report Reanalyses." *Phi Delta Kappan,* vol. LIV (May, 1973), pp. 602-605. Criticizes the policy implications drawn from the Coleman Report by *On Equality of Educational Opportunity* (Mosteller and Moynihan, eds.). Major point is that the impression that more school spending will not improve equality of opportunity is incorrect.

Hurwitz, Emanuel, Jr., and Charles Tesconi, Jr., eds. *Education for Whom?* New York: Dodd, Mead & Co., Inc., 1974. Analyzes the major elements of equal educational opportunity issue with major foci on the role of the judiciary, structure of school finance, and desegregation. Multidisciplinary analysis drawing on sociology, economics, philosophy and political science.

Jencks, Christopher, et al. *Inequality: Reassessment of Family and Schooling in America.* New York: Basic Books, Inc., 1972. Through a reanalysis of recent data on educational opportunity, such as the Coleman Report and the analysis of the author's own research data, the following general conclusions are reached about the effects of schooling on economic opportunity:
1. educational reform cannot bring about equality;
2. genes and I.Q. scores have relatively little effect on success; and
3. school quality has little effect on achievement or on economic success.

Miller, La Mar P., and Edmund W. Gordon, eds. *Equality of Educational Opportunity: A Handbook for Research.* New York: AMS Press, 1974. A collection of materials arranged under five categories: Defining and Assessing Equal Educational Opportunity; Implications of Research and Evaluation; Review of the Literature; Exemplary Evaluation and Research Studies; New Perspectives for Research.

Mosteller, Frederick, and Daniel P. Moynihan, eds. *On Equality of Educational Opportunity.* New York: Random House, 1972. Reassessment and policy implications of the Coleman Report by group of research analysts. Some criticism of Coleman's methodology, but general agreement regarding his findings. A major policy question raised is whether increased school expenditure will positively effect equal educational opportunity.

K. FREEDOM OF CHOICE IN SCHOOLING

Fantini, Mario D. *Public Schools of Choice.* New York: Simon and Schuster, 1974. Defends the potential of public education to accomplish internal reform which can provide the scope and variety needed for public schools to meet variations in student needs and interests. Critical of voucher plan which would prevent the growth of a continuum of public school choices.

Friedman, Milton. "The Voucher Idea." *New York Times Magazine,* vol. 23 (September, 1973), p. 22. Author's outline for program of vouchers in education. Stresses free market competition. Recommends government-funded vouchers to each family for each child. Issues of segregation, parochial schools, and social class are discussed.

Jencks, Christopher. "Education Vouchers." *The New Republic,* vol. 163 (July 4, 1970), pp. 19-21. Supportive explanation of voucher idea, with some discussion of objections to it. Describes Office of Economic Opportunity role in support of voucher experiment.

Levin, Henry M. "Vouchers and Social Equity." *Change,* vol. 5 (October, 1973), pp. 29-33. Explores the voucher concept as it is developing in higher education. This is seen as potentially supportive of greater social equity in higher education and carrying the promise of greater career options for all, that extend beyond the traditional college education.

Mecklenburger, James A., and Richard W. Hostrop, eds. *Education Vouchers: From Theory to Alum Rock.* Homewood, Illinois: ETC Publications, 1972. Selected articles organized in sections dealing with historical development of first the idea of vouchers, and lastly, its practical test in the Alum Rock Elementary School District.

Sizer, Theodore R. "The Case for a Free Market." *Saturday Review,* vol. 11 (January, 1969), p. 34. Reviews concept of "marketplace competition" as a path of educational reform and innovation. Four models analyzed: decentralization, alternative schools, commercial competition, and voucher systems.

L. GENETIC AND ENVIRONMENTAL DETERMINANTS OF INTELLIGENCE

Bodmer, Walter F., and Luigi Luca Cavalli-Sforza. "Intelligence and Race." *Scientific American,* vol. 223 (October, 1970), pp. 19-29. Two geneticists attack Jensen's hereditary intelligence position as scientifically unsupportable. They contend that the genetic components of intelligence cannot be isolated allowing one to conclude that biological inheritance is more important than environmental influences.

Cohen, David K. "Does IQ Matter." *Commentary,* vol. 56 (April, 1972), pp. 51-59. Believes that intelligence does not play the primary role in school success or socioeconomic status. Therefore, the heredity-environment argument is a meaningless exercise in terms of its implications for education.

Eysenck, H. J. *The I.Q. Argument.* Freeport, New York: The Library Press, 1971. Arguement supportive of Jensen position that due to heredity, blacks have inferior intelligence for purposes of traditional schooling. Calls for more and better-funded research on the subject to establish the case more conclusively.

Gage, N. L. "I.Q. Hereditability, Race Differences, and Educational Research." *Phi Delta Kappan,* vol. LIII (January, 1972), pp. 308-312. Disputes the hereditability of intelligence argument through criticism of the data research of Jensen and others. Calls for improved research and development to improve current achievement and attitude among Negro students.

Gartner, Alan, Colin Greer, and Frank Riessman, eds. *The New Assault on Equality: IQ and Social Stratification.* New York: Harper and Row, 1974. Reviews the controversy about the environmental and genetic impact on intelligence and the consequences of the conflicting views for social stratification and equality. Previously published papers by Chomsky, McClellan and others explore the social implications of genetic and environmental interpretations of human achievement.

Jensen, Arthur R. *Educability and Group Differences.* New York: Harper and Row, 1973. Elaboration of aurthor's 1969 argument that there are extensive learning differences between blacks and whites, and that most of the difference is attributable to genetic inheritance.

Jensen, Arthur R. "How Much Can We Boost IQ and Scholastic Achievement." *Harvard Educational Review,* vol. 39 (Winter, 1969), pp. 1-123. The paper that started the current controversy over nature-nurture influences on intelligence and school potential. Jensen contends that genetic influence in intelligence is greater than previously assumed and that the intelligence of blacks places them at a disadvantage to whites in coping with the traditional intellectual demands of the schools.

Richardson, Ken, and David Spears, eds. *Race and Intelligence.* Baltimore: Penguin Books, Inc., 1972. A collection of articles on the relationship of race to intelligence from the disciplines of psychology, biology and sociology. Concepts of intelligence, race, heredity and environment are examined from an editorially neutral viewpoint, although the editors see the present debate as essentially futile in terms of resolution.

Senna, Carl, ed. *The Fallacy of I.Q.* New York: Third Press—Joseph Okpaku Publishing Co., 1973. Seven critiques by scientists, social scientists, and educators of Jensen's thesis on the relationship of intelligence to race.

Shockley, William. "Dysgenics, Geneticity, Raceology: A Challenge to the Intellectual Responsiblity of Educators." *Phi Delta Kappan,* vol. LIII (January, 1972), pp. 297-307. Supports the view that intelligence is primarily influenced by heredity and that there are important racial differences in hereditary intelligence. Shockley believes Negroes less intelligent than whites because of genetic differences.

Zach, Lillian. "The IQ Debate." *Today's Education,* vol. 61 (September, 1972), pp. 40-43, 65-66, 68. Reviews the history of intelligence testing in the United States and concludes that IQ scores should not be used with blind, uncritical faith in them. Intelligence is a rather hazy concept, subject to a variety of interpretations, and tests are not infallible measures of this vague concept.

M. IMPROVING URBAN PUBLIC EDUCATION

Cronin, Joseph M. *The Control of Urban Schools.* New York: The Free Press, 1973. Describes current and historical patterns of urban school governance and control, with suggestions for reform. Data drawn from in-depth historical survey of 14 large city school boards.

Gittell, Marilyn, and Alan Hevesi, eds. *The Politics of Urban Education.* New York: Praeger, 1969. Collection of articles, including documents and case studies, providing theoretical and historical background to understanding current demands for urban education reform. Multi-disciplinary analysis of decentralization, community control and other issues of urban school reform.

Hillson, Maurie, Francesco Cordasco, and Francis P. Purcell, eds. *Education and the Urban Community: Schools and the Crisis of the Cities.* New York: American Book Co., 1969. A sourcebook which assembles materials under seven categories: The City in Modern America; The School and the Urban Ethos; The School and Aspects of the Community Relationship; School Organization; The Schools and the Employment of Youth; Federal Aid to Education; Directions and Possible Remedies.

Hummel, Raymond C., and John M. Nagel. *Urban Education in America: Problems and Prospects.* New York: Oxford University Press, 1973. Emphasizes that problems of urban education are not solely related to the schools and teachers, but involve total range of urban and societal problems. Analysis includes social, political, historical and economic factors. Calls for comprehensive systems approach to solving school problems that involves all segments of society.

Kozol, Jonathan. *Death at an Early Age.* Boston: Houghton Mifflin Co., 1967. Indictment of miseducation perpetrated on minority students by urban public schools. Author's personal experiences and reactions to them as a teacher in Boston elementary school serving black children.

Passow, A. Harry, ed. *Opening Opportunities for Disadvantaged Learners.* Teachers College Press, Columbia University, 1972. Collection of original essays covering a wide range of topics relevant to current urban education: educational parks, compensatory education, and teaching strategies for the urban poor and minorities.

Task Force on Urban Education. *The Urban Education Task Force Report.*

New York: Praeger, 1970. Report of federal government commission chaired by Wilson C. Riles. Presents comprehensive, detailed data about the problems of urban education throughout the nation. Recommends improved financial support as critical, and advocates improved compensatory education and racial/ethnic integration.

Walberg, Herbert J., and Andrew T. Kopan, eds. *Rethinking Urban Education: Sourcebook of Contemporary Issues.* San Francisco: Jossey-Bass Publishers, 1972. Original essays by specialists in different areas of expertise affecting urban education. Psychology and evaluation of learning, sociological, political and economic influences, historical and philosophical foundations of education, all combining to insist on the necessary adaptations to cultural and individual differences.

N. NON-TRADITIONAL HIGHER EDUCATION

Commission on Non-Traditional Study. Samuel B. Gould, ed., *Diversity by Design.* San Francisco: Jossey-Bass, 1973. Comprehensive report on the problems, trends and potential of non-traditional study in higher education. Recommendations in support of lifelong learning, emphasis on service to the learner, new agencies to provide access to counseling, learning and credit, and new faculty orientation.

Cross, K. Patricia, John R. Valley & Associates. *Planning Non-Traditional Programs.* San Francisco: Jossey-Bass, 1974. Reviews the studies of the Commission on Non-Traditional Study and discusses alternatives for the education of school dropouts, housewives, retired persons and others.

Gould, Samuel B., and K. Patricia Cross, eds. *Explorations in Non-Traditional Study.* San Francisco: Jossey-Bass, 1972. First report of the Commission on Non-Traditional Study. The term is defined, groups to be served are identified, new techniques (external degree, testing procedures, National University) are described and future potential is discussed for extending non-traditional education.

Houle, Cyril O. *The External Degree.* San Francisco: Jossey-Bass, 1973. Reviews the philosophy, needs, and practice related to the movement toward external degrees in American higher education and abroad. Wide variety of programs covered and attention to the populations external degrees are intended to serve.

Mushkin, Selma J., ed. *Recurrent Education.* Washington: National Institute of Education, 1973. Report on Georgetown Conference on Recurrent Education, which presents papers given on variety of aspects dealing with implementing life-long learning. Major foci are policy directions, supply and demand, target groups, relation to work, and financial and political implications. Several reports on European practice.

Valley, John R. *Increasing the Options: New Developments in College and*

University Degree Programs. Princeton, New Jersey: Educational Testing Service, 1972. Review of non-traditional and external degree programs nationwide.

O. REFORMING SECONDARY EDUCATION

Brown, Frank B. *The Reform of Secondary Education: A Report to the Public and the Profession*. New York: McGraw-Hill, 1973. Report of National Commission on the Reform of Secondary Education. Thirty-two recommendations dealing with local, state and national levels. Emphasis on greater options, wider participation in establishing goals, objectives and activities, and mutual appraisal of progress. Recommends lowering compulsory attendance age to 14.

Cusick, Philip A. *Inside High School: The Student's World*. New York: Holt, Rinehart & Winston, 1973. Report of author's observations after attending high school for six months. Critical of high school organization and operation. Concludes that most of student's energies are directed toward purposes that are unrelated to the goals of the school.

National Committee on Secondary Education. *American Youth in the Mid-Seventies*. Washington: National Association of Secondary School Principals, 1972. Addresses a number of problems of youth transition to adulthood germane to high schools. Recommends "action learning" as major technique for improving school's role.

Trump, J. Lloyd, and Delmas F. Miller. *Secondary School Curriculum Improvement, Challenges, Humanism, Accountabiltiy*. Boston: Allyn & Bacon, 1973. Reassessment of 1968 high school survey, stressing need to humanize high school and better adjust to needs of society and students.

P. THE ROLE OF THE COMMUNITY COLLEGE

Cross, K. Patricia, *Beyond the Open Door*. San Francisco: Jossey-Bass, 1971. Examines the role of community colleges in particular in providing higher education for the poorer and less academically able students.

Gleazer, Edmund J. *Project Focus: A Forecast Study of Community Colleges*. New York: McGraw-Hill Book Co., 1973. Deals with changes and forecasts in areas of student population, curriculum and instruction, organization and governance, financial support, and community relations.

Kintzer, Frederick. *Middleman in Higher Education*. San Francisco: Jossey-Bass Publishers, 1973. Examination of the role played by the community college as a connecting link with both the high school and senior college, with major emphasis on problems of articulation and transfer from the junior to senior college. Extensive treatment of formal and informal organization for articulation within key states.

Mesker, Leland L., and Dale Tillery. *Breaking the Access Barriers: A Profile of Two-Year Colleges.* New York: McGraw-Hill Book Co., 1971. Carnegie Commission on Higher Education profile of development of community two-year colleges. Strengths, weaknesses, trends, with particular emphasis on the community college's role in expanding diverse higher education opportunity to a wider range of the population that is served by traditional higher education.

Palinchak, Robert. *The Evolution of the Community College.* Metuchen, N.J.: Scarecrow Press, 1973. Documented survey of historical development, current status, problems, and issues in the community college movement.

Q. THE ROLE OF SCHOOL GUIDANCE AND COUNSELING

Brammer, L. M., and H. C. Springer. "A Radical Change in Counselor Education and Certification." *The Personnel and Guidance Journal,* vol. 49 (June, 1971), pp. 803-808. Describes the State of Washington plan for performance-based education and periodic on-the-job evaluation as a basis for certification of school counselors.

Cook, David R., ed. *Guidance for Education in Revolution.* Boston: Allyn and Bacon, Inc., 1971. Collection of original essays aimed at new concepts and strategies for current and future counseling and guidance methods and programs.

Ginzberg, Eli. "The Interface Between Education and Guidance." *Phi Delta Kappan,* LIV (February, 1973), pp. 381-384. Argues for less ambitious goals for school guidance, with particular reference to the matter of career guidance.

Humes, C. W., Jr. "Are Counselors Part of Pupil Personnel Services?" *The School Counselor,* vol. 18 (May, 1971), pp. 316-319. Explores the role conflicts among counselors and other pupil service professions, emphasizing the need for clarity of relationships, and for the counselor, clarity about his own role.

Island, David. "An Alternative for Counselor Education." *Personnel and Guidance Journal,* vol. 50 (May, 1972), pp. 762-766. Present counselor education is ineffective. Should be replaced by "conscientization" in counselor education, in which student's interests form the basis for dialogue with peers. Emphasis on clinical consciousness.

Lewis, M. D., and J. A. Lewis, "Counselor Education: Training for a New Alternative." *The Personnel and Guidance Journal,* vol. 49 (May, 1971), pp. 754-758. Identifies inconsistency and conflict between counselor education in which training assumes that most professional time will be spent counseling and the reality of pseudo-adminstrative, quasi-clerical, and semi-instructional tasks actually performed by counselors. Recommends a new activist approach to counselor training practice.

Menacker, Julius, and Thomas E. Linton. "The Educateur Model: An Effective Alternative for Urban Pupil Personnel Services." *The School Counselor,* vol. 21 (May, 1974), pp. 336-340. Advocates adopting the European "Educateur" system of re-education, re-socialization, and student advocacy as an appropriate response to current confusion over the role of urban school guidance and counseling.

Shertzer, Bruce, and Shelley C. Stone, "Myths, Counselor Beliefs and Practices." *The School Counselor,* vol. 19 (May, 1972), pp. 370-377. Identifies numerous inconsistencies between generally accepted beliefs in counseling and counselor practice. Also, conflicts between personal and professional philosophies.

R. THE SCHOOLING OF EXCEPTIONAL STUDENTS: INTEGRATION OR SEGREGATION?

Cegelka, Walter J., and James L. Tyler, "The Efficacy of Special Class Placement for the Mentally Retarded in Proper Perspective." *Training School Bulletin,* vol. 67 (May, 1970), pp. 33-68. Impartial review of the proper placement of mentally retarded students. Authors examine historic and contemporary theory and research supporting and opposing both special classes for mentally retarded and their integration into normal classrooms.

Dunn, Lloyd M. "Special Education for the Mildly Retarded—Is Much of It Justifiable? *Exceptional Children,* vol. 35 (September, 1968), pp. 5-22. Argues against placement in homogeneous special classes for mildly retarded students. Supports more attention to individual differences within normal classrooms.

Gallagher, James J. "Phenomenal Growth and New Problems Characterize Special Education." *Phi Delta Kappan,* vol. LV (April, 1974), pp. 516-520. Describes the rapid growth of special education during the past decade and the problems and issues that have attended this growth. The trend toward "mainstreaming" of the mildly handicapped is viewed positively, and as one element in the new accommodations being developed between general and special education.

Kirp, David L. "The Great Sorting Machine." *Phi Delta Kappan,* vol. LV (April, 1974), pp. 521-525. Argues that excessive sorting, categorizing and labeling in schooling inhibits humane education. Calls for less sorting, and more care when it is done.

Kolstoe, Oliver P. "Programs for the Mildly Retarded: A Reply to the Critics." *Exceptional Children,* vol. 39 (September, 1972), pp. 51-56. Argues against abandoning special education classes for mildly retarded. Suggests that criticisms of this practice are more related to administrative aspects than to the concept of special classes itself.

Mercer, Jane R. *Labeling the Mentally Retarded: Clinical and Social System*

Perspectives on Mental Retardation. Berkeley, Calif.: University of California Press, 1973. Argues against current practice in labeling students as retarded. Test results and interpretation discriminate against the poor and minorities. Many labeled retarded function effectively away from school, hence no useful social purpose is served by the labeling process.

Pappanikov, A. J., Thomas T. Kochanek, and Melvyn L. Reich. "Continuity and Unity in Special Education." *Phi Delta Kappan,* LV (April, 1974), pp. 546-548. A model of functional levels of diagnosis and intervention based on continuum of functions to be performed, designed to return handicapped children to the mainstream.

S. SEXISM IN EDUCATION

Anderson, Scarvia B., ed. *Sex Differences and Discrimination in Education.* Worthington, Ohio: Charles A. Jones, 1972. Collection of readings on variety of topics related to female sex discrimination in education.

Frazier, Nancy, and Myra Sadker. *Sexism in School and Society.* New York: Harper & Row, 1973. Major emphasis on negative effects on women of sex bias in school and college. Separate analyses for elementary, high school and college.

Levy, Betty, and Judith Stacy. "Sexism in the Elementary School: A Backward and Forward Look." *Phi Delta Kappan,* vol. LV (October, 1973), pp. 105-109, 123. Contends that sex-typing permeates the curriculum, the extra curriculum, teacher behavior, school structure and organization, and is particularly damaging to females.

Saario, Terry N., Carol N. Jacklin, and Carol K. Tittle, "Sex Role Stereotyping in the Public Schools." *Harvard Educational Review,* vol. 43 (August, 1973), pp. 386-416. Examines sex role stereotyping in the areas of elementary school basal readers, achievement tests, and differential curricular requirements for males and females. Argues against sex stereotyping and for more tolerance and flexibility in sex role definitions.

Tidball, M. Elizabeth. "The Search for Talented Women." *Change,* vol. 6 (May, 1974), pp. 51-52, 64. Presents data on accomplishments of women and calls for more attention to necessary changes in education that will better serve the long-neglected educational needs of women.

Trecker, Janice L. "Sex Stereotyping in the Secondary School Curriculum." *Phi Delta Kappan,* vol. LV (October, 1973), pp. 110-112. Points to masculine overemphasis in high school curriculum, particularly, but in no way limited to physical education, vocational and technical programs. Reversing this will require new ways of thinking about women, and the cooperation of teachers, administrators, counselors and educational publishers.

Ulrich, Celeste, " 'She Can Play as Good as Any Boy'." *Phi Delta Kappan,* vol. LV (October, 1973), pp. 113-117. Review of stereotypical assumption and examples of sexual discrimination from physical education and athletics. Calls for reversing present anti-athletic self-fulfilling prophecy for women.

T. SCHOOL FINANCE AND SOCIAL JUSTICE

Berke, Joel S., Alan K. Campbell, and Robert J. Goettel. *Financing Equal Educational Opportunity: Alternatives for State Finance.* Berkeley: McCutchan Publishing Corp., 1972. Report to the New York State Commission on the Quality, Cost and Financing of Elementary and Secondary Education (Fleischman Committee). Analyzes relatiionships between finance and equality of educational opportunity, with special reference to New York.

Berke, Joel S., and Michael W. Kirst. "How the Federal Government Can Encourage State School Finance Reform." *Phi Delta Kappan,* vol. LV (December, 1973), pp. 241-244. Recommends federal financial aid to states for undertaking reforms that will equalize educational opportunities and financial responsibilities.

Coons, John, William Clune III, and Stephan Sugarman, *Private Wealth and Public Education.* Cambridge, Mass.: Belknap Press of Harvard University Press, 1970. Description and criticism of system of public school finance as unjust.

Howe, Harold II, "Anatomy of a Revolution." *Saturday Review,* vol. LIV (November 20, 1971), pp. 84-88, 95. Reviews the arguments surrounding the issue of differential levels of school finance, with particular reference to the California *Serrano* decision. Supports the need for reform of school finance to insure equal financing in order to obtain equal educational opportunity.

Johns, Roe L., Kern Alexander, and Forbis Jordan, eds. *Financing Education: Fiscal and Legal Alternatives.* Columbus, Ohio: Charles E. Merrill, 1972. Extensive national study of school finance practice and problems, and alternate proposals for improvement. Results of federally funded, four-year study by the National Educational Finance Project.

Lekachman, Robert, "Schools, Money, and Politics: Financing Public Education." *The New Leader,* vol. LV (September 18, 1972), pp. 7-14. Supports the "Serrano-Rodriguez doctrine" as a necessary reform of an unjust system of school finance. Considers the appropriateness of full state funding of public schools and the possiblity of spending more money in poor districts than is available for rich districts.

Moynihan, Daniel P. "Equalizing Education: In Whose Benefit?" *The Public Interest,* vol. 29 (Fall, 1972), pp. 69-89. Criticizes current concern over equal distribution of school finances as contributing mainly to increased overall expenditure for schools, which will mainly benefit educators rather than students. Opposes increased government intervention in educational affairs.

Nolte, M. Chester, "The Quest for Educational Equality." *The American School Board Journal,* vol. 159 (july, 1972), pp. 25-26. Discusses the legal implications of the "Serrano-Rodriguez doctrine" particularly the supportive concept that the level of school funding may not be a function of wealth other than the wealth of the state as a whole. Shows the variety of forces (states, federal courts, government, the Constitution) that converge to influence the issue.

Shannon, Thomas A. " 'Rodriguez': A Dream Shattered or a Call for Finance Reform?" *Phi Delta Kappan,* vol. LIV (May, 1973), pp. 587-588. Discusses the issues and future implications of the U.S. Supreme Court decision against the plaintiff Rodriguez, who contended that the Texas system of school finance discriminated against districts with lower levels of school funds, in violation of the 14th Amendment to the U.S. Constitution. The Court ruled that the Texas system did not injure "some suspect class" and that education is not a "fundamental right protected by the U.S. Constitution."

Wise, Arthur E. "Legal Challenges to Public School Finance." *School Review,* vol. 82 (November, 1973), pp. 1-25. Discusses the significance of the Supreme Court's rejection of the plaintiff's argument in *San Antonio v. Rodriguez.* Author predicts this decision indicates an end to federal court support for school finance reform for the foreseeable future.

U. STUDENT ALIENATION

Bettelheim, Bruno, "Student Revolt: The Hard Core." *Vital Speeches of the Day,* vol. 35 (April 15, 1969), pp. 405-410. Takes the position that student alienation is primarily the result of an artificially extended period of adolescence that is exacerbated by the drive for more and higher education for all, particularly at the college level. These students are guilt-ridden, hate themselves and desperately want control and direction.

Bronfenbrenner, Urie. "Childhood: The Roots of Alienation." *The National Elementary School Principal,* vol. LII (October, 1972), pp. 22-29. Takes the position that alienation begins in early childhood. It is caused by adult neglect of children and by the breakdown of the family, community, and neighborhood structures. Children are deprived of meaningful intergenerational communication and of contact with the world of work. Schools contribute to alienation through their insularity.

Bronfenbrenner, Urie. "The Origins of Alienation." *Scientific American,* vol. 231 (August, 1974), pp. 53-61. Estrangement between youth and adults in the U.S. is higher than it has previously been. The causes lie in the rapid and radical changes in the family, which, in turn, have been caused by changes in such areas as business, urban planning, and transportation. The effects are most clearly evident in the schools.

Heath, Douglas H. "Student Alienation and School." *School Review,* vol. 78 (August, 1970), pp. 515-528. Optimistic view of student unrest. Suggests it is an opportunity for reordering educational priorities toward more personalization and broader, more diverse goals in education.

Hendrick, Irving G., and Reginald L. Jones, eds. *Student Dissent in the Schools*. Boston: Houghton Mifflin Co., 1972. Collection of readings exploring the causes, expressions and possible solutions to active expressions of student alienation. Topics include values, drug problem, student rights, dress and grooming school codes, student publications, and racial conflict.

Keniston, Kenneth, *The Uncommitted*. New York: Harcourt, Brace, Jovanovich, 1971. Collection of author's essays over past few years that relate general causes and manifestations of youth alienation to recent evidence of student unrest.

Keniston, Kenneth. *Youth and Dissent*. New York: Harcourt Brace, Janovich, 1971. Collection of author's essays over past few years that relate general causes and manifestations of youth alienation to recent evidence of student unrest.

V. STUDENT DRUG ABUSE

Aubrey, Roger F. *The Counselor and Drug Abuse*. Boston: Houghton Mifflin Co., 1973 (Set VII, Guidance Monograph Series). Advocates drug abuse prevention programs based on both cognitive and affective elements. Stresses development of good decision-making skills and sound value systems in students, leading to a life style taking students beyond drugs.

Blum, Richard H., and Associates, *Students and Drugs*. San Francisco: Jossey-Bass, 1970. Reports psychopharmacological research on nature and correlates of student drug abuse.

[Drug Abuse Survey Project] *Dealing with Drug Abuse*. New York: Praeger Publishers, 1972. Comprehensive report on national pattern of drug abuse, effects of drug abuse, treatment and rehabilitation, and drug abuse education.

Gelinas, M. V. "Classroom Drug Scene." *American Education*, vol. 6 (November, 1970), pp. 3-5. Review of trends among student drug abusers, with recommendations for coping with the problem.

Grant, R. H. "Drug Education: What It is and Isn't." *Journal of Drug Education*, vol. 2 (March, 1972), pp. 89-97. Recommends taking emphasis off information-giving and on promoting peer interaction and role models. Programs must be comprehensive, concerned with self-development.

National Commission on Marijuana and Drug Abuse. *Drug Use in America: The Problem in Perspective*. Washington: U.S. Government Printing Office, 1973. Comprehensive data and analysis of drug problem in America, with specific reference to schools. Commends increase in school drug education, but recommends better education and more meaningful roles for students as more important preventative measure.

W. TEACHER UNIONIZATION

Braun, Robert J. *Teachers and Power*. New York: Simon and Schuster, 1972. History of the American Federation of Teachers; theory and rationale for teacher unionization and collective bargaining; detailed analysis of Newark, N.J. strike.

Carter, Barbara. *Parents and Power: The Story Behind the New York City Teachers' Strike*. New York: Citation Press, 1971. Description and analysis of the strike and the forces (black militants, union leaders, school officials) involved in it.

Lewis, Richard. "Who Will Control the AFT?" *Change,* vol. 6 (May, 1974), pp. 14-17. Analyzes the potentials for unity and divisiveness between the New York AFT local and the national AFT. Predicts that eventual merger with the NEA will reduce the New York AFT local's power base.

Lieberman, Myron. "The Union Merger Movement: Will 3,500,000 Teachers Put It All Together?" *Saturday Review-Education*, vol. LV (June 24, 1972, pp. 50-56. Discusses the implications of potential merger of the American Federation of Teachers and the National Education Association from political, educational, and economic perspectives.

O'Neill, John. "The Rise and Fall of the UFT," in Annette Rubenstein, ed., *Schools Against Children: The Case for Community Control*. New York: Monthly Review Press, 1970. Generally critical review and analysis of union changes from militant social reformism to protection of middle-class wages and professional prerogatives at the expense of the poor and minority students.

Perry, Charles R., and Wesley A. Wildman. *The Impact of Negotiations in Public Education: The Evidence from the Schools*. Worthington, Ohio: Charles A. Jones Publishing Co., 1970. Deals with the nature of the collective bargaining process and its results in schools. Description and analysis of most aspects and issues in school collective bargaining.

X. YOUTH IN A CHANGING SOCIETY

Bronfenbrenner, Urie. *Two Worlds of Childhood*. New York: Russell Sage Foundation, 1970. Comparison of schools and other child-rearing institutions in the U.S.A. and U.S.S.R. The Soviet Union's system inducts youth into adult society by involving the total society in the maturation process. In contrast, the American system isolates the child from society. The U.S.S. R. stresses cooperative themes, while U.S. stresses individualistic themes.

Coleman, James S. "How Do the Young Become Adults?" *Phi Delta Kappan,* vol. LIV (December, 1972), pp. 226-230. Inadequate youth socialization partly caused by lack of participation in process by institutions other than the school. This is needed so schools can, as they should, concentrate mainly on the intellectual process.

Havighurst, Robert J., ed. *American Youth in the Seventies: 74th Yearbook, NSSE.* Washington: National Society for the Study of Education, 1975. A collection of original chapters on youth socialization in contemporary society. Major topics are: Youth as a State of Life; Theoretical and Empirical Background; Youth and Social Institutions; and Pluralism and Youth.

Panel on Youth of the President's Science Advisory Committe. *Youth: Transition to Adulthood.* Washington: U.S. Government Printing Office, 1973. Examines transition from youth to adulthood (ages 14-24) and finds schooling to be too greatly relied upon for effectively promoting this transition. Other strategies and institutions are called for to supplement the school as it traditionally operates. Among these are: continuing part-time evening education; "recurrent education" in which there is alternation between full-time work and full-time schooling; "career education," a pattern of work training, youth communities and education vouchers for adolescents to use at schools, or a wide range of other skill training environments.

Wynne, Edward. "Education and Socialization: A Complex Equation." *Educational Researcher,* vol. 1 (December, 1972), pp. 5-9. Discusses dynamic relationship between education and socialization. Continuation of present policies will produce people unequipped to adequately participate in adult society.

Wynne, Edward. "Socialization to Adulthood: Different Concepts, Different Policies." *Interchange,* vol. 5 (Spring, 1974), pp. 23-35. Maintains that the socialization process for upper-middle class children and adolescents is dysfunctional, as schools and suburbs are poor socializers because of little personal responsibility, meaningful work, and intergenerational contact. Calls for research and development to expand the number and diversity of persons and institutions involved in youth socialization.

PART III:

CHRONOLOGICAL TABLEAUX

XVIII. THE COLONIAL PERIOD (1607-1783)

A. GENERAL WORKS

Bailyn, B. *Education in the Forming of American Society*. Chapel Hill: University of North Carolina Press, 1960. The history of education should be vastly expanded in scope and concern. An excellent bibliographic essay.

Boorstin, D. J. *The Americans: The Colonial Experience*. New York: Random House, 1958. An excellent general work, with considerable information on both formal and informal education.

Bridenbaugh, Carl. *Cities in Revolt*. New York: Capricorn Book, 1964. Carries the history of Colonial American urban life up to the year 1776. Same five cities as his *Cities in the Wilderness*.

Bridenbaugh, Carl. *Cities in the Wilderness*. New York: The Ronald Press, 1938. Life in five major cities of Colonial America. A rich storehouse of educational information. Covers period 1625-1742.

Bridenbaugh, Carl, and Jessica B. Bridenbaugh. *Rebels and Gentlemen*. New York: Oxford University Press, 1962. The people and the city of Philadelphia, including their educational pursuits.

Bruce, Philip A. *Institutional History of Virginia in the 17th Century*. New York: Putnam, 1910. An oldie but goodie. Deals extensively with education in the Virginia colony in the 17th century.

Cremin, L. A. *American Education: The Colonial Experience, 1607-1783*. New York: Harper and Row, 1970. The most recent and certainly the most extensive treatment of Colonial American education in all of its formats. An excellent annotated bibliography.

Curti, Merle. *The Growth of American Thought*. 2nd ed. New York: Harper and Row, 1957. An intellectual history of America, with a good section on Colonial times and the European heritage.

Eggleston, Edward. *The Transit of Civilization from England to America in the 17th Century*. New York: D. Appleton and Co., 1900. A classic work, stresses the diffusion of culture from European roots to the New World. A more modern variation on this thesis is that of Louis B. Wright, *Culture of the Moving Frontier* (1955).

Hindle, Brooke. *The Pursuit of Science in Revolutionary America, 1735-1789*. Chapel Hill: University of North Carolina Press, 1956. The varied scientific interests, training and contributions of the Colonial Americans.

Miller, Perry, ed. *The American Puritans*. New York: Anchor Books, 1956. The prose and poetry of the Puritans, including a section on their literary and educational ideals.

Morgan, E. S. *The Puritan Dilemma*. Boston: Little Brown and Co., 1958. Although this is the story of John Winthrop, it is also an excellent introduction to an understanding of Puritan dogma.

Morison, S. E. *The Intellectual Life of Colonial New England*. New York: New York University Press, 1956. Education, libraries, almanacs, etc., as part of the total intellectual life of Colonial New England.

Newlin, Claude M. *Philosophy and Religion in Colonial America*. New York: Philosophical Library, 1962. The 18th century Puritan mind. For the philosophical thought of the earlier period, may be used with Perry Miller's *The New England Mind in the 17th Century*, and his *The New England Mind: From Colony to Province*.

Parrington, Vernon L. *Main Currents in American Thought: The Colonial Mind, 1620-1800*. New York: Harcourt, Brace and Co., 1927. Although clearly anti-Mather in its tone, it is valuable withal for intellectual history. For another view of Mather, see Otho T. Beall and Richard Shryock, *Cotton Mather: First Significant Figure in American Medicine* (1954).

Rossiter, Clinton. *The First American Revolution*. New York: Harcourt, Brace and World, 1953. A revised version of Part I of the author's *Seedtime of the Republic*. Valuable for the structure of Colonial society, as well as insights into the mind of Colonial America.

Savelle, Max. *Seeds of Liberty: The Genesis of the American Mind*. New York: Alfred A. Knopf, 1948. The influences that combined to form the American mind. Valuable for any studies of American education.

Sutherland, Stella. *Population Distribution in Colonial America*. New York: Columbia University Press, 1936. A very helpful and necessary tool for obtaining an accurate picture of the population of Colonial America.

Wright, Louis B. *The Cultural Life of the American Colonies*. New York: Harper and Bros., 1957. Cultural and intellectual history, including both formal and informal education.

B. FORMAL EDUCATION

1. Schools

Bridenbaugh, Carl. *Myths and Realities: Societies of The Colonial South.* Baton Rouge: Louisiana State University Press, 1952. The last third of the book is particularly valuable, as it deals with the educational activities in the backcountry of the Colonial South.

Burns, N. R. *Education in New Jersey, 1630-1871.* Princeton: Princeton University Press, 1942. A good, solid history of education activities in a middle colony.

Campbell, H. G. "The Syms and Eaton Schools and Their Successors." *William and Mary Quarterly,* vol. 20 (2nd ser., 1940), pp. 1-61. An extensive history of an early (began 1647?) free school in the colony of Virginia.

Clews, E. W. *Educational Legislation and Administration of the Colonial Governments.* New York: Macmillan, 1899. With the exception of Georgia, this work deals with the legislation pertaining to education in the colonies of the New World.

Cole, N. M. "The Licensing of Schoolmasters in Colonial Massachusetts." *History of Education Journal,* vol. 8 (1956), pp. 68-74. How one got approval to teach in Colonial Massachusetts before the days of certification.

Corry, J. P. "Education in Colonial Georgia." *Georgia Historical Quarterly,* vol. 16 (1932), pp. 136-145. Georgia is the least studied (because of lack of primary source material) of the American colonies. This is a survey of educational efforts in Georgia during the Colonial period.

Ford, P. L. *The New England Primer.* New York: Teachers College Press, 1962. A printing of the original New England Primer, with an introduction.

Hendrick, I. G. "A Reappraisal of Colonial New Hampshire's Effort in Public Education." *History of Education Quarterly,* vol. 6 (1966), pp. 43-60. Concludes, upon re-examination of the New Hampshire educational scene in Colonial times, that, all things considered, the state did pretty well by comparison with other states.

Holmes, P. *A Tercentenary History of the Boston Latin School, 1635-1935.* Cambridge, Mass.: Harvard University Press, 1935. A school history of one of America's most venerable institutions, and the alma mater of some of its best known men.

Hooker, R. J. *The Carolina Backcountry on the Eve of Revolution.* Chapel Hill: University of North Carolina Press, 1953. This is the journal of Charles Woodmason, "Anglican Itinerant." Gives a picture of education away from the coastal population centers.

Kilpatrick, W. H. *The Dutch Schools of New Netherland and Colonial New York.* Washington, D.C.: U.S. Government Printing Office, 1912. An older work, but the most satisfactory study of the schools of early New York.

Landrum, G. W. "The First Colonial Grammar in English." *William and Mary Quarterly,* vol. 19 (2nd ser., 1939), pp. 272-285. The grammar was Latin, and the author of this first in English was Prof. Hugh Jones of the College of William and Mary in 1724.

Middlekauff, R. *Ancients and Axioms: Secondary Education in 18th Century New England.* New Haven: Yale University Press, 1963. The persistence of the Puritan education tradition in New England as it adapted to meet the increasing secularization and commercialization of the 18th century.

Plimpton, G. A. "The Hornbook and its Use in America." *Proc. of the American Antiquarian Society,* vol. 25 (1916) pp. 264-272. The great-great granddaddy of the Basal Reader for American children—what it was and how it was used.

Pratt, D. J. *Annals of Public Education in the State of New York, 1626-1746.* Albany, New York: The Argus Co., 1872. In spite of the premature statehood in the title, this is a helpful compendium of records and acts relative to education in New York. Covers Dutch as well as English reigns.

Roobach, A. O. *The Development of the Social Studies in American Secondary Education Before 1861.* Philadelphia: University of Pennsylvania Press, 1937. This work provides an extensive review of the literature of the topic, and describes Colonial attempts to put social studies into the curriculum.

Seybolt, R. F. *The Evening School in Colonial America.* Urbana: University of Illinois Press, 1925 A survey, using primary sources (newspapers) of the extent and nature of the evening schools of Colonial America.

Seybolt, R. F. *The Private Schools of Colonial Boston.* Cambridge, Mass.: Harvard University Press, 1935. The varied and often fascinating offerings of the "private venture schools" of Colonial Boston, gathered from their newspaper advertisements and announcements.

Seybolt, R. F. *The Public Schools of Colonial Boston, 1635-1775.*

Cambridge, Mass.: Harvard University Press, 1935. From town meeting minutes, records, diaries, etc., Seybolt documents the growth of the public schools of Colonial Boston.

Seybolt, R. F. *Source Studies in American Colonial Education: The Private School*. Urbana: University of Illinois Press, 1925. The innovative role played by the Colonial American private schools relative to curricular changes in response to public needs.

Shipton, C. K. "Secondary Education in the Puritan Colonies." *New England Quarterly*, vol. 7 (1934), pp. 646-661. Argued that there was a continued concern with education in 18th century New England, and that it was transformed to meet a changed situation in that century.

Smith, C. J. "Plan For an Academy . . ." *William and Mary Quarterly*, vol. 3 (2nd ser., 1923), pp. 52-57. An interesting proposal for a Colonial (1770) academy.

Smith, L. A. H. "Three Spelling Books of American Schools, 1740-1800." *Harvard Library Review*, vol. 16 (1968), pp. 72-93. One learns more from spelling books than how to spell. This is a content analysis of three early American spellers.

Smith, W. "The Teacher in Puritan Culture." *Harvard Educational Review*, vol. 36, No. 4 (1966), pp. 394-411. This article traces the sources of American attitudes towards teachers, the influence of Puritan ideology on teaching, and of Harvard College.

Tully, Alan. "Literacy Levels and Educational Development in Rural Pennsylvania." *Pennsylvania History*, vol. 39 (July, 1972), pp. 301-312. Takes a rather jaundiced view of the state of education and literacy in rural Pennsylvania in the years 1729-1775.

Woody, T. *Early Quaker Education in Pennsylvania*. New York: Teachers College, 1920. A careful and authoritative history of the Quaker educational efforts in Pennsylvania.

2. Higher Education

Blair, J., and Fouace, S. "The Charter and Statutes of the College of Willam and Mary in Virginia." *William and Mary Quarterly*, vol. 22 (1st ser., 1914), pp. 281-296. These are the statutes for 1736. For the statutes of 1758, see the *William and Mary Quarterly*, vol. 16 (1st ser., 1908), pp. 239-256.

Brinton, H. H. "The Quaker Contribution to Higher Education in Colonial America." *Pennsylvania History*, vol. 25 (1958), pp. 234-250. In the area of higher education, the major and characteristic contribution of the Quakers was in the field of practical and scientific studies.

Broderick, F. L. "Pulpit, Physics and Politics: The Curriculum of the College of New Jersey, 1746-1794." *William and Mary Quarterly,* vol. 6 (3rd ser., 1949), pp. 42-68. The curricular evolution of Princeton as it developed from the experience of the "log cabin colleges."

Bronson, W. C. *The History of Brown University, 1764-1914.* Providence: Published by the University, 1914. The standard history of one of the nine Colonial American colleges.

Cheyney, E. P. *History of the University of Pennsylvania.* Philadelphia: University of Pennsylvania Press, 1940. The book spans the years from 1740-1940, and the early chapters provide good material for Colonial American studies.

Cohen, I. B. *Some Early Tools of American Science: An Account of the Early Scientific Instruments and Mineralogical and Biological Collections in Harvard University.* Cambridge, Mass.: Harvard University Press, 1950. An extremely valuable work on science and education in the Colonial College. Gives far more information than the title might lead one to think.

Come, D. R. "The Influence of Princeton on Higher Education in the South Before 1825." *William and Mary Quarterly,* vol. 2 (3rd ser., 1945), pp. 359-396. The philosophy of higher education espoused by Princeton in Colonial times, and its influence in the South (particularly Virginia).

Dexter, F., ed. *Documentary History of Yale University* . . . New Haven: Yale University Press, 1916. Primary source materials for the years 1701-1745.

Durin, R. "The Role of the Presidents in the American Colleges of the Colonial Period." *History of Education Quarterly,* vol. 1, No. 2 (June, 1961), pp. 23-31. A rapid survey of the presidents of the Colonial American colleges—their duties and their accomplishments.

Haller, M. "Moravian Influence on Higher Education in Colonial America." *Pennsylvania History,* vol. 25 (1958), pp. 214-222. The Moravian church group and the extent of its educational activities in Colonial America, as well as the educational philosophy of the Moravians.

Hornberger, T. *Scientific Thought in the American Colleges*: 1638-1800. Austin: University of Texas press, 1945. Chronicles the changing place of science in the Colonial college curriculum with considerable detail.

Knight, E. W. "Early Opposition to the Education of American Children Abroad." *Education Forum,* vol. 11, No. 2, Pt. 1 (1946), pp. 193-204.

Kraus, J. W. "The Development of a Curriculum in the Early American Colleges." *History of Education Quarterly,* vol. 1, No. 2 (June, 1961), pp. 64-75. The development of curriculum from a 17th century Cambridge model to distinct variations by the latter part of the 18th century.

McAnear, B. "The Raising of Funds by the Colonial Colleges." *Mississippi Valley Historical Review,* vol. 38, No. 4 (March, 1952), pp. 591-612. The start of "shoestring financing" in higher education. Lotteries and the like.

Middleton, A. P. "Anglican Contributions to Higher Education in Colonial America." *Pennsylvania History,* vol. 25 (1958), pp. 251-268. The Anglican universities of Cambridge and Oxford provided the chief models for the American college in Colonial America.

"Minutes of the College Faculty, 1758." *William and Mary Quarterly,* vol. 1 (2nd ser., 1921), pp. 24-26. The minutes of a faculty meeting at the College of William and Mary in 1758. They read not unlike those of a modern college faculty. For the minutes of other years' meetings, see *William and Mary Quarterly,* 1st ser., vols. 1-5, 13-15.

Morison, S. E. *Harvard College in the 17th Century.* (2 vols). Cambridge, Mass.: Harvard University Press, 1936. A monumental study of a Colonial college in its formative years. Morison has amassed an amazing amount of material. May be used with his *The Founding of Harvard College* (1935).

Morison, S. E. *Three Centuries of Harvard.* Cambridge, Mass.: Harvard University Press, 1946. For those who do not have Morison's abiding fascination with Harvard, this is the shorter history of Harvard College.

Rand, E. K. "Liberal Education in 17th Century Harvard." *New England Quarterly,* vol. 6 (1963), pp. 525-551. Examines the *Ars Liberalis* at Harvard College in the 17th century, and what it was like to study them there.

Richardson, L. B. *History of Dartmouth College.* 2 Vols. Hanover: Dartmouth College Publications, 1932. The standard history of Dartmouth College.

"Speeches of Students of the College of William and Mary, Delivered May 1, 1699." *William and Mary Quarterly,* vol. 10 (2nd ser., 1930), pp. 323-337. The speeches recorded were made in conjunction with a fund-raising campaign for the college. They contain interesting educational insights from the student point of view.

Tewksbury, D. G. *The Founding of American Colleges and Universities Before the Civil War, with Particular Reference to the Religious Influences Bearing Upon the College Movement.* New York: Bureau of Publications, Teachers College, Columbia University, 1932. With this title, what more can one say? It is a classic work on the topic.

Walsh, J. J. *Education of the Founding Fathers of the Republic.* New York: Fordham University Press, 1935. A detailed study of the Colonial

American colleges, and the Scholasticism that Walsh finds therein. See also his "Scholasticism in the Colonial Colleges," *New England Quarterly,* vol. 5 (1932), pp. 443-532, for a shorter version of the argument.

Wertenbaker, T. J. Princeton: Princeton University Press, 1946. The standard history of Princeton, covering the years 1746-1896.

C. INFORMAL EDUCATION

1. The Family

Calhoun, A. W. *A Social History of the American Family From Colonial Times to the Present* (3 Vols.) Cleveland: The Arthur M. Clark Co., 1917-1919. The classic and still the most comprehensive work on the American family.

Demos, J. *A Little Commonwealth: Family Life in Plymouth Colony.* New York: Oxford University Press, 1970. An excellent work of careful and detailed microanalysis of a New England community, along the lines suggested by Morgan.

Demos, J. "Notes on Life in Plymouth Colony." *William and Mary Quarterly,* vol. 22 (3rd ser., 1965), pp. 264-286. A microanalysis of a Colonial American community, utilizing court, marriage, church and other local records.

Earle, Alice M. *Child Life in Colonial Days.* New York: Macmillan, 1899. The daily happenings in the lives of the children of Colonial America—from education through funerals.

Earle, Alice M. *Home Life in Colonial Days.* New York: Macmillan Co., 1898. Much detailed information on the Colonial American home and the activities therein.

Glubok, S., ed. *Home and Child Life in Colonial Days.* New York: The Macmillan Co., 1969. An abridgement of Alice Morse Earle's *Home Life in Colonial Days* and her *Child Life in Colonial Days.*

Greven, P. J., Jr. "Family Structure in 17th Century Andover, Mass." *William and Mary Quarterly,* vol. 23 (3rd ser., 1966), pp. 234-256. Stresses the essential "nuclear" quality of the 17th century Puritan family structure.

Greven, P. J., Jr. "Historical Demography and Colonial America." *William and Mary Quarterly,* vol. 24 (3rd ser., 1967), pp. 435-454. The application of demographic techniques to family research in Colonial American history.

Kiefer, Sister M. "Early American Childhood in the Middle Atlantic

Area." *Pennsylvania Mag. of History and Biography*, vol. 68 (1944), pp. 3-37. The middle colonies, and what it was like to grow up there in Colonial times.

Matthews, W. *American Diaries: An Annotated Bibliography of American Diaries Written Prior to 1861*. Boston: J. S. Canner and Co., 1959. A helpful reference book for access to primary sources on family life.

Moller, H. "Sex Composition and Correlated Culture Patterns of Colonial America." *William and Mary Quarterly*, vol. 39 (2nd ser., 1945), pp. 113-153. The relative shortage of women in Colonial America, and the social consequences of the phenomenon.

Morgan, E. S. "New England Puritanism: Another Approach." *William and Mary Quarterly*, vol. 18 (3rd ser., 1961), pp. 236-242. The other approach suggested herein is a study of Puritan life on a microanalytical, township basis.

Morgan, E. S. *The Puritan Family* (Rev. ed.). New York: Harper and Row, 1966. Provides the Puritan viewpoint on education, children, child rearing, etc.

Morgan, E. S. *Virginians at Home: Family Life in the 18th Century*. Chapel Hill: University of North Carolina Press, 1952. Attempts to do for a Southern colony what he did for the New England colonies in *The Puritan Family*.

Rothman, D. J. "A Note on the Study of the Colonial Family." *William and Mary Quarterly*, vol. 23 (3rd ser., 1966), pp. 627-634. Raises provocative questions about the Colonial American family, *i.e.,* was "family tribalism" the cause of the weakening of the Puritan structure of government?

Saveth, E. N. "The Problem of American Family History." *American Quarterly*, 21 (1969), pp. 311-329. This article provides an excellent and extensive review of the literature relating to the American family.

2. Books and Libraries

Cantor, M. "The Image of the Negro in Colonial Literature." *New England Quarterly*, vol. 36 (1963), pp. 452-477. Through informal education, the foundations of both pro and anti-slavery thought was laid in the Colonial period.

Dexter, F. B. "Early Private Libraries in New England." *Proc. of the American Antiquarian Society*, N.S. vol. 18 (1907), pp. 135-147. The extent, variety, etc., of the books in the private libraries of the colonists of early New England.

Kiefer, M. *American Children Through Their Books, 1700-1835.* Philadelphia: University of Pennsylvania Press, 1948. The rising status of children as revealed by the books that were written for them.

Lamberton, E. V. "Colonial Libraries of Pennsylvania." *Pennsylvania Mag. of History and Biography,* vol. 42 (1918), pp. 193-234. A survey of the Pennsylvania area in terms of the existing libraries of Colonial times.

Powell, W. S. "Books in the Virginia Colony before 1624." *William Marshall Quarterly,* vol. 5 (1948), pp. 177-184. The very earliest books available to the Virginia colonists for their informal education.

Salisbury, S. "Early Books and Libraries in America." *Proc. of the American Antiquarian Society,* vol. 5 (1884), pp. 171-215. What was available and where it was available in terms of reading material in Colonial America.

Smart, G. K. "Private Libraries in Colonial Virginia." *American Literature,* vol. 10 (1938), pp. 24-52. The extent, variety, etc., of book holdings in the private libraries of Colonial Virginia.

Wright, L. B. *The First Gentlemen of Virginia: Intellectual Qualities of the Early Colonial Ruling Class.* San Marino, Calif.: The Huntington Library, 1940. Essentially a study of the books owned (and presumably read) by the elite of Colonial Virginia.

Wright, T. O. *Literature And Culture in Early New England.* New York: Russell and Russell, 1966. This is a reprinting of the 1920 edition of Wright's book. It deals specifically and well with the extent of informal education in 17th and 18th century New England.

3. Other Instruments of Education

Baldwin, Alice M. *The New England Clergy and the American Revolution.* New York: Frederick Ungar Pub. Co., 1958. Traces the educational influence of the Colonial New England clergy. Numerous examples of the content of sermons.

Chroust, A. H. *The Rise of the Legal Profession in America.* (2 Vols.) Norman: University of Oklahoma Press, 1965. The early, informal apprenticeship education of the legal profession in America.

Gummere, R. M. "The Classical Element in Early New England Almanacs." *Harvard Library Review,* vol. 9 (1955), pp. 181-196. The almanacs as informal education instruments, and the classical element that was in them.

Miller, S. "A Brief Retrospect of the 18th Century . . ." *William and Mary Quarterly,* vol. 10 (3rd ser., 1953). A reprinting of Miller's book, published in 1803, which gives a history of informal education. Only the first part of the book is reprinted.

Seybolt, R. F. *Apprenticeship and Apprenticeship Education in Colonial New England and New York.* New York: Teachers College, 1917. The influence of apprenticeship education on the formal education of the schools. Fine source of documents.

Shryock, R. H. *Medicine and Society in America, 1660-1860.* New York: New York University Press, 1960. An excellent study of the development of medical education, initially via the informal apprenticeship system.

Sidwell, R. T. "Writers, Thinkers and Fox Hunters . . ." *History of Education Quarterly,* vol. 8 (1968), pp. 275-288. Educational theory as it was learned in Colonial America through the almanacs of the times.

Winslow, O. E. *Meetinghouse Hill, 1630-1783.* New York: The Macmillan Co., 1952. The Colonial American church as an instrument of informal education.

D. POLITICAL MINORITIES (WOMEN, BLACKS, NATIVE AMERICANS, AND POOR)

Adams, E. C. *American Indian Education: Government Schools and Economic Progress.* New York: King's Crown Press, 1946. The only overview of Indian educational history. A limited work, it provides a fine outline of the topic.

Barth, P. J. *Franciscan Education and the Social Order in Spanish North America (1501-1821).* Chicago: University of Chicago Press, 1945. Efforts by the Franciscan Fathers to educate the Indians via formal schooling.

Benson, M. *Women in Eighteenth-Century America: A Study of Opinion and Social Usage.* New York: Columbia University Press, 1935. Valuable work to understand the position and theories regarding women in 18th century America.

Bullock, H. A. *A History of Negro Education in the South: From 1619 to the Present.* Cambridge, Mass.: Harvard University Press, 1967. Not very helpful for the Colonial scene, but it does present an overview of the area.

Crane, V. A. *The Southern Frontier, 1670-1732.* Ann Arbor: University of Michigan Press, 1929. Valuable for the understanding of Anglo-Indian affairs in the Colonial South.

Davis, J. L. "Roger Williams Among the Narragansett Indians." *New England Quarterly,* vol. 43 (1970), pp. 593-604. Roger Williams received an education from the Indians that formed a basis for his social critiques.

Dexter, E. A. *Colonial Women of Affairs* . . . 2nd rev. ed. Boston and New York: Houghton Mifflin Co., 1931. Women of note in Colonial America, the education they received and what they accomplished in business and the professions.

Earle, A. M. *Colonial Dames and Good Wives*. New York: Frederick Ungar Pub. Co., 1962. A re-print of an earlier edition, this is a highly informational social history of women in Colonial America.

Frost, S. E., Jr. "Higher Education Among the American Indians During the Colonial Period." *History of Education Journal*, vol. 9 (1958), pp. 59-66. Some ill-conceived ventures in higher education among the Indians.

Gookin, D. "Historical Collections of the Indians in New England." *Mass. Hist. Society Collections*, vol. 1 and 2 (1806). A printing of Gookin's 1674 work dealing with the educational efforts of John Eliot among the Indians. Also gives information on the educational work among the Indians by lesser known Puritan ministers.

Grant, A. *Memoirs of an American Lady*. 2 Vols. New York: Dodd, Mead and Co., 1901. An excellent picture of Colonial American life from a female point of view. Includes information on formal and informal education.

Greene, L. J. *The Negro in Colonial New England*. New York: Columbia University Press, 1942. One of the few works on the topic. Provides some specific information on education of Black people.

Jernegan, M. W. *Laboring and Dependent Classes in Colonial America, 1607-1785* . . . Chicago: University of Chicago Press, 1931. The classic work on the education of the poor, slaves and servants of Colonial America.

Johnson, E. P. "Early Missionary Work Among the North American Indians." *Papers of the American Society of Church History*, vol. 3 (2nd ser., 1912), pp. 13-29. An overview of missionary work with the Indians, including educational. The various denominational history journals are valuable sources for Indian educational history.

Jordan, W. D.   *White Over Black*. Chapel Hill: University of North Carolina Press, 1968. Chronicles the attitudes of White towards Black people through the years 1550-1812. Essential for an understanding of Black education.

Kellaway, W. *The New England Company, 1646-1776: Missionary Society to the American Indians*. New York: Barnes and Noble, 1961. Christianity and education among the Indians of Colonial New England.

Kemp, W. W. *The Support of Schools in Colonial America by the Society for the Propagation of the Gospel in Foreign Parts*. New York: Teachers College, 1913. The educational activities of the S.P.G., particularly interesting regarding New York. The S.P.G. supported schools for several marginal groups.

Klingberg, F. *American Humanitarianism in Colonial New York.* Philadelphia: The Church History Society, 1940. The work of the S.P.G. of the Church of England in Colonial New York.

Klingberg, F. *An Appraisal of the Negro in Colonial South Carolina.* Washington, D.C.: Associated Publishers, 1941. Contains, among other things, the history of the "Charleston Negro School" from the year 1743. The school was an S.P.G. venture.

Knight, E. W., ed. *A Documentary History of Education in the South Before 1860.* 5 Vols. Chapel Hill: The University of North Carolina Press, 1949. A valuable collection of documents relating to the Colonial South. Many documents dealing with the education of marginal groups.

Leonard, E. A. *The Dear-Bought Heritage.* Philadelphia: University of Pennsylvania Press, 1965. Colonial women; their lives, work and the education they received.

Mann, H. *The Female Review: The Life of Deborah Sampson.* New York: Arno Press, 1972. This is a reprint of a 1797 edition, and is the story of a woman who fought in the American Revolution under the name of Robert Shurtlieff. Tells of her education and her adventures.

McCallum, J. D. *Eleazar Wheelock.* Hanover: Dartmouth College Publications, 1939. The biography of the great Colonial American educator of the Indians and the founder of "Moor's Charity School." (Moor put up the money.)

McCallum, J. D., ed. *The Letters of Eleazar Wheelock's Indians.* Hanover: Dartmouth College Publications, 1932. The letters of the students of "Moor's Charity School" (for Indians), which later became Dartmouth College.

Morris, R. B. *Government and Labor in Early America.* New York: Columbia University Press, 1946. Excellent descriptions and documentation of the educational provisions in the trades and apprenticeship agreements.

Nash, G. "The Image of the Indian in the Southern Colonial Mind." *William and Mary Quarterly,* vol. 29 (3rd ser., 1972), pp. 197-230. Anglo-Indian interaction in the Colonial South for 150 years. Extensive treatment, and necesssary to understand educational outlook.

Pennington, E. L. "The Rev. Francis Le Jau's Work Among Indians and Negro Slaves." *Journal of Southern History,* vol. 1 (1935), pp. 442-458. The S.P.G. and its work with both Indians and Blacks.

Pennington, E. L. "Thomas Bray's Associates and their Work Among the

Negroes." *Proc. of the American Antiquarian Society,* NS., vol. 48 (1939), pp. 311-403. Some of the schools established by the Bray Associates for Blacks in Colonial America.

Robinson, W. S., Jr. "Indian Education and Missions in Colonial Virginia." *Journal of Southern History,* vol. 18 (1952), pp. 152-168. The best account of "Henrico College," an effort at Indian education in the 17th century Virginia colony.

Sheehan, B. W. "Indian-White Relations in Early America." *William and Mary Quarterly,* vol. 26 (3rd ser., 1969), pp. 267-286. A review essay which is critical and extensive regarding the literature on Anglo-Indian relations in early years.

Smith, Marie H. *Higher Education for the Indians in the American Colonies.* Unpublished M.A. Thesis, New York University, 1950. Limited to higher education, but one of the very few sources for this era.

Spruill, J. C. *Women's Life and Work in the Southern Colonies.* New York: Russell and Russell, 1969. Reprint of a 1938 edition. This is a most helpful work for the southern Colonial woman; her life, work, and a considerable amount of information about her education.

Stander, G. *The History of the Founding of Jesuit Educational Institutions in the Colony of New York.* Unpublished M.S. Thesis, City College of New York, 1933. Famed mostly for their work in New France, the Jesuits also did educational work in New York. For the educational work of the Jesuits with the Indians, the multi-volume *Jesuit Relations* is a rich source.

Staub, J. S. "Benjamin Rush's Views on Women's Education." *Pennsylvania History,* vol. 35 (1967), pp. 147-157. The amazing Dr. Rush and his early advocacy of education for women.

Tyler, L. G. "Education in Colonial Virginia: Poor Children and Orphans." *William Marshall College Quarterly, Hist. Mag.,* vol. 5 (1897), pp. 219-223. The educational provisions for those from "the other side of the tracks" in Colonial Virginia.

Vaughan, A. T. *New England Frontier: Puritans and Indians, 1620-1675.* Boston: Little, Brown and Co., 1965. Tells the story of Harvard's Indian College as well as other Puritan attempts to educate the Indians.

Wells, G. F. *Parish Education in Colonial Virginia.* New York: Teachers College, 1928. Education for the poor in Virginia via apprenticeship and county-parish work schools.

Whiting, H. F. *The Old New York Frontier.* New York: C. Scribner's Sons, 1902. The old New York frontier, including some information about missionary schools for the Indians.

Winslow, O. E. *John Eliot: "Apostle to the Indians."* Boston: Houghton Mifflin Co., 1968. The best biography of the remarkable teacher who devoted 50 years of his life to Indian education in New England.

Woodson, C. C. *The Education of the Negro Prior to 1861.* 2nd ed. Washington, D.C.: The Associated Publishers, 1919. About the only extensive treatment of the topic for Colonial America. Has an extensive appendix with documents.

Woody, T. *A History of Women's Education in the United States.* 2 Vols. New York: Octagon Books, 1966. Originally published in 1929, this is the best work to date on the history of the education of women in the United States.

E. IDEAS AND PEOPLE

Anderson, D. R. "The Teacher of Jefferson and Marshall." *South Atlantic Quarterly,* vol. 15 (1916), pp. 327-343. The story of Thomas Wythe and his famous pupils.

Best, J. H., ed. *Benjamin Franklin on Education.* New York: Teachers College, 1962. Selected writings of Franklin on education. Essay on Franklin's education ideas.

Boorstin, D. J. *The Lost World of Thomas Jefferson.* New York: Henry Holt and Co., 1948. The Jeffersonian view of the world, including "the quest for useful knowledge."

Brookes, G. S. *Friend Anthony Benezet.* Philadelphia: University of Pennsylvania Press, 1937. The biography of the great Quaker educator who was vitally interested in the education of marginal groups.

Brumbaugh, M. G. *The Life and Works of Christopher Dock.* Philadelphia: Lippincott, 1908. Includes an English translation of the famous *Schul-ordung.*

Burnaby, Rev. A. *Travels through the Middle Settlements in North America in the Years 1759-1760.* Ithaca: Cornell University Press, 1960. Comments on education, both formal and informal, in the colonies of Virginia, Maryland, Pennsylvania, New York, Massachusetts, New Hampshire, and Rhode Island.

Cohen, S. S. "Benjamin Trumbull, The Years at Yale." *History of Education Quarterly,* vol. 6 (1966), pp. 33-48. The college days of a Colonial American student, 1755-1759.

Conroy, G. P. "Berkeley and Education in America." *Journal of the History of Ideas,* vol. 21 (1960), pp. 211-221. The practical influences of the famous philosopher upon Yale, Harvard and King's Colleges—his gifts, books, etc.

Dexter, F. B. *Biographical Sketches of the Graduates of Yale College, With Annals of the College History, Oct. 1701-June 1792.* 4 Vols. New York: Henry Holt, 1885-1907. This work, in conjunction with Sibley on Harvard graduates, gives biographical information on a number of Colonial American school teachers.

Earle, A. M., ed. *Diary of Anna Greene Winslow: A Boston School Girl of 1771.* Boston: Houghton Mifflin Co., 1894. One of the more easily accessible diaries of a Colonial American school pupil.

Farish, H. D., ed. *The Journal and Letters of Philip Vickers Fithian.* Williamsburg, Va.: Colonial Williamsburg, Inc., 1957. The fascinating journal of a tutor on a Southern Colonial plantation, 1773-1774.

Fowle, W. B. "Memoirs of Caleb Bingham." *American Journal of Education,* vol. 5 (Sept., 1858), pp. 325-349. One of America's forgotten teachers, who was a famous pedagogue in his own day in Colonial America.

Gegenheimer, F. A. *William Smith: Educator and Churchman, 1727-1803.* Philadelphia: University of Pennsylvania Press, 1943. The life and educational ideas of the one-time provost of the College and Academy of Philadelphia.

Gould, E. P. *Ezekiel Cheever: School Master.* Boston: The Palmer Co., 1904. The biography of the New England teacher who was honored by Cotton Mather in the latter's *Corderius Americanus . . .* (1708).

Gould, E. P. "John Adams as a Schoolmaster." *Education,* vol. 9 (1889), pp. 503-512. Adams' comments (from the diary he kept) on the time that he spent as a school teacher.

Hindle, B. "The Quaker Background and Science in Colonial Philadelphia." *Isis,* vol. 46 (1955), pp. 243-250. The Quaker scientists (Bartram, Logan, et al.) and how their Quakerism related to their interest in science.

Hornberger, T. "Samuel Johnson of Yale and King's College." *New England Quarterly,* vol. 8 (1935), pp. 378-397. Illustrative of the relationship of science and religion in Colonial America.

Jackson, J. "A Philadelphia Schoolmaster of the Eighteenth Century." *Penn. Mag. of History and Biography,* vol. 35 (1911), pp. 315-332. The professional life and accomplishments of Colonial American teacher David James Dove.

Lee, G. C., ed. *Crusade Against Ignorance: Thomas Jefferson on Education.* New York: Teachers College, 1961. An excellent source of the educational ideas of the multi-talented Mr. Jefferson.

Morgan, E. S. *The Gentle Puritan: A Life of Ezra Stiles, 1727-1795.* New

Haven: Yale University Press, 1962. The biography of President Stiles of Yale.

Morison, S. E. *Builders of the Bay Colony*. Boston: Houghton Mifflin Co., 1930. Contains, among other things, a good essay on Harvard's first president, Henry Dunster.

Morison, S. E. "The Harvard Presidency." *New England Quarterly,* vol. 31 (1958), pp. 435-446. Some interesting vignettes about the men who occupied the office of the president.

Olmstead, D. "Timothy Dwight as a Teacher." *American Journal of Education,* vol. 5 (1858), pp. 567-585. A sketch of Yale's great teacher and president by one of his former students.

Parsons, F. "Ezra Stiles of Yale." *New England Quarterly,* vol. 9 (1936), pp. 286-316. Yale's famous president and teacher—a great scholar and a genuine "character."

Riley, E. M., ed. *The Journal of John Harrower: An Indentured Servant in the Colony of Virginia, 1773-1776*. Williamsburg, Va.: Colonial Williamsburg, Inc., 1965. One of the more interesting and informative diaries of a Colonial American teacher.

Schlesinger, E. B. "Cotton Mather and his Children." *William and Mary Quarterly,* vol. 10 (3rd ser., 1953), pp. 181-189. The home life of C. Mather and the education that he provided to his children. For further information on this aspect of Mather, see *The Diary of Cotton Mather.*

Seybolt, R. F. "Schoolmasters of Colonial Boston." *Pub. of the Colonial Society of Mass. (Transactions,* 1927-1930), pp. 130-156. Brief biographical information and listings of some Boston teachers in Colonial Boston.

Seybolt, R. F. "Schoolmasters of Colonial Philadelphia." *Pennsylvania Mag. of History and Biography,* vol. 52 (1928), pp. 361-371. Who taught school in Colonial Philadelphia. Excellent source material.

Sibley, J. L. *Biographical Sketches of Graduates of Harvard University in Cambridge, Mass.* 3 Vols. Cambridge, Mass.: William Sever, 1873-1885. These three volumes are a monumental guide to the lives and fortunes of Harvard graduates.

Tolles, F. B. *Meeting House and Counting House*. Chapel Hill: University of North Carolina Press, 1948. The Quaker merchants of Colonial Philadelphia, 1682-1783, including their ideas about the process of education.

Tolles, F. "Philadelphia's First Scientist: James Logan." *Isis,* vol. 47 (1956), pp. 20-30. The story of the man who helped make Quaker Philadelphia the scientific capital of Colonial America.

Tucker, L. "President Thomas Clap of Yale College." *Isis,* vol. 52 (1961), pp. 55-77. The great Yale educator and his scientific emphasis. Science and math at Yale College.

XIX. THE GROWTH OF THE AMERICAN REPUBLIC (1783-1865)

A. THE RISE OF THE COMMON SCHOOL

1. Aspirations of the Revolutionary Generation

Arrohead, Charles F., ed. *Thomas Jefferson and Education in a Republic.* New York: McGraw-Hill, 1930. Excerpts from Jefferson's writings on education with an introductory essay by the editor.

Fitzpatrick, Edward A. *The Educational Views and Influence of De Witt Clinton.* New York: Teachers College Press, 1911; reissued by Arno Press, 1970. The status of education in New York from 1785 to 1805 followed by Clinton's intellectural and political contributions to the extension of educational opportunity. The author ranks Clinton "with Mann and Barnard in a trinity of educational leadership in the United States."

Hansen, Allen O. *Liberalism and American Education in the Eighteenth Century.* New York: Macmillan, 1926. An analysis of plans for a system of education befitting a new republic set forth by Benjamin Rush, Noah Webster, Nathaniel Chipman and others.

Honeywell, Roy J. *The Educational Work of Thomas Jefferson:* Cambridge: Harvard University Press, 1931. Still considered by many to be the best work on Jefferson's educational ideas and activities. A most useful ninety-page listing of sources is provided.

Kuritz, Hyman. "Benjamin Rush: His Theory of Republican Education." *History of Education Quarterly,* vol. 7 (Winter, 1967), pp. 432-51. An analysis of Rush's writings on education. The author finds Rush motivated by a blend of hope and fear for the nation's future, espousing in his essays a mixture of educational liberalism and social conservatism.

Lee, Gordon C., ed. *Crusade Against Ignorance: Thomas Jefferson on Education.* New York: Teachers College Press, Columbia University, 1962. An introductory essay, "Learning and Liberty: The Jeffersonian Tradition in Education," followed by a collection of Jefferson's letters, essays and legislative proposals in which his educational views and proposals are enunciated. Number 6 in the Classics in Education series.

Messerli, Jonathan. "The Columbian Complex: The Impulse to National Consolidation." *History of Education Quarterly,* vol. 7 (Winter, 1967), pp. 417-31. A review of efforts by political and intellectual leaders following the Revolution to foster a comprehensive system of schooling which would promote a national culture and secure the newly established republican form of government.

Rudolph, Frederick, ed. *Essays on Education in the Early Republic.* Cambridge: Harvard University Press, 1965. Essays written between 1786 and 1799 by Benjamin Rush, Noah Webster, Robert Cowin, Samuel Knox and others.

Shoemaker, Ervin C. *Noah Webster: Pioneer of Learning.* New York: Columbia University Press, 1936. A thorough study that clearly illustrate's Webster's contributions to American education.

Warfel, Harry R. *Noah Webster: Schoolmaster to America.* New York: Macmillan, 1936. This is the best biography of Webster to date. The influence of Webster's textbooks and dictionary on American education.

2. Leaders of the Crusade

Brubacher, John S. *Henry Barnard on Education.* New York: McGraw-Hill, 1931. Henry Barnard's views and influence on education and the politics of educational reform. Barnard as hero of the common school movement.

Carter, James G. *Essays Upon Popular Education.* Boston: Bowles and Dearborn, 1826; reissued by Arno Press, 1970. The writings of one of the first fathers of the common school movement. His arguments for quality public education ring remarkably fresh to the modern reader.

Cremin, Lawrence A., ed. *The Republic and the School: Horace Mann on the Education of Free Men.* New York: Teachers College Press, Columbia University, 1951. A brilliant biographical essay, "Horace Mann's Legacy," by Cremin followed by excerpts from Mann's twelve annual reports. Number 1 in the Classics in Education Series.

Filler, Louis, ed. *Horace Mann on the Crisis in Education.* Antioch, Ohio: Antioch Press, 1965. Selections from Mann's writings and addresses chosen to illustrate his philosophy of public education and the problems with which he was forced to contend in his crusade for the common school.

Foster, Frank C. "Horace Mann as Philosopher." *Education Theory,* vol. 10 (January, 1960), pp. 9-25. Addresses the question of Mann's status as a philosopher. Considers him as an instrumentalist, a phrenologist and an experimentalist. Thought-provoking article.

Hackensmith, Charles W. *Biography of Joseph Neef: Educator in the Ohio Valley, 1809-1854*. New York: Carlton, 1973. A biography of the man who did much to popularize Pestalozzianism in America. His experiences at New Harmony and his associations with William Maclure and Robert Owen are described, but little in-depth analysis of the man and the social forces that shaped his ideas and actions.

McClintock, Jean, and Robert McClintock, eds. *Henry Barnard's School Architecture*. New York: Teachers College Press, Columbia University, 1970. Barnard's views on school architecture as a vehicle for educational reform. A valuable bibliography of Barnard's sources and interpretive essays by the editors are included. Number 42 in the Classics in Education series.

[Horace Mann] *Life and Works of Horace Mann*. Boston: Lee and Shepard, 1891, 5 vols. The most complete collection of Mann's works.

Mann, Mary Peabody. *Life of Horace Mann*. Boston: Walker, Fuller, 1865. A tribute to Mann by his wife and co-worker.

Messerli, Jonathan. *Horace Mann: A Biography*. New York: Alfred A. Knopf, 1972. A scholarly, well-written biography which finally presents Mann in human rather than saintly garb. The work is also to be valued for its depiction of the social setting from which a great era of reform emerged.

Messerli, Jonathan C. "Horace Mann at Brown." *Harvard Educational Review*, vol. 33 (Summer, 1963), pp. 285-311. Mann's years at Brown depicted, despite his own disclaimers, as significant to his intellectual and social development. Also offers an interesting portrait of collegiate life and studies during the early nineteenth century.

Messerli, Jonathan C. "Horace Mann's Childhood: Myth and Reality." *The Educational Forum*, vol. 30 (January, 1966), pp. 159-68. A description and analysis of Mann's youth based upon sound research. Messerli takes issue with much of the rags-to-riches romanticism found in earlier studies.

Minnich, Harvey C. *William Holmes McGuffey and His Readers*. New York: American Book Co., 1936. A biography of McGuffey designed to accompany Minnich's *Old Favorites from the McGuffey Readers*.

Monroe, Will S. *The Educational Labors of Henry Barnard*. Syracuse: C. W. Bardeen, 1893. The facts are there as is the hero.

Tharp, Louise Hall. *Until Victory: Horace Mann and Mary Peabody*. Boston: Little, Brown, 1953. A romantic story aimed at a mass audience. Yet, well told and based on sound, scholarly research.

Williams, E. I. F. *Horace Mann: Educational Statesman*. New York:

Macmillan, 1937. Horace Mann as hero triumphant. Undocumented, but provides a good bibliography.

3. Ideas, Issues and Conflict

Bidwell, Charles E. "The Moral Significance of the Common School." *History of Education Quarterly,* vol. 3 (Fall, 1966), pp. 50-91. A sociological analysis of class and moral values as factors in the common school movements of Massachusetts and New York. Strong support for those who view "status rivalry" as a key ingredient in the rise of the public schools. An important study.

Bourne, William O. *History of the Public School Society of New York, Portraits of the Presidents of the Society.* New York: William Wood, 1870; reissued by Arno Press, 1971. A highly detailed study of New York City's philanthropically sponsored school system (1805-1853), including an interesting, though biased, view of the PSS's position in its controversy with the city's Catholics, 1840-42. Numerous original documents are included.

Carlton, Frank Tracy. *Economic Influences upon Educational Progress in the United States, 1820-1850.* Madison: University of Wisconsin Press, 1908; reissued with foreword by Lawrence A. Cremin. New York: Teachers College Press, Columbia University, 1965. A classic in the history of education. Carlton was one of the first to point to the relationship between social and economic conditions and the movement for public schools. Number 27 in the Classics in Education series.

Cremin, Lawrence A. *The American Common School, an Historic Conception.* New York: Teachers College Press, Columbia University, 1951. Though Cremin's interpretations have been challenged, the work stands as the most scholarly and complete treatment of the common school movement. The development of public education in the context of social, economic and political history.

Culver, Raymond B. *Horace Mann and Religion in the Massachusetts Public Schools.* New Haven: Yale University press, 1929; reissued by Arno Press, 1970. An examination of Horace Mann's contributions to the secularization of the public schools in Massachusetts.

Curoe, Philip R. V. *Educational Attitudes and Policies of Organized Labor in the United States.* New York: Teachers College, Columbia University Press, 1926; reissued by Arno Press, 1970. Organized labor as a major initiator of the common school movement. Early chapters treat the period prior to the Civil War.

Dunn, William K. *What Happened to Religious Education: The Decline of Religious Teaching in the Public Elementary School, 1776-1861.* Baltimore: Johns Hopkins Press, 1958. A description and analysis of the decline of religious teachings in the public schools, 1776-1861. A scholarly, well-written work.

Finegan, Thomas E. *Free Schools: A Documentary History of the Free School Movement in New York State.* Albany: The University of the State of New York, 1921; reissued by Arno Press, 1971. Documents depicting the key issues in the struggle to attain free public schooling in New York State.

Gershenberg, Irving. "Southern Values and Public Education: A Revision." *History of Education Quarterly,* vol. 10 (Winter, 1970), pp. 413-22. Gershenberg provides evidence to support his contention that "the South's educational backwardness cannot be attributed to any lack of interest . . . on the part of the people . . . [but rather] to the lack of interest and/or commitment to public education by those who exercised political power in the South."

Greene, Maxine. *The Public School and the Private Vision.* New York: Random House, 1965. An important book. The views on education of social reform leaders (Jefferson, Carter, Mann and others) contrasted with those of leading literary figures including Emerson, Thoreau, Hawthorne and Melville.

Jackson, Sidney L. *America's Struggle for Free Schools: Social Tension and Education in New England and New York, 1827-1842.* Washington: American Council in Public Affairs, 1941. Depicts the movement for common schools as a largely conservative reaction to Jacksonian democracy, a device for status maintenance.

Jackson, Sidney. "Labor, Education and Politics in the 1830's." *Pennsylvania Magazine of History and Biography,* vol. 66 (July, 1942), pp. 279-93. Organized labor's contributions to the launching of the common school movement with primary emphasis upon New York City.

Jones, Howard Mumford, ed. *Emerson on Education: Selections.* New York: Teachers College Press, Columbia University, 1966. Essential reading for those interested in the philosophical roots of open education. As Robert Ulich stated, "Emerson closes the circle of the great idealists Rousseau, Pestalozzi, and Froebel, on whom all the essential concepts of modern, or progressive education are based." Number 26 in the Classics in Education series.

Kaestle, Carl F. "Common Schools Before the 'Common School Revival': New York Schooling in the 1790's." *History of Education Quarterly,* vol. 12 (Winter, 1972), pp. 465-500. Independent, tuition-charging primary schools and free charity schools provided the rudiments of education. Evidence is presented to support the contention that "the decision to give public aid to the city's free charity schools . . . proved to be a crucial preliminary to the creation of the nineteenth century public school system."

Kaestle, Carl F. *The Evolution of an Urban School System: New York City 1750-1850.* Cambridge: Harvard University Press, 1973. Largely concerned with the systemization of schooling in the period 1800 to 1850. In the spirit of recent revisionist writing, Kaestle depicts educational development as a response by conservative forces to what they perceived as dangerous trends in society: immigration, intemperance, crime, vagrancy.

Katz, Michael B. *The Irony of Early School Reform: Educational Innovation in Mid-Nineteenth Century Massachusetts.* Cambridge: Harvard University Press, 1968. A work that did much to launch the recent revisionist movement in the history of education. Katz's interpretation of the age of school reform denies the validity of the labor-education thesis as well as the more popular depiction of a liberal, humanitarian movement. His case studies describe a middle class reform imposed upon a reluctant community for largely selfish reasons.

Lannie, Vincent P., and Bernard C. Diethorn. "For the Honor and Glory of God: The Philadelphia Bible Riots of 1840." *History of Education Quarterly,* vol. 8 (Spring, 1968), pp. 44-106. An analysis and description of the causes and events surrounding the bloody conflict between nativists and Catholics over Bible reading and religious exercises in the public schools of Philadelphia. A dark chapter in the history of the common school movement.

Lannie, Vincent P. *Public Money and Parochial Education: Bishop Hughes, Governor Seward, and the New York School Controversy.* Cleveland: Press of Case Western University, 1968. A detailed study of the attempts of the Catholic community of New York City to obtain public financial support for its schools in the face of opposition from the publicly financed, privately controlled Public School Society and anti-Catholic public opinion. Among the results of the controversy was the establishment in the city of a system of publicly controlled district schools.

Lannie, Vincent P. "William Seward and the New York School Controversy, 1840-1842: A Problem in Historical Motivation." *History of Education Quarterly,* vol. 6 (Spring, 1966), pp. 52-71. Lannie takes the position that Governor Seward's efforts on behalf of the education of Catholic children were motivated by an "essentially humanitarian impulse" rather than by self-serving political ambition as implied in John W. Pratt's analysis. See Pratt citation below.

Messerli, Jonathan C. "Controversy and Consensus in Common School Reform." *Teachers College Record,* vol. 66 (May, 1965), pp. 749-59. School committee records as valuable sources for investigating the motives and issues involved in the common school movement. Messerli insists that scholars in search of the truth must go beyond the tracts of the antagonists to "less controversial" materials.

Messerli, Jonathan. "Localism and State Control in Horace Mann's Reform of the Common Schools." *American Quarterly,* vol. 7 (Spring, 1965), pp. 104-112. The author denies the sufficiency of the "hero" thesis or economic or ideological determinism for analyzing Mann's ideas, motives and actions.

Monroe, Will S. *History of the Pestalozzian Movement in the United States.* Syracuse: C. W. Bardeen, 1907; reissued by Arno Press, 1969. The spread of Pestalozzianism in Europe and its transfer to the United States. Chapters devoted to Maclure, Neef and Harris and to the early experiments in Philadelphia, New Harmony and Oswego. An extensive bibliography is included.

Pawa, Jay M. "Workingmen and Free Schools in the Nineteenth Century: A Comment on the Labor-Education Thesis." *History of Education Quarterly,* vol. 11 (Fall, 1971), pp. 287-302. Takes issue with labor-education thesis of Curoe, Carlton and others, which emphasized a significant role by labor in the establishment of free public education. Finds the base of the common school movement primarily in the urban middle class.

Pratt, John W. "Governor Seward and the New York School Controversy, 1840-1842." *New York History,* vol. 42 (October, 1961), pp. 351-64. A brief, well-written account of the religious and political controversy which eventually led to the establishment of a public school system in New York City.

Pulliam, John. "Changing Attitudes Toward Free Public Schools in Illinios, 1825-1860." *History of Education Quarterly,* vol. 7 (Summer, 1967), pp. 191-208. An analysis of the arguments on both sides of the free school issue and the factors which led to the eventual success of the common school movement in Illinois. A case study in many ways illustrative of developments in the other states of the old Northwest.

Ravitch, Diane. *The Great School Wars: New York City, 1805-1793.* New York: Basic Books, 1974. Chapters one through eight of this highly acclaimed work provide a vivid account of the development, amidst religious and political controversy, of public education in New York City during the first sixty years of the nineteenth century. This is social and educational history at its best.

Schultz, Stanley K. *The Culture Factory: Boston Public Schools, 1789-1860.* New York: Oxford University Press, 1973. The bureaucratization of urban public schooling. Schultz, in step with recent revisionist educational historians, views public schools established to provide social control over the poor and the foreign elements of our cities.

Smith, Timothy. "Protestant Schooling and American Nationality, 1800-1850." *The Journal of American History,* vol. 53 (March, 1967), pp. 679-95. The role of Protestant educational activities in helping to shape the American's conception of his nationality. Educational developments in New York City and Illinois during the first half of the nineteenth century are offered as case studies.

Taylor, William R. "Toward a Definition of Orthodoxy: The Patrician South and the Common Schools." *Harvard Educational Review,* vol. 36 (Fall, 1966), pp. 412-26. The growth and decline of the common school movement in the ante-bellum South in the context of Southern intellectual history. An interesting, revealing study.

Thursfield, Richard E. *Henry Barnard's American Journal of Education.* Baltimore: Johns Hopkins Press, 1937. The *Journal* was a significant force for educational reform. In its pages laymen were urged on to support the expansion and improvement of public schools, and teachers were informed of advances in the area of curricula and teaching.

Tyack, David. "The Kingdom of God and the Common Schools." *Harvard Education Review,* vol. 36 (Fall, 1966), pp. 447-69. An analysis of the crucial role of Protestant clergymen in the establishment of American common schools with Oregon used as a case study.

Vinovskis, Maris A. "Trends in Massachusetts Education, 1826-1860." *History of Education Quarterly,* vol. 12 (Winter, 1972), pp. 501-29. The author presents and analyzes Massachusetts educational statistics from 1826 to 1860. This and additional studies of a similar nature, he explains, are essential if we are to determine the contribution of education to economic development.

Welter, Rush. *Popular Education and Democratic Thought in America.* New York: Columbia University Press, 1962. An important study of the growth of education within the context of the nation's social, political and intellectual development. Students of the period 1783-1865 will find chapters two through eight pertinent.

4. "The District School As It Was"

Burton, Warren. *The District School As It Was.* Boston: Lee and Shepard, 1850; reissued by Arno Press, 1970. Rev. Burton's mostly fond recollections of his boyhood schooling in rural America during the early national period. Delightful reading.

Commager, Henry Steele, ed. *Noah Webster's American Spelling Book.* New York: Teachers College Press, Columbia University, 1958. Commager's interpretive essay "Schoolmaster to America" followed by a facsimile of *The American Spelling Book,* the famous "bluebacked speller." Number 17 in the Classics in Education series.

Eggleston, Edward. *The Hoosier School-Master.* New York: C. Scribner's, 1883. Reissued: New York: Hill and Wang, 1957. A novel depicting the struggles and triumphs of a young schoolteacher in rural Indiana prior to the Civil War. Enjoyable reading and instructive for students interested in the status of teachers in American society.

Elson, Ruth M. *Guardians of Tradition: American Schoolbooks of the 19th Century.* Lincoln: University of Nebraska Press, 1964. America's values and attitudes reflected in her schoolbooks. An interesting, informative, sometimes amusing, often shocking study.

Johnson, Clifton. *Old-Time Schools and School Books.* New York: Macmillan, 1904. Schooling from the colonial period to the Civil War as revealed in curricula, methods of teaching, student life, and particularly the content of textbooks. Numerous illustrations and extensive excerpts from schoolbooks. Interesting reading.

Minnich, Harvey C. *Old Favorites from the McGuffey Readers.* New York: American Book Co., 1936. Reissued, Detroit: Gale Research Co., 1969. Some of the most popular stories selected from the six graded McGuffey Readers.

Mosier, Richard D. *Making of the American Mind: Social and Moral Ideas in the McGuffey Readers.* New York: Kings Crown, 1947. Rev. ed., 1965. Mosier discusses the values and beliefs promoted by the McGuffey readers and the impact of these texts on the minds of American youth.

Sloane, Eric. *The Little Red Schoolhouse: A Sketchbook of Early American Education.* New York: Doubleday, 1972. A little book of thirty-two pages describing the architecture and life-style of the one-room school house. The author finds the old far superior in many ways to our modern, graded, Bible-free public schools.

Soderbergh, Peter A. "Old School Days on the Middle Border, 1849-1859–The Mary Payne Beard Letters." *History of Education Quarterly,* vol. 8 (Winter, 1968), pp. 497-504. Charles Beard's mother presents a view of schooling during Indiana's frontier period. Background historical information is provided by the editor.

B. THE AGE OF THE ACADEMY AND THE BIRTH OF THE HIGH SCHOOL

Belting, Paul Everett. *The Development of the Free Public High School in Illinois to 1860.* Springfield, Illinois: State Historical Journal, 1919; reissued by Arno Press, 1970. Adapted from a Ph.D. thesis, the work provides a valuable case study of the high school movement in its early years.

Brown, Elmer Ellsworth. *The Making of Our Middle Schools.* New York: Longmans, Green, 1914; reissued by Arno Press, 1970. Reissued with a new introduction by Maurie Hillson and F. Cordasco, Totowa, N.J.: Littlefield, Adams, 1970. Still the most complete survey of the history of secondary education from the Colonial period to the beginning of the twentieth century. Particularly useful for those interested in pre-Civil War developments.

Franklin, John Hope. *The Militant South, 1800-1861.* Cambridge: Harvard University Press, 1956. The social forces which created, in the author's view, a peculiarly violent character to the antebellum South. An extremely interesting discussion of military schools and their contributions to Southern bellicosity.

Grizzell, Emit D. *Origin and Development of the High School in New England Before 1865.* New York: Macmillan, 1923. A detailed, narrowly conceived history of the early high school movement. The author contends that the roots of the institution are essentially American rather than Prussian, as some have claimed.

McLachlan, James. *American Boarding Schools: A Historical Study.* New York: Scribner, 1970. A definitive history of the elite boarding schools for boys which dot our northeastern coast. A scholarly, readable, important study.

Sizer, Theodore, ed. *The Age of the Academies.* New York: Teachers College Press, Columbia University, 1964. An important interpretive essay by Sizer precedes several documents illustrating the history of the academy movement. Number 22 in the Classics in Education series.

C. GROWTH AND FERMENT IN COLLEGIATE AND PROFESSIONAL EDUCATION

1. The Age of the College

Allmendinger, David F., Jr. "The Strangeness of the American Education Society. Indigent Students and the New Charity: 1815-1840." *History of Education Quarterly,* vol. 11 (Spring, 1971), pp. 3-22. The emergence of a national organization complete with professional bureaucracy to provide financial aid for college-bound students.

Borrowman, Merle. "The False Dawn of the State University." *History of Education Quarterly,* vol. 1 (June, 1961), pp. 6-22. Thomas Cooper at South Carolina, Horace Holley at Transylvania and Philip Lindsley at the University of Nashville—prophets of an institution whose time has not yet arrived.

Crane, Theodore Rawson, ed. *The Colleges and the Public, 1787-1862.* New York: Teachers College Press, Columbia University, 1963. Sixteen contemporary essays and documents preceded by an historiographical essay by the editor. Number 15 in the Classics in Education series.

Eddy, Edward D., Jr. *Colleges for Our Land and Time: The Land Grant Idea in American Education.* New York: Harper and Row, 1957. The best single work on the subject. Early chapters deal with the development of the idea and the political struggles leading to the passage of the Morrill Act.

Faherty, William B., S.J. "Nativism and Midwestern Education: The Experience of Saint Louis University, 1832-1856." *History of Education Quarterly,* vol. 7 (Winter, 1968), pp. 447-58. The deterioration of Catholic-Protestant cooperation in education brought about by the nativist movement of the 1840's and 50's.

Florer, John H. "Major Issues in the Congressional Debate of the Morrill Act of 1863." *History of Education Quarterly,* vol. 8 (Winter, 1968), pp. 459-78. Justin Morrill's brilliant maneuvering through Congress of the Act providing for land grant colleges. Many of the arguments were strikingly similar to those associated with the federal aid-to-education bills of the 1960's.

Hans, Nicholas. "The Project of Transferring the University of Geneva to America." *History of Education Quarterly,* vol. 8 (Summer, 1968), pp. 246-51. Birth, development and demise of the plans of Francis D'Ivernois and Thomas Jefferson to transfer the University of Geneva, complete with faculty, to the United States. Initially it was to be established as a state university in Virginia, later a federal university in Washington, D.C.

Hofstadter, Richard, and Walter P. Metzger. *The Development of Academic Freedom in the United States.* New York: Columbia University Press, 1955. Part One, "The Age of the College," by Richard Hofstadter, traces the history of academic freedom from the colonial period through the Civil War. As the authors point out, this period in actuality marked the "prehistory of academic freedom" in the United States, an era of denominational colleges in which intellectual freedom was rarely demanded or permitted and yet an era in which the first stirrings were heard.

Hofstadter, Richard, and Wilson Smith. *American Higher Education: A Documentary History.* Chicago: University of Chicago Press, 1961, 2 vols. The most complete collection of documents relating to the history of higher education in the United States. The editors provide introductions and bibliographic guides. See Parts I through VI for the period 1787-1865.

Nash, Paul. "Innocents Abroad: American Students at British Universities in the Early Nineteenth Century." *History of Education Quarterly,* vol. 1 (June, 1961), pp. 32-44. Despite the pleas of cultural nationalists,

Americans in significant numbers continued to study medicine at Edinburgh and London and, to a lesser extent, theology at Edinburgh. Article presents impressions of these institutions by American visiting students.

Naylor, Natalie A. "The Ante-Bellum College Movement: A Reappraisal of Tewksbury's *The Founding of American Colleges and Universities.*" *History of Education Quarterly,* vol. 13 (Fall, 1973), pp. 261-74. Evidence is presented to support the author's contention that the data, interpretations and conclusions in Tewksbury's classic, oft-cited work need revision. Further, she urges greater attention to agencies other than the colleges that were providing higher education—academies, female seminaries, normal schools, etc.

Norwood, William F. *Medical Education in the United States Before the Civil War.* Philadelphia: University of Pennsylvania Press, 1944; reissued by Arno Press, 1971. From the time of colonial practitioners of physic to the rise of medical schools prior to the Civil War. Changing concepts of medical training and regional and national developments are discussed.

Paulston, Roland G. "French Influence in American Institutions of Higher Learning, 1784-1825." *History of Education Quarterly,* vol. 8 (Summer, 1968), pp. 229-45. An examination of French influence on American intellectual life and institutional structure, the reasons for its presence and eventual decline. As examples of this influence, the University of the State of New York, the University of Michigan and the University of Virginia are discussed in some detail.

Perry, Charles M. *Henry Philip Tappan: Philosopher and Universtiy President.* Ann Arbor: University of Michigan Press, 1933; reissued by Arno Press, 1971. A first-rate biography of one of the pioneer reformers of American higher education. Tappan struggled unsuccessfully to establish Michigan as a research-oriented university whose curriculum would be attuned to the needs of a dynamic society.

Power, Edward J. *Catholic Higher Education in America: A History.* New York: Appleton-Century-Crofts, 1972. Part one details the founding of Catholic higher education in the United States. A rather uncritical "upward and onward" study in the Cubberley manner.

Rose, Earle D. *Democracy's College: The Land Grant Movement in the Formative Stage.* Ames, Iowa: Iowa State College Press, 1942; reissued by Arno Press, 1970. A comprehensive study of the land grant college idea and the political efforts to secure passage of the Morrill Act. Author's style is rather pedantic.

Rudolph, Frederick. *The American College and University, A History.* New York: Knopf, 1962. An exceptionally fine single-volume history of American higher education. Chapters two through eleven treat the period from 1787 to 1865.

Schmidt, George P. *The Old Time College President.* New York: Columbia University Press, 1930. The role and influence of the American college president from 1760 to 1860. Well-documented with an extensive bibliography. An interesting, colorful study.

Tewksbury, Donald G. *The Founding of American Universities and Colleges Before the Civil War.* New York: Teachers College, 1937; reissued by Arno Press, 1970. A much-cited study of the founding of "denominational colleges" and state universities in the decades between the Revolution and the Civil War.

2. Teacher Education, Formal and Informal

Hall, Samuel R. *Lectures on School-Keeping.* Boston: Richardson, Lord Holbrook, 1829; reissued by Arno Press, 1970. Used by generations of teacher trainees in the normal schools. Interesting reading for today's students of education.

Mattingly, Paul H. "Educational Revivals in Ante-Bellum New England." *History of Education Quarterly,* vol. 11 (Spring, 1971), pp. 39-71. The role of teachers' institutes as a major force for the professional training and inspirational uplift of common school teachers during the 1840's and 1850's.

Norton, Arthur O. *The First State Normal School in America: The Journals of Cyrus Peirce and Mary Swift.* Cambridge: Harvard University press, 1926. The journals provide a first-hand glimpse into not only the methods and curricula of the early normal schools but student and faculty life as well. Other documents relating to the establishment of normal schools in Massachusetts are provided.

Page, David P. *Theory and Practice of Teaching: Or the Motives and Methods of School-Keeping.* 7th ed. Syracuse, N.Y.: Hall and Dickens, 1848; reissued by Arno Press, 1970. A popular textbook in the early normal schools. Page drew heavily from Mann's Annual Reports, liberally quoting from them in his text.

D. EDUCATING POLITICAL MINORITIES

1. Blacks

Andrews, Charles C. *The History of the New York African Free Schools* . . . New York: M. Day, 1830; reprinted by Negro University Press, 1969. A fascinating, first-hand account of the struggles and successes of a significant, early venture in schooling for blacks.

Fuller, Edmund. *Prudence Crandall: An Incident of Racism in Nineteenth*

Century Connecticut. Middletown, Connecticut: Wesleyan University Press, 1971. The story of a heroic but futile attempt to provide schooling for blacks in a quiet, seemingly respectable Connecticut town during the 1830's.

Litwack, Leon F. *North of Slavery: The Negro in the Free States, 1790-1860*. Chicago: University of Chicago Press, 1961. Chapter four, "Education: Separate the Unequal," provides a vivid portrait of the status of education for Northern black youth in the decades preceding the Civil War.

Ruchkin, Judith P. "The Abolition of 'Colored Schools' in Rochester, New York, 1832-1856." *New York History*, vol. 51 (July, 1970), pp. 377-93. The decision of Rochester's blacks to seek separate schools for their children, and Frederick Douglass' campaign to have such schools abolished.

Woodson, Carter. *The Education of the Negro Prior to 1861*. Washington, D.C.: Associated Publishers, 1919; reissued by Arno, 1968. Still undoubtedly the best work on the subject. Woodson concerned himself with informal as well as formal agencies of education, with the Southern slave as well as the Northern freedman.

2. Women

Beecher, Catherine, and Harriet Beecher Stowe. *The American Woman's Home: Or, Principles of Domestic Science*. Boston: H. A. Brown, 1869; reissued by Arno Press, 1971. Pioneers of the women's rights movement, the sisters uphold the traditional roles of women, but stress the dignity, importance and complexity of home management. The work served for decades as a guide to child care, family health and domestic civility.

Cross, Barbara M., ed. *The Educated Woman in America*. New York: Teachers College Press, Columbia University, 1965. Excerpts from the writings of three pioneers of the woman's education movement, Catherine Beecher, Margaret Fuller and M. Carey Thomas, with a forty-eight page introductory essay by the editor. Number 25 in the Classics in Education series.

Riley, Glenda. "Origins of the Argument for Improved Female Education." *History of Education Quarterly*, vol. 9 (Winter, 1969), pp. 455-70. Industrialization's impact on the status, roles and self-image of women. Writers in ladies' magazines and guidebooks idealize women as wives, mothers and teachers and call for improved education to prepare them for these noble callings.

Woody, Thomas. *A History of Women's Education in the United States*. New York: The Science Press, 1929. 2 vols. A detailed study, though today's advocates of women's rights may find some of the author's comments rather patronizing. The early national period is treated in volume one.

E. EDUCATION OUTSIDE THE SCHOOL

Bode, Carl. *The American Lyceum: Town Meeting of the Mind.* New York: Oxford University Press, 1965. The best and most complete treatment of the Lyceum movement.

Ditzion, Sidney. *Arsenals of a Democratic Culture.* Chicago: American Library Association, 1947. Begins where Jesse Shera's study left off and expands the treatment to include national developments. Particularly fine analysis of the contributions of Everett, Ticknor and Wayland.

Gratton, C. Hartley, ed. *American Ideas About Adult Education, 1710-1951.* New York: Teachers College Press, Columbia University, 1956. For students of the early national period, documents relating to mechanics' institutes, lyceums and libraries are included. Number three in the Classics in Education series.

Hayes, Cecil B. *The American Lyceum: Its History and Contribution to Education.* Washington: Government Printing Office, 1932. A documented history of the lyceum movement with little in the way of analysis of causes and effects.

Horlick, Allan S. "Phrenology and the Social Education of Young Men." *History of Education Quarterly,* vol. 11 (Spring, 1971), pp. 23-38. Phrenology accepted as a science and employed as a self-help, career guide by young men seeking success and status and by employers seeking the best men for their firms.

Shera, Jesse H. *Foundations of the Public Library: The Origins of the Public Library Movement in New England, 1629-1855.* Chicago: University of Chicago Press, 1949. The roots and development of the public library movement in New England. An in-depth, scholarly study.

Wishy, Bernard. *The Child and the Republic: The Dawn of Modern American Child Nurture.* Philadelphia: University of Pennsylvania Press, 1968. A history of child rearing as revealed through didactic literature for parents and teachers and books written specifically for children. The first half of the volume deals with the period prior to 1860. A must for those interested in the history of education as more than a study of schooling.

F. EDUCATION, SOME BROAD VIEWS

Binder, Frederick M. *The Age of the Common School, 1830-1865.* New York: John Wiley, 1974. Educational history within the context of the nation's social and political development. Both formal and informal education are considered as are the unique conditions of women, blacks, and

Catholics.

Butler, Vera. *Education as Revealed by New England Newspaper Prior to 1850.* Temple University, 1935; reissued by Arno Press, 1970. Developments in education as perceived through newspaper articles of the day. Chapters devoted to colleges, academies and the common school. Extensive annotated bibliography.

Curti, Merle. *The Social Ideas of American Educators.* New York: Scribner, 1935. Reprinted with an additional chapter on the last twenty-five years, Totowa, N.J.: Littlefield, Adams, 1959. An outstanding series of biographical essays on some of America's leading educators. Curti was one of the first to challenge the idea that the school alone can be a panacea for the nation's social ills. Chapter Two, an overview of the period 1800-1860, and chapters Three, Four and Five, dealing with Mann, Barnard and the education of women, are of significance for students interested in the "Growth of the American Republic."

Eaton, Clement. *The Freedom-of-Thought Struggle in the Old South.* New York: Harper and Row, 1964. Chapter three, "A Dark Cloud of Illiteracy," and chapter nine, "Academic Freedom Below the Potomac," combine to provide a detailed description and interpretation of the status of education in the antebellum South.

Knight, Edgar W. *A Documentary History of Education in the South Before 1860.* 5 vols. Chapel Hill: University of North Carolina Press, 1949-1953. An essential source for students of the history of Southern education.

Madsen, David L. *Early National Education, 1776-1830.* New York: John Wiley, 1974. Madsen provides a broadly conceived view of education, examining "the political, social, artistic, economic, and scholarly activities of early American society that influenced the conduct and subject matter of education."

XX. THE EXPANSION OF AMERICAN EDUCATION
(1865-1900)

A. AMERICAN SOCIETY

Beard, Charles, and Mary Beard. *The Rise of American Civilization*. New York: The Macmillan Company, 1927. Political and economic viewpoints related to cultural and social history.

Boorstin, Daniel J. *The Americans: The Democratic Experience*. New York: Random House, 1973. America of the average man—the meaning of the many and often unnoticed revolutions occurring in homes, farms, factories, schools and stores.

Carlton, Frank Tracy. *Economic Influences upon Educational Progress in the United States, 1820-1850*. Madison: University of Wisconsin Press, 1908. Emphasis on the determination of educational trends by economic forces. Preparation of the nation for the Civil War and reconstruction. Bibliography.

Chamberlain, John. *The Enterprising Americans: A Business History of the United States*. New York: Harper & Row, 1963. Development of business, industry, commerce and technology in the United States. Good bibliography.

Elson, Ruth Miller. *Guardians of Tradition: American Schoolbooks of the Nineteenth Century*. Lincoln: University of Nebraska Press, 1964. How the white Protestant value system was reflected in textbooks. A study of one thousand volumes which contributes to an understanding of the formation of the American character.

Hacker, Louis M. *The Shaping of the American Tradition*. New York: Columbia University Press, 1947.

————. *The Triumph of American Capitalism: The Development of Forces in American History to the End of the Nineteenth Century*. New York: Columbia University Press, 1940. Broad view of the force of economic developments in American life.

Holbrook, Stewart H. *Dreamers of the American Dream*. Garden City, N.Y.: Doubleday and Company, 1957. Visionaries, pioneers, fanatics, patient doers working for dreams of what they wanted in America: utopian communities, nutrition, temperance and suffragette movements, institutional reform for the handicapped and prisoners, labor unions.

Hopkins, Charles H. *The Rise of the Social Gospel in American Protestantism, 1865-1915.* New Haven: Yale University Press, 1940. Doctrinal and ideological stands in American Protestantism's development of emphasis on social welfare.

Kirkland, Edward C. *Industry Comes of Age: Business, Labor, and Public Policy, 1860-1897.* New York: Holt, Rinehart & Winston, 1961. Interpretation of one section of American economic history.

Marty, Martin E. *Righteous Empire: The Protestant Experience in America.* New York: Dial Press, 1970. "A devastating critique of the role of the churches in American life . . . from within the mainstream of life of those same churches."

Nevins, Allan. *The Emergence of Modern America, 1865-1878.* New York: The Macmillan Company, 1927. Broad, inclusive discussion.

Schlesinger, Arthur M. *The Rise of the City, 1878-1898.* New York: The Macmillan Company, 1933. The transit from agricultural to urban America.

Shannon, Fred A. *The Farmer's Last Frontier, 1860-1897.* New York: Farrar and Rinehart, 1945. General agricultural history mingled with some social history. Urban impact on rural life.

Tarbell, Ida M. *The Nationalizing of Business, 1878-1898.* New York: The Macmillan Company, 1946.

Vassar, Rena, ed. *Social History of American Education.* 2 vols. Chicago: Rand McNally & Company, 1965. Anthology, volume 2—1860 to the present.

Veblen, Thorstein. *The Theory of the Labor Class.* New York: The Macmillan Company, 1899. Influential criticism of finance capitalism and its abuses.

Welter, Rush. *Popular Education and Democratic Thought in America.* New York: Columbia University Press, 1962. Traces evolution of education in terms of representative schools of political and social theory.

Wish, Harvey. *Society and Thought in Modern America: A Social and Intellectual History of the American People from 1865.* New York: Longmans, Green and Co., 1952. Discusses the passing of the frontier, the influence of Darwinism, the growth of the Labor Movement, and the urbanization and industrialization of American life and thought.

B. THE AMERICAN MIND

1. General

Curti, Merle. *The Growth of American Thought.* 3rd ed. New York: Harper & Row, 1964. An outstanding full-scale survey of American intellectual history.

————. *The Social Ideas of American Educators: With a New Chapter on the Last Twenty-five Years.* Totowa, N.J.: Littlefield, Adams, 1959. Social and intellectual history of American education, with notices of such educators as Booker T. Washington, William T. Harris, Bishop Spalding, G. Stanley Hall, Willam James, and others.

Hendricks, James Dale. "The Child—Study Movement in American Education, 1878-1914: An Historical Interpretation of an Educational Piety in Industrial America." Unpublished Doctoral dissertation, Columbia University, 1969. Study of the new view of the child as it developed.

Hofstadter, Richard. *Social Darwinism in American Thought.* Philadelphia: University of Pennsylvania Press, 1945. Evaluation of social thought derived from evolutionary theory, and its impact on American society. Covers whole range of social and economic thought.

Parrington, Vernon L. *Main Currents in American Thought, Vol. III, The Beginnings of Critical Realism in America, 1860-1900.* New York: Harcourt, Brace & World, Inc., 1930. Good chapter on impact of determinism on American thought—an American classic of the social interpretation of literature.

Reisner, E. H. *Nationalism and Education since 1789.* New York: The Macmillan Company, 1925. Good account—material on administration and supervision.

Silver, Harold. *Robert Owen on Education.* Cambridge: Cambridge University Press, 1969. An account of the utopian community at New Harmony, Indiana and how it influenced education.

Turner, Frederick Jackson. *The Frontier in American History.* New York: Henry Holt & Company, 1950. Thesis, often disputed but influential, that the open frontier offered Americans cheap land, shaped their ideas of government, contributed to developing of institutions, breaking down conservative society, encouraging initiative and political democracy and equalitarianism, and advancing the Federal structure of government and the exercise of national authority.

Wishy, Bernard. *The Child and the Republic: The Dawn of Modern American Child Nurture.* Philadelphia: University of Pennsylvania Press, 1968. Nineteenth century views of child nurture, home care, and religious and moral life, contradictions of a culture at odds with itself, debate about the nature and destiny of the child in nineteenth century literature.

2. Educational Movements

Adams, John. *The Herbartian Psychology Applied to Education.* Boston: D. C. Heath and Company, 1897. Discussion of theory widely adopted in the training of teachers.

Barnard, Henry. *Pestalozzi and His Educational System.* Syracuse, N.Y.: C. W. Bardeen, 1881. Discussion by the noted educator of a system of educating children popular in nineteenth century teacher training.

Brubacher, John S. *Henry Barnard on Education.* New York: McGraw–Hill Book Company, 1931. The educational thought of an outstanding educator, educational journalist, and first United States Commissioner of Education.

Buchner, E. F. *The Educational Theory of Immanuel Kant.* Philadelphia; J. B. Lippincott Co., 1904. The source of Idealism's influence on education in the nineteenth century.

Dearborn, Ned Harland. *The Oswego Movement in American Education.* New York: Arno Press, 1969. Reprint of study of the Oswego Normal School and its preeminence and prestige in education. The course of Pestalozzianism as it came to American and was spread by Oswego. Detailed, specific.

De Garmo, Charles. *Herbart and Herbartians.* New York: Charles Scribner's Sons, 1896. Discussion of Herbartian educational theories by an outstanding disciple and publicist for the movement.

Fletcher, S. S., and J. Welton, eds. *Froebel's Chief Writings on Education.* New York: Longmans, Green and Company, 1912. Discussion of the theories and practice of the founder of the kindergarten movement.

Hollis, Andrew P. *The Contributions of the Oswego Normal School to Educational Progress in the United States.* Boston: D. C. Heath and Company, 1898. The work of Edward Sheldon at Oswego.

Monroe, Will S. *History of the Pestalozzian Movement in the United States.* New York: Arno Press, 1969. (reprint) A time-tried history of the influence of Pestalozzi in education of teachers and children.

3. Journalism and Libraries

Davis, Sheldon Elmer. *Educational Periodicals during the Nineteenth Century.* Washington: United States Bureau of Education, Bulletin 28, 1919. (Reprinted, 1970) Reactions of educators to educational developments in the nineteenth century.

Milne, James Mollison. *History of Educational Journalism*. Syracuse, N.Y.: C. W. Bardeen, 1893. Information regarding pedagogical reviews, particularly with reference to free schools.

Mott, Frank Luther. *American Journalism*. 3rd edition. New York: The Macmillan Company, 1962. A well-known, perhaps the best, history.

————. *A History of American Magazines*. Cambridge: Harvard University Press, 1938-1968. 5 vols. Comprehensive and essential guide to periodicals of the latter half of the nineteenth century, and beyond.

Thompson, C. Seymour. *Evolution of the American Public Library, 1653-1876*. Metuchen, N.J.: The Scarecrow Press, 1952.

4. Educational Theory and Philosophy

James, William. *Pragmatism, A New Name for Old Ways of Thinking*. New York: Longmans, Green & Co., Inc., 1907. The classical presentation of what has been acclaimed as the "native American philosophy."

Kennedy, Gail, ed. *Pragmatism and American Culture*. Boston: D. C. Heath and Company, 1950. Discussion of the impact of Pragmatism on the American social order.

Krug, Edward A., ed. *Charles W. Eliot and Popular Education*. New York: Teachers College, Bureau of Publications, Columbia University, 1961. Essays on the thought and influence of a renowned president of Harvard University.

Luqueer, F. L. *Hegel as Educator*. New York: Columbia University Press, 1896. Discussion of Idealism in education.

Mead, George H. *Movements of Thought in the Nineteenth Century*. Chicago: University of Chicago Press, 1936.

Partridge, G. E. *Genetic Philosophy of Education*. New York: Sturgis and Walton, 1912. G. Stanley Hall's educational philosophy abstracted from his psychological works.

Persons, Stow, ed. *Evolutionary Thought in America*. New Haven: Yale University Press, 1950. Includes essays by Scoon and Northrop on the impact of Darwin on American thought and philosophy.

Spalding, John Lancaster. *Means and Ends of Education*. Chicago: McClurg and Company, 1897. Bishop Spalding, Catholic educator and activist, was also a philosopher whose thought and work were influential among American educators.

Wiener, Philip P. *Evolution and the Founders of Pragmatism*. Cambridge: Harvard University Press, 1949. Explores the role of the Metaphysical Club on the development of Pragmatism.

5. Psychology and Education

Boring, Edwin G. *History of Experimental Psychology*. New York: Appleton-Century-Crofts, 1950. Written with considerable interpretation, the student's most satisfactory introduction to the field.

Brennan, R. E. *History of Psychology*. New York: The Macmillan Company, 1945. Written from the Roman Catholic viewpoint.

Harris, William Torrey. *Psychology Foundations of Education*. New York: D. Appleton & Company, 1901. Superintendent of St. Louis public schools, United States Commissioner of Education, psychologist, philosopher, Harris introduced the kindergarten and vocational education into the schols of his time, played a large role in the NEA, and greatly influenced American education.

James, William. *Talks to Teachers on Psychology*. New ed. New York: Henry Holt & Co., 1938. (originally, 1900) James held that psychology was a science while teaching was an art. An educational classic.

————. *Principles of Psychology*. Cleveland: World Publishing Company, 1948. (originally, 2 vols. 1890) Indispensable for the student of education.

Spencer, Herbert. *Education: Intellectual, Moral, and Physical*. New York: D. Appleton & Co., 1860. Influential in the development of American education, Spencer emphasized mental training, forcefully presenting the views of the foremost thinkers of his time.

Strickland, Charles, and Charles Burgess. *Health, Growth, and Heredity: G. Stanley Hall on Natural Education*. New York: Teachers College, Bureau of Publications, Columbia University, 1965. An early experimental psychologist and head of Clark University, Hall was among the first to make psychological studies of the child and the adolescent.

Wilson, Louis N. *Granville Stanley Hall*. New York: G. E. Stechert & Co., 1914. A study of the life and work of Hall.

C. IMMIGRATION

Berger, Morris Isaiah. "The Settlement, the Immigrant, and the Public School: a Study of the Influence of the Settlement Movement and the New Migration upon Public Education, 1890-1924." Unpublished Doctoral dissertation, Columbia University, 1956. Study of the beginnings of the new migration and education.

Brown, Francis J., and Joseph S. Roucek, eds. *One America: The History, Contributions, and Present Problems of our Racial and National Minorities.* 3rd edition. Englewood Cliffs, N.J.: Prentice-Hall, Inc., 1952.

Erickson, Charlotte. *Invisible Immigrants: The adaptation of English and Scottish Immigrants in Nineteenth Century America.* Miami: University of Miami Press, 1972.

Handlin, Oscar. *The Uprooted.* Boston: Little, Brown & Co., Inc., 1951. The meaning of immigration from the viewpoint of American society and that of the human beings who were immigrants. Social and personal implications of separation from old cultures and involvements in new, for millions of immigrants who form the basis of the American population.

————, ed. *Children of the Uprooted.* New York: George Braziller, 1966. Influences of ethnic derivation on second-generation Americans as seen in their writings.

————, ed. *Immigration as a Factor in American History.* Englewood Cliffs, N.J.: Prentice–Hall, Inc., 1959. Selected source materials concerning the old world background of immigrants, their economic adjustment and cultural contributions, the position of the immigrant in American politics.

Hansen, Marcus L. *The Immigrant in American History.* Cambridge: Harvard University Press, 1940. The historical role of the immigrant in American life: introduction of differences of outlook and culture greatly modifying the basic Anglo-Saxon heritage and the whole pattern of American life. Essays edited by Arthur M. Schlesinger after Hansen's death.

Hartmann, Edward G. *The Movement to Americanize the Immigrant.* New York: Columbia University Press, 1948. American response to the new immigration—an attempt, through education and other means, to metamorphize various ethnics into white Anglo-Saxon Protestants.

Higham, John. *Strangers in the Land: Patterns of American Nativism 1860-1925.* New Brunswick: Rutgers University Press, 1955. The ebb and flow of American nativist response to immigration, the story of public fear and prejudice in action.

Hutchinson, E. P. *Immigrants and their Children, 1850-1950.* Census Monograph Series. New York: John Wiley & Sons, 1956.

Jones, Maldwyn Allen. *American Immigration.* Chicago: University of Chicago Press, 1960. A good survey with some material concerning the impact of the immigrant on the schools.

D. LABOR

Commons, John R., *et al. History of Labor in the United States.* 4 vols. New

York: The Macmillan Company, 1916-1935. Most analytical of the general histories of American labor.

Curoe, Philip R. *Educational Attitudes and Policies of Organized Labor in the United States*. New York. Teachers College, Bureau of Publications, Columbia University, 1926. From the organization of the Mechanic's Union of Trade Associations in Philadelphia, 1828 to 1925. Identifies perennial educational problems of organized labor as apprenticeship training, child labor, educational implications of the shorter working day. A thorough historical study which requires supplementation by more recent researches.

Douglas, Paul H. *Real Wages in the United States, 1890-1926*. Boston: Houghton Mifflin Co., 1930.

Ensign, Forest C. *Compulsory School Attendance and Child Labor*. Iowa City: Athens Press, 1921.

Ware, Norman J. *The Labor Movement in the United States, 1860-1895*. New York: D. Appleton, 1929. Good post-bellum study of labor.

E. SECULARIZATION OF AMERICAN LIFE AND EDUCATION

Adams, Herbert B. *The Church and Popular Education*. Baltimore: Johns Hopkins Press, 1900.

Billington, Roy Allen. *The Protestant Crusade, 1800-1860*. New York: The Macmillan Company, 1938. Study of the origin of American nativism, and the steps which led toward secularization of the schools.

Brown, Samuel W. *The Secularization of American Education: As Shown by State Legislation, State Constitutional Provisions and State Supreme Court Decisions*. New York: Teachers College, Bureau of Publications, Columbia University, 1912. Religion played a prominent role in early American education. Study of some of the steps and how they were taken toward secularizing American education, and of the Protestant approach to secularization.

Confrey, Burton. *Secularism in American Education*. Washington: Catholic University of America Press, 1931. A Catholic approach to state and church positions in the struggle to secularize public education during the nineteenth century.

Curran, Francis X. *Major Trends in American Church History*. New York: America Press, 1946. Discussion, among others, of increasing secularism in American Protestantism—written by a Catholic.

————. *The Churches and the Schools: American Protestantism and Popular Elementary Education*. Chicago: Loyola University Press, 1954. The surrender to the state by American Protestantism during the nineteenth century of the control of popular education, a move unique in history.

Dunn, William Kailer. *What Happened to Religious Education?* Baltimore: The Johns Hopkins Press, 1958. Documents and discusses the decline of religious teaching in public elementary schools from 1776 to 1861—the foundation of increasing secularization of public education.

Sizer, Theodore R., ed. *Religion and Public Education*. Boston: Houghton Mifflin Company, 1967. Discussions concerning the place of religion in public education. Thesis—there resulted a tangle of threads crossing the traditional lines of inquiry (legal or constitutional, philosophical, theological, historical, psychological, social). Reports of Conference on the Role of Religion in Public Education held at Cambridge, Massachusetts in May, 1966.

Whittmore, L. B. *The Church and Secular Education*. Greenwich, Conn.: The Seabury Press, 1960. Study of the educational effects of separation of church and state, concluding there were both debits and credits.

F. DEVELOPMENT OF EDUCATION

Beale, Howard K. *A History of Freedom of Teaching in American Schools*. New York: Charles Scribner's Sons, 1941. Unique and scholarly account treating of school practices concerned with teachers' ideas, minority group teachers, personal conduct of teachers, freedom of choice in methods and materials. Discusses problems in private, parochial, and black schools. Forces lessening academic freedom and safeguards of that freedom are also discussed.

Cremin, Lawrence A. *The American Common School: An Historic Conception*. New York: Teachers College, Bureau of Publications, Columbia University, 1951. Development of the public school during the first half of the nineteenth century. Extensive bibliography.

––––. *The Genius of American Education*. Pittsburgh: University of Pittsburgh Press, 1965. Concerned fundamentally with purpose in education, suggesting that the animating spirit of education lies in its commitment to popularization.

––––. *The Transformation of the School: Progressivism in American Education, 1876-1957*. New York: Alfred A. Knopf, Inc., 1961. Development of Progressivism from the very roots of the movement in America, as part of a larger movement in the history of the United States. Well documented, extensive bibliographical note.

––––. *The Wonderful World of Ellwood Patterson Cubberly: An Essay on the Historiography of American Education*. New York: Bureau of Publications, Teachers College, Columbia University, 1965. Discussion of the beginnings of American educational history, its influence on education as well as on the writing of educational history.

Edwards, Newton, and Herman G. Richey. 2nd ed. *The School in the American Social Order.* Boston: Houghton Mifflin Company, 1963. Good example of the increasing attention to the social background of education.

Greer, Colin. *The Great School Legend: A Revisionist Interpretation of American Public Education.* New York: Basic Books, Inc., 1972. Educational history in the new mode.

Hawkins, Hugh. *Between Harvard and America: The Educational Leadership of Charles W. Eliot.* New York: Oxford Press, 1972. Harvard in the late nineteenth century and the remarkable man who was its president for forty years. Focal points of this penetrating study analyze the relationship between universities and American society.

Karier, Clarence J. *Man, Society, and Education.* Chicago: Scott, Foreman and Company, 1967. Study of concepts of human nature and society, with the school as center, assuming that the way men defined themselves and their ideal society has important implications for educational thought and practice. Covers 1865-1965, discussing pragmatic, psychological, and humanistic conceptions of man and society, the nature of the child, and Supreme Court decisions on education.

Katz, Michael B. *The Irony of Early School Reform: Educational Innovation in Mid-Nineteenth Century Massachusetts.* Boston: Beacon Press, 1968. Revisionist, suggesting that modern public school systems arose as a conservative response to industrialization, contradicting the view that public education resulted from the working class, and holding this myth hindered reform and contributed to social problems rife in urban schools.

Kennedy, Millard Fillmore, and Alvin F. Harlow. *Schoolmaster of Yesterday: A Three-Generation Story, 1820-1919.* New York: McGraw-Hill Book Company, Inc., 1940. Deals with the old school more than with the new. Valuable as a corrective to idealized history of education.

McCluskey, Neil G., S. J. *Public Schools and Moral Education: The Influence of Horace Mann, William Torrey Harris, and John Dewey.* New York: Columbia University Press, 1958. Suggests American education is caught in an unresolved ambiguity, schools being responsible for character education with no common view as to what it should be.

Minnich, H. C. *William Holmes McGuffey.* New York: Macmillan, 1936. Life and work of the writer/editor of the McGuffey *Readers* which provided American children with moral codes and a taste for fine literature.

Monroe, Paul. *The Founding of the American School System.* New York: Hafner Publishing Co., 1971. Reprint of a compilation of sources and documents, useful for making available material which might be inaccessible, but also for revealing certain basic assumptions of the compiler.

Mosier, Richard D. *Making the American Mind: Social and Moral Ideas in the McGuffey Readers.* New York: King's Crown Press, Columbia University, 1947. Ideas and values fostered by the McGuffey readers, tracing their spread throughout the United States from 1836 to 1900. Reveals McGuffey's ideas on Christianity.

Perkinson, Henry J. *The Imperfect Panacea: American Faith in Education, 1865-1965.* New York: Random House, 1968. Examines the American concept that education is the cure-all of social, political, and economic problems. Interpreting the possibilities and resonsibilities of education, Perkinson concludes that schools have been unable to solve national problems and as yet their true function is misunderstood.

Reisner, E. H. *The Evolution of the Common School.* New York: Macmillan, 1930. History of elementary education from the Middle Ages, emphasizing the nineteenth and twentieth centuries in America.

Slosson, Edwin E. *The American Spirit in Education.* New Haven: Yale University Press, 1921. Abbreviated account offering material usually not included in other texts: Washington, DeWitt Clinton, Catholic education.

Thomas, Russell. *The Search for a Common Learning: General Education, 1800-1960.* New York: McGraw-Hill Book Company, Inc., 1962. Part I discusses historical background of general education in American colleges, 1800-1930, social forces changing the character and aims of American colleges, and problems of general education in the growth of American public schools and universities.

G. ADULT EDUCATION

Bode, Carl. *The American Lyceum: Town Meeting of the Mind.* New York: Oxford University Press, 1956. A complete and scholarly study of the first major adult education program in the United States, 1820 to the Civil War.

Gould, Joseph E. *The Chautauqua Movement.* New York: State University of New York, 1961. One of America's most successful means of informal education. Discusses the birth of the movement, William R. Harper, the University of Chicago, difficulties. Postscript plus useful notes and some illustrations. Subtitle: An Episode in the Continuing American Revolution.

Grattan, C. Hartley, ed. *American Ideas about Adult Education, 1710-1915.* New York: Bureau of Publications, Teachers College, Columbia University, 1959.

Hayes, Cecil B. *The American Lyceum: Its History and Contribution to Education.* Washington: United States Office of Education, Bulletin No. 12, Government Printing Office, 1932. Sketchy history of the Lyceum from 1826 to about 1913 and its contributions to the advancement of public education. Useful source materials and Appendix include the Lyceum's

Constitution and By-Laws, Resolutions, list of lectures and essays, names of many who aided the movement.

Hopkins, Howard C. *History of the Y.M.C.A. in North America*. New York: Association Press, 1951. The Y.M.C.A., started as a Christian movement to keep young men in the church, initiated physical education and sports, classes in various subjects, reading rooms, Bible classes.

Johnson, Alvin. *The Public Library*. New York: American Association for Adult Education, 1938.

Kniker, Charles Robert. "The Chautauqua Library and Scientific Circle, 1878-1914: *An* Historical Interpretation of an Educational Piety in Industrial America." Unpublished Doctoral dissertation, Columbia University, 1969.

Noffsinger, Samuel. *Correspondence Schools, Lyceums, and Chautauquas*. New York: Macmillan, 1926.

Nordhoff, Charles. *The Communistic Societies of the United States*. New York: Schocken Books, 1875. Brings to life the daily existence of Harmonists, Shakers, Oneidas, Auroras, Zoarists, and all those communities inspired by Holy Writ and a vision of the City Beautiful. Re-education of people into a commune system.

Pence, Owen Earle. *The Y.M.C.A. and Social Need*. New York: Association Press, 1939. Examination of some internal and some external factors making for continuity and change in the American Y.M.C.A., an agency for informal education. Traces the founding and development to the 1930's. Selected references.

Richmond, Rebecca. *Chautauqua, an American Place*. New York: Duell, Sloane and Pearce, 1943. Brief history of the town where the Chautauqua movement began and grew to maturity. Simple, well-illustrated book provides insights into a unique American educational institution.

Wittlin, Alma S. *The Museum: Its History and its Task in Education*. London: Routledge & Kegan Paul, 1949. A documented history of the museum as an agency of adult education.

H. MINORITIES AND EDUCATION

Berry, Brewton, ed. *The Education of American Indians: A Survey of the Literature*. Prepared for the Special Subcommittee on Indian Education of the Committee on Labor and Public Welfare, United States Senate. Washington: Government Printing Office, 1969. A thorough overview.

Bond, Horace Mann. *The Education of the Negro in the American Social Order*. New York: Prentice-Hall, 1934. A standard work on Negro education during the 1880's and 1890's.

Bullock, Henry Allen. *A History of Negro Education in the South: From 1619 to the Present*. Cambridge: Harvard University Press, 1967. The most recent and, considered by many, the most inclusive history of education for Negroes in the South.

Calam, John. *Parsons and Pedagogues: The SPG Adventure in American Education*. New York: Columbia University Press, 1971. A specialized study dealing with the education of Indians and others by the Society of the Propagation for the Gospel.

Coates, Lawrence George. "A History of Indian Education by the Mormans, 1830-1900." Unpublished Doctoral dissertation, Ball State University, 1969.

Franklin, John Hope. *From Slavery to Freedom*. New York: Alfred A. Knopf, 1937. Good general guide to the study of Negroes and the schools.

Frazier, E. Franklin. *The Negro in the United States*. Rev. ed. New York: Macmillan, 1957. An early useful study by a Negro sociologist.

Knight, Edgar W. *Public Education in the South*. Boston: Ginn and Company, 1922. The attempt of Southern states to set up a system of education for Negroes.

Manuel, Herschel T. *Spanish Speaking Children of the Southwest: Their Education and the Public Welfare*. Austin: University of Texas Press, 1965.

Pratt, Richard Henry. *Battlefield and Classroom: Four Decades with the American Indian, 1867-1904*. New Haven: Yale University Press, 1964.

Swint, Henry Lee. *The Northern Teacher in the South, 1862-1870*. Nashville, Tenn.: Vanderbilt University Press, 1941. Motives and work of Northern teachers, and of the societies and organizations which supported them, in educating freed Negroes in the South. Southern reaction to educating Negroes under a program advanced by radical legislatures. Biographical and statistical data, bibliography.

Thorpe, Earl E. *The Mind of the Negro: An Intellectual History of Afro-Americans*. Baton Rouge, La.: Ortlieb Press, 1961. An ambitious study which leaves unanswered a number of provocative questions.

Washington, Booker T. *Tuskegee and its People*. New York: D. Appleton, 1908. Story of a poineer Negro school by its founder.

West, Earle H., ed. *The Black American and Education*. Columbus, Ohio: Charles E. Merrill, 1972. Sources and statements on Negro educational development, problems, and issues in the United States from 1680 to 1970.

Woodward, C. Vann. *Origins of the New South, 1877-1913*. Baton Rouge: Louisiana State University Press, 1951. The Negro and the schools during the period of reconstruction.

I. AGRICULTURAL, MECHANICAL, AND INDUSTRIAL EDUCATION

Anderson, Lewis Flint. *History of Manual and Industrial School Education.* New York: D. Appleton, 1926. Part I discusses the history of manual and industrial education from its origins in Europe, while Part II emphasizes its development in the United States.

Barlow, Melvin L. *History of Industrial Education in the United States.* Peoria, Ill.: Charles A. Bennett Co., 1967.

Bennett, Charles A. *Manual and Industrial Education up to 1870.* Peoria, Ill.: The Manual Arts Press, 1926. Begins with the Renaissance and includes chapters on Fellenberg, Pestalozzi, industrial schools for the poor, apprenticeship, "The Mechanical Institute Movement," higher technical education, and the development of art education in relation to industry. Important documents quoted; illustrated.

————. *History of Manual and Industrial Education, 1870-1917.* Peoria, Ill.: Manual Arts Press, 1937. Discusses the beginnings of vocational education in the schools.

Clark, Harold F., and Harold S. Sloan. *Classrooms in the Factories: An Account of Educational Activities Conducted by American Industry.* New York: Distributed by New York University Press for the Institute of Research, Fairleigh Dickinson University Press, 1958. Surveys the field, reviewing the origin of corporation teaching, its extent and nature, and its impact on traditional American education. Discusses type of subject matter taught, teachers and students, reasons behind this significant development.

Douglas, P. H. *American Apprenticeship and Industrial Education.* New York: Columbia University Press, 1921.

Hawkins, Layton S., Charles S. Prosser, and John C. Wright. *Development of Vocational Education.* Chicago: American Technical Society, 1951. History of vocational education from its beginning in primitive America to 1951. Emphasis on thirty-year period following the enactment of the Vocational Education Act in 1917.

James, Edmund Janes. *Origins of the Land-Grant Act of 1862 and Some Account of its Author.* Urbana: Illinois University Press, 1910. Traces the sources of the epoch-making land grant legislation.

Powell, G. E. *Industrial Education and the Establishment of the University, 1840-1870.* Urbana: University of Illinois Press, 1918. Links the establishment of the University of Illinois to the development of industrial education.

Ross, Earle D. *Democracy's College: The Land Grant Movement in the Formative State*. Ames: Iowa State College Press, 1942. Accounts of the movement for public education, demand for technical education, efforts to pass the Morrill Land Grant Act and additional federal grants, control of the program by the states, aims and organization of the colleges, relationships between the colleges and the federal government.

Scott, Roy V. *The Reluctant Farmer: The Rise of Agricultural Extension Education to 1914*. Urbana: University of Illinois Press, 1970. Surveys the rise of agricultural extension education in the United States from the 1880's to 1914, examining attempts by the farm press, local agricultural clubs, country fairs, and colleges to improve farming devices.

Shannon, Fred A. *The Farmer's Last Frontier: Agriculture, 1860-1897*. New York: Farrar & Rinehart, 1945. A general history of agriculture in the United States, plus some incidental social history.

Stombaugh, Roy. *A Survey of the Movements Culminating in Industrial Arts Education in Secondary Schools*. New York: Bureau of Publications, Teachers College, Columbia University, 1936. Identifies certain major movements in industrial arts education and their influence on present theory and practice, from 1871 when the Boston Whittling School was established to date published. Eight trends identified. Good bibliography.

Struck, F. Theodore. *Foundations of Industrial Education*. New York: John Wiley & Sons, 1930. Traces the development of the idea of industrial education from the Middle Ages to about 1930, discussing especially commissions, associations, legislation, apprenticeship, guidance, training and certification of teachers.

True, Alfred Charles. *A History of Agricultural Education in the United States, 1785-1925*. Washington: Government Printing Office, 1929. From the development of early agricultural schools in Europe in the eighteenth century, tracing development of agricultural education through colleges, secondary schools, elementary schools. Emphasis on Morrill Land Grant Act of 1862 and the consequent growth and development of collegiate agricultural education. Good bibliography, illustrations.

J. NON-TAX-SUPPORTED EDUCATION

1. General

Beach, Fred F., and Robert T. Will. *The State and Nonpublic Schools*. Misc. No. 28, United States Office of Education. Washington: Government Printing Office, 1958.

Kraushaar, Otto F. *American Non-Public Schools: Patterns of Diversity*. Baltimore: Johns Hopkins University Press, 1972. Uniquely informative and comprehensive, if not entirely thorough. A study of the past, the problems, and the prospects of religious and secular private schools in the United States.

2. Jewish

Pilch, Judah. *A History of Jewish Education in America.* New York: American Association for Jewish Education, 1969.

Yapko, Benjamin L. "Jewish Elementary Education in the United States from Colonial Period to 1900." Unpublished Doctoral dissertation, The American University, 1958.

3. Catholic

Buetow, Harold. *Of Singular Benefit: The Story of Catholic Education in the United States.* New York: Macmillan, 1970.

Burns, James A., and Bernard J. Kohlbrenner. *A History of Catholic Education in the United States.* New York: Benziger Brothers, 1937. Burns' classical history of Catholic education, as revised by Kohlbrenner.

Dawson, Christopher. "Education and Christian Culture," reprinted in *The Catholic Mind,* vol. 52 (April, 1954), 193-203. Analysis of the cultural desert of English and American Catholicism of the eighteenth and nineteenth centuries, together with specific suggestions to revive the life of such culture.

De Hovre, Frans. *Catholicism in Education.* New York: Benziger Brothers, 1934. Discussion of Catholic philosphy and Catholic education, basic principles of life and pedagogy, and the thought of representative Catholic educators of the nineteenth and twentieth centuries: Bishop Spalding, Felix Dupanloup, Cardinal Newman, Cardinal Mercier, and Otto Willmann.

Diggs, M. A. *Catholic Negro Education in the United States.* Houston: Standard Printing and Lithographing Company, 1936.

Klinkhamer, Sr. Marie Carolyn. "Historical Reasons for the Inception of the Parochial School System." *The Catholic Educational Review,* vol. 52 (February, 1946), 73-94. Short, incisive analysis of conditions attendant upon the beginnings of parochial schools for Catholic children.

McCluskey, Neil G. *Catholic Education in America: A Documentary History.* New York: Bureau of Publications, Teachers College, Columbia University, 1964. Introduction by Lawrence A. Cremin, stating that since Roman Catholic education in the United States is second only to the public school system in size and scope, American education cannot be understood apart from it. Traces intellectual basis for Catholic education from Bishop John Carroll's early pronouncements in the 1790's to more recent pastorals of the American hierarchy.

Schuler, Paul Julian. *The Attitudes of American Catholics toward Progressive Education in the United States, 1892-1917.* Notre Dame, Indiana: University of Notre Dame Press, 1969.

4. Protestant

Curran, Francis X. *The Churches and the Schools.* Chicago: Loyola University Press, 1954. American Protestantism and popular elementary Education: surrender by American Protestantism during the past century of the control of popular elementary education to the state, a unique development in the history of Christianity, which has traditionally claimed this right. Investigation of causes.

Harris, J. Henry. *Robert Raikes: The Man and his Work.* New York: E. P. Dutton, 1899. Presents the founder of the Sunday School movement and his work in England and America.

Hartzler, J. E. *Education among the Mennonites of America.* Danvers, Ill.: Central Mennonite Publishing Board, 1925.

Rice, E. W. *The Sunday School Movement, 1780-1917, and the Sunday School Union, 1817-1917.* Philadelphia: American Sunday School Union, 1917. Survey of the work of the Sunday Schools in American culture.

Sherrill, Lewis J. *Presbyterian Parochial Schools, 1846-1870.* New Haven: Yale University Press, 1932. Survey by an authority of Protestant equivalents in early nineteenth century of the Catholic parochial schools.

5. Private Secular

Brickman, William W. "The Historical Background of the Independent School in the United States." *The Role of the Independent School in American Democracy.* Milwaukee, Wis.: Marquette University Press, 1956. Excellent review of the background and history of the private independent school.

Chamberlain, Ernest B. *Our Independent Schools: The Private School in Education.* New York: American Book Company, 1944.

Cole, Robert Danforth. "Private Secondary Education for Boys in the United States." Unpublished Doctoral dissertation, University of Pennsylvania, 1928. Broad, general picture of private secondary education, including general statistics, the legal basis of private schools, personnel, organization and administration, results obtained, present and probable future trends. Numerous tables and helpful bibliography.

McLachlan, James Stuart. "The Education of the Rich: the Origin and Development of the Private Prep School, 1778-1916." Unpublished Doctoral dissertation, Columbia University, 1966.

XXI. HISTORY OF AMERICAN EDUCATION IN THE TWENTIETH CENTURY

A. AMERICAN SOCIETY IN THE TWENTIETH CENTURY

1. The American Setting

Berthoff, Rowland. *An Unsettled People: Social Order and Disorder in American History*. New York: Harper and Row, 1971. A study and analysis of American social history. Reaching into the twentieth century, Part Three is entitled "The Reconstituted Society, 1875-1945."

Filler, Louis. *The Muckrakers: Crusaders for American Liberalism*. Chicago: Henry Regnery, 1950. On the crusades of the muckrakers, their social causes and accomplishments as presented in their writings.

Gabriel, Ralph Henry. *The Course of American Democratic Thought*. New York: Ronald Press, 1956. On the history of human dignity, common principles underlying society and America's mission in furthering the peace and security of its citizens. The twentieth century is included in Parts IV and V. Part IV: American Democratic Thought is Conditioned by the Coming of a New Intellectual Age; Part V: The American Democratic Faith Survives in a Time of Revolution and Violence.

Handlin, Oscar. *John Dewey's Challenge to Education: Historical Perspectives on the Cultural Context*. The John Dewey Lectureship, No. 2. New York: Harper and Brothers, 1959. Presents John Dewey in his nineteenth century cultural setting and, by showing his reactions against this setting, clarifies the differences between the nineteenth and twentieth centuries, especially in the field of education.

Hofstadter, Richard. *Anti-intellectualism in American Life*. New York: Vintage Books, 1962. Discusses the role of schools in anti-intellectualism. Part I: Introduction; Part II: The Religion of the Heart; Part III: The Politics of Democracy; Part IV: Conclusion.

Kellogg, Charles Flint. *NAACP: A History of the National Association for the Advancement of Colored People*. Baltimore: Johns Hopkins Press,

1967. (Two volumes) A history of the efforts of the NAACP to educate and rally black Americans to deal legally with American society in order to achieve total integration.

Lasch, Christopher. *The New Radicalism in American (1889-1963): The Intellectual as a Social Type*. New York: Vintage Books, 1965. On the improvement of the quality of American culture and the rise of the intellectual class. Included are chapters on Jane Addams, on "Woman as Alien," on Mabel Dodge Luhan, on Randolph Bourne, on "Politics as Social Control," on *"The New Republic* and the War," on Lincoln Concord and Colonel House, and on Lincoln Steffens.

Lynch, Hollis R. *The Black Urban Condition: A Documentary History, 1866-1971*. New York: Thomas Y. Crowell, 1973. Cities in the South, North, North Central regions and Border areas are all studied to provide a context for the black urban condition. Dealing with the twentieth century: Part 2: The Twentieth Century: Pre-World War I; Part 3: World War I to the Depression; Part 4: The Depression and the New Deal; Part 5: World War II to 1959; and Part 6: The Sixties and After.

Mowry, George E. *The Era of Theodore Roosevelt and the Birth of Modern America: 1900-1912*. New York: Harper Torchbooks, 1958. On the administration of Theodore Roosevelt and the social ideas of his times. Includes chapters on diplomacy, political developments, administrative leadership, Progressivism, and the growth of urbanization.

Mowry, George E. *The Urban Nation: 1920-1960*. New York: Hill and Wang, 1965. Describes the transformation of American life through urbanization and the mass-production-consumption economy.

Potter, David M. *People of Plenty: Economic Abundance and the American Character*. Chicago: University of Chicago Press, 1954. Describes the influence of American economic abundance upon the national character. Part I: The Study of National Character; Part II: Abundance and the Shaping of American Character.

Wecter, Dixon. *The Hero in America: A Chronicle of Hero-Worship*. Ann Arbor: University of Michigan Press, 1963. On the importance of hero worship, its meaning and object in America. Chapters directly related to the twentieth century include: "The Unknown Soldier: Hero of the World War," "Gods from the Machine: Edison, Ford, Lindbergh," and "Champion of the New Deal."

2. Cultural Influences and Their Expression

Birnbaum, Lucille C. "Behaviorism in the 1920's." *American Quarterly*, vol. 7 (Spring, 1955), pp. 15-30. Describes the ready acceptance of behaviorism in the United States during the 1920's.

Bontemps, Arna, ed. *The Harlem Renaissance Remembered*. New York: Dodd, Mead, 1972. A collection of essays which analyze the social causes of, participants in, and cultural results of the Harlem Renaissance.

Brown, Dorothy M. "The Quality Magazine in the Progressive Era." *Mid-America,* vol. 53 (July, 1971), pp. 139-159. Through excerpts, quotes, and analysis the "quality" magazines are shown to have warned the readers of the deep malaise of spirit in America.

Bryant, Ira B., Jr. "News Items about Negroes in White Urban and Rural Newspapers." *The Journal of Negro Education,* vol. 4 (April, 1935), pp. 169-178. Shows a comparison of the methods of presenting news about blacks in 1932 and in 1912 as well as a study of the influence of political and professional status on black news.

Erisman, Fred. "L. Frank Baum and the Progressive Dilemma." *American Quarterly,* vol. 20 (Fall, 1968), pp. 616-623. The OZ books reflect the difficulty of rural social adaptation to an urban world far removed from the ideal world desired by rural Americans.

Hansen, Chadwick. "Social Influences on Jazz Style: Chicago, 1920-30." *American Quarterly,* vol. 12 (Winter, 1960), pp. 495-507. A study of the social pressures on the black migrant to Chicago to abandon the traditions of jazz and to adopt the popular music of the white middle class.

Heald, Morrell. "Business Thought in the Twenties: Social Responsibility." *American Quarterly,* vol. 13 (Summer, 1961), pp. 126-139. Explains why the identification of new social problems led to a period of trial and error in business practice, to efforts to find new solutions, and to an increased awareness of the need for social justification of business practices.

Horowitz, Helen L. "Varieties of Cultural Experience in Jane Addams' Chicago." *History of Education Quarterly,* vol. 14 (Spring, 1974), pp. 69-86. On the philosophy of and practice at Hull House as a place of culture and middle-class values, acting as an educational mission to the immigrant population.

Janosik, G. Edward. "Suburban Balance of Power." *American Quarterly,* vol. 7 (Summer, 1955), pp. 123-141. On the information gap in political literature which emphasized city ward politics at a time when suburban communities were gaining domination.

Kenkel, William F. "Marriage and the Family in Modern Science Fiction." *Journal of Marriage and the Family,* vol. 31 (February, 1969), pp. 6-14. The depiction of families in science fiction is often unsatisfactory but the use of technology to support man can be valuable.

Levy, Betty. "The School's Role in the Sex-Role Stereotyping of Girls: A

Feminist Review of the Literature." *Feminist Studies,* vol. 1 (Summer, 1972), pp. 5-23. On the educational and social influence in schools which promote behavioral differences between boys and girls.

Mottram, Eric. "Living Mythically: The Thirties." *Journal of American Studies,* vol. 6 (December, 1972), pp. 267-287. On the depiction of life in the 1930's in various media of communications.

Phillips, J. O. C. "The Education of Jane Addams." *History of Education Quarterly,* vol. 14 (Spring, 1974), pp. 49-68. On Jane Addams' efforts to propagate an international ethic of female values and humanity such as she had already done in Chicago.

Rodnitzky, Jerome L. "Getting the Ear of the State: A Pioneer University Radio Station in the 1920's." *History of Education Quarterly,* vol. 8 (Winter, 1968), pp. 505-509. On the problems of an educational radio station in getting funded and determining programs.

Saveth, Edward N. *American Historians and European Immigrants, 1875-1925.* New York: Russell and Russell, 1965. Ideas of racial superiority inherent in northern European and Teutonic origins, which were developed in the nineteenth century, are traced in the writings of Theodore Roosevelt, Woodrow Wilson and twentieth-century historians.

Seeger, Charles. "Music and Class Structure in the United States." *American Quarterly,* vol. 9 (Fall, 1957), pp. 281-294. On the interrelationships of music and society and a description of the changes as America developed in the twentieth century.

Soderbergh, Peter A. "Bibliographical Essay: The Negro in Juvenile Series Books, 1899-1930." *Journal of Negro History,* vol. 58 (April, 1973), pp. 179-186. Shows that the "series" books presented a black stereotype which influenced millions of readers.

Witham, W. Tasker. *The Adolescent in the American Novel, 1920-1960.* New York: Frederick Ungar, 1964. Adolescent experiences with sex, family, education and preparation for life are analyzed as they are presented in American novels.

3. Educational Thought in Twentieth Century American Society

Berkman, Richard L. "Students in Court: Free Speech and the Functions of Schooling in America." *Harvard Educational Review,* vol. 40 (November, 1970), pp. 567-595. A study of the trends in court decisions reflecting traditional disciplinarian concepts of education.

Bowers, C. A. *The Progressive Educator and the Depression: The Radical Years.* New York: Random House, 1969. On the efforts of liberal educators in the 1930's to make the schools agents of social change.

Butts, R. Freeman. "Public Education and Political Community." *History of Education Quarterly,* vol. 14 (Summer, 1974), pp. 165-183. The author expresses his belief in the need for additional history of education which is not too extremely conservative or radical.

Carbone, Peter F., Jr. "The Other Side of Harold Rugg." *History of Education Quarterly,* vol. 11 (Fall, 1971), pp. 265-278. An analysis of the social planning which Rugg foresaw as improving the quality of American life.

Chambers, Gurney. "Michael John Demiashkevich and the Essentialist Committee for the Advancement of American Education." *History of Education Quarterly,* vol. 9 (Spring, 1969), pp. 46-56. On the life of the man who played a key role in establishing the Essentialist movement.

Conant, James Bryant. *Shaping Educational Policy.* New York: McGraw-Hill, 1964. On the development of national educational policies.

Curti, Merle. *The Social Ideas of American Educators with New Chapter on the Last Twenty-Five Years.* Totowa, New Jersey: Littlefield, Adams, 1959. On the ideas and accomplishments of a number of American educators chosen to portray national trends. Part II has chapters on twentieth-century figures such as Booker T. Washington, Bishop Spalding, G. Stanley Hall, William James, Edward Lee Thorndike, and John Dewey.

"Doing History of Education, a Discussion." *History of Education Quarterly,* vol. 9 (Fall, 1969), pp. 329-375. A series of articles on the need to carve a new role for educational history.

Douglass, Harl R., ed. *Education for Life Adjustment: Its Meaning and Implementation.* New York: The Ronald Press, 1950. A series of essays on the purposes of life adjustment education and the ways in which the teaching of various subject areas should be changed in order to meet these purposes.

Dworkin, Martin S., ed. *Dewey on Education: Selections.* Classics in Education, No. 3. New York: Bureau of Publications, Teachers College, Columbia University, 1959. On the life and influence of John Dewey. Selections include: "My Pedagogic Creed," "School and Society," "The Child and the Curriculum," "Progressive Education and the Science of Education," and Dewey's "Introduction to *The Use of Resources in Education* by Elsie Ripley Clapp."

Hiner, N. Ray. "Professions in Process: Changing Relations Between Historians and Educators, 1896-1911." *History of Education Quarterly,* vol. 12 (Spring, 1972), pp. 34-56. In order to gain a larger place in the schools for their discipline, historians argued for an enlargement of the school's place as a social institution, an argument in which some educators joined for different reasons.

Karier, Clarence J. "Elite Views on American Education." An essay in *Education and Social Structure in the Twentieth Century* edited by Walter Laqueur and George L. Mosse. New York: Harper Torchbooks, 1967, pp. 149-163. An analysis of the thought of Edward L. Thorndike, Irving Babbitt, and Lawrence Dennis, who were selected for analysis because they represent three significant conservative positions.

Karier, Clarence J. *Man, Society, and Education: A History of American Educational Ideas.* Glenview, Illinios: Scott, Foresman, 1967. On ideas in society, among educators, and organizations which affect education. Chapters on twentieth-century ideas include: "Humanist Conceptions of Man and Society," "A Fascist and a Communist View of the Function of the American School," and "The United States Supreme Court and Education."

Mower, O. Hobart. "Learning Theory: Historical Review and Re-interpretation." *Harvard Educational Review,* vol. 24 (Winter, 1954), pp. 37-58. Advances the hypothesis that learning theory must ground itself in the reflex-arc concept, in conditioning, and in solution learning as well as in personality theories.

Phillips, Richard C. "The Historical Development of the Term, Experience Curriculum." *History of Education Quarterly,* vol. 5 (June, 1965), pp. 121-130. An explication of the use given the expression "experience curriculum" by educators during the twentieth century.

Rubin, Barry. "Marxism and Education—Radical Thought and Educational Theory in the 1930's." *Science and Society,* vol. 36 (Summer, 1972), pp. 171-201. Describes the increasingly key role played by the educational system in shaping consciousness and social strata.

Soderbergh, Peter A. "Charles A. Beard and the Public Schools, 1909-1939." *History of Education Quarterly,* vol. 5 (December, 1965), pp. 241-252. On the continuous writings and comments by Charles A. Beard about the public schools.

Strickland, Charles E., and Charles Burgess, eds. *Health, Growth, and Heredity: G. Stanley Hall on Natural Education.* Classics in Education, No. 23. New York; Teachers College Press, 1965. On the life and influence of G. Stanley Hall, both selections from his writings and analysis. Part I: Evolution and Psychology; Part II: Child Study; Part III: The Child-Centered School; Part IV: Health, Sex and Morals.

Timpane, P. Michael. "Educational Experimentation in National Social Policy." *Harvard Educational Review,* vol. 40 (November, 1970), pp. 547-566. A defense of the idea that experimentation must be accompanied by active need of the educational services provided by the experiment in order to be successful.

Tyler, Ralph W. "National Assessment: A History and Sociology." *School and Society,* vol. 98 (December, 1970), pp. 471-477. On a number of continuing efforts to evaluate education as it is offered in the schools.

Welter, Rush. *Popular Education and Democratic Thought in America.* New York: Columbia University Press, 1962. A survey history of the relationships between popular education and democratic thought in which the final section deals with "Twentieth-Century Innovations."

White, Morton. *Social Thought in America: The Revolt Against Formalism.* With a new preface and an epilogue. New York: Harper, 1958. A study of the intellectual pattern of an era including pragmatism, institutionalism, behaviorism, legal realism, economic determinism, the "new history."

Winters, Elmer A. "Man and His Changing Society: The Textbooks of Harold Rugg." *History of Education Quarterly,* vol. 7 (Winter, 1967), pp. 493-514. On the development and popularity of books published under the direction of Rugg.

Wirth, Arthur G. *John Dewey as Educator: His Design for Work in Education (1894-1904).* New York: John Wiley, 1966. On the period of John Dewey's life when he was at the University of Chicago as Chairman of the Departments of Philosophy, Psychology, and Education, was directing his University Laboratory School and developing his educational theories in conjunction with practice. Part I: The Theory: Philosophical and Psychological; Part II: Curriculum and Methodology in the Laboratory School.

Woelfel, Norman. *Molders of the American Mind: A Critical Review of the Social Attitudes of Seventeen Leaders in American Education.* New York: Columbia University Press, 1933. Analyzes the ideas of educators who had influenced the author. Section One: Some Implications of Contemporary Social Change; Section Two: Analysis of the Viewpoints of American Educators; Section Three: Interpretive Criticism of the Viewpoints of American Educators; Section Four: Suggestive Strategic Considerations for American Educators.

4. Education Outside the Schools

Carlson, Robert A. "Americanization as Early Twentieth-Century Adult Education Movement." *History of Education Quarterly,* vol. 10, pp. 440-464. On the role of Americanization and the attitudes of Americanizers working with immigrants and the industrial poor.

Gower, Calvin W. "The Civilian Conservation Corps and American Education: Threat to Local Control?" *History of Education Quarterly,* vol. 7 (Spring, 1967), pp. 58-70. On the struggle between the CCC and national public school organizations to determine whether the CCC should play a significant role in providing education for American youth.

Linton, Thomas E. *An Historical Examination of the Purposes and Practices of the Education Program of the United Automobile Workers of America, 1936-1959.* Ann Arbor: The University of Michigan School of Education, 1965. On the role of education in unions. Part I: Political Power and Industrial Conflict Influence the Development of the Early Education Program; Part II: Education During the Second World War: A Time of Conservativism and Prosperity for the UAW; Part III: Education as Persuasion: Political Conformity Replaces Political Dissent.

Starr, Mark. "Workers' Education." *Harvard Educational Review,* vol. 21 (Fall, 1951), pp. 243-264. A description of the influence of publications from the National Association of Manufacturers and the effort of workers' education to counteract that influence.

B. AMERICANS AND THEIR SCHOOLS

1. The Americans from Overseas: Their Experience

Beck, Earl R. "The German Discovery of American Education." *History of Education Quarterly,* vol. 5 (March, 1965), pp. 3-13. The views of Germans during the 1920's and 1930's give a new perspective of American education at that time.

Handlin, Oscar. *The Uprooted: The Epic Story of the Great Migrations that Made the American People.* New York: Grosset & Dunlap, 1951. Brings the life of immigrants into close immediacy by treatment of historical facts as an epic narrative. Treats ocean crossings, work, religion, ghettos, generational differences, alienation and restriction.

Handlin, Oscar. *This Was America: True Accounts of People and Places, Manners and Customs as Recorded by European Travelers to the Western Shore in the Eighteenth, Nineteenth, and Twentieth Centuries.* New York: Harper Torchbooks, 1949. Materials have been divided according to topics. Part One: The Sources of American Nationality; Part Two: The Consequences of Expansion; Part Three: Urban America; Part Four: The Burdens of Maturity.

Higham, John. *Strangers in the Land: Patterns of American Nativism 1860-1925.* Corrected and with a new Preface. New York: Atheneum, 1965. A history of American attitudes toward immigrants and immigration. Twentieth-century ideas and events are presented in Chapter 5: The Return of Confidence; Chapter 6: Toward Racism: The History of an Idea; Chapter 7: The Loss of Confidence; Chapter 10: The Tribal Twenties; and Chapter 11: Closing the Gates.

Jones, Maldwyn Allen. *American Immigration.* Chicago: The University of Chicago Press, 1960. On the massive immigration into the United States and its influence on social ideas and institutions. Includes chapters on nativism, distribution of population, sources, life styles, and restriction.

Mohl, Raymond A., and Neil Betten. "Paternalism and Pluralism: Immigrants and Social Welfare in Gary Indiana, 1906-1940." *American Studies,* vol. 15 (Spring, 1974), pp. 5-30. Describes the social efforts of and influences upon a variety of social welfare agencies and is of particular interest to educational history because of location of the study.

O'Brien, Kenneth B., Jr. "Education, Americanization and the Supreme Court: The 1920's." *American Quarterly,* vol. 13 (Summer, 1961), pp. 161-71. On the social ferment resulting from Americanization and the meaning of the Supreme Court rulings on education in the 1920's.

Smith, Timothy L. "Immigrant Social Aspirations and American Education, 1880-1930." *American Quarterly,* vol. 21 (Fall, 1969), pp. 523-543. An investigation of the reasons for immigrant concern about education.

Ware, Caroline F. *Greenwich Village, 1920-1930: A Comment on American Civilization in the Post-War Years.* New York: Harper Colophon Books, 1965. Describes the interrelationship of traditional American life and the lives of immigrant newcomers. Part I: Community; Part II: People; Part III: Institutions.

2. Regional Efforts to Establish Schools

Atherton, Lewis. *Main Street on the Middle Border.* Chicago: Quadrangle Paperbacks, 1966. On the unique character of small-town America, especially in the midwest. Includes sections on churches, schools, lodges, politics, holidays, culture, and hopes.

Dabney, Charles William. *Universal Education in the South.* Vol. II, "The Southern Education Movement." Chapel Hill: University of North Carolina Press, 1936. In reprinted form, New York: Arno Press and The New York Times, 1969. On the organized, philanthropic effort to provide universal education in the South.

Fuller, Edgar, and Jim B. Pearson, eds. *Education in the States: Historical Development and Outlook.* A Project of the Council of Chief State School Officers. Washington, D.C.: National Education Association of the United States, 1969. Traces the developments since 1900 of each of the fifty state departments of education and the central school agencies of Puerto Rico, American Samoa, Guam, the Panama Canal Zone, and the Virgin Islands.

Gershenberg, Irving. "Southern Values and Public Education: A Revision." *History of Education Quarterly,* vol. 10 (Winter, 1970), pp. 413-422. An economic argument is developed to show that whites in the

South attended school as much as was available to them.

Murphy, Jerome T. "Title V of ESEA: The Impact of Discretionary Funds on State Education Bureaucracies." *Harvard Educational Revew,* vol. 43 (August, 1973), pp. 362-385. Shows that a major problem with federal aid to education can be found in the administering of public bureaucracies.

Tyack, David B. "The Tribe and the Common School: Community Control in Rural Education." *American Quarterly,* vol. 24 (March, 1972), pp. 3-19. On the issue of school control in rural communities.

3. Special Interest Groups: The American Context

Baron, Harold M. "Race and Status in School Spending: Chicago, 1961-1966." *The Journal of Human Resources,* vol. 6 (Winter, 1971), pp. 3-24. The civil rights movement and the availability of federal funds have partially equalized expenditures for education.

Clift, Virgil A. "The History of Racial Segregation in American Education." *School and Society,* vol. 88 (April 23, 1960), pp. 220-229. Racial segregation in American schools had a long history but was being challenged even before the 1954 Supreme Court ruling.

Cordasco, Francesco, and Rocco G. Galatioto. "Ethnic Displacement in the Interstitial Community: The East Harlem (New York City) Experience." *The Journal of Negro Education,* vol. 40 (Winter, 1971), pp. 56-65. Describes the successive displacement of ethnic groups in East Harlem during the twentieth century and the experiences of the groups resulting from displacement.

Duker, Sam. *The Public School and Religion: The Legal Context.* New York: Harper & Row, Publishers, 1966. On the Supreme Court cases affecting public education from 1923 to 1964.

Fellman, David, ed. *The Supreme Court and Education.* New York: Bureau of Publications, Teachers College, Columbia University, 1960. On the influence of the Supreme Court in education. Part I: Education and Religion; Part II: Education and Racial Segregation; Part III: Academic Freedom.

Ginzberg, Eli, and Associates. *Educated American Women: Life Styles and Self-Portraits.* New York: Columbia University Press, 1966. On the interactions of education, work, life styles, and socialized expectations in a group of educated women. Includes chapters on the purposes of the study, the methods used, observations and analysis of the findings especially as related to the fulfillment and functioning of the subjects.

Glazer, Nathan, and Daniel Patrick Moynihan. *Beyond the Melting Pot:*

The Negroes, Puerto Ricans, Jews, Italians, and Irish of New York City.
Cambridge, Massachusetts: 2nd ed. M.I.T. Press, 1970. On the role of
ethnicity in New York City with a section on the social influences and
attitudes affecting each ethnic group.

McPherson, James M. "White Liberals and Black Power in Negro
Education, 1865-1915." *The American Historical Review,* vol. 75 (June,
1970), pp. 1357-1386. Describes the conflicting goals of education,
academic standards and self-determination in early black public schools.

Somerville, Rose M. "Family, Life and Sex Education in the Turbulent
Sixties." *Journal of Marriage and the Family,* vol. 33 (February, 1971),
pp. 11-35. On the changes in sex education offerings, the social pressures
which brought them about, and the resulting difficulties.

Valenti, Jasper J., Paul A. Woelfl, and James O'Shaughnessy. "A Double
Revolution? The Supreme Court's Desegregation Decision." *Harvard
Educational Review,* vol. 25 (Winter, 1955), pp. 1-17. An exploration of
the historical basis for fears caused by the "Brown" integration decision
for the security of all private schooling.

C. SCHOOLS IN AN URBAN SOCIETY

1. The Twentieth Century Urban School Situation

    Cohen, Sol. "Urban School Reform." *History of Education Quarterly,*
    vol. 9 (Fall, 1969), pp. 298-304. On the need to explore new questions,
    new areas, and new political issues in twentieth-century urban history.

    Cordasco, Francesco, Maurie Hillson, and Henry A. Bullock, eds. *The
    School in the Social Order: A Sociological Introduction to Educational
    Understanding.* Scranton, Pennsylvania: International Textbook, 1970. A
    description of schools in the modern social order. Includes chapters on
    "Social Class and Education," "Social Selections: Educational
    Aspirations," "Education and the Minority Child," "Teachers and the
    Teaching Profession."

    Flexner, Abraham, and Frank P. Bachman. *The Gary Schools: A General
    Account.* New York: General Education Board, 1918. A summary of a
    series of reports on the platoon schools: 1: Organization and
    Administration; 2: Costs; 3: Industrial Work; 4: Household Arts;
    5: Physical Training and Play; 6: Science Teaching; and 7: Measurement
    of Classroom Products.

    Fuller, Edgar, and Jim B. Pearson, eds. *Education in the States:
    Nationwide Development Since 1900.* Washington: National Education
    Association, 1969. Combines essays by educational administrators on
    important issues relating to educational administration and supervision in
    educational history.

Gittell, Marilyn, and Alan G. Havesi, eds. *The Politics of Urban Education*. New York: Praeger, 1969. Describes the struggle for power in urban schools. Chapter I: Community Power Struggle; II: Education and Race; III: Education and Politics: Case Studies; IV: School Governance and Reform; V: Community Control of the Schools.

Katz, Michael B., ed. *School Reform: Past and Present*. Boston: Little, Brown, 1971. Presents excerpts and essays from the nineteenth and twentieth centuries on: "The Public School and the City," "The Uses of Pedagogy," "Black Education in the Urban North," and "The Triumph of Bureaucracy in Urban Education."

Krug, Edward A. *The Shaping of the American High School*. Vol. I. New York: Harper & Row, 1964. Vol. II, 1920-1941. Madison, Wisconsin: University of Wisconsin Press, 1972. Describes social and political developments, changes in the American high school, and the thinking of those most immediately responsible for the changes.

Larson, Richard G. "School Curriculum and the Urban Disadvantaged: A Historical Review and Some Thoughts About Tomorrow." *The Journal of Negro Education*, vol. 38 (Fall, 1969), pp. 351-360. Reviews the expressed concerns about curriculum for disadvantaged youth and finds they have been expressed in areas such as developmental characteristics and organization rather than in relationship to content.

Lazerson, Marvin. *Origins of the Urban School: Public Education in Massachusetts, 1870-1915*. Cambridge: Harvard University Press, 1971. A study of the social values and ideas leading to the development of the kindergarten, manual training, vocationalism and citizenship education.

Lazerson, Marvin. "Urban Reform and the Schools: Kindergartens in Massachusetts, 1870-1915." *History of Education Quarterly*, vol. 11 (Summer, 1971), pp. 115-142. As kindergartens became institutionalized they changed from maintaining a delicate balance between freedom and order to having a main commitment to control.

Mehl, Bernard. "The Conant Report and the Committee of Ten: A Historical Appraisal." *Educational Research Bulletin*, vol. 39 (February 10, 1960), pp. 29-38, 56. Describes the similarities and differences between the reports on the American high school by Conant and by the Committee of Ten.

Merelman, Richard M. "Public Education and Social Structure: Three Modes of Adjustment." *The Journal of Politics*, vol. 35 (November, 1973), pp. 798-829. American educational history is shown to be consistent with an incremental model of organizational evolution.

Miller, Harry L., and Roger R. Woock. *Social Foundations of Urban Education*. Hinsdale, Illinois: Dryden Press, 1970. A description of conflicts in twentieth century urban schools and suggested readings. Part I: Social and Economic Influences on the Urban School; Part II: The Schools and Their Communities.

Rudy, Willis. *Schools in an Age of Mass Culture: An Exploration of Selected Themes in the History of Twentieth-Century American Education.* Englewood Cliffs, N.J.: Prentice-Hall, 1965. Chapters include themes on "The Child–Centered School," "Education for All," "Church, State and School," "May 17, 1954," "Evaluation of American Education by Foreigners," "The 'Cold War' Among American Educators," and "The School in the Making of Modern America."

Schwartzman, David. "The Contribution of Education to the Quality of Labor 1929-1963." *The American Economic Review,* vol. 58 (June, 1968), pp. 508-514. A modification is developed of E. F. Denison's estimate that three-fifths of the increased output of labor between 1929 and 1957 was due to increased education.

Sinclair, Upton. *The Goslings: A Study of the American Schools.* Pasadena, California: Upton Sinclair, 1924. Presents Sinclair's personal views of the political and social corruption, injustice, and degeneration of the American schools in the twentieth century.

Social Class Structure and American Education. Harvard Educational Review. A special issue, vol. 23. A series of papers on the relationships of social classes and American education. Part I (Summer, 1953): "The Nature of Social Classes: Theory and Empirical Studies," and "The Function of Public Education in Relation to Social Stratification"; Part II (Fall, 1953): "The Curriculum, Teacher and Administrator in Relation to Social Stratification"; "Educational Measurement in Relation to Social Stratification"; "A Critique of the Special Issues"; and "Social Class and Education: An Annotated Bibliography."

Sutherland, Neil. "The Urban Child." *History of Education Quarterly,* vol. 9 (Fall, 1969), pp. 305-311. A presentation of the idea that curriculum and school practice have been studied adequately and that it is necessary to turn attention to the urban child in his/her social setting.

Toffler, Alvin, ed. *The Schoolhouse in the City.* New York: Praeger, 1968. Brings together the papers presented at a July, 1967 conference at Stanford University on problems of urban decay. Part I: The City; Part II: The System; Part III: The Schoolhouse.

Tyack, David B. "Growing Up Black: Perspectives on the History of Education in Northern Ghettos." *History of Education Quarterly,* vol. 9 (Fall, 1969), pp. 287-297. On the questions which need research and the sources which can be investigated in order to understand the black, urban experience in northern cities.

Wirth, Arthur G. *Education in the Technological Society: The Vocational-Liberal Studies Controversy in the Early Twentieth Century.* Scranton: Intext, 1972. Describes the thinking and practice of a number of educators and groups who were involved in the vocational education controversy. Part I: American Education in the Technological Society: Issues and Initial Responses; Part II: Interest Group Pressures for a New Education in an Industrial Society; Part III: Public School Responses to Pressures for Vocationalizing Education; Part IV: Philosophical Issues: Education and the Industrial State.

2. Social Pressures and the Schools

Berg, Ivar. With the assistance of Serry Gorelick and Foreword by Eli Ginsberg. *Education and Jobs: The Great Training Robbery.* Boston: Beacon Press, 1971. A sociological study of recent educational practices and social expectations. Chapters include: "Education in Economic Perspective," "Job Requirements and Educational Achievement," "Demographic and Managerial Requirements," "Educational Achievements and Worker Performance," "Educational Achievements and Job-Related Attitudes," "The Blue-Collar Worker: A Special Case," and "Education and Public Service."

Berrol, Selma C. "William Henry Maxwell and a New Educational New York." *History of Education Quarterly,* vol. 8 (Summer, 1968), pp. 215-228. A description of the role played by Maxwell in ensuring that all children had an opportunity to have public education and that the school would make some effort to fit the child.

Bowers, C. A. "Social Reconstructionism: Views from the Left and the Right, 1932-1942." *History of Education Quarterly,* vol. 10, pp. 22-52. On the interrelationships between pedagogy and politics and the conservative reaction to this interrelationship.

Cremin, Lawrence A. "Toward a More Common School." *Teachers College Record,* vol. 51 (February, 1950), pp. 308-319. Describes the twentieth century attacks against the belief that education alone will provide freedom and equality.

Herbst, Jurgen. "High School and Youth in America." An essay in *Education and Social Structure in the Twentieth Century* edited by Walter Laqueur and George L. Mosse. New York: Harper Torchbooks, 1967, pp. 165-182. On the changes of social expectations of the high school and its relationship to adolescence throughout the twentieth century.

Karier, Clarence J. "Liberalism and the Quest for Orderly Change." *History of Education Quarterly,* vol. 12 (Spring, 1972), pp. 57-80. A description of the ideological conflict between beliefs and practices faced by the American liberal educator.

Karier, Clarence J., Paul C. Violas, and Joel Spring. *Roots of Crisis: American Education in the Twentieth Century*. Chicago: Rand McNally, 1965. Brings together a series of essays which emphasize a new analysis of influences affecting education in the twentieth century. Chapters include: "Business Values," "Social Control," "Testing for Order," "Deschooling," "Indoctrination Debate," "Academic Freedom," "The Cold War," "Youth Culture," and "Anarchism."

Katz, Michael B. *Class, Bureaucracy, and Schools: The Illusion of Educational Change in America*. New York: Praeger, 1971. An analysis of school reform efforts in both the nineteenth and twentieth centuries with suggestions for a new historical approach to historical writing.

Kilpatrick, William H., ed. Written in collaboration by Boyd H. Bode, John L. Childs, H. Gordon Hullfish, John Dewey, R. B. Raup, and V. T. Thayer. *The Educational Frontier*. New York: D. Appleton-Century, 1933. Combines a series of jointly planned essays on the social-economic situation in the early 1930's, and on the influences of this situation on education. I: The Confusion in Present-Day Education; II: The Social-Economic Situation and Education; III: The New Conception of the Profession of Education; IV: The New Adult Education; V-VII: The School: Its Task and Its Administration—I, II, III; VIII: Professional Education from the Social Point of View; IX: The Underlying Philosophy of Education.

Laslett, Barbara. "The Family as a Public and Private Institution: An Historical Perspective." *Journal of Marriage and the Family*, vol. 35 (August, 1973), pp. 480-492. Shows that the tendency toward privacy of the twentieth century family may be only an historical phase in an institution which changes to meet strains of society.

Perkinson, Henry J. *The Imperfect Panacea: American Faith in Education, 1865-1965*. New York: Random House, 1968. Shows that Americans have placed too much faith in public education as a single remedy for social problems. Twentieth century sections include chapters on the relationships between schools and "The Negro," "The City," "Economic Opportunity," and "The Government."

Rosenthal, Alan, ed. *Governing Education: A Reader on Politics, Power, and Public School Policy*. Garden City, New York: Doubleday, 1969. Describes the political pressures which influence public school decisions. Part One: Politics and Public Education; Part Two: Community Influence on Public School Policy; Part Three: The Government of Education.

Rossi, Peter H., and Alice S. "Background and Consequences of Parochial School Education." *Harvard Educational Review*, vol. 27 (Summer, 1957), pp. 168-199. It is shown that circumstances in the public schools gave rise to the need for parochial schools which, in turn, affect the public schools in a variety of ways.

Shostak, Arthur B. "Education and the Family." *Journal of Marriage and the Family,* vol. 29 (February, 1967), pp. 124-139. Historically the school and family have enjoyed a symbiotic relationship but today the school is venturing into traditional areas of family dominance.

Spring, Joel. With a foreward by Ivan Illich. *Education and the Rise of the Corporate State.* Boston: Beacon Press, 1972. On the relationships of school and state. Chapters include: "The Philosphy of the Corporate State," "Factory Life and Education," "The Classroom as Factory and Community," "Extending the Social Role of the School," "The Radical Reaction to the Public Schools," and "The Meaning of Schooling in the Twentieth Century."

Strong, Bryan. "Ideas of the Early Sex Education Movement in America, 1890-1920." *History of Education Quarterly,* vol. 12 (Summer, 1972), pp. 129-161. A description of the changes in sex education brought about by the changing sexual mores of society.

Sutherland, Arthur E. "The Supreme Court and the Public School." *Harvard Educational Review,* vol. 24 (Spring, 1954), pp. 71-85. The relationship between the Supreme Court and the public schools is discussed.

Tyack, David B., ed. *Turning Points in American Educational History.* Waltham, Massachusetts: Blaisdell, 1967. Includes historical analysis and documentary selections dealing with significant issues in American education. Twentieth century issues are: "Becoming an American: The Education of the Immigrant"; "Growing up Black: The Education of the Negro"; "Democracy, Bureaucracy and Education: John Dewey and the Redefinition of the Common School"; "The People's College: The Emergence of the High School"; "The Education of Teachers and the Teaching of Education."

3. Social Efficiency and the Progressive Movement

Bowers, C. A. "The Ideologies of Progressive Education." *History of Education Quarterly,* vol. 7 (Winter, 1967), pp. 452-473. Describes the interrelationships of educational theories and political movements during the first third of the twentieth century.

Callahan, Raymond E. *Education and the Cult of Efficiency: A Study of the Social Forces that have Shaped the Administration of the Public Schools.* Chicago: University of Chicago Press, 1962. The concept of scientific management is shown to have created a social setting for economic evaluation of learning and the development of "efficient" modes of teaching.

Cohen, Sol. "The Industrial Education Movement, 1906-17." *American Quarterly,* vol. 20 (Spring, 1968), pp. 95-110. On the inclusion of vocational courses in the public high schools for the purpose of serving the masses and alleviating child labor.

Cohen, Sol. *Progressives and Urban School Reform: The Public Education Association of New York City, 1895-1954.* New York: Bureau of Publications, Teachers College, Columbia University, 1964. A study of planning by earnest volunteers. The contents range from a chapter on "Roots of Reform,1880-1895" through "Hey-Day 1917-1931" and "The Perils of Prosperity, 1932-1940" to "Defender of Progressivism 1940-1954."

Cremin, Lawrence A. "John Dewey and the Progressive-Education Movement, 1915-1952." *The School Review,* vol. 67 (Summer, 1959), pp. 160-173. John Dewey became a spokesman of the progressive education movement but did not, as is frequently charged, direct the movement.

Cremin, Lawrence A. "The Origins of Progressive Education." *The Educational Forum,* vol. 24 (January, 1960), pp. 133-140. Progressive education had its origins, according to the author, in the reform movement before World War I.

Cremin, Lawrence A. "The Progressive Movement in American Education: A Perspective." *Harvard Educational Review,* vol. 27 (Fall, 1957), pp. 251-270. The need for reform in the schools brought about the progressive movement in education.

Cremin, Lawrence A. *The Transformation of the School: Progressivism in American Education, 1867-1957.* New York: Vintage Books, 1961. Relates the progressive movement in education to the political progressive movement. Part I: The Progressive Impulse in Education, 1876-1917, and Part II: The Progressive Era in Education, 1917-1957.

Drost, Walter H. "Clarence Kingsley—'The New York Years.' " *History of Education Quarterly,* vol. 6 (Fall, 1966), pp. 18-34. On the career in education which led Kingsley to advocate social efficiency in schools and to chair the committee which produced the "Cardinal Principles Report."

Drost, Walter H. *David Snedden and Education for Social Efficiency.* Madison: University of Wisconsin Press, 1967. Relates the work of Snedden to the educational movement which he helped create. Includes a history of his family life, his years as a professor and Commissioner of Education in Massachusetts, and an analysis of his theories and his role in American education.

Feldman, Egal. "Prostitution, the Alien Woman and the Progressive Imagination, 1910-1915." *American Quarterly,* vol. 19 (Summer, 1967), pp. 192-206. Presents evidence to show that the attack on prostitution and the vigorous defense of young immigrant women were part of the effort to make way for the "New Woman."

Graham, Patricia A. *Progressive Education: From Arcady to Academe: A History of the Progressive Education Association, 1919-1955*. New York: Teachers College Press, 1967. On the differences in progressivism before World War I and after, this volume provides a picture of the Association and its efforts toward child-centered pedagogy.

Hays, Samuel P. *The Response to Industrialism: 1885-1914*. Chicago: University of Chicago Press, 1957. On the period of great social change at the turn of the century and its portent for life in the twentieth century. Includes chapters on "The Shock of Change," "Organize or Perish," "The Individual in an Impersonal Society," "The Politics of Adjustment," and "The Rise to World Power."

Johanningmeier, Erwin V. "William Chandler Bagley's Changing Views on the Relationship between Psychology and Education." *History of Education Quarterly*, vol. 9 (Spring, 1969), pp. 3-27. On the life of Bagley and his changing views about education as it related to social efficiency.

Joncich, Geraldine M., ed. *Psychology and the Science of Education: Selected Writings of Edward L. Thorndike*. New York: Bureau of Publications, Teachers College, Columbia University, 1962. On Thorndike's tremendous contributions to educational planning and social efficiency. Part I: Psychology as Science; Part 2: Education as Science; Part 3: Intellect and Learning, Worth and Progress; Part 4: Measurement.

McBride, Paul W. "The Co-Op Industrial Education Experiment, 1900-1917." *History of Education Quarterly*, vol. 14 (Summer, 1974), pp. 209-221. Evidence is mustered to show that the co-op education movement may have been exploitative and seeking to instill docility in pupils.

Osofsky, Gilbert. "Progressivism and the Negro: New York, 1900-1915." *American Quarterly*, vol. 16 (Summer, 1964), pp. 153-168. Shows that as blacks moved to northern cities, the public became increasingly aware of the practical difficulties faced by the blacks in daily life and an attitude of supportive reform developed.

Rice, J. M. *Scientific Management in Education*. New York: Hinds, Noble and Eldredge, 1914. Reprint, New York: Arno Press and The New York Times, 1969. Shows methods of applying scientific management to education by organizing use of time and gives correlations in spelling, arithmetic and language between social origins and test results.

Spring, Joel. "Education and Progressivism." *History of Education Quarterly*, vol. 10 (Spring, 1970), pp. 53-71. A description of the development of education for a specific skill and the progressive reaction.

Stevens, Edward W., Jr. "Social Centers, Politics, and Social Efficiency in the Progressive Era." *History of Education Quarterly,* vol. 12 (Spring, 1972), pp. 16-33. On the various efforts to tackle urban problems and the inability of those making the efforts to deal with the problems of democracy in education.

Swift, David W. *Ideology and Change in the Public Schools: Latent Functions of Progressive Education.* Columbus, Ohio: Charles E. Merrill, 1971. Combines the issues of progressive education, control, autonomy, personnel and support.

Venn, Grant, assisted by Theodore J. Marchese, Jr. *Man, Education and Work: Postsecondary Vocational and Technical Education.* Washington: American Council on Education, 1964. On the development of vocationally-oriented education at the secondary and postsecondary levels. Chapters are: "Man, Education, and Work"; "The Development of Vocational and Technical Education"; "Vocational and Technical Education in Secondary and Higher Education"; "The Federal Government and Vocational and Technical Education"; "Manpower Needs, Present and Future"; "Major Issues in Vocational and Technical Education"; "Conclusions and Recommendations."

4.　Teachers and Superintendents in the Urban Society

Berube, Maurice R., and Marilyn Gittell. *Confrontation at Ocean Hill-Brownsville: The New York School Strikes of 1968.* New York: Praeger, 1969. Brings together documents and opinions on teachers' strikes, racism, and community control.

Braun, Robert J. *Teachers and Power: The Story of the American Federation of Teachers.* New York: Simon and Schuster, 1972. An expository history of the A.F. of T. from Chicago to Ocean Hill-Brownsville given without documentation.

Callahan, Raymond E. *Changing Conceptions of the Superintendency in Public Education, 1865-1964.* Cambridge: New England School Development Council, 1964. A series of lectures which review the development of public school superintendents as educational leaders, business managers, educational statesmen, and educational realists.

Cole, Stephen. *The Unionization of Teachers: A Case Study of the UFT.* New York: Praeger, 1969. A history of teacher unions with a focus on the UFT. Includes chapters on: "The Growth of Teacher Militancy," "History of the Teacher Union Movement in New York City," "Social Control: The Reaction of Authorities to the Union Movement," and "Teaching and Other Professions: Conditions Leading to Unionization."

Issel, William H. "Teachers and Educational Reform During the Progressive Era: A Case Study of the Pittsburgh Teachers Association."

History of Education Quarterly, vol. 7 (Summer, 1967), pp. 220-233. A study of the contributions made by teachers to improve education and to strengthen the teacher association and a call for more studies in order to determine national practice.

Lieberman, Myron. "Teachers Strikes: An Analysis of the Issues." *Harvard Educational Review,* vol. 26 (Winter, 1956), pp. 39-70. The legal and practical situation of teachers' unions is considered.

Peltier, Gary L. "Teacher Participation in Curriculum Revision: An Historical Case Study." *History of Education Quarterly,* vol. 7 (Summer, 1967), pp. 209-219. On the unusual practice of encouraging teachers to participate in curriculum revision and its results.

Stinnett, T. M. *Turmoil in Teaching: A History of the Organizational Struggle for America's Teachers.* New York: Macmillan, 1968. The strategies, conflicts and weapons used in the drive to organize teachers in the 1960's.

AUTHOR INDEX

A Note about This Book

The text of this book was set on an IBM Selectric Composer System in the type face,Press Roman. The book was composed by Ted Little of Live Gold Inc., New York and was printed and bound by Braun & Brumfield, Inc., Ann Arbor, Michigan. The following people on the publisher's staff contributed to the publication of this book: Gabriel Hornstein, Martin Smolar, and Elizabeth M. Burke.

DATE D

6.15.'82